I HEAR YOU KNOCKIN'

The Sound of New Orleans Rhythm and Blues

Jeff Hannusch
a.k.a. Almost Slim

Swallow Publications, Inc.

Copyright © 1985 by Jeff Hannusch

All rights reserved. No part of this book may be reproduced or transmitted in any form or by any means, electronic or mechanical, including photocopying, recording or by any information storage and retrieval system, without permission in writing from the Publisher.

Swallow Publications, Inc.
P.O. Drawer 10
Ville Platte, Louisiana 70586
318/363-2139

Second Printing, 1987
Third Printing, 1989
Printed in the United States of America

LIBRARY OF CONGRESS
CATALOGING IN PUBLICATION DATA

Hannusch, Jeff aka Almost Slim
 I Hear You Knockin'; The Sound of
New Orleans Rhythm and Blues

  Bibliography: p.
  Discography: p.
  1. Music, Popular (Songs, etc.) New Orleans and Louisiana - History and criticism.

84-51112
ISBN 0-9614245-0-8

Acknowledgments

It would require literally another chapter to list everyone who has helped me, but I must be brief. Besides everyone cited in the text I must thank in particular: Connie Atkinson, whose encouragement, foresight and so much more, made this book possible; Kathleen Joffrion, my wife, who has put up with all of my idiosyncracies; Nauman Scott and Pat Berry, for providing the opportunity to be heard; Louis Nugent, Ronnie Brinkman and Dave Booth for direction; Rico and Lee Crum for the photos; Tipitina's, The Maple Leaf, Jimmy's and the Fairmont, for the free admissions; Mike Ledbetter, the greatest musical journalist ever, for inspiration; Leo Gosserand for his friendship and curiosity; Walter Brock at WWOZ community radio; Alpertine Washington and Leona Robinson Kelly, just for being there; Mason Ruffner and Willie Cole. Others who gave invaluable help are my parents, John and Helen Hannusch, Hammond Scott, Chris Strachwitz, Jimmy Augustine, Bunny Matthews, Jerey Fletcher, Peter Guralnick, Pierre Trudeau, Robin Leary, Murray Burt, Linda Matys, Sonny Schnideaux, John Kelly, Scott Billington and the folks at Rounder, Mr. Cross, Don Leedy, Jim Glasscock, Gatemouth Brown, Marcia Ball, Emil Jackson, Gordon DeSoto, Billy Dell, Ted Carroll, Chester Malmstedt, John Berthelot, Cleon Floyd, Joop Viser, Senator Jones, Allison Kaslow, Lynn Abbott, Dan Forte, and of course, Floyd.

Note: the following books have been used for reference: *Walkin' To New Orleans*, John Broven; *Deep South Piano*, Karl Get zur Heide; *Lost Highway & Feel Like Going Home*, Peter Gualnick; *The Story of the Blues*, Paul Oliver; *Top Pop Records, 1955-1970* and *Top Rhythm & Blues Records, 1949-1971*, Joel Whitburn; *New Orleans Rhythm and Blues Record Label Listings*, Ray Topping; *Blues Records, 1943-1966*, Mike Ledbitter and Neil Slaven; *The Sound of Philadelphia*, Tommy Cummings.

In addition, various of the following magazines or newspapers were consulted: *Wavelength, Blues Unlimited, Louisiana Weekly, Fig-*

aro, *Living Blues, Goldmine, The Music Reporter, Gambit, Rolling Stone, The Times-Picayune, The States-Item, New Orleans Magazine, Whiskey, Women, and..., Ebony, Billboard, Cashbox* and *Dixie*.

This book is respectfully dedicated to "Tuts" Washington, a great musician, a gentleman and a friend.

Mr. G on Bourbon Street

CONTENTS

Foreword: By Joe Banashak

Introduction 1

Part One: THE PIANO PLAYERS 3
   Tuts Washington: "Thank You Music Lovers" 5
   Professor Longhair: Going To The Mardi Gras 15
   Huey "Piano" Smith: Don't You Just Know It 35
   James Booker: The Piano Prince of New Orleans 45
   Allen Toussaint: Southern Knight 55

Part Two: THE PIONEERS 69
   Roy Brown: The Good Rockin' Man 71
   Mr. Google Eyes: The Nation's Youngest Blues Singer 83
   Dave Bartholomew: The Man Behind The Big Beat 95

Part Three: THE RECORD MEN 105
   Cosimo Matassa: New Orleans' Recording Giant 107
   Dr. Daddy-O: New Orleans' First Black Radio Personality .. 119
   Johnny Vincent: The Ace Records Man 127
   Joe Banashak: The Record Man 135
   Marshall Sehorn: The Mind Behind The Music 161

Part Four: NEW ORLEANS BLUES 169
   Bill Webb: "They Call Me Boogie Bill" 171
   Guitar Slim: The Things That He Used To Do 177
   Earl King: Still Letting The Good Times Roll 189

Part Five: WOMAN'S VIEWPOINT 205
   Shirley Goodman: Sweetheart Of The Blues 207
   Dorothy Labostrie: New Orleans Songstress 219
   Irma Thomas: The Soul Queen of New Orleans 225

Part Six: THE SECOND LINE 237
   Lee Allen: Cookin' With Mr. Lee 239
   Smiley Lewis: I Hear You Knockin' 245
   James Crawford: "Sugar Boy" 259
   Johnny Adams: The Tan Canary 267
   Bobby Mitchell: I'm Gonna Be A Wheel Someday 281

Part Seven: THE HIT MAKERS 289
   Chris Kenner: Man of 1,000 Dances 291
   Bobby Marchan: Is There Something On Your Mind? 301
   Frankie Ford: Feel Like Jumpin' 307
   Jessie Hill: Puttin' Some Disturbance On Your Mind 317
   King Floyd: Back In The Groove? 325
   Ernie K-Doe: The In-Kredible K-Doe 333
   Lee Dorsey: Still Working In A Coal Mine 343

EPILOGUE 351
   Winnie's Lounge: Where The Music Plays On 355
   Appendix A:
    New Orleans R&B Singles Chart Entries 1949-1971 359
   Appendix B: Important Rhythm and Blues Clubs 365
   Appendix C: Album Discography 367

PHOTO CREDITS 374

INDEX 375

Roy Brown and Chubby Newsom, Lake Charles, 1949

Foreword
by
Joe Banashak

When I came to New Orleans approximately thirty-five years ago, my first desire was to sit and listen to Dixieland music. Like most newcomers, I spent much time in the French Quarter where the Dixieland beat was played in almost all the nightclubs back then. Needless to say I enjoyed every moment and every earful. But there was also another beat and style of music emerging in New Orleans and not found in the French Quarter. It was a style and sound that became known as rhythm and blues (R&B); it caught my ear along with the gospel spiritual music and blues of the day, very infectious and interesting.

As the years went by, I began getting involved with recording this newer music that was coming out of New Orleans and once again its name was changed, this time to rock and roll. Through the years of 1959 to 1965, it seemed to reach its pinnacle, but little did I realize its popularity would last so long.

I am continually amazed at the longevity of this type of music. In the days of producing records and music, I am sure none of us thought of the future life of these sounds. If we had, we would have taken more pictures and gleaned more history and biography from the artists and musicians. Fortunately, the younger people who became collectors of this music got so involved and interested, they felt a need to search for the history and write about it, such as Jeff has done between the covers of this book.

I am delighted to have been a part of the New Orleans Sound and a part of this book along with the biographies of the other New Orleans music makers. With excitement and great anticipation I look forward to your reading and enjoying *I Hear You Knockin': The Sound of New Orleans Rhythm and Blues* along with me.

Bobby Mitchell, 1983

Introduction

From the perspective of the mid-1980s, it is difficult to imaging the time when New Orleans rhythm and blues played a major part in the popular music spectrum. It is for this reason that I've written these portraits of many of New Orleans' most important rhythm and blues artists. Besides paying my own personal tribute, I hope I can draw attention to their talent and their contribution to the wealth of New Orleans music. In other words, simply to say thanks.

Long before I ever considered writing about New Orleans rhythm and blues, I avidly listened to it. I don't remember if it was one of Roy Brown's emotion-laced blues, one of Professor Longhair's rhumba-boogies, or a smoky Lee Allen sax break, but that warm melodic sound drew my attention like a magnet. New Orleans seemed like such a magical place; not because of the lures of the French Quarter or Mardi Gras, but because people like Smiley Lewis, Guitar Slim, and Archibald and Fats Domino actually lived there!

I wish I personally could have been in the studio when Dave Bartholomew made his first record, or when Dr. Daddy-O spun his first 78, but, of course, age and geographic considerations have made that impossible. Instead, I have had to rely on the words of others to tell the first-hand story of New Orleans rhythm and blues. I've tried to keep my own views and interpretations at a minimum and to intersperse enough factual information to emphasize a point and to aid the reader's understanding of the book.

Rather than attempt a "Complete History of New Orleans Rhythm and Blues," which was ably covered in the scope of John Broven's *Walkin' To New Orleans*, hopefully this collection of profiles will show a historical perspective. I apologize in advance for omissions, but circumstances have prevented me from including every key artist; hopefully they can be included in a second volume. Also, the duplication of material was unavoidable at times. Rather than choose to view this as a flaw, the gracious reader will use this information to interrelate the stories.

Lastly, more important than any story or any book, is The Music. If this book causes you to go out and listen to one of these artists or to go and buy one of their records, then this book has served its purpose.

Jeff Hannusch a.k.a. Almost Slim
New Orleans, Louisiana
May 30, 1984

Part One:

THE PIANO PLAYERS

Without a doubt, the piano has been the most important instrument as far as the development of New Orleans rhythm and blues is concerned. In the days that preceded the jukebox, New Orleans was teeming with piano players that entertained in cafes, barrooms, beauty shops, at picnics, fish fries, movies and, of course, the infamous Storyville brothels.

The pianists usually fell into two distinct categories. The schooled, sophisticated pianists that played a variety of styles and came to be known as "professors," and the cruder barrelhouse piano players that only played the blues. The professors most often worked solo in the brothels (which was a great honor) or were absorbed by jazz/dance bands. A number of pianists that were considered "professors" made recordings before World War II, including Clarence Williams, Buddy Christian, Spencer Williams, and of course Jelly Roll Morton, perhaps the most famous of all the New Orleans professors.

The barrelhouse pianists often consisted of semi-professionl musicians who often played merely for drinks, or for whatever tip was thrown on the piano. Some of the barrelhouse players, like Champion Jack Dupree, Archibald and Professor Longhair (who never was able to make a living strictly from music until the last years of his life) thankfully were recorded, but hundreds more never were. "Sullivan Rock," Frank Duston, "Rocker," "Drive 'Em Down," "Kid Stormy Weather," "Boogus" (who apparently could only play the black keys on the piano) and Robert Bertrand are dead and gone, to be remembered only by the dwindling number of musicians who were active during the first half of the century.

But with barrooms and brothels galore, there were many opportunities for work and a number of occasions for the pianists to exchange ideas and styles. Quite often a number of musicians would assemble in one joint and have "bucking" contests to see who was the best and fastest piano player. Through this musical competition and comparison of ideas, New Orleans absorbed a variety of styles and developed its own unique piano tradition.

Since the piano was the foundation of the black music that

evolved in New Orleans after World War II, it would only seem obbious that the city would develop a rhythm and blues style that differed from other urban centers. Not surprisingly, it would be the pianists like Professor Longhair, Fats Domino and Allen Toussaint who would serve as the major driving forces behind the music.

TUTS WASHINGTON
"Thank You Music Lovers"

Isidore "Tuts" Washington, Jr., was born in New Orleans, January 24, 1907, the son of Juanita Howard and Isidore Washington, St. Tuts had an older sister who died before his birth, and an "outside" brother fathered by Isidore Sr. "I'm a creole," affirmed Tuts, "so there will never be a shadow of doubt in your mind. I come up on the corner of Eighth and Franklin [now Simon Bolivar Street]. Most of my peoples is dark, but my pa's grandpa was an Indian, and I got his color.

Tragedy struck Tuts' life early, when his mother died under mysterious circumstances when he was just six. "The doctor said she drank some coffee that was poisoned," explains Tuts. "I don't know if someone would have poisoned her purposely," he says but adds quickly, "People were a lot more superstitious in them days, that could have had something to do with it."

Even though Tuts spent a relatively short period of life with his mother, there was apparently much love in the family, and he still speaks fondly of her, although he does admit, "She was real strict. My ma's the one that started calling me 'Tuts.' I don't know but she just did." Photographs of Juanita show a dark-skinned, well-dressed, handsome woman with a glint of no-nonsense in her eyes.

Tuts' father, a house painter, begrudgingly had to put his son in the care of his wife's sister, Rosetta Howard, who lived further downtown, near the intersection of Josephine and Clara Streets. "I don't need to tell you things was different in those days. You could buy a sack of groceries for a dollar, and a big bag a' crackers for a nickel. There wasn't all this killin' and stealin' you got today. A man could walk the streets any time o'day. I used to play in the alley behind the Leidenheimer's Bakery where they baked the French bread loaves. The bakers would give us kids donuts and bread all the time and I'd run back and give 'em to my aunt."

Like any child growing up in New Orleans, Tuts was exposed to a great deal of music. "There was plenty of it around," says Tuts. "There was always bands out in the street, 'cause nearly everybody got waked by a band then. On weekends, sometimes there'd be two or three bands out on the corner tryin' to 'buck' each other to see which one was best. All us kids would run behind the bands, they call it second linin' today. I liked to hear the 'Tin Roof Blues.' [sings] 'Don't you get too funky 'cause your water's on.' That was kicks.''

It wasn't too long before Tuts became interested in making his own music. "The first thing I learned to play was the harmonica and the drums. Every quarter I'd get, I'd run to the corner and buy a harmonica—Hohner Marine Band harmonica. I got to where I played one pretty good, but my aunt made me quit playin' em 'cause she said they would make my lips too big."

But it was an upright piano sitting in his aunt's front room that eventually drew most of Tuts' attention. "I was 10 years old when I first started playing the piano. No one taught me to play, not even how to play a C chord. That's why I believe it was a gift from God. I always could play anything I heard. When I was a kid, I was a good whistler. Every time I heard a song that I liked, I'd whistle it all the way home, then I'd sit down and 'find it' on the piano. I got to the point where *good* piano players would come and ask me to show them things to play.

"I started out playin' the blues, 'cause that was what the people liked to hear. I'd sneak around the joints and listen to 'em play the blues and boogie woogie. They had a gang of blues players then; see, every joint had a piano in it 'cause this was before they even had radios and jukeboxes. People wanted to hear something while they were drinkin'—that's why they had all these piano players out there. Not every joint could afford to get a band, so you had a lot of these guys out here hustlin' for change and a few drinks. I didn't play in the joints when I was real young, but I used to go 'round the corner to the Gallo Theatre [on Claiborne Ave.]. I played there when the movies would be showing. Fish fries, too. People would give fish fries to raise money and hire me to play to entertain the people. Made a couple a'dollars and got all I could to eat and drink, that's all I was lookin' for then. Just a good time."

As a child, Tuts was sent to a private "colored" school in Uptown New Orleans on Franklin Avenue run by a group of Lutheran teachers. "It cost my pa ten cents a week to send me to school. I remember I learned to read from a McGuffey's reader—it was a real good book for learnin'. I only played hooky one day, but I got caught by one of the teachers. 'Essedor'—I hated to hear that—'where have you been?' Well, she gave me a whippin' and then she told my pa. Then he tore my ass up too. I never played hooky again."

Tuts only completed the sixth grade, although he contends, "My

Tuts at 20

education was just as good as anyone who graduated from a public high school. I quit school to go to work. I started shinin' shoes for the rich white folks in front of the Crescent Billiard Hall, where Kolb's Restaurant is now on St. Charles Avenue [on the lake side of the 100 block]. I was makin' seven dollars a week. Man, I thought I was rich."

Even though Tuts had barely reached his teens, he began playing in bands whose members were far older than himself, and also began "hangin' out" in joints. "I never had any problems playin' with bands. I played with all of our best dixieland bands in the twenties—Kid Punch, Kid Rena, plenty of 'em."

Tuts also joined the large number of "barrelhouse" pianists that circulated throughout the city. "Right away I knew I didn't just want to be a blues player, there was a gang of them around. If you wanted to get a good job that paid some money, you had to play more than the blues, you had to be able to play anything the people wanted.

"See, in them days the [red light] district was still open. Now I'm not just talkin' about the white district on Basin Street, but the colored district in, in behind Rampart Street [Perdido Street]. We used to have a joint in back of the precinct that we called the 'Fuck Around.' I run up on a gang of blues players there in the Twenties.

'Black' Merineaux, Fats Pichon, Little Brother Montgomery, Burnell Santiago, Kid Stormy Weather, Hezekiah—they was all blues players. Some nights there'd be three or four of us in there and we'd 'buck' each other to see which one was best. Some nights they'd raid the joint and I'd have to run out the back door 'cause I wasn't old enough to be in there. I'd come at all hours of the night and my aunt would be so mad. She'd say, 'Tuts, where you been?' and she'd beat the hell out of me."

Tuts' reputation as a good player spread, and although his aunt wasn't too happy about the late hours he was keeping, she eventually consented to let her nephew take proper lessons from a "professor." "Everybody that passed the house and heard me play would say, 'That boy is good, he ought to be takin' lessons.' Finally, when I was 18, my pa sent me to a teacher. I only went one day, the teacher told my pa, 'I can't teach this boy nuthin'. He already plays better than a tenth grade pianist.' So I just carried on the way I had been, sneakin' in the joints and tryin' to learn what I could by ear."

As Tuts grew to be an adult, he spent most of his life developing his style and soaking up the nightlife that New Orleans had to offer during the 1930's. "A piano player had it made in them days. Women would fight over a piano player. See, the district was open, women were turnin' tricks and they had plenty money. They wanted their men to look good. I had women buy me gold belt buckles, rings, silk shirts, new suits and all kinds of shit. Man, they'd be putting money in your pocket and fightin' with each other to do it.

"I was mostly playin' by myself in the colored joints. Now a lot of them Italians had speakeasy joints. They hired nothin' but colored bands. The colored joints didn't hire too many bands because they could only afford a piano player. Bourbon Street, too. They hired nothin' but colored bands in those days.

"Now I bummed around plenty in my day, that's when I was drinkin' liquor. Mostly I bummed on Rampart Street, 'cause Rampart was nothin' but joints. I'd get me a half pint of gin, sit up in a joint and maybe play some piano and then walk down the street to the next joint. Do that all day long. Things was happenin' in them days. There was gambling and prostitution, but it seemed like a person had a chance to make some money then."

The man who came to influence Tuts' piano style the most was Joseph Louis "Red" Cayou. Cayou was two years Tuts' senior and was inspired by Jelly Roll Morton, who visited his house. Cayou played with a jazz trio at the Big 25, but mostly played solo piano in the honky tonks and gaming houses. "Red Cayou was the best

Smiley Lewis, Herman Seale, Tuts Washington
El Morocco Club, 1947

thing we had around here," declares Tuts flatly. "He had long hands and bowed legs. Red could walk into any joint in town and run anybody offa the piano. Piano players were scared to play when Red walked in the door. He fingered the hell out of the piano. Played so fast you couldn't even see his hands. That sumbitch was electric! That's where I got my left hand. He used to tell me, 'You son of a bitch, I'm gonna run you offa that piano.' He played in the tonks, but he played 'round those whorehouses over on Basin Street before they closed them down. Red left here around '25 and moved to Oakland, California. He never did come back. I got to visit him once out there, but he died in a car wreck in 1947."

Before Tuts reached his twenties, he began leaving town to play piano in New Orleans dance bands. Tuts recalls playing with Captain John Handy, "Son" Johnson, Isaiah Morgan, Kid Clayton, Papa French, Kid Rena, and Louis Demain, who all led bands at the time and, according to Tuts, played "for whites and coloreds."

During the 1930's Tuts could most often be found in one of the tiny clubs that lined South Rampart Street or occasionally with a dixieland group, led by the likes of Kid Sheik, Alton Purnel, or Thomas Jefferson. While on Rampart Street, Tuts imparted much to a number of up-and-coming pianists. "I taught a lot of these fellows," assures Tuts. "When I was playing at the Kotton Club, Fess [Roy Byrd, a.k.a. Professor Longhair] used to come in and watch me at the piano. He'd rub smut on his lip so it would look like a mustache and he could look older and fool the owners. I tried to show him some of these strides that I play, but he couldn't make it. He had to make a fist and roll his lefthand to cover what I could cover."

Not long after, Tuts began his most memorable musical association, one with Overton Lemons, of course better known as Smiley Lewis. "I had been knowin' Lewis from when I played with Thomas Jefferson back in the Thirties. I was playin' on Rampart Street, and Lewis would always stop by to see me on his way home from workin' in the Quarter with Noon Johnson and 'Papoose' [Walter Nelson]. He use' to say, 'Man, I wish I could play with someone that's as good as you, Tuts.' He use' to sing a few tunes with me, 'cause I always did like his voice.

"I took a job with Kid Ernest at the Boogie Woogie Club in Bunkie, Louisiana. It was during the war, and things had slowed up around New Orleans, so I took the job. The man that owned the club wanted a vocalist, so I talked Kid and his brother into hiring Lewis. We played around Bunkie and Marksville, Louisiana, for the best part of two years. When I came home I had $800 in my pocket."

Tuts was present on Smiley's first recording, "Turn On Your Volume" b/w "Here Comes Smiley" that was recorded in 1948 for Deluxe Records. "We had the best trio around New Orleans," confirms Tuts. "Nobody could beat Smiley singin' blues or standards. We played all around town, The Gypsy Tea Room, the El Morocco, the Dew Drop, all 'round town.

"We started bummin' around the J&M Studio. I remember they had an old German-made upright piano that I liked to play. I wrote a lot of those numbers for Smiley then that I never got credit for. I wrote 'The Dirty, Dirty People Done The Poor Boy Wrong,' and I gave Smiley the words to 'Tee-Nah-Nah.' That was one of those prison songs they used to sing up in Angola. 'Tee-Nah-Nah' went everywhere; every time I turned around I heard it on the box. We travelled all over on that record. Florida, Mississippi, Oklahoma— Melvin Cade was bookin' us—we went to so many places I had to write my aunt just to let her know where I was. In fact I did so much travelling then that I'm not too crazy about travelling now.

"I stayed with Smiley 'till around '51. Smiley just got too big-

Archibald and Tuts Washington

headed and ornery. He got to the point where you couldn't tell him nuthin'. We had had words a bunch of times so I left the trio and then Dave Bartholomew ran behind him and got him to make all those records for the Imperial Recording Company."

Curiously, even though he lived through the most active recording period in New Orleans and scores of inferior musicians were recorded, Tuts was never inclined to make recordings of his own. "I never did have to make no records," points out Tuts. "I always been havin' a name around New Orleans for my playin' ability. Now a lot of these boys that get a record out, they need one to get a name. But they get a bass guitar and a drum to fill out their sound. I never did need that. They got a name offa that rock 'n' roll, that teenaged music. They got them loud guitars on there and that high hollerin' and screamin'. But you can't call that music—that's just a bunch of damn noise."

After Tuts split with Smiley, he joined Papa Celestin's Dixieland Band, replacing his talented cousin, Jeanette Kimball, on piano. "Papa Celestin had the most popular band in New Orleans. His band was even a member of the white union, and no other black band did that until the unions merged in the Seventies. We mostly played on Bourbon Street at the Paddock Lounge. Once we went over to Texas and I was supposed to go to Germany to play for Eisenhower. But Jeanette asked for her job back, and I let her have it because it was hers to start out with. I got a job playin' with Andrew Anderson playin' down in Grand Isle, Louisiana, at a resort."

Despite his aversion to recording, Tuts was often sought out by other New Orleans pianists for "tips," and served as an inspiration for most of the city's renowned pianists. "A lot of these Johnny-come-lately piano players came to hear me. I remember Fats Domino when he was just a li'l ole fat boy. I had a job down at the Club Desire with Smiley and he come around beggin' me to play 'The Honeydripper.' But Fats can't play nothin' but that 6/8 time. He got lucky and came along with that 'Blueberry Hill' in these teenaged times. He needed that band behind him to sound good.

"I used to go over to James Booker's house when he was a boy. His grandmother was a personal friend of mine. We used to drink together. He was like Fess, he would sneak in the joints and listen to me play. He was a pretty good little piano player, I have to give him that, he was one of the only guys that was good enough to play on Bourbon Street. But that dope brought him down. I saw him when he come out of the penitentiary with a patch over his eye. He saw me on Bourbon Street and he gave me a big hug. I said, 'Where you been, James?' He said, 'Over the hill, Pops.' It's too bad he got mixed up in that dope."

Throughout the latter half of the Seventies, Tuts played with his old friend Thomas Jefferson at the Maison Bourbon and occasionally played house parties for New Orleans' more well-to-dos. In 1979, he participated in *Piano Players Rarely Ever Play Together*, a documentary film produced by Stevenson Palfi, which also featured Professor Longhair and Allen Toussaint. "It was to show three generations of piano players," explains Tuts. "By me being the oldest, the other ones learned from me. I'm the one that sold that picture. Now I told you about Fess, I knew about Allen when he lived back in Gert Town and learned offa Ernest Penn. Allen got his name from writin' music for other people."

In 1980, Tuts began a two-year engagement at the Bayou Room, an elegant lounge inside Pontchartrain Hotel on St. Charles Avenue. At the time, this observer wrote:

"He plays the piano three nights a week, from Thursday to Saturday, for the cocktail crowd in the Pontchartrain Hotel's Bayou Bar. The majority of his audience consists of affluent New Orleanians with a smattering of conventioneers sporting plastic lapel cards, waiting to dine in the St. Charles Avenue hotel's elegant dining room.

"The Steinway baby grand is scarred from the endless splash of drinks and burning cigarettes. Tuts Washington sits behind its keyboard letting the standards flow, and the requests pour in all night long. 'How High The Moon,' 'Canadian Sunset,' 'Sentimental Journey,' 'Hello Dolly.' Tuts is never at a loss for crowd pleasers in the Bayou Bar.

"Occasionally he will tap his Storyville roots and launch into a blistering boogie woogie that will recall the pioneers of boogie woogie piano from the 1920's, Jimmy 'Papa' Yancey and Pinetop Smith. The years roll away as Tuts' hands fly over the piano keys, seemingly faster than a man of 74 years of age should be able to play.

"Just about this time, conversation at the bar and the crowded tables ceases. Attention focuses on the little man with the odd tuft of hair (a coif which in Storyville would have identified him as a house pianist). He finishes with a flourish of stride and polite applause. He reaches for his polished ivory cigarette holder and calmly lights another Kool. Finally a smile creases his face and he proclaims, as always, 'Thank you, music lovers!'

"Couples return to their conversations as Tuts returns to his steady stream of standards. Everybody drinks up, some leave a tip at the piano, but all leave with a smile. That's the earmark of a successful player's evening. A good piano player brings it all together.''

In March of 1983, at the age of 76, Tuts finally made his first solo recordings, which resulted in the *New Orleans Piano Professor* album that was issued on the Rounder label. Tuts finally consented to recording after Rounder complied with the stringent specifications laid down by the New Orleans Musicians Union. During the two days of recording, Tuts surprisingly reacted like a studio veteran, putting down more than twenty completed piano solos, and one vocal, the risque "Papa Yellow's Blues."

"I'm glad I finally made one," says Tuts. "I'm proud of it. Everybody that heard it said they liked it, white and colored. I even sold some in my neighborhood and the people said that they enjoyed it. See, I mixed it up, I'm versatile, I didn't just put the blues on there, I mixed in some of them standard numbers.

"I believe my playin' is better than it was twenty or thirty years ago. I'm not as fast, but I'm still fast enough. I know more now, 'cause I keep studyin'. I goes down to Werlein's and buy books to study it. A good piano player's got to keep studying and improving. If you don't, you're not worth a damn anymore.''

PROFESSOR LONGHAIR
Going To The Mardi Gras

Professor Longhair's life read much like a modern day fairy tale. As a musician and as an individual, Professor Longhair was the kind of personality Hollywood should drool over. Here was a man who had risen from abject poverty, who with a combination of talent and [both good and bad] luck—became perhaps the most influential figure in the chronicles of the city's music. Then he sank into obscurity for years, only to be rediscovered by an eager group of young music fans who gave him the acclaim and credit he truly deserved. Sadly, though, he died on the very eve of what would be his greatest commercial success. But even in Fess' death, sorrow wasn't the only emotion one felt. Unlike so many other deserving rhythm and blues figures, Longhair had beaten the odds and collected his rightful dues—even if only partially.

Professor Longhair gave his life and his music to New Orleans. Invariably he is remembered with love and respect in the city. His music influenced such people as Allen Toussaint, Smiley Lewis, Dr. John, The Meters, Fats Domino, Huey Smith, James Booker, and even the New Orleans modern day rock group, The Radiators.

As a musician his style was clearly limited, but his sound was so unique and off the wall it didn't really matter. His appeal lay in his offbeat songs and an instantly identifiable piano style, which he once described as a blend of "rhumba, mambo and Calypso." When he sang his voice tended to crack when he sought the higher register, but it remained curiously appealing. He even whistled like a possessed mockingbird. Given the rudiments of a small group, or even just a good drummer, Professor Longhair could really "Walk Your Blues Away."

For many years Professor Longhair was a mysterious legend among blues collectors around the world. His handful of mesmerizing records sent us on a frenzied search for these scratchy discs. When at last he was rediscovered and brought back to musical life, he oh so pleasantly surprised everyone. So often subjects of the rhythm and blues revival had suffered from the years of inactivity and were very much a disappointment once they performed again in public.

But not Professor Longhair. It seemed as though he was just calmly waiting for someone to pay attention to him again. If anything, Longhair's playing [like a fine wine] had improved with age. In 1979 he could incite a crowded Tipitina's just as he had done at the Caldonia Inn three decades previously. Once you'd seen him, you could never lose the picture of him flailing away at the piano, with his head turned sideways wailing the lyrics of "Tipitina," or whistling the intro to "Mardi Gras in New Orleans."

Professor Longhair was born Henry Roeland Byrd on December 19, 1918, the son of Ella Mae Byrd and James Lucius Byrd. His birthplace was Bogalusa, Louisiana, a small paper milling town in Washington Parish that hugs the Pearl River near the Mississippi-Louisiana border.

Ella Mae had one other older son, Robert, but she bore no other children. Shortly after "Roy" was born, James deserted his wife, and Ella Mae brought her sons to New Orleans. They settled into a downtown tenement, behind Rampart Street near Girod Street, that was later razed during the 1950s to make room for the new City Hall and Federal Buildings.

As a youth, Roy Byrd used to tap dance for tips on Bourbon and Rampart Street. Along with his pals Harrison Hike and Streamline Isaac (Byrd was called Whirlwind), the trio "hamboned," and split the change that was thrown into the street. From there the trio began making "music" by banging out rhythms on discarded orange crates and lard cans. Usually Whirlwind and Harrison would play the pans, while Longhair accompanied them by tapping out the rhythm with his feet. This was the depression, so Longhair could be found both day and night trying to hustle some loose change. Longhair recalled that these street-corner antics deepened his interest in music.

Ella Mae Byrd was capable of playing a number of instruments herself, and she showed her son the rudiments of each. Longhair's first real instrument was a guitar that his mother bought him. But he soon abandoned it because it made his fingers sore and the strings were always breaking. During the mid-Thirties Longhair began hanging out in clubs and joints in his neighborhood, especially Delpee's, located on Calliope and Franklin (now Loyola). Delpee's used to feature piano players, and Longhair began watching and listening, thereby inspiring him to play. Robert Bertrand, Kid Stormy Weather, Little Brother Montgomery, Drive 'Em Down, Sullivan Rock and Tuts Washington all came under Longhair's early scrutiny. Tuts Washington still vividly recalls Longhair poking his

South Rampart, 1940's

head in the Rampart Street joints and begging lessons from "Father Tuts." "I tried to show Fess some of these strides that I plays," points out Tuts. "But he couldn't make it. Fess had to roll his left hand to cover what I can. Fact is that's how he came up with his style."

Longhair once recalled he danced with a group that included Tuts Washington, "Bama" on trumpet, and a drummer. One night the drummer was ill and he played the drums while Harrison and Streamline danced. Tuts encouraged Longhair, telling him he could "keep a pretty good beat." Longhair scraped together enough money to buy a drum kit, piece by piece. Eventually, though, he lost his interest in the drums because they were too difficult to carry around. This intensified his interest in piano, and obviously he wouldn't have to carry a piano around. Tuts began showing Longhair some songs because "he played too good not to be playing something."

Sullivan Rock (Rocky Sullivan) was always cited as his major influence. Longhair met the barrelhouse pianist in a speakeasy around 1936. He soon found himself following Sullivan Rock into the Rampart Street bars and saloons. Sullivan Rock, who died around 1940, eventually showed him how to play "Pinetop's Boogie

Woogie." Once Longhair found out how to put the song together, he started adding his own embellishments, finding he had a natural talent. Thereafter, when he was not hustling nickels and dimes on the street corner, Longhair could be found banging out a tune on a battered piano somewhere on Rampart Street.

As Longhair and his pals got to be better dancers, they began to get hired by the Lincoln and Palace Theatres on the weekends. They had worked out an act that included perilous acrobatics, tricks, and dancing up and down four-foot walls. He even had a spell with the C.J.K. Medicine Show working as a dancer in blackface, and as an errand boy. But he quit after a month because the comedian would throw pies in his face during the show. Also during his teens Longhair developed a passionate interest in playing cards. His reputation as one of the city's best coon-can players is well known. For most of his life Longhair would "support" himself and his family by gambling.

As his piano playing developed, he began luring other musicians to accompany him. His first professional job was at the Cotton Club, on Rampart Street, with Champion Jack Dupree. The relationship of Dupree and Longhair has for the most part been overlooked. Dupree, though eight years older, learned to play from Longhair in exchange for singing lessons. Dupree's writing style also impressed him, as Longhair often confirmed.

During the late Thirties Longhair also accompanied Sonny Boy Williamson (Rice Miller), whom he greatly admired, at Dudly Monroe's popular New York Inn, down the street from the Cotton Club. Longhair began concentrating more on his piano playing and singing after a "tricky knee" curtailed his tap dancing—but not his gambling career.

In 1937, Longhair joined the Civilian Conservation Corps—C.C.C.—one of Roosevelt's W.P.A. projects. In exchange for $50 a month, plus room and board, he was required to work with the crews that built the levees, graded the roads, dug spillways, and cut down trees and weeds along the highways. On top of that, he was also expected to drill and attend C.C.C. classes. Longhair was shrewd enough to realize he could avoid an awful lot of this work by entertaining some of the other workers on the recreation hall's piano. Although he stayed in the C.C.C. only six months, it left a deep impression on his developing style. Longhair remembers being impressed by the way the Latin groups that he heard would play with calypso and rhumba beats.

When his C.C.C. term finished, he returned to New Orleans,

picking up pretty much where he left off, supporting himself by playing coon-can. Whenever he was broke, he'd pick up a piano-playing job so he could make enough to get back into a card game. He even gave boxing a whirl, but went back to the card table after he had his front teeth knocked out in an alley.

Longhair attempted to enlist in 1940, but was turned down because of his bad knee. But when America entered World War II, he was drafted into the army in 1942, and was stationed at Camp Claiborne in Alexandria, Louisiana. Although he completed basic training, he was never shipped overseas because he developed a hernia and a burst appendix—both of which required operations. While in the army hospital he had little else to do but brush up on the recreation room's piano. He also exchanged a lot of ideas with other patients about anything and everything. After spending eight months in the hospital, he was given a medical discharge in 1944.

Things were slow when Longhair got back to New Orleans since most of his coon-can buddies were still in uniform. For awhile he had a stake in a cafe called "Jimmy Hicks' Barbeque Pit," near the corner of Rampart and Howard. Hicks needed a cook, but couldn't afford to hire one. So Longhair bought himself a cookbook, and Hicks took him on as an equal partner. The two partners built up the business, offering soul food and plate lunches. To supplement his income, Longhair set up his own profitable punchboard hustle selling tries on cheap trinkets.

During his stint as a restaurant entrepreneur, Longhair married his first wife (though reluctantly), Beulah Walker. Though they stayed together less than a month, Longhair couldn't manage to get a divorce until 1975, the day before he married his second wife, Alice Walton Byrd.

When business wasn't too heavy around the "Barbeque Pit," Longhair played on the piano Hicks had bought for the cafe. Hicks' mother-in-law was an invalid and sat in the restaurant, where Longhair would play "Just A Closer Walk With Thee," and other hymns for her. Hicks bought out Longhair just after the war was over, apparently because he was jealous of his punchboard hustle. So Longhair returned to his old haunts, playing coon-can, and hustling up a piano job when he needed the money.

Longhair kept his playing at a minimum until the explosion of recording activity took place in New Orleans during 1948, and he decided he wanted to make some noise too.

As Longhair tells the story, he got his first break at the Caldonia Club, then located at the corner of St. Claude and St. Philip Street.

Apparently he stepped in the club one night while the local king, Dave Bartholomew, and his orchestra, was playing. During the intermission the group's pianist, Salvador Doucette, stepped down, and Longhair got permission to sit in. Once he started playing, the crowd went wild over the new sound, and the club began to fill up with extra customers. The club's owner, Mike Tessitore, noticed the extra business, and promptly fired Bartholomew and hired Longhair on the spot! So Longhair recruited a band that included Eddie Jones (Apeman Black?) on tenor sax, Walter "Papoose" Nelson on guitar, and "Big Slick" (John Woodrow?) on drums. Tessitore was taken with the band's slick appearance and longish hair, and first gave Longhair his romantic pseudonym.

Whatever the true facts, the entertainment page of the April 3, 1948 *Louisiana Weekly* announced: "Biggest female impersonator show in town at the Caldonia, with music by the Three Hair Combo, featuring Professors Longhair, Shorthair, and No Hair!" The group remained a regular fixture around the Caldonia for most of 1948.

By 1949, bigger things were on the horizon. Besides the Caldonia Inn job, Longhair worked across the river at Kohlmen's Tavern in Algiers as Henry Long Hair, with Joe Mingo, M.G. Stevens and the Frog Trio. He even hosted a big Jax Beer party at the Pepper Pot in Gretna, honoring Dr. Daddy-O, who still recalls their initial meeting: "Fess was the kind of performer that gave me a gut reaction the first time I saw him. They made him wear these long-toed shoes, because he would kick on the piano so hard, he would break the front of it. All the club owners liked him because he drew a good crowd and they made a lot of money."

In October of 1949, he was approached by Jesse Erickson, who was looking for talent to record on his Dallas based Star Talent label. Longhair was recorded in a makeshift studio, set up in Joe Prop's Bar, located on the corner of St. Peter and Villere streets. A standard four-song session took place which included "She Ain't Got No Hair," "Bye Bye Baby," "Professor Longhair's Boogie," and the original "Mardi Gras In New Orelans." At the end of the session, Erickson asked the group whom he should credit the records to. Robert Parker and Longhair came up with the unforgettable "Professor Longhair and his Shuffling Hungarians." But before the records could break, they were withdrawn from sales because Erickson had held non-union sessions, thereby depriving the public of some of the finest music ever recorded in New Orleans.

Longhair's "rhumba, mambo and calypso" style of playing was already fully developed, especially on his anthem "Mardi Gras In

Vocal
BMI 1:56
ebb pub.

MISERY
(R. Byrd)
PROFESSOR LONGHAIR
106

New Orleans." Longhair first got the tune together at the Pepper Pot, after deciding that since there were songs about Christmas and other holidays, why not write one about New Orleans' biggest celebration?

After the Star Talent fiasco, Longhair came to the attention of William B. Allen, who owned a radio shop and ran the local Mercury Records distributorship on the corner of Basin and North Claiborne. Longhair and his group used to rent their P.A. from his shop, and Allen approached them one day representing Mercury Records. In late 1949, a session was arranged at the National Recording company in the Godchaux building on Canal Street. Recording some of the same tunes he had for Star Talent, Longhair [in order to avoid possible legal problems with Star Talent] reverted to his real name, Roy Byrd and his Blues Jumpers, which included John Woodrow, Robert Parker and Walter "Papoose" Nelson. One of them, the hilarious "Hadacol Bounce"—"cleans your teeth, makes your eyeballs bright"—had to be withdrawn from the market, because it was considered a commercial for the popular southern patent medicine. But "Baldhead," his Mercury remake of "She Ain't Got No Hair," was indeed good enough to reach #5 (for 2 weeks) on the national R&B charts during August of 1950.

Longhair recalls he wrote the song about a girl that used to frequent the Pepper Pot.

In April of 1950, the *Louisiana Weekly* commented: "Roy Byrd, who plays the most unusual piano blues that you ever heard, and the first male recording artist contracted to Mercury Records, and his band the Blues Jumpers, are featured Easter Sunday Night, April 8th, at the San Jacinto Hall. For engagements call Raymond-8222."

Even before his Mercury release made the charts, Longhair was approached in the Pepper Pot by Jerry Wexler and Armet Ertegen of Atlantic Records. They lured Longhair into the J&M Studio with a mere $100. Ten sides were cut in early 1950, from which three singles were released. Included was a popular remake of "Mardi Gras In New Orleans," credited to Roy "Baldhead" Byrd. The second, "Professor Longhair Blues" and "Walk Your Blues Away," credits Professor Longhair and his Blues Scholars. And the third, "Hey Little Girl," and "Willie Mae," simply credits Roy Byrd. The continuous change of his name couldn't have helped his national sales, but everybody knew who he was in New Orleans and bought his records in good quantities.

Longhair changed labels again in 1951, this time signing on with Federal—a King Records subsidiary—through the aid of Joe Assunto, who later ran Joe's One-Stop Record Shop on Rampart Street. Four sides were released, including the powerful "Curly Haired Baby" and the superb blues "Gone So Long," which features Longhair's patented two-fisted keyboard attack. Not surprisingly, he had a small hit with the latter in Texas and Louisiana.

During 1952, Longhair made a short midwestern tour with Dave Bartholomew and Fats Domino. When the group stopped in St. Louis, Longhair was recorded in a tavern by the tiny Wasco label. Once again his name was changed, this time to Robert Boyd. Two sides were issued, "East St. Louis Baby"—an altered version of "Mardi Gras In New Orleans"—and "Boyd's Bounce," but it sold poorly.

Earl Palmer, who played drums on the tour, recalled that even though Fats had hot records out, Longhair stole his thunder with his wild onstage antics that included his walking on the keyboard. Apparently he also won a good portion of Fats' earnings too, playing coon-can in the back seat of Fats' Cadillac!

Atlantic decided to try once again, and a session was arranged in November of 1953. With the regular J&M Studio unit of Lee Allen, Red Tyler, Earl Palmer and Frank Fields, Longhair cut four of his best sides including his much remembered "Tipitina," which rose as high as #2 in the New Orleans R&B charts. But because Longhair rarely worked any place but the tiny nightspots in New Orleans, Atlantic (and for that matter his other record companies) had trouble moving his records outside the Gulf Coast.

During the mid-Fifties, Longhair suffered a mild stroke which affected his playing. As a result he had to curtail his performing. The burden of raising his family fell on his "wife," Alice Walton Byrd, who took in laundry. The only money Longhair could manage was from his coon-can winnings.

By 1955 he had recovered sufficiently to accompany Edgar "Big Boy" Myles and the Sha-wees on his Specialty sides. Included on the session was a top notch rework of Longhair's "Who's Been Fooling You."

Longhair next entered the studio in 1957, recording six sides for Ebb, a label owned by Art Rupe's (Specialty's owner) ex-wife. The session was arranged by Dick Stergel, who ran one of the local independent record distributorships. Longhair cut three stinging singles, including the unforgettable "Looka No Hair," and two excellent ballads, "Misery" and "Cry Pretty Baby." He even managed another local hit with the rollicking "No Buts, No Maybes."

In 1958, Longhair found himself on the newly-formed New Orleans' Ron label, run by Joe Ruffino. After a nice ballad, "If Only I Knew," he had another hit with the definitive version of "Go To The Mardi Gras," which still gets plenty of airplay locally during Carnival season. But it seemed as if it was Longhair's last fling with the big time. Jobs grew further apart as his style suddenly seemed dated compared to newcomers like Ernie K-Doe, Lee Dorsey, and Irma Thomas, who were now dominating the New Orleans scene.

Most of his work revolved around Carnival and the occasional job playing solo in neighborhood bars. Longhair must have still cut an exciting profile though, resplendent in his fish-tailed tuxedo. Sadly, things went from bad to worse as on Carnival day of 1960 he was arrested on the bandstand of the San Jacinto Club for suspicion of drug possession.

He didn't return to the studio again until 1962, when Wardell Quezergue produced a session for Rip Roberts' Rip label. Quezergue tried to update Longhair's style—i.e. "Whole Lot Of Twistin'"—but the records failed miserably—musically and financially.

His 1963 switch to Watch Record was a vast improvement. This time Quezergue kept things simple, and Longhair produced strong versions of his old "Baldhead," and Big Jay McNeely's "There Is Something On Your Mind."

He returned to the studio again in 1964 to be produced by Quezergue and Earl King. Earl still recalls the session: "Fess was about ready to give it up. In fact he had, as far as personal appearances went. He was just hangin' out at the One Stop sweepin' up and that.

"I had wrote this song 'Big Chief' in school. So when we went to work on this project for Professor Longhair, I got to thinkin' about the Mardi Gras, and went back to my book. I had the idea to record Fess with a lot of bass because I never thought he had been recorded right. So me and Wardell got together, and he wrote out the horn arrangement for fifteen pieces.

"Meantime, me, Fess and Smokey Johnson got together and rehearsed it. So when we got to the studio, Fess thought there was gonna be just four pieces, but there was all these musicians hangin' around the studio. So Fess turns to me and says, 'Earl, what are all these guys doin' here? I guess they're waitin' for the next session huh?'

"I said, 'Probably so.' So Fess gets in behind the piano and plays his little intro, then Smokey and the rhythm section falls in, then all of a sudden where the big crash of horns come in, Fess stops playin' —Bam! He says, 'What is that!?!'

"I said, 'Well that's the rest of the guys that's gonna be on the session.' So we took a fifteen minute break for Fess to compose himself. Fess says, 'Man we don't really need all them.'

"I said, 'I know but they gonna play man.' So after he got his head together he was all right."

"Big Chief" temporarily transformed the previously downcast Longhair according to King. "Fess reached a new energy level. The Professor gained a new adrenalin. One week he was totally out of it, and then the next he was all enthusiastic about being musical again, and he would be playin' again every day."

According to Earl, although "Big Chief" has always been associated with Mardi Gras in New Orleans, it wasn't geared at all to the Carnival season when it was originally released. "London Records leased it before it ever came out. Their intention wasn't to make it a Mardi Gras record. That's why the title 'Big Chief' was put on it instead of something else connected with the Mardi Gras thing. At the time the promotional aspect was very nil. They just released it period. I think the Professor was victimized because at the particu-

A GIANT IN NEW ORLEANS!! #1

"IF I ONLY KNEW"

b/w

CUTTIN' OUT

by

Professor Longhair

RON #326

BIG IN NEW ORLEANS, HOUSTON, NASHVILLE

NOTICE TO RETAIL RECORD DEALERS: *If you are unable to secure our merchandise from our distributors, please contact us.*

DEEJAYS: FOR COPIES WRITE US

RON RECORDS, INC.

(DIVISION OF RIC RECORDS, INC.)
630½ BARONNE ST.   NEW ORLEANS, LA.   JAckson 2-3224

---

lar time that company had some hot groups then. They wasn't too impressed with any newcomers where they had to spend a big budget promoting.

"The first year they were weird around here; the stations wouldn't even play it. The next year, though, people around here started gettin' into it, and the year after it got a little better, and so on."

Sadly, Longhair's enthusiasm didn't last after "Big Chief" had apparently flopped. To make matters worse, Watch followed up with the horrific "Third House From The Corner" and "Willie The Prince." "Man that was the most ridiculous stuff—I was just furious," seethes Earl, recalling the record. "Fess didn't have anything to do with that. Joe Assunto wanted to do something totally out in left field, and that's what he did. That should never have followed 'Big Chief.'"

Musically, Longhair just sank further into obscurity. Without a record company, he almost totally abandoned playing. It was a sad sight to see him, stooped and in poor health, cleaning up around the One-Stop. "The record companies missed out on Fess," points out Earl King. "They just thought of him as a good musician with a few good songs and forgot about him. There was a whole lot left in Fess, he had a lot of new ideas and approaches. It didn't take a whole lot to stir him up and excite him, but they didn't stick around to find it out."

By 1969, rumors of his whereabouts began circulating around New Orleans and Europe. Stories concerning Longhair described him as bald, semi-bald, dead, crippled, in California, unable to play and retired.

Noted English journalist Mike Leadbitter managed to track down the mysterious Longhair at his 1522 South Rampart Street address in early 1970 and described their meeting: "He was down and out, and very sad, as neglect, frustration and poor health had taken their toll. The man we met was no longer a big recording artist, but an old man forgotten by the recording industry."

Longhair also came to the attention of two young New Orleans music enthusiasts, Quint Davis and Allison Minor Kaslow. "I'd grown up with the great mass of people that subliminally knew about Professor Longhair from hearing 'Go To The Mardi Gras' every year," reflects Davis.

"But not having ever seen him, I didn't know if he was a real entity or not. The way I got started on Professor Longhair was the first time George Wein came down to do the Jazz and Heritage Festival in 1970. I took George down to the H&R Bar on Second and Dryades, to see the Wild Magnolias. We went into the Sweet Shop next door and I played 'Go To The Mardi Gras' on the jukebox, and George stopped right there. George is a pianist—and he said, 'If you're gonna do a festival in New Orleans you better get that guy.'"

Longhair proved to be an elusive target, as Kaslow, who was then working at the Tulane Jazz Archives, points out: "It took almost a year for Quint and me to find him. There was this sense of mysteriousness about him from the first time I heard his name. The jazz people at Tulane didn't think he was too great because he wasn't strictly a jazz musician. Everytime we saw somebody on the bus with long hair or long fingers, we'd get excited and think it must be him."

The duo's persistence paid off as Davis eventually tracked Longhair down: "I'd heard he (Longhair) used to come around Assunto's —The One-Stop (on S. Rampart St.)—and he'd come in every year around Mardi Gras and borrow some money. One day I was in there asking about him, and he walked in right behind me. Someone said, 'That's him,' and I grabbed his hand and said, 'I've been looking for you.'

"He wasn't playing at all then; he was in a totally depreciated state physically, along with poverty and rejection. When he sat down, he couldn't get up. When he did stand up, his knee would rattle around until it set into a groove so he could walk. He had a vitamin deficiency, he had no teeth, no digestion, and he couldn't go to the bathroom. He didn't eat because he couldn't chew or digest anything.

"But he always had this great spirit to endure no matter what. I mean he had to be 55 years old and living in that little house without a pot to piss in, to start over with nothing for an unknown public, and really believe he could have a reincarnation with all that work ahead of him. So I followed it up and got him to play the Jazz Festival gig at Congo Square."

As things turned out, the 1971 New Orleans Jazz Festival was to be the major turning point in Longhair's career. "The first time I saw him he came hobbling through Congo Square with Sheba the drummer," continued Kaslow. "He looked just terrible. He had short hair and a suit on that had been pressed so many times it was shiny. But when he played it was like nothing I'd ever heard before. I'd been around a lot of the blues people, but Byrd was so hip and so full of energy it was different. I couldn't believe here was all that talent seemingly going to waste."

Davis concurred: "I got 'Blind' Snooks Eaglin to play with Fess for that first appearance. You've got to remember the Jazz Festival wasn't a big thing back then; there was hardly anybody there. But when Fess got up to play that upright piano, everything literally stopped. All the musicians and all of the people came over to the stage where Fess was playing."

Longhair was the unabashed sensation of the 1971 Jazz Festival as he sent shockwaves of rhythm through the dumbfounded audience. "He was like a different person after that," says Kaslow. "It was like he was suddenly ten years younger. He was the hippest person you'd ever want to meet."

Longhair also became the target for a number of would-be managers and hangers-on not long after that first Jazz Festival appearance. According to Kaslow, "All of a sudden everyone wanted to take care of his business. They were just driving him nuts. But Fess, being such a nice guy, he was afraid to be mean, even to the people who were obviously trying to take advantage of him. One guy who wanted to manage him would come around to Byrd's house all the time, and when he did, Byrd would lock himself in the armoire and not come out until he left!"

It was eventually Davis who acted as Longhair's manager and confidant: "There really wasn't much work at all in the beginning," recalls Davis. "There wasn't the club scene like today where people actually went out to listen to New Orleans music. Once a month Fess might get a job out at Freddie Domino's Bar in the Ninth Ward. We did the National Folk Festival that year (1971), but the real interest didn't come until later."

Davis feels that one of the keys that further boosted Longhair's "second" career was the demo session he arranged in 1972. "Me and Parker Dinkins (who formed the short-lived Ahura Mazda label) took Fess, Snooks, Big Will and Sheba into a studio in Baton Rouge and cut 34 songs. That was the session that Jerry Wexler (Atlantic Records president) and Albert Grossman (then managing The Band) heard. When they heard on the tapes that he was playing his living ass off and that the music was there, some different forces came together. Wexler arranged the first European tour (in 1973) to Paris and Montreux with Toussaint and the Meters, which was filmed, recorded and was a killer. That was a big thing; it opened up to a lot of people that there was actually a Professor Longhair.

"Grossman invited us up to Woodstock. We did some sessions that were supposed to come out on Bearsville, but in the end it didn't work out. I don't exactly know why—we did some killer sessions—but nothing ever came out. Grossman's got all the tapes.

"You see Grossman's big; I mean he's just physically big, and that's the way he functioned. He moved with a lot of force. He created this hell of a community up there (Woodstock). He had Todd Rundgren, The Band, Paul Butterfield, the Full Tilt Boogie Band and Foghat. He built the first really advanced studio there; he was managing and he had the label.

"He seemed real interested, and he initially made the investment; ($25,000 according to Kaslow) and that money was crucial. It paid for the Baton Rouge session. I bought Fess some clothes, a car and a piano.

"We got there (Woodstock) a day early or something, and they put us up in this house that wasn't finished; it didn't have electricity or a phone, and they told us to hang on for a day or so until they got it together. Well, if you're a 23-year-old Caucasian rock fan and were told to hang on in Woodstock that was one thing, but I was there with 'Blind' Snooks Eaglin and Professor Longhair, and they didn't think things were happening at all. I'll never forget Snooks standing by the window and saying the sound of the snow falling on the roof bothered him.

"When we were there we did one strange session with some guy and then we did a whole afternoon with the Full Tilt Boogie Band, but it just wasn't happening. So I took them to New York and did a session with George Davis on bass, 'Honey Boy,' on drums and Earl Turbinton on saxophone. That was, I'd say, his best session ever.

"We did another session in Memphis later with Zigaboo (Modeliste) on drums and that session was a mother too."

Nonetheless, these recordings have yet to see the light of day, while bootleg albums that contain inferior recordings of live European concerts have proliferated. "Grossman's just not interested," claims Kaslow. "He just doesn't realize the importance of Professor Longhair. Grossman just doesn't know how to deal with black artists."

"I don't understand it either," adds Davis. "They've got the stuff just sitting up there. But I'll tell you what, I'd just like them to send a dub of those sessions to me—that was some of the best Professor Longhair material you'd ever want to hear."

In the meantime Atlantic records issued the landmark "New Orleans Piano" album as part of their six-part "Blues Originals" series. The album collected his Atlantic sessions dating from 1949 and 1953. The LP met with deserved world-wide acclaim, and Longhair gained even broader attention, which further speeded up his metamorphosis.

"Fess was a lifelong professional musician," emphasized Davis. "He was dedicated to his art form so he always had all that style. But when his health started getting better and he started to walk good, he really started taking care of business. He started asking, 'Did we get the deposit? What about a piano? Who is this musician?' I started taking him to the VA Hospital, because they had his medical records. He started taking vitamins, he started eating cheese, drinking milk, wearing glasses and seeing the dentist. But how he was able to walk again and kick the piano was really miraculous. Having all those spiritual and mental juices back and to be physically active at the piano—man it made all the difference in the world to him."

Longhair remained an intensely loyal family man throughout periods of both feast and famine. "His family life was the one stable thing beyond all else in his life," adds Davis. "Alice Walton Byrd was a rock. She could keep a family together. You see there were three generations of Alice's family in the house. There was her mother and her grandmother who laid in a bed in the back of the house. She must have been a hundred. There were kids and relatives always running in and out of the house, and Fess felt like he

ENGLAND'S
PIPEMAKERS
H.W. MARVEN
REGISTERED PLUMBER
W. DEBICKI

was responsible for all of them. Next to being out there playing, the biggest thing in his life was coming home with some money to give Alice."

Jobs began picking up for Longhair by the mid-Seventies, according to Davis. "We booked a few concerts jobs around town like at the Warehouse, but they weren't too frequent. Fess was still playing cards to get the rent money. Then we got a job at Crazy Shirley's on Bourbon Street, which was pretty nice because it was just a couple of hours in the afternoon. The first club stuff was at Jed's. Jed Palmer was the first person to book him at Mardi Gras and ask a dollar at the door. See, people in New Orleans just never paid a cover charge to see music."

Davis rented a house at 1517 South Rampart Street which was to serve as a rehearsal hall and studio for Longhair and Davis' other musical project, the Wild Magnolias. Little by little, all of Longhair's family moved into the second house, and it was here that tragedy befell Longhair when the house burned to the ground, ironically during the 1974 New Orleans Jazz Festival. "Everything burned," sighed Davis. "I mean every damn thing. There was nothing left but ashes. A four-story clapboard got torched just behind the house and everything around it went up. After all we'd done and all we'd built up, all he had left were the clothes on his back. And he wore those same clothes for weeks because he had nothing else to wear. He was miserable because there was no insurance on the contents and I think he felt it was my fault. But it was just one of those things where I just didn't think about insurance."

A hastily-arranged benefit took place at the Warehouse the Monday after the festival with the likes of Allen Toussaint, Earl King, Dr. John and Tommy Ridgley. Unfortunately, only a thousand people showed up and less than $4,500 was raised. Realizing that Longhair was in a jam, Phillippe Rault of the French Barclay label offered him $750 to record an album with Clarence "Gatemouth" Brown. The tragedy seemed to have no effect on Longhair's music, as the resulting *Rock 'n' Roll Gumbo* album was among his most satisfying modern efforts.

Starting over again was no easy task, but Longhair persisted. Besides Jed's, Davis began booking dances at the 501 Club, and another European tour was arranged for 1975. Around this period, Longhair's management reverted to Kaslow when Davis' commitment to organizing the growing New Orleans Jazz Festival began taking up most of his time.

Under Kaslow's direction, Longhair increased the size of his band, even adding a steel drummer, and upped his personal appearance fee. Longhair also came to the attention of Paul McCartney, who was recording an album at New Orleans' Sea-Saint Studio in 1976. McCartney hired Longhair to play a private party aboard the Queen Mary and arranged to record the performance for Harvest records, a subsidiary of Capitol. "Byrd had no idea who Paul McCartney was," recalls Kaslow with a laugh. "He had never even heard of the Beatles. Even though he'd been to Europe and all across the country, his world was right there on Rampart Street with his family."

In 1977, an ambitious group of young New Orleanians tired of having few places for Longhair to play in town organized their money and ideas and opened the old 501 Club and renamed it Tipitina's after one of Longhair's most popular numbers. His rousing performances at that venue are still a legend by all those who were lucky enough to have ever seen him there.

Despite all odds, Professor Longhair had finally made it. He was able to buy a house on Terpsichore Street not far from his former South Rampart Street address. In 1978, Kaslow claims he made $32,000. "Byrd finally got to the point where he didn't have to struggle; he was making a comfortable living. You never saw a happier man. He was always lending money out to his friends or buying diapers for some woman in the neighborhood."

One of Longhair's favorite non-musical activities was buying and using CB equipment (some of it apparently illegal). Many evenings when he had nothing better to do he would herd up some of his grandchildren in his Cadillac and drive the streets of New Orleans listening in to the CB, or go listen to music at Tipitina's with his crippled friend, Richard.

Longhair usually stayed busy either by working at Tipitina's or the other Uptown music clubs. On occasion he'd jet off to London or New York or Chicago or Los Angeles—wherever they wanted to hear his unique music. During November of 1979, a long overdue recording session was arranged at Sea-Saint Studio by Alligator, a Chicago label noted for its blues releases, with one of Longhair's proteges, Dr. John, helping out on guitar.

"He'd never been more satisfied with anything he'd recorded," sighs Kaslow, who helped produce the *Crawfish Fiesta* album. "Everything went perfectly. Byrd was so pleased that he couldn't wait for it to come out."

But, sadly, he would never live to see it. On January 30, 1980, he died of a heart attack less than twenty-four hours before the album hit the record stores.

His widow, Alice Walton Byrd, recalls his last night: "The evening he passed, he was riding around with that fellow in the wheelchair, Richard. He came home and laid down. Then he got up around 10 o'clock and took his little grandson down by Picou's (an all night Mid City bakery) to get a dozen twisters. He came back and I thought it was peculiar that he didn't want no coffee, no twister, no nothin'.

"He laid down on the bed. So I went in the kitchen and Alvin (a son who lives in the upstairs apartment) had come in from work, and I told Alvin to shut the door and be careful to lock it.

"He (Longhair) said, 'Alice who you talkin' to?'

"I said, 'I'm talkin' to Alvin. I told him to lock the door.'

"He said, 'Oh, I heard you.'

"So I ate some rice kind of late that night, and I came into the kitchen after doin' my dishes. So I told Byrd, 'You know I got a heartburn.'

"He said, 'Darlin' you eat too late.'

"So I said, 'Maybe you're right.'

"Then I heard him cough.

"I said, 'Byrd?'

"He didn't moan, he didn't groan, but I seen my mother die and I knew right away he was gone."

So ended the life of one of New Orleans' most popular and celebrated musicians. His wake and funeral nearly crushed the tiny Majestic Funeral Home on Dryades Street. The second line that followed Longhair to the Gentilly cemetery stretched an unprecedented ten blocks.

Some of the city's musical magic was buried with Professor Longhair that cold grey day in February. It's no secret that the condition of New Orleans' rhythm and blues scene has suffered since his untimely death.

Kaslow probably offered the best eulogy of Longhair and New Orleans' loss when she stated: "He just created that happy music. Hearing it again on record is just not the same. He was one of a kind."

HUEY "PIANO" SMITH
Don't You Just Know It

Since the early 1950s, Huey "Piano" Smith's name has been synonymous with good time New Orleans rock and roll. But before his own solo career was launched, he paid his dues in a myriad of bands and recording sessions, working as a dependable sideman.

Although Huey's musical career went a lot further than many of his New Orleans contemporaries, it has nonetheless been dotted with bad luck, mistakes, and senseless business deals. Huey himself feels that his best ideas were "stolen" from him, resulting in his fall into virtual obscurity in the late 1960s.

Today Huey Smith no longer plays music. Instead, he is content to stay close to his small house in Baton Rouge, working occasionally as a gardener and studying the Bible. Although he would be considered the logical heir to carry on the piano tradition of New Orleans since the death of Professor Longhair, Huey has no such ambition, preferring to live a simple, uncluttered life outside of the public eye.

Born in New Orleans on January 26, 1934, and raised in the Garden District, Huey's interest in music stemmed from visits as a six year old to his aunt (who lived on the same South Robertson Street block), and listening to his uncle play blues on an upright piano. Huey recalls his early fascination for the piano: "I used to sit up on the piano stool and play 'til the neighbors used to bang on the walls for me to knock it off. When I was about seven or eight, I began makin' songs up like 'Robertson Street Boogie.'

"I had a pal back then who had straight hair; they used to call him 'Slick,' and I was 'Dark.' So we used to play around at the piano as 'Slick and Dark,' as a duo.

"My father used to give me money to take lessons every week at Greywall School of Music, but I didn't ever go. I kept that music money and learned from my sister, who took piano lessons from the lady next door."

Smith's earliest influences were Dinah Washington, Ivory Joe Hunter, Bull Moose Jackson, Charles Brown — even Hank Williams, whom he heard via the radio and on jukeboxes. But the man who had the greatest influence on Huey, and whom he admires to this day, is Louis Jordan. "I tried to hear all of his records. When I couldn't, me and all the kids in the neighborhood would go down to the Lincoln Theatre and see him in those shorts, like 'Saturday Night Fish Fry,' and 'Reet, Petite and Gone.' If you ask me, that's where rock and roll started — it was with Louis Jordan."

At the age of 15, Huey was introduced to a fellow a little bit older than himself, Eddie Jones a.k.a. Guitar Slim, who had recently arrived from Greenwood, Mississippi, through Willie Nettles, who was playing the drums with Huey. The trio became fast friends and began playing clubs around New Orleans, getting their first foothold at the Tiajuana. After Percy Stovall began booking the group, they began appearing at some other clubs and occasionally filling out-of-town engagements.

Huey began to consider himself very much a professional musician, sometimes working two jobs a night and making as much as $24 an evening. "We had fun getting on stage," confirms Huey. "It sure wasn't work, and we were getting paid too! Didn't have to put no boots or gloves on. Girls looking at you, one on each side of the piano. Well I started falling asleep in school and missing classes in my junior year. I never did go back to graduate."

Huey claims he was present on Slim's first recording (credited to Eddie Jones and his Playboys) "Bad Luck Is On Me," but he is barely audible. He is also present on Slim's 1952 session recorded for Jim Bullet Records, while the group was on tour in 1952. The session produced a fair-sized hit with "Feelin' Sad," which insured plenty of work throughout the south.

Huey got his first chance to record in June of 1953, when Savoy held a giant audition at the J&M Studio. Huey cut the bluesy "You Made Me Cry" and "You're Down With Me" with Lee Allen on sax, Billy Tate on guitar, Roland Cook on bass and Charles Williams on drums. Both sides focus on Huey's pounding piano technique and straining youthful voice. Although the Savoy record didn't sell, Huey fondly recalls his landlady buying a copy and singing "You Made Me Cry" in the hall outside his door, completely unaware her tenant was the one she was singing along to!

Despite the passing notoriety of his own record, Huey stayed on with Guitar Slim, as Slim's star began to brighten. When Slim signed on with Specialty Records in 1954, Huey was dropped in favor of Ray Charles for the "Things I Used To Do" session, but remained in the band temporarily. After Slim's new manager, Frank Pania, matched the newly-made hitmaker with Lloyd Lam-

Huey "Piano" Smith, 1958

bert's more experienced band for important out-of-town engagements, the two friends were forced to part, to the apparent dismay of both. Although their careers took them in different directions, they remained close friends until Slim's death in 1959. Huey recalls crying uncontrollably when he heard the news of Slim's death.

After splitting with Slim, Huey decided to get his own group together. Since Huey wasn't very confident about his singing, he hired Earl King as a vocalist, who was also learning the rudiments of the guitar. Together with Roland Cook, the group worked sporadically around New Orleans.

Huey began to supplement his nightclub work with regular recording session dates. Huey recalls supplying the piano on Little Richard's first Specialty session (including "Tutti Frutti"), Lloyd Price, George "Blazer Boy" Stevens, and also contributing the catchy intro to Smiley Lewis' hit, "I Hear You Knockin'." Smiley took a liking to the young pianist, and often used him in his band for personal appearances.

Huey's real break came when Johnny Vincent left Specialty and formed his own label, Ace, in 1955. Vincent heard Huey and Earl at the Club Tiajuana, and at Doc's, a "voodoo shop" on Dryades Street run by Victor "Doc" Augustine, where many musicians hung out and rehearsed. Vincent convinced Huey and Earl to drive up to Jackson, Mississippi to do a recording session because he had purchased inexpensive studio time at Lillian McMurray's Trumpet Studio, on Farish Street.

The session produced Ace's first big hit, "Those Lonely, Lonely Nights," by Earl King. Huey's rolling piano is very much in the forefront of the performance. The record sold strongly along the Gulf Coast, and together with the royalties generated from Johnny "Guitar" Watson's cover version, Vincent was able to record other New Orleans artists, including Huey.

Always quick to cash in on any angle, Vincent had printed on Earl King's record, "Piano by Fats," more than subtly referring to Fats Domino, who was then burning up the charts. Huey wasn't very taken with Vincent's idea though. "Fats!" he seethes, "I was trying to make a name for myself. What does he wanna put out some lil' 'Fats' on for?"

Vincent eventually gave Huey an opportunity to record, but not the way Huey anticipated. "Eddie Bo had recorded for Johnny, but he had gone with another company (Apollo). Bo cut 'I'm Wise,' for this other company, which sounded like Little Richard's 'Slippin' 'n' Slidin',' and it was startin' to hit. Well, Johnny decided he'd better get something out on Bo quick, but he only had one side ['My Love Is Strong'].

"So I had this song, 'We Like Mambo,' and Johnny quickly grabbed me and said, 'Let's cut that for the flip side.' But when the record came out, my side said by Eddie Bo. Johnny said, 'Oh the printer made a mistake.'

"I felt bad because the record made a lil' local noise. I was comin' up, and here was this thing I had done, with someone else's name on it." Smith finally got Vincent to change the label on the record's second pressing (Ace 515) crediting Huey Smith. But the damage was already done. "The nightclubs were calling for Eddie Bo, not Huey Smith. There was nothing I could do." Eddie Bo in fact began featuring "We Like Mambo," on his shows, to further Huey's chagrin!"

Huey had to wait until his second Ace release "Little Liza Jane," to taste success. "My voice wasn't that good," concedes Huey, "but I could get by with a couple of catchy lines. When I got to the studio, Johnny wanted me to play the music and then put the vocals down later. But I said, 'No way. In no shape or form!' I didn't want another record comin' out with my music and someone else's name on it. Fact I got up and went home. Johnny had to come get me and bring me back.

"As it turned out I did a verse, 'Izzacoo' [Gordon] did a verse, and Dave Dixon did a verse. It did real well locally, the football marching bands use' to play it. So I was encouraged by that."

While playing one night at the Club Tiajuana, Huey met a young singer from Youngstown, Ohio, Bobby Marchan, who led a troupe of female impersonators, "The Powder Box Revue." Huey wrote some numbers for Marchan, who had also previously recorded for Ace. One of the songs Huey penned for Marchan was "Little Chickee Wah Wah."

When he wasn't in the studio, Huey kept himself busy grinding out one-nighters on the Gulf Coast and New Orleans, often working behind Earl King and Smiley Lewis, who were working as a package show, or else playing with his own small group.

Smith recalls this hectic period, which, as it turned out, changed the direction of his career: "One night we'd be in Lake Charles. Then we'd all pile into a station wagon — band equipment and everything — and play the next night in Opelousas. Then we'd come back and work as the house band at the Dew Drop.

"Anyway, Shirley and Lee came up hittin' with 'Let The Good Times Roll,' and they were lookin' for a band to go on the road with. So Frank sent us out with them, and we got some new uniforms and started rehearsing. We went to Atlanta and New York, to do a show for Alan Freed at the Brooklyn Paramount.

"We came back into town one weekend and Johnny was in town, so he rushed me into the studio. I was tryin' to pick up on some catchy lines, and Chuck Berry had this line 'I got rockin' pneumonia, sittin' down at a rhythm revue,' in a song, and Roy Brown had some line about 'young man rhythm.' So I started thinkin' about opposite lines like 'kissin' a girl that's too tall.' So we came up with 'Rockin' Pneumonia And The Boogie Woogie Flu,' that night right in the studio.

"Well I had to go right back out on the road with Shirley and Lee. But after a couple of weeks I heard that the record was hittin' back home, from Bobby Marchan, while we were both in Baltimore.

"Bobby's record ['Chickee Wah Wah'] was also high in the charts, and he was workin' at the Royal too, opening for Shirley and Lee. My record was lookin' to be a national seller, so I figured maybe I could start a group with Bobby, 'cause he was a good showman.

"So Bobby said, 'Yeah, why don't we go back to New Orleans and start a group?' Well, I didn't have enough money, but when Bobby got paid, we bought two train tickets for New Orleans and I gave my notice to Billy Diamond, who was the group's manager. They sent for Allen Toussaint to take my place.

"We organized a group, and Frank Pania started bookin' us. In a couple of weeks we were playin' the Apollo Theatre with Shirley and Lee. It was great because I didn't have to play the piano all night. I just had to play three or four numbers. I was really enjoyin' the business then."

After an extended stay on the R&B charts, "Rockin' Pneumonia" shot into the *Billboard* Hot 100 in August of '57, where it peaked at #52 during a 13-week stay. Marchan and Huey came up with the idea of Clowns, somewhat basing their style on the colorful Coasters, who were also popular at the time. Huey concentrated on writing and arranging, while Marchan took the vocal lead and ran the group's business.

After falling short with their next release "Just A Lonely Clown," Huey and the Clowns came up with a massive two-sided hit in "High Blood Pressure" and "Don't You Just Know It," which stayed 13 weeks on the Hot 100, the latter climbing to #9. It was one of the biggest records of 1958. During this period, Huey's Clowns consisted of Marchan, Willie Nettles, James Rivers, Raymond Lewis, Curley Moore, Gerri Hall, "Scarface" John Williams, Robert Parker and even Jessie Hill for a short time.

A BACK-TO-BACK HIT!

EVEN BIGGER THAN "ROCKIN' PNEUMONIA"
A Billboard Spotlight—Oct. 7

"JUST A LONELY CLOWN"
b/w
"FREE, SINGLE and DISENGAGED"

HUEY SMITH

ACE RECORDS
PHONE 2-6804
227 CULBERTSON AVE.
JACKSON, MISSISSIPPI

ACE #538

Even with the Clowns being one of the top rock and roll attractions in the country, and being featured in cameos on *American Bandstand*, Huey stopped touring with the group and remained home to work on new material. Bobby Marchan took the Clowns on the road, and James Booker replaced Huey on personal appearances. "He was so close to Huey you couldn't tell the difference," commented Marchan.

Apparently the Clowns were really something to see, pulling a series of vaudevillian stunts and generally stirring up the audience.

The event that leaves Huey Smith feeling the most bitter about the music business is the release of his song, "Sea Cruise." According to Huey, Johnny Vincent stole the song from him and gave it to Frankie Ford. "When I did the 'Sea Cruise' track," recalls Huey, still infuriated to this day, "I did the lead vocal with one of the other guys. In my mind it was the one that was gonna throw me over the hump.

"But Johnny, and Frankie Ford's manager, Joe Caronna, liked it too. So Johnny came to me and said, 'Hey, let Frankie do this.'

"I said, 'No way.'

"But Johnny said there was nothing I could do about it. It was comin' out on Frankie.

"Now the flip side was supposed to be called 'Loberta,'" continued Huey lividly, "Not 'Roberta!' I didn't even know no Roberta. Johnny couldn't even hear it. He kept the voices in there singin' 'Loberta' and Frankie's singin' 'Roberta.'

"At that stage of the game I decided I was gonna teach Frankie some songs, thinking that maybe I could make some money at that, so I taught him 'Alimony.' But Johnny always had it in his mind he was gonna beat somebody out of something. I never got any royalties out of Johnny at the time.

"He'd say, 'It's comin', it's comin'.'

"Oh I'd get some little money, like two or three hundred, but I wanted some real money. So when my contract ran out in 1959, I decided I wasn't gonna record for him no more. But he had these tracks I had already laid down, so he could put stuff out on me whenever he wanted to."

Through Dave Bartholomew, Huey moved over to Imperial, cutting eight sides and moonlighting a few sessions for Joe Caronna and Frankie Ford's Spinit label. Huey continued to employ such catchy phrases as the titles "Sassy Sarah?" and "The Little Moron," would indicate. They were fine records, but, saleswise, they were duds. Huey feels Imperial wouldn't push his records because they might adversely affect the sales of their bread and butter man — Fats Domino.

While still signed to Imperial in 1962, Vincent dug out a track Huey had previously recorded. Vincent added some vocals, and Ace had a surprise hit with "The Popeye," which was also a popular dance in New Orleans. Huey relates that Imperial was upset about the success of the Ace record, and subsequently dropped him. Oddly enough, Huey made his way back to Vincent's label.

But Huey's glory days were over, as far as being a rock and roll artist were concerned. Although a fine Christmas album was released (and withdrawn from sales when it was deemed sacreligious) and a few odd sessions took place, Huey couldn't get another hit. He survived by going back out on the road, working fraternity parties and one-nighters throughout the early 1960s. Huey continued to stick it out with Ace until the label crashed in 1964.

With Ace Records behind him, Huey formed his own record company, with the aid of Carlton Picou. Some of Vincent's record business wit must have rubbed off on Huey, as his first 1965 release credits Shindig Smith & the Soul Shakers.

Joe Banashak, at Instant Records, became interested in Huey, and signed him as an artist and producer. "Coo Coo Over You,"

Huey, left, with the Pitter Pats

and "You Ain't No Hippy," did well for Huey in New Orleans. He also produced sides by Larry Darnell, Lee Bates and Skip Easterling. It's easy to write off Huey's post-Ace records as out-of-date. But the same wit and spontaneity of his earlier work are evident on his Instant releases. Unfortunately, Huey's inability to create national hits was magnifying a developing drinking problem.

When the New Orleans music business all but came to a standstill in the late Sixties, Huey abandoned music entirely, and began studying the Bible. He was baptized into the Jehovah's Witnesses congregation, hoping it would help him overcome his developing alcohol problem.

"I had to get away from places like the Dew Drop," emphasized Huey. "I wanted to protect myself and further my Bible studies. Every once in awhile, someone would approach me about music, but I told them I wasn't interested. So I started looking for secular work."

For a short time in 1970, Huey worked as a janitor at a K&B drugstore. But after getting some back royalties from Vincent in an ongoing legal battle, Huey bought a pickup truck and some gardening equipment. He started "Smith's Dependable Gardening Service," and worked in and around New Orleans, throughout most of the Seventies.

In 1979, Huey was approached by Marshall Sehorn, who was interested in recording him at Sea-Saint. For a while it seemed that Huey was really going to make a comeback. He had an album in the can that Sehorn was trying to release, and he and his old partner Bobby Marchan teamed up with David Lastie's rocking band, and were truly the highlight of the 1979 New Orleans Jazz and Heritage Festival.

But Huey fell off the wagon again, and ended up getting disfellowshipped from his congregation. As a result, Huey shelved his music career again, quit his gardening job, and moved to Baton Rouge, where his wife found work as a grade school teacher. After Huey was able to demonstrate that he had mended his ways, he was reinstated by the Jehovah's Witnesses.

Then, in early 1981, it seemed Huey had all his problems straightened out. He had a lawyer and a number of friends trying to get back his copyrights for songs he had sold to Vincent. Jobs were lined up, and he was writing and practicing again. But just when things looked the best, Huey found out Sea-Saint sold his session to Charly Records in England, without his knowledge. When Huey inquired about how much money he would receive for the album, he was presented a bill for $30,000 for studio time and expenses! Not only that, they had overdubbed the original tapes, and they sounded terrible.

For Huey, this was the straw that broke the camel's back. He started drinking once again, and the important gigs that were lined up turned into disasters.

He retreated to Baton Rouge after the 1981 New Orleans Jazz Fest vowing never to play again.

To further cloud the issue, Bobby Marchan claims that MCA Records has a standing offer of a $60,000 advance if Huey and Bobby will sign to do an album.

Will Huey "Piano" Smith try it again? Of course any answer is speculation, but it seems perhaps the man has just been burned once too often, and sadly we may never hear that happy sound he created again.

JAMES BOOKER
The Piano Prince of New Orleans

During the 1981 New Orleans Jazz Festival, James Booker held 3,000 people aboard the riverboat S.S. *President* completely spellbound. The assorted audience of blues freaks, jazz buffs and boogie woogie lovers stomped their feet and clapped their hands in appreciation. His style was by turns flashy and starkly introspective in the manner of every great New Orleans pianist since Jelly Roll Morton. Booker's versions of "All Around The World" and "Something You Got" were interspersed with outrageous extracts from Tchaikovsky and Rachmaninoff.

Then Booker flaunted his nimble-fingered technique on the Longhairish "One Hell Of A Nerve," which he sang in a half-falsetto voice, and played an unnerving blues version of "Black Night." He sang an inspired version of his anthem "Junco Partner" before climaxing his set with a classical melange of "A Taste Of Honey" and "Malaguena." It was a brazen display of his talent and the performance ended with thunderous applause and shouts for encore. Booker stood up to acknowledge the applause, bowed politely, and exited quietly.

Two days later, James Booker was committed to the psychiatric ward of Charity Hospital. The police had found him wandering in the French Quarter babbling incoherently. The three-piece suit he wore on the *President* was encrusted with dried vomit when the police picked him up under the suspicion he was "high on something."

Such tales concerning James Booker are common around New Orleans; many of them are entrusted to local musical folklore. His tragic, on-again-off-again escapades invite comparisons with pioneer jazzman Buddy Bolden, who, like Booker, was referred to as a musical genius, but was unable to sort out his personal life. Bolden died in the state madhouse, Booker died in the emergency ward of Charity Hospital — in his own private madhouse.

Conceivably the finest New Orleans keyboardist of his era, James Carroll Booker III was born at Charity Hospital, December 17, 1939 (the same year Jelly Roll Morton died, he once pointed out). His parents were James Booker Jr., himself a pianist and a Baptist preacher, and Ora Cheatham. At an early age J.C. (as his family referred to him) was sent to nearby Bay St. Louis, Mississippi, to be raised by an aunt. J.C.'s aptitude for music was apparent at the age of six, when he began taking lessons, often in the company of his older sister Betty Jean.

J.C. was a fast learner and he read and played well enough to be considered a child prodigy. But even though his training was in the classics, J.C.'s consuming interest was the blues, and he would play it often. At the age of ten his studies were interrupted when he was run down by a speeding ambulance, severely fracturing his leg. The accident had long-term effects on J.C. as it permanently affected his walk and while recovering, he was first introduced to the drug morphine.

J.C.'s father died in 1953, and he rejoined his mother, along with his sister, in New Orleans. He enrolled in Xavier Preparatory School, where fellow classmate Allen Toussaint recalls, "Booker was the head of the class in math, Spanish and music. He could just play more piano than anyone."

Betty Jean began singing on a live Sunday morning gospel program over WMRY and she took the opportunity to show her brother around the studio and meet deejay Ernie the Whip. J.C. was given an audition, which he passed with flying colors, and he was promptly installed as a regular Saturday afternoon attraction, playing both blues and gospel.

Soon after, he formed his first group, Booker Boy and the Rhythmaires, which included school buddies Art Neville and Curtis Graves, who were also installed on WMRY with Booker.

Pianist Tuts Washington recalls Booker from that period; "I was a personal friend of his mother and his grandmother. I used to go over to his house when he was just a little boy. He used to sit and watch me play in the living room. Then he started sneaking into the joints and watching me play like Fess did. He learned fast."

Pianist Edward Franks, an ex-boyfriend of Betty Jean's, who worked Imperial recording sessions for Dave Bartholomew, was impressed by Booker's feeling and playing technique. He helped arrange an audition with Bartholomew, who was likewise impressed and recorded the 14-year-old doing "Thinking About My Baby" and "Doing The Hambone," which was issued on Imperial. The record failed to sell, but it sharpened Booker's musical ambitions and it led to session work at Cosimo's studio.

"Booker sounded more like Fats than Fats did," recalls Cosimo. "Dave used to get Booker to play the piano on some of Fats' tracks.

James Booker, 1956

A BIG INSTRUMENTAL!
A REAL TWISTER!
LITTLE BOOKER'S "GONZO"
TOP POPS...
ON ALL THE CHARTS—
A-HITTING AND A-SPREADING
ACROSS THE U.S.A.
PEACOCK-1697
BIG! BIG! BIG! BIG!
PEACOCK- RECORDS
2809 Erastus St. Houston 26, Texas

Fats was on the road a lot, so when he came back to town it was easier for Dave to just get Fats to do the vocals."

Booker continued to do spot gigs around New Orleans while still in school, but on weekends he would occasionally go out of town with Shirley and Lee, Earl King or Smiley Lewis. In 1956, he was approached by Paul Gayten, who was then an A&R man for Chicago's Chess Records. Chess was hoping to capitalize on the growing rock and roll trend, and hoped that a young artist like Booker might catch on. "You Need Me" and "Heavenly Angel" were recorded on Chess by Arthur and Booker. Arthur was supposed to have been Art Neville, but he was unable to make the session, so Arthur Booker (no relation) was called in to substitute. The record sold poorly and Booker was subsequently dropped by the label.

"Of course I was disappointed," Booker once said. "I haven't got over it yet. I thought I should have been selling thousands of records. As far as I'm concerned every one of my records should have been number one."

Booker didn't give up, however. Upon graduation from Xavier Prep in 1957, he joined Joe Tex's band, which worked the Southern nightclub circuit, often traveling as far as Georgia, Arkansas and Texas. When Tex signed with Ace Records, he suggested to Ace's

47

owner Johnny Vincent that he should record his keyboardist as well.

Thanks largely to Bill Doggett and his success with instrumentals like "Honky Tonk" and "Slow Walk," the Hammond organ came into vogue as a rhythm and blues instrument. Booker picked up on the instrument quickly, and soon became New Orleans' foremost organist.

In 1958, Johnny Vincent, the owner of Ace, decided to cut an instrumental with Booker doubling on piano and organ. Under the guise of Little Booker, "Teenage Rock" and "Open The Door" were released with Charles Williams, Lee Allen, Red Tyler and Frank Fields completing the session. Both sides used the same rhythm track with Booker's organ featured on "Teenage Rock," but, to Booker's dismay, Joe Tex's voice dubbed on "Open The Door."

"I sure didn't stay long at Ace," said Booker. "I walked into the studio and Johnny Imbragulio — yeah that's his real name — had Joe Tex singing on my track. I didn't like the way they were doing business. I had a three-year contract but I got out of it because my mother signed it because I was under age."

Even though Booker reflected that "it was a productive period for me," it was also the period when he first started to experiment with hard drugs. Never one to hide his drug dependency, Booker commented, "I was frustrated and started shooting dope as a form of rebellion. I was playing music so that I could get enough money to buy dope."

After Booker parted with Ace and Joe Tex, he did a short tour with Shirley & Lee, before returning to New Orleans and working a few spot R&B gigs and organ gigs on Bourbon Street. Earl King recalls that during this period Booker's behavior was beginning to raise some questions. "Booker just started acting foolish. One night we had a real important job and the whole band went down to Rampart street to get measured up for uniforms. So when it comes time to play, in comes Booker wearing a dirty t-shirt and a greasy pair of dungarees. At first we just ignored it, but he got worse and worse. You'd be driving to a gig and Booker would be in the back seat trying to start some kind of humbug. Finally one night I put him out of my car; I just got tired of his foolishness.

"One time Little Richard was staying at the Dew Drop, and he used to have this robin's-egg blue Cadillac convertible. Him and Booker used to drive up and down Canal Street, hollering and carrying on like the two biggest sissies in the world."

In 1958, Booker was hired by Bobby Marchan to work with Huey Smith and the Clowns. Booker sat in for Huey, who preferred to stay home and work in the studio rather than go on the road.

In 1959, Booker abandoned New Orleans and playing gigs, enrolling in music at Southern University in Baton Rouge, hoping that college studies might help him conquer an increased drug dependency. Just 20, James Booker was far older than his years.

The following year Don Robey, of Duke/Peacock Records in Houston, came to New Orleans in search of an A&R man. On Earl King's recommendation, he approached Booker. Booker declined, preferring the more settled college life, but returned an old favor by suggesting Earl Frank's name. Despite declining Robey's offer, his interest in R&B was rekindled when Dee Clark and Phil Upchurch came through Baton Rouge looking for an organist. Booker dropped out of school two months short of graduation and joined their band.

As luck would have it, the tour broke up in Houston, and Clark pawned the band organ to Don Robey. Robey saw that Booker was in a jam so he asked him to work a few dates at his club, the Golden Peacock, and to sit in on some sessions with Larry Davis and Little Jr. Parker.

While in the studio, Robey suggested that they try to tape a few instrumentals, with the idea that maybe they could come up with a single. Eventually they came up with two sides, but they couldn't come up with suitable titles for the record. Edward Frank suggested "Gonzo," which was Booker's nickname, that originated from the lead character in the movie *The Pusher*. Booker suggested the flip be titled "Cool Turkey," and the single was released on Peacock. Surprisingly Robey missed the obvious reference to drugs (or did he?), but the real surprise was when the record climbed as high as number 10 in *Billboard's* R&B charts, and number 43 on the pop chart in December 1960, becoming one of Robey's biggest sellers ever.

"I was a successful failure with Don D. Robey," pointed out Booker. "I sold him all my rights before I even recorded 'Gonzo.' "

Even though Booker eventually cut a total of five singles for Peacock, he and Robey had parted company by 1962, when it was apparent that they couldn't come up with a successful follow-up.

Once again Booker took to the road, and although he admitted he was "shooting so much dope that my memory was cloudy," he still recalled working with Roy Hamilton, B.B. King and Little Richard in California and in Las Vegas.

The year 1962 saw him sitting in on Lloyd Price's hit "Misty" and recording an album under the guise of the Lloyd Price Band. He also did some sessions with Wilson Pickett for Price's Double L label. Booker continued to gig with Pickett and occasionally his old pal Joe Tex.

His nomadic existence continued throughout the mid-Sixties, which only compounded his dependency on drugs and alcohol. During the late Sixties he settled in New York for two years where he played on sessions with Aretha Franklin, who recorded Booker's "So Swell When You're Well," and King Curtis. "I did about an album's worth of material for Atlantic," said Booker. "I put together a trio and we sounded very ragtime. Jerry Wexler produced it but it was never released."

In 1968, producer Richard Perry used Booker on Fats Domino's *Fats Is Back* album on Reprise. On it Booker plays some stunning Domino-like piano take-offs and fills.

In 1970, the long hard years of drug addiction caught up with Booker and he was arrested in front of the Dew Drop Inn for possession of heroin and sentenced to two years at Angola. While in prison Booker organized the prison's music program and worked in the library. After serving only six months, he was paroled with his old friend Joe Tex signing the release papers.

Once granted his freedom, Booker returned to New Orleans where he began working once more on Bourbon Street. The early Seventies was a notoriously slow period for musicians in New Orleans and a frustrated Booker apparently broke parole, and headed for the greener pastures of New York. While there he recorded with Maria Muldaur, Ringo Starr (on *Beaucoup of Blues),* Jerry Garcia, and the Doobie Brothers. He even worked with Lionel Hampton's orchestra occasionally around the Big Apple.

Then Booker turned up in Downington, Pennsylvania, of all places, where he played jazz in a cocktail lounge for nearly a year. "Yeah I really liked it," he pointed out. "It was real quiet and I was trying to get myself together."

Next, producers Leiber and Stoller found Booker and sent him to Los Angeles to record with Charles Brown, and on T-Bone Walker's last album, *Very Rare,* released on Warner Brothers. Then it was on to Cincinnati where he made some sessions for King Records.

Booker didn't reappear in New Orleans until after his legal problems were straightened out in 1975. When he returned, he was wearing a patch where his left eye had once been. Booker has told more than one writer he lost it in a scuffle over session money in New York, but he also admitted to some of his friends that the loss of his eye was due to his use of a dirty syringe.

Whatever the facts, Booker's real break was just around the corner, and came via his first appearance at the 1975 New Orleans Jazz and Heritage Festival. On stage, Booker donned an exotically styled cape, an eye patch emblazened with a gold star, and a garish wig. He naturally puzzled most of the audience throughout his 45-minute cameo. In the audience was Norbert Hess, a German musicologist and promoter, who thought enough of his playing to arrange to bring him to Europe for the 1975 Berlin Rhythm and Blues Festival, and some other European dates.

When he got back to the States, he was contacted by producer Joe Boyd (he had met Booker earlier at a Geoff Muldaur session) who wanted to record Booker in a solo setting. Boyd came to New Orleans to record the *Junco Partner* album, but apparently couldn't get a note out of Booker until the pianist was sufficiently loaded.

The album was released on the English Island label in December 1976 and met with much critical acclaim on both sides of the ocean. Booker promoted the album by touring England and Germany, where he also took the opportunity to record a live album for the Aves label. That same year, Booker had himself committed to a New Orleans addiction clinic, where he completed a methadone treatment program.

"The star on my eye patch is there to represent my victory over my heroin addiction," he once pointed out. Truly the late Seventies were a very productive period for Booker. He toured in Europe again in 1977, where he recorded yet another live album in Zurich, which eventually won a Grand Prix de Disque de Jazz award. In 1978 he appeared at the highly acclaimed Montreaux Jazz Festival.

After returning from Montreaux, Booker rarely, if at all, left New Orleans. Instead he installed himself in a number of clubs and worked occasional sessions at SeaSaint Studio. He dispensed with the wigs and flashy capes for a calmer, more staid appearance. But besides the physical change, some sort of deeper emotional change was taking place inside James Booker. He rarely exhibited his once out-going, witty personality; instead he withdrew into a shell of suspicion and mistrust. He went through a series of managers, or "contacts" as he referred to them, and his behavior grew more and more erratic. He was known to leave the stage during the middle of a set and disappear for days, he often vomited on the piano, neglected to pay his cab fares, and he frequently turned himself into the psychiatric ward at Charity Hospital. It seemed like no matter what stunt Booker pulled, it only reinforced his "mad genius" reputation.

In October 1982, Booker completed the recording session which resulted in the *Classified* album, released on the Rounder label. Booker originally came to Rounder's attention in 1981, when they leased his live Swiss album for U.S. distribution. At the time of the session Booker had been working regularly in New Orleans at the Maple Leaf Bar with a tight combo that included saxophonist Alvin "Red" Tyler, drummer Johnny Vidacovich and bassist Jim Singleton. The group was well rehearsed and Booker sounded great in this disciplined setting. Booker, and his manager John Parsons, assured Rounder producer Scott Billington that he was indeed ready to make an album. Despite the misgivings by many people in the local music business—because of Booker's unpredictable behavior—Billington budgeted a three-day session at Ultrasonic Studio in New Orleans.

The week before the session, Booker had a seizure on the street and was rushed to Charity Hospital in an ambulance. Parsons moved Booker to Southern Baptist Hospital, hoping Booker would recover sufficiently to still make the session. Billington cancelled and rescheduled the project a number of times before a doctor gave Booker the final go ahead, but he was warned that his liver was practically nonfunctional, and that his next drink might be his last.

The first day of the session was a disaster. Booker refused to play any of the numbers the group had rehearsed, instead listlessly banging out fragments of classical pieces, refusing to sing altogether.

The second day was clearly ten times worse than the first. Booker refused to play at all, retreating to a corner of the studio where he stared at the walls. Eventually Booker telephoned Earl King and Cyril Neville, in an attempt to bolster his own self-confidence, but to no avail. At one point Billington and Red Tyler physically picked up the frail pianist and placed him behind the keyboard in an attempt to get him to play. After two days, Rounder had only three usable tracks. Billington had already decided to scrap the project in disgust, but Red Tyler talked him into giving Booker one more chance.

On the final day, like magic, Booker showed up over an hour before the rest of the musicians. He reeled off some of the most astounding piano solos, almost before the recording engineer could turn on the tape machine. Booker cut four tunes before the band had even set up. Once they joined in, Booker was even further inspired. After just four hours, Booker had laid down enough material for more than one album.

As the session was concluding, even Booker allowed himself a rare, satisfied smile as the other musicians filed out of the studio. Billington pumped Booker's hands vigorously, looking as if a great weight had been taken from his shoulders. Booker returned once more to the piano and launched into a storming version of Professor Longhair's "Big Chief." Halfway through the tour-de-force, while the tape machine was running, Booker halted his playing to look at his watch. He then stood up, announced he had to go to the bank before it closed to cash his session check, and promptly walked out the door.

Two days later Booker disappeared into thin air. He failed to appear for his Maple Leaf gigs and he hadn't returned to his French Quarter apartment. Finally, after searching the city morgue and the jail, John Parsons located him in the New Orleans House of Detention, where he was being held on a disturbing the peace charge. Parsons bailed him out on a Saturday afternoon and he played that night at the Maple Leaf where he sounded better than ever.

After the release of the album, Booker took a job filing and typing at a City Hall office, to supplement his weekly Monday night job at the Maple Leaf. Things went well for Booker until the summer of 1983, when he began drinking heavily again and got fired from the City Hall job and his performances at the Maple Leaf grew more and more erratic.

In October 1983, Booker got it together enough to appear the picture of decorum for a local cable television broadcast. On October 31, he made his last public appearance, playing before five paying customers at the Maple Leaf. He didn't show up for his next gig on November 7.

On Tuesday November 8, 1983, he was pronounced dead at 1:32 p.m., the cause of death an apparent heart and lung failure.

During the last two months of his life Booker had taken to hanging out at a small bar on Orleans Street, where he drank and often scored low-grade cocaine. On the morning of his death he was in the bar and took what turned out to be a lethal dose of cocaine. It was apparent that Booker was in some sort of trouble and someone at the bar drove Booker to Charity Hospital, where they placed him in a wheelchair, and left him in a hallway where he was found by an orderly. There seemed to have been some mixup in the emergency room and Booker remained unattended until he was discovered dead.

Booker's wake was the Thursday evening after his death, at the Rhodes Funeral Home, on Washington Avenue, ironically not far from the studio where he recorded his last album. The wake was a disspirited affair, sparsely attended by mostly friends, musicians and family members. There were few floral arrangements, the tributes were few, and the feeling of "let's get the thing over with" pervaded everything. Booker was dressed in a dark suit and wore sunglases, his face wore a week old beard, and as far as dead bodies go, his looked none too good.

The next morning dawned cold and grey. Booker was whisked away in a silver hearse after a brief, informal ceremony. His coffin was placed in a family vault in Providence Memorial Park, on Airline Highway in Metairie, Louisiana.

ALLEN TOUSSAINT
Southern Knight

Allen Toussaint opens the door to his posh Fairmont Hotel suite, and he bids you to enter with a slight bow and an uneasy smile. He is dressed immaculately as always, a diamond studded gold medallion stands out against his silver raw silk suit and open-toed Birkenstock sandals. He perches himself on an expensive couch, switching glances from the nearby spinet piano and the chilled bottle of unopened champagne which rests on the polished oak table that separates him from the interviewer.

Despite his renown, detailed profiles of Toussaint's life are rare. He is as reserved with journalists as he is with the spotlight. It's only over the last few years through the prodding of his business partner Marshall Sehorn that Toussaint has become more of a public personality, even if reluctantly.

Toussaint has been made available to selected journalists on this day by Robyn Leary, who is coordinating his rare one-week engagement at the Fairmont Hotel's elegant Blue Room. The previous evening's performance was described by Toussaint as "opening night blues," as the high powered nightclub routine at times bogged down in inappropriate flash and awkwardness. Like this afternoon's interview, Toussaint looked as if he'd rather be playing the piano alone in his office back at his studio.

After the perfunctory exchange of greetings and odd bits of information, Toussaint settles back, accepting the interview as a matter of course. His furrowed brow and flared nostrils give him a passive expression which hides just what he's thinking. Although Toussaint doesn't expand freely, his answers are always precise and articulate, but always with a trace of "Let's get this over with" in his voice.

As a songwriter, producer, vocalist, arranger, pianist and half-owner in a prestigious studio, Toussaint's reputation long ago reached legendary status. He could have easily become a "superstar" by the mid-Seventies, but he remained indifferent to the demands of international popularity. Instead he preferred to stay in the background, writing and producing in New Orleans for a myriad of other artists and on occasion for himself.

Allen Toussaint was born January 14, 1938. He spent the first 23 years of his life in "Gerttown," at 3041 College Court, which is located on the lakeside of Earhart Boulevard, between Xavier University and Jefferson Davis Parkway, primarily a black New Orleans suburb. "It was a shotgun house like every other one on the block," he begins. "The streets weren't paved in those days, and that's where we'd play. People used to keep chickens and animals in the backyards. It was definitely a lot of fun for a kid growing up. It was a typical ghetto."

According to Toussaint, his rearing was "very Catholic." His father, Clarence, worked on the railroad and played trumpet in his off hours. His mother Naomi Neville Toussaint, played piano and raised the three Toussaint children — Vincent, Allen and Joyce.

An upright piano was part of the family's furniture, and Toussaint remembers very little of life before he began trying to play it. His sister studied classical music, and she taught the 12-year-old Allen the rudiments of the instrument. He tried formalized lessons once, but abandoned them after his progress was minimal, and he realized he learned more by listening to the radio. He also tried his hand at drums, trumpet and trombone, but always ran back to the piano.

Toussaint cites his early influences as Albert Ammons, Ray Charles, Lloyd Glenn and "especially Professor Longhair." He also mentions a mysterious local musician, Ernest Penn, as a major inspiration. Penn was a contemporary of pianist Tuts Washington, who recalls "bumming" with Penn. "Penn could play a lot of different instruments," says Tuts. "He could play a lot of piano — blues piano — but when I played with him he played guitar or banjo. He was murder on that banjo. He could play that banjo about a thousand miles behind his head. A lot of musicians liked to play with Penn because he was a good showman. He contracted syphilis and his family disowned him. He moved back to College Court where he taught Allen. He ended up killing himself."

"I started my first band with Little Snooks [Snooks Eaglin] when I was 13," recalls Toussaint. "It was called the Flamingoes. We used to practice in my parents' front room. We played at high school dances, parties and things like that."

While in his early teens, Toussaint began to sneak into the Dew Drop, where he was introduced to many of the top local R&B performers who occasionally invited him onstage to play. A number of musicians, including Earl King and Tommy Ridgley, recall seeing Toussaint enter the weekly Dew Drop talent shows at the time.

Allen Toussaint, 1968

It was in fact Earl King who Toussaint claims "gave me my first break. Huey Smith was playing in Earl's band at the time and for some reason he couldn't make a gig. We played in Prichard, Alabama. That was the first big time professional job I played."

After attending both Booker T. Washington and Cohen high schools, Toussaint dropped out of school midway through tenth grade to satisfy his insatiable interest in music. During the summer of 1957, he was once again called on to replace Huey Smith, this time in Shirley and Lee's band. Smith abandoned the group in Baltimore to push his own record, "Rockin' Pneumonia," which was just beginning to break nationally. Toussaint stayed on the road with Shirley and Lee for several months, completing the tour. "That was the last time I really worked as a gig musician," he reflects. "I started getting into other things when I got back. The road was okay, but I couldn't see much future in it."

In 1957, after the stint with Shirley and Lee, Dave Bartholomew heard about a talented young pianist and went down to the Dew Drop one evening to check Toussaint out. Bartholomew was impressed enough to offer Toussaint his first taste of studio work. "Dave needed someone to play tracks for Fats Domino," he explains. "He heard me and realized that I could play just like anybody. Fats was on the road and Dave needed the tracks right away because he sent them right out to the West Coast. So I went down to Cosimo's and played on 'Young School Girl,' 'I Want To Know,' and a few other tunes. It was a real honor.''

Toussaint found himself being called into the studio with an increasing frequency. "I started getting a lot of calls to come by the studio and play background sessions. Then after awhile I got the chance to do some arrangements, producing you might say, but we didn't use that word then. I began to get real busy."

Earl King arranged an audition for Toussaint with Johnny Vincent at Ace Records, but Vincent felt Toussaint's style wasn't commercial enough. "All Johnny could hear was Huey Smith at the time," says Earl. "That would have been a real bonus for Johnny if he had grabbed Allen first."

Toussaint did, however, eventually write and arrange some sides for Alvin "Red" Tyler on Ace, and he arranged and played on Lee Allen's smash instrumental "Walkin' With Mr. Lee." In 1958, Danny Kesler and Murray Sporn, a couple of talent scouts with major label connections, came to New Orleans to look for people to record. According to local legend, people were lined up around the block from Cosimo's studio after Kesler and Sporn ran an ad in the local papers saying "Talent Auditions: People Wanted." The duo hired Toussaint to accompany the hundreds of aspiring recording artists. After three days, Kesler and Sporn gave up auditioning people after being frustrated by the mediocre talent that came to the studio. However, they were impressed with Toussaint's playing and decided to sign him to a publishing and album deal.

Toussaint was a bit unnerved by the chore of writing and arranging enough songs for an album, but realized it might be the break he needed. With "Red" Tyler in town, Toussaint went into the studio February 26, 1958, to make his first solo recordings. Kesler and Sporn were in a hurry to get back to New York, so the session had to be completed in two days, with many of the compositions being made up on the spot. The tapes were taken to New York, where Kesler and Sporn came up with the titles for the twelve instrumentals Toussaint recorded. The ensuing album, *The Wild Sound of New Orleans* by "Al Tousan," was leased to RCA. It commercially didn't live up to anyone's expectations, but is now a prized collector's item. Musically it serves as an interesting showcase for the then 20-year-old pianist who mimicked a variety of piano styles including Longhair and Albert Ammons. The album also contained a bouncy instrumental called "Java," which six years later became Dixieland trumpeter Al Hirt's ticket to national recognition.

Toussaint viewed the album as a way of "opening the door" to the highly competitive music business. Late in 1958, Toussaint wrote and arranged Lee Dorsey's local hit "Love of Lovers" for the Valiant label, which was later leased to ABC nationally. The record confirmed to Toussaint that he should channel all his musical energies towards producing and arranging rather than "gigging."

"I felt like that's what I wanted to be doing," he says. "I felt more comfortable producing than trying to go out on the road to pursue a solo career. As a producer, I felt like a sideman, but an important sideman, one who is able to push the artist. That's what I wanted to do. I wanted to be the man behind the artist."

In early 1960, Toussaint met Joe Banashak and Larry McKinley of Minit records. He showed up at Minit's talent audition once again to provide accompaniment for auditioning vocalists. "I'd been recording behind a few people and I'd written a few songs," says Toussaint, "but I wasn't doing it for one company in particular, just whoever called me. When Minit started, I went down one evening to play for some people they were auditioning. When we finished, Joe Banashak asked me if I could work with the company until Harold Batiste was able to get back to New Orleans. At the time Harold was out on the West Coast working for Specialty. Joe explained that it was just a temporary thing, but Harold never came back. So I just made the best of the situation."

Just twenty-two, Toussaint was given full control of the sessions. Generally, he wrote the material and arranged and played it on the early Minit releases. "A lot of these tunes we'd get together in the front room of my parents' house. It used to be a lot of fun back then; it seemed like we didn't have anything to worry about. Irma, K-Doe, Aaron Neville, Benny Spellman — we used to really jam back. Generally we'd rehearse during the day and go over to the studio at night.

"I had no qualms about turning the sessions over to Allen," points out Banashak. "That was his job. I looked at it like, he made the records and it was my job to sell them.

"When I first met Allen, he was involved in a professional agreement with Allen Orange. Allen Orange was a vocalist who wrote some material with Allen. The partnership didn't last very long because we only did one record on them (Allen & Allen, "Heavenly Baby" b/w "Tiddle Winks"). Allen Orange left town after that. I think he might have gone to Nashville.

"Allen always carried himself with quiet elegance. He used to wear ruffled shirts and diamond pins, even in the studio. And when there was a session, Allen always showed up late. He drove flashy Cadillacs and a Harley Davidson. I think he had a preconceived idea about how a star should look and act. He never used to say too much or ask many questions, but he was always listening and taking things in. Just about anything he tried his hand at he could master. A lot of people don't know it, but Allen is one of the best pool shooters around. He really used to constantly amaze me. He didn't have that good of an education, but he picked things up from other people real fast."

Toussaint's first national production hit turned out to be Jessie Hill's surprising "Ooh Poo Pah Doo," which Toussaint arranged, but oddly didn't write. "I didn't like 'Ooh Poo Pah Doo'," explains Toussaint. "I didn't think it made sense. I thought songs had to be more expressive. But when I saw the effect it had on other people, I began to look at things differently."

After "Ooh Poo Pah Doo," the hits started to flow fast and furiously. Toussaint proved to be a one-man hit factory, turning out a staggering number of commercially great and artistic records. Besides the Minit successes of K-Doe, Spellman, Aaron Neville, the Showmen and Irma Thomas, he also produced Lee Dorsey's "Ya Ya" on Fury, and Clarence Henry's "But I Do," on Argo. Of course Toussaint was also responsible for the sessions recorded for Banashak's other label, Instant, including the early Chris Kenner hits.

"I'd always had R&B in mind when I was writing those early records," points out Toussaint. "I got inspiration from a lot of different places. A lot of those tunes I wrote with what I call 'The soft-shoe approach.' In most cases I wrote with a certain artist in mind for each song. Irma's songs were written for her. The Aaron Nevilles and the Benny Spellmans too. They were written with their individual approach to singing in mind. I had trouble writing specifically for K-Doe and Chris Kenner; I had a hard time getting a feel for the type of material they sang best."

One of the ongoing mysteries concerning Toussaint is why he used his parents' names, C. Toussaint and Naomi Neville, instead of his own on his songwriter's credits. Toussaint claims, "I signed a publishing agreement with Danny Kesler who leased me out to RCA. When I became of age, they (Kesler and Sporn) didn't live up to their end of the agreement, so the contract was null and void.

However, to get out of it, it called for some court negotiations. Well I couldn't wait until they got through with the legal proceedings, so to keep new material coming out, I used a pseudonym to keep from getting tied up. I used Clarence Toussaint on a few things, but it didn't seem like it was far enough away from my name. So I used my mother's maiden name, Naomi Neville (no relation to the musical Neville family) because I certainly trusted her."

However, Joe Banashak tells a different story. Banashak claims Toussaint used a writer's alias because the IRS was giving him problems; and the name change was meant to throw them off the scent.

Whatever the reason, Toussaint spent the rest of the early Sixties writing and producing sessions for Banashak on Minit, Instant and later ALON, which was formed as Toussaint's own label. "ALON wasn't my name," he explains. "It was the initials of N.O., L.A., spelled backwards. I was doing a lot of local people on ALON like Benny Spellman, Joe Harper and Eldridge Holmes up until I went into the army. We didn't have any hits so to speak. But I felt like we had some fine records."

The heyday for Instant/Minit/ALON pretty much ended in January of 1963, when Toussaint entered the army. "I'd had a few deferrments," says Toussaint, "but they just hang over your head. So rather than try to get another one, I just went in. I had a good time in the army. I was stationed at Fort Hood, over in Texas. I went through basic training, but in the evening I played in the service club. I was assigned to the soldier's chorus right away, working under Ron Ensore. I used to come back home on weekends and we'd got back into the studio sometimes, but it wasn't the same. We lost some of the momentum."

At the beginning of his army stint, Toussaint grew despondent about writing, partially because he wasn't receiving writer's royalties from BMI for his material. But through Banashak's intercession, Toussaint was paid a large portion of royalties meant for "Naomi Neville." A rejuvenated Toussaint formed an instrumental group on the base called The Stokes, which consisted of of Ronald C. Inzer-trombone, Hugh Preston Jr.-sax, Sam Lillibridge-trumpet, Carl Hays, Jr.-guitar, Aldo Vennari-drums, Al Fayard-percussion, and, of course, Toussaint on piano. Banashak encouraged Toussaint to write catchy instrumentals similar to the successful "Java" which Al Hirt was then having a hit with. Banashak often travelled to Houston where The Stokes were recorded, for releases on ALON. Among the first titles the group recorded was "Whipped Cream," which eventually became a major hit for Herb Alpert, and became the theme song for the popular television program, "The Dating Game." On occasion, Toussaint was able to return to New Orleans and produce the odd session on Instant or ALON.

Toussaint drops his reserve, offering a rare insight into his personality, while describing an incident which took place near the end of his military hitch: "I got a check in on some record royalties and I got it cashed. Me and some friends that were in The Stokes went in to Dallas to perform. While we were there, I wanted to buy a new car because I was about to get out.

"I thought I'd get a Cadillac, because I had Cadillacs before I went into the army. Well this was '65, when they cut the fins off the Cadillacs, and I thought they just looked ridiculous. So I went around and looked at other cars. I saw this Bonneville and I thought it was just really sharp. So I went in a dealership to buy one.

"I was gonna pay a sizeable downpayment in cash because the notes would be cheaper. This salesman at the Pontiac dealership told me just how much the car would be. He spoke with kind of a condescending attitude, but that didn't concern me, I was concerned about the car. When he asked me how much I was gonna put down on it, I told him, and said I'd pay it in cash. He said, 'No, you don't understand, the downpayment is a large amount of money.' So I said, 'That's all right. I can handle that.' So he left and came back and said, "Well, if you had a little more it would make your note a lot less.' So I said, 'Yes, I can handle that.' Then he said he had to go speak to his supervisor again.

"Well, these trips he was making was to call the police. When the police got there, they took us to jail and put us all in separate rooms. This was 1965, not the Thirties! It was like Dragnet. They questioned each of us: 'Where did you get the money?' That kind of stuff. I guess they were suspicious because I was the only black guy in the band. After an hour and a half, they let us go. What had happened was that a bank had been robbed, and they were checking to see if we had anything to do with it. Finally, they called Joe Banashak in New Orleans to see if I was telling the truth.

"Once they let us go, I went right back to the same place and bought the car! I really did. I know a lot of people would ask, 'Why would you?' Well, I just resumed the same speed and did what I set out to do. That's just the way I operated in those days."

Once discharged, Toussaint returned to New Orleans and resumed producing sessions for Banashak on Instant and ALON. But Toussaint says he felt uncomfortable continuing the same relationship he'd had with Banashak and began to look elsewhere. "When I came out of the service, one of the problems I felt was that things hadn't progressed enough while I was away. A lot of the artists that we'd had — I'm talking about Aaron Neville, K-Doe and Irma Thomas — were no longer with us. A lot of record distributorships had folded or changed hands, but that didn't really worry me because I was just interested in the music. Things just didn't feel progressive.

"There were no bad vibes between Joe and me, I just felt it was time to dissolve the partnership. I had no idea I would get into another partnership as soon as I did with Marshall (Sehorn). I just knew it was time to get out of that one."

Toussaint's relationship with Sehorn goes back to the 1961 Fury sessions when Sehorn was looking for someone to write and arrange for Lee Dorsey and Bobby Marchan. In 1965, Sehorn brought Dorsey to Banashak and Toussaint and arranged for them to produce a session on Dorsey which he hoped to lease. The sessions yielded the hit "Ride Your Pony," but, more importantly, it provided the opportunity for Sehorn and Toussaint to lay the groundwork for an agreement.

Once "Ride Your Pony" was leased to Amy/Bell Records and began to take off, Sehorn and Toussaint cemented their agreement; Toussaint broke his contract with Banashak and began producing exclusively for "Marsaint Music." Sehorn was able to strike an agreeable deal with Amy/Bell to provide product on Dorsey, which turned out to be very profitable for all parties involved.

It is on Dorsey's records that many feel Toussaint's best work is found. Toussaint himself feels that Dorsey is the perfect medium for his music. "Lee has certainly inspired a lot of my writing," he says," like 'Working In A Coal Mine.' Who else but Lee Dorsey could pull a song off like that! 'Ride Your Pony,' 'Everything I Do Gonna Be Funky,' 'Sneakin' Sally Through the Alley' — those songs would probably never have been written if it hadn't of been for the kind of guy that Lee is. He just inspires all kinds of ideas that no one else does. I can always see Lee moving through the world and me back there watching and writing about it."

With substantial royalties coming in from Dorsey's hits, Sehorn and Toussaint were able to form their own corporation called "Cinq Sou," meaning five cents in Creole French, which later was to become Sansu Enterprises. With Sehorn the hustling boisterous front man and Toussaint the reclusive musical genius, they established the Sansu, Kansus, Deesu, and Tou-Sea labels. They set up an office on St. Phillip Street and employed Cosimo's relocated Jazz City Studio on Camp Street. Between the two of them, Toussaint and Sehorn were able to record a major portion of the local talent available. "We really were busy in those days," confirms Toussaint. "People would just come in off the street and audition in those days. If they were good enough we'd try and record them. But let's face it, it was easier then. Making a record was a less costly venture. You used to be able to do a session for $600. Today that same session would cost you $70,000."

Even though Sehorn landed a national distribution deal with Amy/Bell for Sansu and Tou-Sea, other than Betty Harris' "Near To You," the duo had to be content with only local success in the late Sixties on their house labels. Nonetheless, a number of classic sides were committed to wax. People like Eldridge Holmes, John Williams, Curley Moore, Warren Lee, Ray Algere, Zilla Mays, Diamond Joe, Willie West and Willie Harper made great records that were played in New Orleans.

By 1970, national success was established for Sansu by leasing a number of productions to major labels. Besides Dorsey's material going to Amy/Bell, and later Polydor, Wilbert Harrison was recorded for Buddah, Aaron Neville was recorded for Mercury, and Sansu's biggest find, the Meters, went to Josie and later to Warner Brothers.

The year 1971 was a busy year for Toussaint. New albums were recorded by Dorsey, K-Doe and Lou Johnson, the latter of whom was recorded for Volt. The Band was impressed with Toussaint's talent, and they had him arrange "Life Is A Carnival" on their *Cahoots* album. More importantly, however, it was the year that Allen began stepping out as a solo artists. His reluctance to produce his own records had been cast aside only on the original RCA album, and the occasional single on Amy and ALON. Toussaint's haunting "From A Whisper To A Scream" was released on the Tiffany label as a single, which drew much critical acclaim. An album soon followed on Scepter, simply entitled *Toussaint*, which was a fine showcase for the talent he usually kept screened behind other artists. Another album was planned for Scepter, but, according to Toussaint, they had a falling out over "business and music."

The following year, *Life, Love and Faith* was released on Warner

Brothers' subsidiary label, Reprise. Although the album had its moments, generally it didn't live up to the expectations of the Scepter album, as Toussaint sounded forced and commercialized.

"I've *never* really considered myself a solo artist," he points out. "I mean I have records out on my own, but that's not my destiny. I think I probably could if I were to try, and maybe a lot of people would like to see me go in that direction. But I've spent most of my life playing for myself and playing behind other artists. I enjoy that a lot more than being out front.

"I do it from time to time, but it's just an enjoyable diversion. The public appreciates it, even though I don't think I deserve it, and I'm most thankful for it. But it's not my vocation or occupation. I much prefer being on my own. To tell you the truth, I get very uncomfortable when I hear my voice. I'm just not a limelight performer."

In August of 1973, the Toussaint/Sehorn partnership entered a new era with the opening of the ultra-modern Sea-Saint Studio in the quiet Gentilly neighborhood of New Orleans. Sea-Saint grew from necessity, as New Orleans hadn't had a decent studio since Cosimo's Jazz City Studio was forced into bankruptcy and all of its equipment sold at a sheriff's auction.

The state-of-the-art recording facility was financed by government loans, a group of financial backers that comprised Sansu Enterprise, and the fruits of Toussaint's and Sehorn's publishing and recording success. But, ironically, for a man who drives a Rolls Royce, owns part of a recording studio, and has even written a song called "Viva La Money," Toussaint disdains from taking money or business. "I don't concern myself with money," he claims. "I just worry about music. The premise of my relationship with Marshall is that he takes care of the business and I take care of the music. Marshall's the go-getter. He invites me in on the business and gives me total respect. But, personally, money doesn't mean that much to me."

The opening of the studio meant a redirection of Toussaint's talents and energies. The emphasis on recording local singles was all but abandoned, as more profitable deals with major labels were sought for the studio. Initially, the studio signed a lucrative long-term agreement with Warner Brothers, which contracted large blocks of time for their artists, and inked Toussaint and the Meters to exclusive recording contracts.

The first production hit to come out of Sea-Saint was the Pointer Sisters' "Yes We Can," on Blue Thumb. It was followed soon after

Allen Toussaint, 1972

by LaBelle's massive hit "Lady Marmalade." The combination of these two successes, a short time apart, drew much attention from the national music press. Quite suddenly the words "genius" and "brilliance" were being used to describe Toussaint and his music. With increasing frequency, artists of both large and small stature journeyed to New Orleans for his magic musical touch.

The mid-Seventies clearly proved to be Toussaint's most productive in terms of commercial writing, recording and producing. King Biscuit Boy, Z.Z. Hill, Frankie Beverly, Etta James, Gladys Knight and Joe Cocker all recorded albums that were produced by Toussaint, bringing further credibility to him and the studio.

Impressed by Toussaint's productions for others, Paul McCartney recorded an album with his group Wings in New Orleans, which proved to be a real feather in the studio's cap, and only served to underline Toussaint's reputation.

"I don't think any of those artists came here looking for a New Orleans sound," says Toussaint. "I like to think beyond that. I've always tried to collect every sound that's come my way. I never wanted to be, say, just a blues player. I have to do different things or I swiftly get bored.

"New Orleans has a lot of good music, but if you listen to the national heartbeat, it becomes obvious why the world doesn't like many of our things today. A lot of New Orleans things have that around-the-corner feel, and that's not going to go over elsewhere. You've got to have higher expectations than just New Orleans.

"It's not necessary for me to physically leave New Orleans to work. I don't think I'd ever do that, but it is necessary for my work to leave New Orleans. It needs to be packaged and sold elsewhere for it to be successful. It's like Coca-Cola. They wouldn't be such a big company if they only sold Cokes in New Orleans. Music is the same way."

Eventually, even if reluctantly, Toussaint's career as a solo artist blossomed. His 1975 Warner Brothers album *Southern Nights* finally flaunted the artistry that was every bit equal to the man's lofty reputation that was built by helping others. He even occasionally overcame his aversion to live performances, developing a flashy, fast paced show that became one of the highlights of the annual New Orleans Jazz and Heritage Festival.

Glen Campbell's subsequent cover of "Southern Nights" turned into one of the biggest international hits of 1977, becoming Toussaint's biggest composing success ever, which only put his talent in greater demand. Before the decade was completed, Toussaint had overseen albums by Lee Dorsey, Joe Cocker, The Neville Brothers, Albert King, Boz Scaggs and Dr. John.

Oddly enough, Toussaint's 1978 *Motion* album (to date his last contemporary effort) was produced by Jerry Wexler and recorded in Los Angeles. "As an artist, I don't really know just who I am," he explains, referring to his solo material. "I really don't know what people expect of Allen Toussaint the performer. That's why I'd have to say I prefer someone else to produce my records. They can see things more objectively."

The new decade has seen a slowdown in product flowing out of Sea-Saint. In 1980, Toussaint produced albums by Eric Gale, Ramsey Lewis, Mylon LeFevre and Patti LaBelle, but none reached any degree of national success. Since then, things have been uncharacteristically silent at Sea-Saint. Warner Brothers didn't renew their contract with the studio, and Toussaint hasn't had a new album on the market for more than half a decade. In 1983 two albums' worth of material were recorded by Carla Baker and a young group, Cinnamon, but only one unsuccessful single on Baker was released.

According to Toussaint, a number of albums' worth of material on himself and other artists is on the shelf at Sea-Saint, which

Sehorn hopes to lease for a lucrative sum. One effort Toussaint has put a lot of effort into is a gospel album, which he feels is quite promising. Toussaint points out he is now a reborn Christian and that his renewed belief in God has changed his thinking about the direction of music.

As of this writing, Toussaint seems poised to move once again in another direction. Although, characteristically, he won't show his hand, he does speak freely of the upcoming musical "renaissance" that he expects to happen in New Orleans soon. "You used to have to come here (New Orleans) to get certain things done. But it's not the same anymore, it's really crowded out there. I think New Orleans is going to enjoy a new heyday, but it's going to be different than the ones in the past. We've always enjoyed a certain luxury in New Orleans by not abiding to the national rules. The best thing about New Orleans has always been the difference, not the sameness. It's the same with our music. But in order to survive in today's music world, New Orleans will have to broaden its horizons and stop thinking in terms of just itself. We'll have to just survive."

Part Two:

THE PIONEERS

By 1947, black America's musical tastes were changing. People were demanding a faster-paced music to dance to, one that had an increasing emphasis on the rocking boogie rhythms. New Orleans, always a hotbed of musical activity, was no exception.

But in New Orleans, a raunchier, downhome music was emerging, one that simultaneously was rooted in Dixieland jazz, the barrelhouse-blues piano style, and the infectious street parade rhythms. Add to this the influence of gospel quartets, and the advent of electrical amplification, and you had a music developing that was to sound totally unique.

With none of the major record companies interested in exploiting the situation, New Orleans was a ripe musical plum waiting to be picked by the independent record companies. There was hot competition among the scores of independent labels, as they tried to stay one step ahead of each other. Rather than the music changing independently of the record companies, the companies accelerated the synthesis of New Orleans rhythm and blues by striving for a more successful musical formula.

The pioneers of early New Orleans rhythm and blues were all firmly rooted in the music of another era, but they used it to create a new music. Without a Roy Brown or a Dave Bartholomew, the music might have turned out differently. But New Orleans rhythm and blues grew, it became increasingly popular and became one of America's most distinct musical styles.

ROY BROWN:
The Good Rockin' Man

The importance of Roy Brown is perhaps best put into perspective when deejay Dr. Daddy-O says, "If I had to put my finger on an exact moment when rhythm and blues started in New Orleans, I'd have to say it was when Roy Brown came out with 'Good Rockin' Tonight.' That really turned things around for music in New Orleans. 'Good Rockin' Tonight' was the first instance where New Orleans felt there was such a thing as black music.' "

It isn't overstating the fact to say that Roy Brown was America's first soul singer. A true master of "the slow burn," Roy sang the blues with a passion matched by no one. Roy Brown was one of the first singers to adapt the untamed vocal approach of gospel singers to the twelve-bar blues format.

"Roy was a blues singer's blues singer," says Mr. Google Eyes, one of Roy Brown's contemporaries. "Nobody could 'worry' a word or a phrase quite like he could. Roy Brown could make you laugh and cry during the same song. He just had that kind of emotion when he sang.

"Even though he had a lot of big records, I don't think Roy Brown ever got the credit he deserved. If you listen to Johnny Ace, Little Milton, Bobby Bland, or B.B. King, you can tell they've listened to Roy Brown since they were kids. And Jackie Wilson — man sometimes you can't even tell the two apart."

His singing notwithstanding, Roy Brown was a top-notch songwriter, employing both humor and deep-seated emotion to tell his story. He remains one of the great blues lyricists of all time. While his songs illustrated life in black America in the Forties and Fifties, they have also stood the test of time. Not only did his material help springboard the careers of Elvis and Buddy Holly during the Fifties, it has been translated in the Eighties by the likes of the Blasters, the Honeydrippers and Joe Ely.

Roy Brown was born in New Orleans on September 10, 1925, the son of True Love Brown (who was of Negro-Algonquin Indian parentage) and Yancy Brown. Yancy moved his family to Eunice, Louisiana, a small St. Landry Parish town, while Roy was quite young, to seek work as a plasterer. True Love directed a church choir, and she encouraged young Roy's early interest in music.

At the age of 12, Roy organized his own spiritual quartet that performed many original songs he had written. He always credited this period as the beginning of his rhythmic singing. In fact, he remembers his mother giving him a whipping after church one night for "jazzing up a spiritual."

Living in an agricultural area of the state, Roy was in the fields early, earning a living cutting cane, harvesting rice and chopping cotton. To make the time pass more quickly he joined his coworkers in singing spirituals. On his off hours Roy began jotting down ideas for new spirituals.

True Love died when Roy was just 14, and he and his father moved on to Houston, where Roy attended high school. After graduation he moved to Los Angeles, where he trained to be a pro boxer. As a welterweight, Roy claimed to have won 16 of 18 bouts before hanging up his gloves because he hated the sight of blood!

Singing was still a consuming interest, and in 1943, Roy entered an amateur show at the Million Dollar Theatre. Imitating his favorite vocalist Bing Crosby, Roy won first prize for singing "I Got Spurs That Jingle, Jangle, Jingle." After this first taste of success, Roy started singing in all the theaters that had amateur nights, winning a number of prizes.

Brown returned to Houston in 1943 to be inducted into the army, but was rejected because he had flat feet. While there he began singing in a few Sixth Ward clubs, and came to the attention of a visiting Shreveport club owner, who was impressed at the way Roy handled songs like "Stardust" and "Temptation." He hired Roy for a then-stratospheric sum of $125 a week, because he felt Roy would be a good novelty since he sounded white.

It was during his nine-month stay at "Billy Riley's Palace Park" that Roy actually started to sing the blues. After seeing the audience throw money on the bandstand when the other singers on the show sang blues, Roy quickly learned "When My Man Comes Home" and Billy Eckstine's "Jelly Jelly."

Up until then, Brown was content to do all of Bing Crosby's material. It wasn't until he was spurned by his band, The Coot Lewis Combo, that he began to really concentrate on singing blues. Roy maintained that he just didn't like singing the blues.

After the Shreveport club burned down in 1946, Roy moved to Galveston, Texas, where he got a job singing with Joe Coleman's band. He stayed with Coleman for four months, doing Ink Spots and Crosby imitations. Galveston pianist Candy Green still remem-

**Roy Brown and the Mighty Men
Greystone Ballroom, 1947**

bers Roy from those days. "Roy had a real smooth polished voice in those days," says Green, "but he wasn't singin' no blues; strictly ballads and Sinatra stuff."

After the short stay with Coleman's band, Roy organized his own combo, called the Mellowdeers, and went to work at Mary Russell's Club Grenada, a notorious Galveston gaming house. Roy managed to secure air time on radio station KGBC, until then an unheard of acomplishment for a group of black musicians in 1946. Roy's theme was Bing's "There's No You," and he was generally called on to croon the ballads, while another band member handled the more rhythmic numbers.

It was during the KGBC radio days that Roy claims to have written his trademark tune, "Good Rockin' Tonight." According to Roy, he wrote the song for the group's trumpeter Wilbert Brown to sing over the air. At the last second, Wilbert passed out, just as the announcer was introducing the song. Roy took the cue and began shouting and using a falsetto — a perfect contradiction to his crooning style. The song caused an immediate stir, and the station's switchboard lit up with people asking who this new singer was. However, Candy Green claims, "No, Roy didn't write that tune. He had a piano player named Joel Harris who wrote it. Joel wasn't a full-time musician, he was a schoolteacher who just moonlighted for some extra bread. He wrote it and gave it to Roy."

Whatever the circumstances, Roy added the tune to his repertoire, and it became one of his most requested numbers back at the Club Grenada. The group was even surreptitiously recorded during one of their broadcasts, and two sides, "Deep Sea Diver" and "Bye Baby Bye" were issued on Bob Quinn's Gold Star label once Roy hit the big time in 1947. Roy left the Mellowdeers and Galveston, and not long after headed for his birthplace. Candy Green laughs when recalling the circumstances: "Roy had to leave town fast 'cause he got himself caught fooling around with another club owner's girl. He split owing a lot of people money. But when he came back a couple of years later a star, he had a big line of people comin' backstage, and there he was with a big roll of money payin' everybody off!"

When Roy got to New Orleans in March 1947, he was dead broke. Noticing that "Mr. Blues" — Wynonie Harris — was at the Dew Drop on Rampart Street, he wrote the lyrics to "Good Rockin' Tonight" down on a paper sack, hoping to interest Harris in buying the song outright. After being snubbed by Harris, his band let Roy do the song during the intermission. Harris' band was taken with Roy's tune, and one of the band members suggested he take the song down to Cecil Gant, who was playing down on Jackson Avenue at Foster's Rainbow Room, and who might be able to help him. Roy took his advice and sang the song to Gant during one of his breaks. Gant was so taken with "Good Rockin' Tonight" he called Jules Braun, one of the co-owners of DeLuxe, at 4 a.m., and made Brown sing it over the phone. Braun told Gant to give Roy $100, get him a room at the Dew Drop, and keep an eye on him, because Braun was coming down to New Orleans later that week to record Paul Gayten and Annie Laurie.

The next night, Roy was sitting in with Gant's band at the Dew Drop, Savoy Records' Herman Lubinsky spotted him, and offered him $125 to record. Roy quickly consented, taking Lubinsky's cash, but, strangely, Lubinsky never returned to get Roy to sign a contract.

Two days later, Gant took Roy over to the Jung Hotel to meet Braun. Braun asked Roy if he could write three other songs by next week to make up a session. Roy went back to his room and penned "Lollipop Mama," "Miss Fanny Brown" and "Long About Midnight." Later that afternoon he called Braun and told him he had the rest of the songs written. Braun was skeptical at first, but told

Roy to meet him down at the J&M Studio the next morning, where he had scheduled a Paul Gayten/Annie Laurie session.

Sure enough, Braun went for the songs, and Bob Ogden's band was brought in to back Roy on "Good Rockin' Tonight." Apparently Cosimo Matassa, the engineer, was having trouble with the microphones on the session, and Roy had to stoop down and sing into the piano's microphone.

Immediately after the session, Braun took his masters back to Linden, New Jersey. Roy was hired by Ogden to sing down at the Black Diamond Restaurant on North Galvez and Conti streets, along with Sporty Johnson, Myrtle Jones and Alma Parnell. By May, "Good Rockin' Tonight" was released, and the entire revue moved on to the more prestigious Robin Hood club, on Jackson Avenue and Loyola.

When the record first came out, some of Roy's friends brought him to a club on Rampart Street to hear it. Without realizing that it was his own voice coming out of the jukebox, he commented that he thought it was a pretty good record. But once he realized just who it was that was singing, he spent the rest of the afternoon playing "Good Rockin' Tonight" on the jukebox. The impact of "Good Rockin' Tonight" was immediate in New Orleans, although it didn't enter the national charts until early the following year. Roy soon became the hottest musical item in the city.

Not long after, he left Ogden's band and teamed up with Clarence Samuels, a blues shouter from Texas whose recordings appeared on Decca. Billing themselves as the "Blues Twins," the pair worked with Edgar Blanchard's band at the Down Beat Club on Rampart Street. The duo jammed the club every night in return for $4 a week, and a room over the club. In August 1947, the *Louisiana Weekly* reported: "Clarence Samuels and Roy Brown sing some real hip music as 'The Blues Twins.' Both singers really throw themselves into the sessions, rebobbing and versing groovy tunes. The Down Beat is rocking from the early PM until hours after daybreak." Dr. Daddy-O recalls that Roy and Samuels would sing from on top of the bar so they could get more people in the Down Beat!

As "Good Rockin' Tonight" got bigger and bigger, so did the demand for Roy's personal appearances. Even though the owner of the Down Beat raised Roy to $10 a week, he was lured away with a $50-a-night guarantee by the owner of the Starlight Club, on Lowerline and Forshey Street.

At the Starlight Roy formed his own band led by Teddy Riley on trumpet. Other band members included Frank Parker, drums; Tommy Shelvin, bass; Edward Santino, piano; and the colorful LeRoy "Batman" Rankin on tenor sax. Roy was offered a tour of the West Coast as "Good Rockin' Tonight" began getting a national foothold, but he preferred staying at the Starlight, occasionally taking engagements at other local clubs. The *Louisiana Weekly* reported in November 1947: "Everybody's talking about Roy Brown, that great blues singer, and papa of 'Good Rockin' Tonight.' For this reason he is being featured at The Club Rocket for a big dance November 2, and is also being held over indefinitely, after breaking all attendance records at the Starlight Hotel and Cafe."

With "Good Rockin' Tonight" in the charts, DeLuxe Records rushed Roy back into the studio for more sides. By the end of 1947, Roy had recorded twenty-two titles for the Braun Brothers, eight of which were committed to wax. Among the best were "Miss Fanny Brown" and "Mighty, Mighty Man."

When Roy's records started hitting the national charts, he and his group The Mighty Mighty Men hit the road to cash in, travelling first to Nashville, where they made an unheard of $2,500 for one night. Bandleader Teddy Riley picks up the story: "We didn't play to nuthin' but packed houses. Roy was so popular, there was even a guy out there making a living impersonating him [Clarence Samuels]. Sometimes we'd play over thirty nights in a month. We drove all over the country in a Cadillac limousine. It was never like work. Roy was a lot of fun, but he worked harder than anybody.

"You talk about talented. Roy probably wrote over a thousand songs that never got published. Man we played on a bunch of big records — "Whose Hat Is That," "Brown Angel," "Boogie At Midnight" — oh, just lots of them. We played all the big theatres, the Apollo, the Howard, all over California and each year we did a big show at Wrigley Field in Chicago. For awhile George Weinberg booked us on a package show with Roy Milton, called it 'The Battle of the Blues.' From 1947, when I joined Roy, until 1954, when I left over a misunderstanding, we were steady on the road. New Orleans was just a base."

Recordingwise, things were just as busy. Since Roy Brown and The Mighty Mighty Men stayed on the road so much, many sessions had to be arranged in Dallas and the King studios in Cincinnati. Between November 1949 and August 1951, Roy had an incredible string of successes, with no less than six records making the national R&B top ten. The string started with "Boogie At Mid-

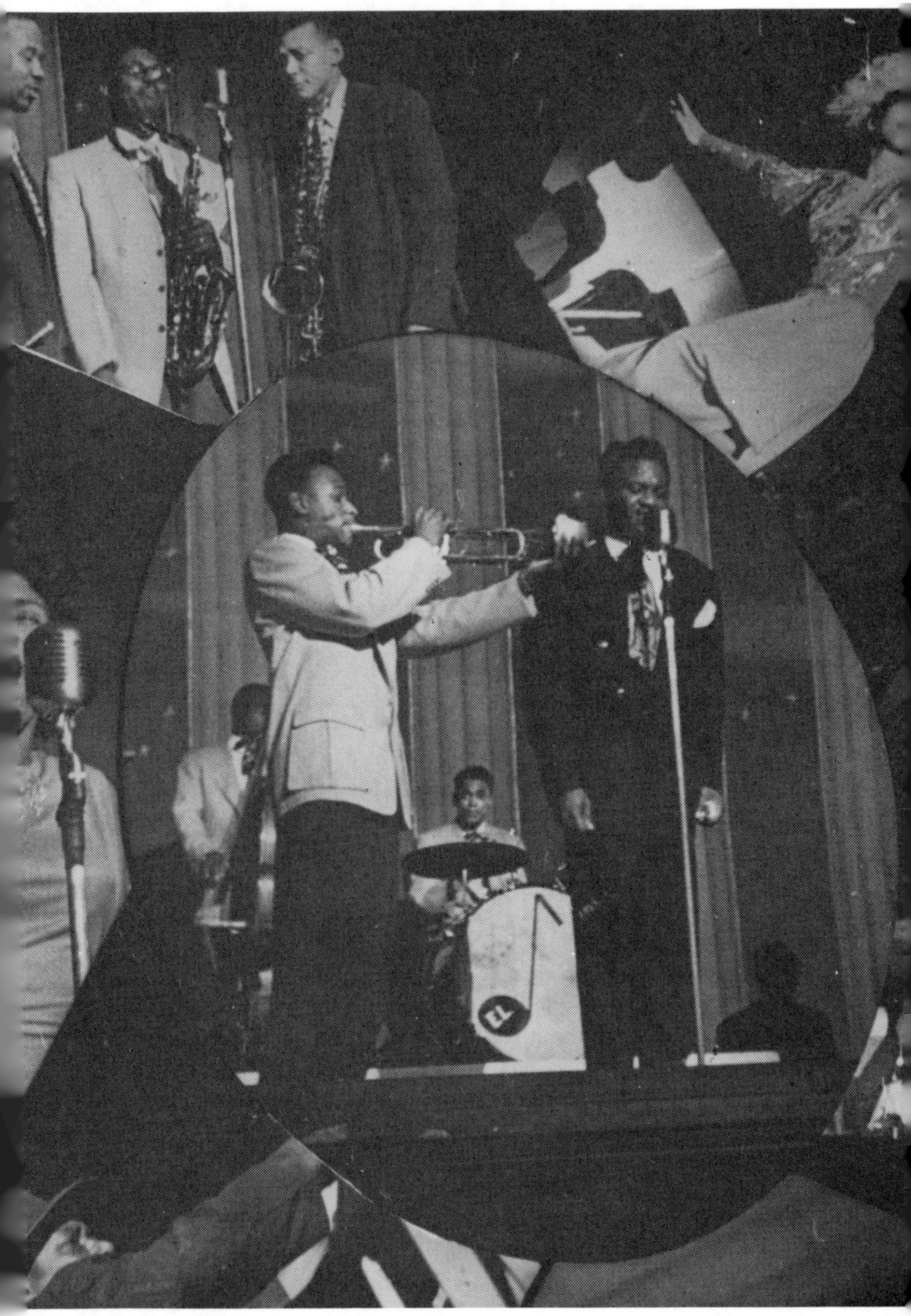

night," which climbed to number three, and was followed by his biggest hit, the impassioned "Hard Luck Blues," which climbed to number one during the summer of 1950. Other chart records were "Love Don't Love Nobody," a number two hit in September 1950; the two-sided smash "Long About Sundown" b/w "Cadillac Baby," which respectively rose to number eight and number six in November 1950; and "Big Town," a number eight R&B record from August 1951. Whether it was a smoldering blues or a pulsating jump number, Roy Brown could lead his listener to any emotion.

By 1952, King Records had bought up Roy's contract and the rest of the DeLuxe label. However, Roy's stay at King wasn't to his liking. Although King had the facilities to promote and distribute R&B records that were second to none, owner Syd Nathan had a reputation for not paying royalties. Even though Roy was paid in advance for his sessions, he claims he never got the performance royalties he should have gotten and, in fact, wasn't even registered with B.M.I. until 1957.

Roy Brown's King recordings from the early Fifties were of his expected high quality, but he couldn't repeat his early national success with DeLuxe. Nonetheless, songs like "Old Age Boogie," "Grandpa Stole My Baby," "Laughin' But Cryin'," "Trouble At Midnight," and "Black Diamond" still sold heavily enough in New Orleans, Texas, and most of the Deep South to warrant more sessions by King.

On the road, Roy Brown and The Mighty Mighty Men were still setting all kinds of attendance records. "We definitely had the top band out there," declares Teddy Riley. "We were cutting fifteen-piece bands like Basie and Eckstein. Batman used to get up on the bar and up in the rafters to play. Man, we had those people going crazy."

Brown and his group toured extensively off their hits. Besides playing the country's largest theaters, they barnstormed across the country playing everything from baseball parks to tobacco warehouses. The group must have made quite a sight as they went through choreographed dance steps in matching brightly colored suits while going through their latest hits.

In 1953, at the height of his career, Roy found out he was being defrauded by his personal manager, Jack Pearl. Pearl, Syd Nathan, King Record's president, and Ben Bart, his booking agent at Universal Attractions, had arranged to book Roy's jobs with a pair of dissimilar contracts. Roy was shown a contract with a smaller guarantee than was actually paid by the promoter, with the extra money being pocketed by Pearl and his conspirators.

Roy fought back by turning Pearl into the musicians' union for defrauding him out of his percentages. Universal Attractions, in turn, decided to make it hard on Roy by booking him simultaneously at opposite ends of the country, thereby giving him a "no-show" reputation.

Roy was forced to take matters into his own hands and began booking himself throughout the South, often paying for promotion out of his own pocket. Once while touring California during late 1954, Roy happened to turn on the radio and hear a white hillbilly singer named Elvis Presley singing "Good Rockin' Tonight." Although no one could have predicted it, Presley would soon have a shattering effect on Roy Brown's career and the rest of the music industry.

By 1956, rock and roll had dropped the bottom out of Roy's record sales. What was needed was a systematic about-face in his recording attempts. Luckily, Roy was able to get a release from King, and he signed a one-year contract with Imperial Records.

"Roy was doing pretty bad when rock and roll came in," recalls Dave Bartholomew, who signed and produced Roy for Imperial. "See Roy was more or less an older type of blues singer, and that was dying out. I was living in back of St. Bernard Avenue, and Roy lived just around the corner. He came by my house one night and said, 'Man, can you get me with Imperial?'

"We did a cover on 'Party Doll' [originally recorded by Buddy Knox, a Texas rockabilly artist on Roulette]. We got the word from California to cover it, and it didn't do too bad. After that we did 'Let The Four Winds Blow.' It was just an audition tape, we were foolin' around the studio when we did it. Well, Chudd [Imperial Records' owner] puts the goddamn record out. It was all out of time and tempo, the record just wasn't right, but he still did 1,000,000 on it. I didn't think it was hittin' on shit. There was another thing I cut on him, 'Saturday Night,' but nothin' after that. I'd have to say I got Roy on the tail end of his career. It wasn't long after that he had those run-ins with the law and moved to California."

Roy's brief sojourn at Imperial helped revitalize his sagging career. "Party Doll" surprised everybody, and it became his first record to hit the *Billboard* Hot 100, if only for two weeks, peaking at 89, in April 1957. On "Party Doll," Roy was given a schmaltzy pop arrangement, but he still managed the occasional patented vocal roll. "Let The Four Winds Blow," though, was another story. This time Roy was perfectly relaxed as he romped through the Bartholomew arrangement. It turned into Roy's biggest Imperial hit, going to #38 nationally during its 15-week stay in the summer of 1957. Brown also managed some of the rockingest sides Bartholomew ever produced. Some of Roy's Imperial sides like "Saturday Night," "Hip Shakin' Baby," and "I'm Ready To Play" came as close as any black singer did to the white rockabilly sound.

His 1957 successes put Roy back on the road as a member of many R&B package shows, headlining with the likes of Ray Charles, Big Joe Turner, Etta James and Larry Williams. Roy kept up his road touring until around 1959, when his records again faded from popularity. Imperial wouldn't pick up Roy's option because Roy claimed the IRS was auditing him, and Imperial didn't want them looking into their books too.

By 1959, Roy had found himself back on King Records for two sessions recorded in Cincinnati. Even though he managed a stunning "School Bell Rock," in the best Chuck Berry tradition, and a stirring "Ain't Got No Blues Today," sales were negligible and Roy was sadly sinking out of sight. To top it off, the IRS was after him, and he also was arrested in New Orleans by the FBI in February 1960 for defrauding a promoter out of $200 by impersonating B.B. King over the phone and trying to get him to wire him money in New Orleans.

After this embarrassment, Rubin Cherry's Memphis-based Home Of The Blues label expressed interest in recording Roy and brought him to Memphis to record at Sun Records Studio with the Willie Mitchell band. The records did well in Memphis and New Orleans, especially the storming "Rocking All The Time," which was very reminiscent of his past DeLuxe glories. They brought him back for one more session in 1961 that produced "Oh So Wonderful," a hilarious duet with Mamie Dell. Soon after, Roy moved to California where he shied away from performing, seeking employment as a door-to-door salesman, hawking everything from household utensils to encyclopedias. There were some obscure but fine releases on DRA, Connie and Mobil, but they just sold locally. Fats Washington even recorded him on behalf of Chess Records, but the session has remained unissued.

Teddy Riley commented on Roy Brown's demise, "I guess things just came too fast for him, and when they started to slip away he couldn't handle it." Dave Bartholomew agreed adding, "Roy thought he was broke. But you see he had a good wife, she knew how to get things done. She had a nursery out in California and they were doing very well, very well. She was the kind of woman who knew how to hold on to a dollar. Roy lived very well, he wasn't hurtin'."

In 1967, after a chance meeting with former Savoy representative Lee Magid, Brown arranged to cut a session for ABC-Bluesway. "New Orleans Woman" and "Standing On Broadway" were pulled for a single, doing moderately well. Roy was in tremendous form on the Bluesway session, screaming and bellowing with great enthusiasm and delight. An album was planned, but strangely it didn't see the light of day until 1973.

During the late Sixties more singles were released on small labels like Gert, Summit and Tru-Love, but really nothing much happened for Roy other than picking up weekend gigs in Orange County. By 1970 things started to turn around again. That same year he was chosen to close the Monterey Jazz Festival along with the Johnny Otis Revue. The performance, which was recorded on Epic, gave notice to the rest of the world that Roy Brown wasn't a spent force.

Brown was so exhilarated by his Monterey success that he began writing new material, and he and co-producer Miles Greyson recorded it on their newly-formed Friendship label. One of the titles, "Love For Sale," caused such a stir that Mercury leased it, but just missed getting it into the national R&B charts. The record was his biggest seller since "Let The Four Winds Blow." The follow-up, "Mail Man Blues," did almost as well.

Not long after, Roy signed with Jimmy Holiday at 20th Century Fox to do an album. Sadly, nothing ever materialized from the agreement. However, in 1976, Route 66 Records in Sweden reissued a collection of his DeLuxe sides that actually made the top ten best-seller list in that country! Undoubtedly the high point of Roy's career was his highly acclaimed European tour of 1978. European audiences had rediscovered the champion blues shouter of the Forties and Fifties, and Roy "Good Rockin' " Brown was their hero. Roy packed them into European theatres just as he had packed black theaters during the height of his DeLuxe days.

Route 66 put together another collection of vintage material, and new recordings were made with a Swedish band. When he returned home, Americans began taking notice too, and he got recording and personal appearance offers.

It is indeed ironic that Roy Brown's last public appearance should be in his hometown, New Orleans, the town that he had given so much to. After a twenty-year absence, Roy set the 1981 New Orleans Jazz Festival crowd on its ear with powerful versions of "Good Rockin' Tonight" and "Love For Sale." Even the normally composed Dave Bartholomew allowed, "He sounded real good! Better than he did twenty years ago." For the first time in twenty-six years Roy was reunited with his old bandleader Teddy Riley, who concurred with Bartholomew's opinion.

Roy returned to San Fernando to his wife and daughter. New Orleans singer Joe Jones, who was close to Roy in California, spoke of his last days: "Roy was so proud of his daughter. She was the joy of his life, and getting her through college was the biggest thing for Roy. She graduated on Friday night, and Roy had a heart attack and died on the following Sunday evening. He must have died happy."

MR. GOOGLE EYES
The Nation's Youngest Blues Singer

Whenever New Orleans musicians get together to recall the early days of rhythm and blues, inevitably the name Joe August, also known as Mr. Google Eyes or simply Mr. G, crops up. Performers like Johnny Adams, Earl King, Ernie K-Doe, King Floyd and Deacon John have cited him as an early inspiration.

Although he didn't attain the recording success of many of his New Orleans contemporaries, Mr. G's recordings predate those of Fats Domino, and are among the finest examples of early New Orleans rhythm and blues.

These days Mr. G, or simply G, as his friends refer to him, lives quietly with an aunt in a tiny cottage deep in the Ninth Ward section of New Orleans. His trim physique, bright eyes, and full head of salt-and-pepper hair betray the fact he recently turned 50. Most of his time is spent heading a political organization — Blacks That Give A Damn — that aids kids in trouble and lobbies local politicians. But Mr. G likes nothing better than recalling the early New Orleans R&B days. Proud of his checkered career, he is eager to recall, gleefully at times, his past and always has one more humorous anecdote to tell.

Born Joseph Augustus in New Orleans on September 13, 1931, he spent the first 10 years of his life Uptown, where he got his initial taste of music. "There used to be shows over on Washington Avenue at the Lincoln Theater — vaudeville I guess you'd call it. We called 'em 'Midnight Rambles.' Used to be a lot of comedians, Lollypop, Sporty Johnson, Alma Parnel. Sometimes they'd come by the house to eat. I was just a little guy, but right then I liked their style of life. I wanted to be just like 'em.

"Then we moved over into the Iberville Projects when they first opened in 1940. My grandmother got me singin' in the choir of the First Emmanuel Baptist Church. That's where I got my bottom from."

An only child, Joseph was close to both his mother and his grandmother. To bring some extra money into the household he hustled up a part time job, which as it turned out drew him even closer to a professional music career. "I must have been twelve when I got a job across the street workin' for old man Dooky Chase. I used to deliver sandwiches on my bicycle.

"Well, his son Edward had a band, so I hung around the house listening to it. I spent more time around there than in my own home. Fact, old man Dooky practically raised me."

Being staunch church going Baptists, Mr. G's mother and grandmother weren't too happy about him getting involved with music, especially the blues. "My family was dead set against it. My grandmother said I'd be workin' for the devil, so they wouldn't buy me an instrument. I wanted a set of drums too. Everybody in the neighborhood had a horn or a saxophone. The next best thing I had was my voice, so that was my instrument. Music to us was a natural thing. We used to set up out in the courtyard and start playin' — right there in the middle of the project.

"From workin' around Dooky Chase, I got to meet lots of musicians like Fats Pichon. He would stop in after work in the mornin' and get a hot sausage po-boy. I told him I wanted to be a performer too, and would ask him questions about it."

It was while working at Dooky Chase's that the teenaged Joseph August was stuck with the "Google Eyes" tag. "When I wasn't on the bicycle, old man Dooky would call me in the kitchen and ask me to help him cook. They had a window between the kitchen and the dining room, where the waitresses would come and pick up food. They had some pretty women," he says with a whistle, "and I would just sit there and stare. One night Dooky caught me and said, 'Come on, you better get your google eyes out of there!' That night they started to rib me, and it got back to the neighborhood and it stuck."

Although barely a teenager, the ambitious youngster managed to work his own way into bands and clubs. "When I had a night off, I'd go help Dooky Chase's band [Chase sponsored a popular jazz band during the Forties] by carrying the instruments into the dances, and I talked 'em into lettin' me sing a few numbers. I used to get my behind whipped for stayin' out late, but I made $3 a night!"

Once he had his foot in the door there was no way to stop the eager Google Eyes, who had yet another trick up his sleeve. "I saved all my money up and put the down payment on a PA set from Johnny's Music Shop on Rampart Street. At that time very few bands had PA sets. Even Paul Barbarin didn't have one. He had about the best band in town and he had to go borrow one. It was in a black cabinet; it had one 12-inch speaker. See, some of the young-

LEROY'S
(AIR CONDITIONED)
Silver Palace
GENERAL TAYLOR
AND WILLOW STREETS
PHONE TW. 5-9115

—PRESENTS—
EVERY WEDNESDAY NIGHT
"LITTLE GIANT OF SHOW BUSINESS"

Joe "Mr. G" August

*Columbia - RCA - Duke
Recording Artist*

ALONG WITH
*Other Top
Entertainers*

"GOLDEN BOY" JOE "Mr. G" AUGUST

er guys who started bands didn't have 'em, so they would come to me. That put me in demand — they sure couldn't have the PA unless I sang.

"The only way my mother would let me sing the blues through it, and bring it in the house, was to let the church use it on Sunday. So with my PA, I could make $3 a night, and get into the clubs when the rest of the kids my age had to peep in the window."

The PA set aside, Google Eyes was quickly making a name for himself as an exciting, talented blues singer, as he made the rounds of the city's clubs. "I started workin' the Downbeat Club on Rampart Street around 1947, singing opposite Roy Brown. Worked at the Robin Hood on Jackson Avenue with Paul Gayten and Annie Laurie. This was when I was 14 years old. With that PA, I was welcomed everywhere."

Although Roy Brown, Paul Gayten and Annie Laurie recorded first, Mr. Google Eyes was right on their heels. "I was gettin' a good reputation around town. I was in and out of the Dew Drop, The Pelican, Foster's, the Plum Room. I was workin' at Fosters with Wynonie Harris, and did a 'Battle of The Blues' with Billy Eckstine at the Club Desire. In fact, he was the first one to call me Mr. G, 'cause they were callin' him Mr. E.

"Deluxe records came down here first to record Paul [Gayten] and Roy [Brown], but I recorded for the Coleman Brothers from Newark, New Jersey, on Coleman Records. They were the only black record company in the country at that time I believe.

"They were a spiritual label up 'til then, and Bill Coleman came down to look for talent while he was here trying to set a record distributorship with William B. Allen. Coleman came in a club one night and heard me sing, and said, 'That's who I want to record.' In fact, he passed up Larry Darnell for me."

Only 15 at the time, his first record proclaimed "Mr. Google Eyes — the world's youngest blues singer," and it turned out to be one of his biggest. "We did 'Poppa Stoppa's Be-Bop Blues,' and 'Real Young Boy (Just 16 Years Old).' It was big. I came up with the song with Poppa Stoppa's name on it, so he would play it on the radio. I wrote that with Miss Elsie Montgomery, who was Little Brother Montgomery's wife. I remember him playin' on this old beat up piano in there while we got it together.

"You see, Coleman was smart. I come up with the song 'No Wine, No Women' — that was my second record. Then he got me to cut a radio spot singin' it for Monogram Wine. It was a great advertisement. Got paid a case of wine for it and I didn't even drink!"

"I had another big record with 'Rock My Soul.' I did four records for Coleman, with Lee Allen and Paul Gayten backin' me."

Unlike other New Orleans artists, Mr. G fared well with his record company. "I made more money with Coleman than Deluxe paid Paul Gayten and Roy Brown. Coleman knew the business. The first record took off with such a bang that five days later they took me up to sing at a hotel they owned in Newark. At first my mother sure didn't want me to go, but they gave her $750 — see 'cause I was still a minor — so she changed her mind. Guys like Roy Brown didn't get but $50."

Even if Google Eyes' records didn't sell in the quantities of his other New Orleans rivals, they greatly enhanced his popularity, and made him one of the city's top rhythm and blues attractions. "I always had work, I was makin' more money than everybody. I was just really lucky."

Things just kept rolling for the world's youngest blues singer, as the prestigious Columbia Records bought out his Coleman contract. "Coleman was good to me, but being a small company they could only go so far distributing, and they knew it. Columbia had only two or three black people on the whole damn label. But they

COLUMBIA

Mfrd. under Pats. Pending Trade Marks Reg. U.S. Pat. Off. Marcas Registradas Made in U.S.A.

DEMONSTRATION RECORD

For perfect tone
use Columbia Needles

38667
(CO 41895)

FOR YOU MY LOVE
Jump Blues with Vocal
- Gayten -
MR. GOOGLE EYES
Accompanied by Billy Ford and his
Musical V-8's

wanted to experiment, so they bought out my contract. That's when we did 'For You My Love,' that Paul Gayten wrote. I did that with Billy Ford's band; Coleman had picked 'em for me.

"We did all right with the records. I had four on Columbia, and I was real happy with the sound. But there was one problem with Columbia. I found out a lot of people couldn't get my records because the distributors were prejudiced. People were askin' for my records at the record shops, but the shops couldn't get 'em. One time I was in Atlanta and was lookin' for my latest record. I come to find out the guy who sold blues records wouldn't carry Columbia, because they were a white record company."

During the early Fifties, Mr. G settled down in Newark, to be near the studio. "I married a girl from Newark. It [Newark] was my jumpin' off point 'till 1956. I worked New York, and all over the country, but I got back to New Orleans pretty much. I'd either stay with my mother, or Frank Pania put me up at the Dew Drop. Whenever I came to town Frank said I had a job there.

"Shaw was bookin' me out of New York, and he got me with Al Hibbler and we toured a bit, and made some records. Bill Cook started managin' me, and he got me into the Be Bop set at The Birdland, with Charlie Parker, Gene Ammons and Miles Davis."

His sets at The Birdland led Mr. G to one of the high points of his career as he proudly relates: "Count Basie's wife was in the club one night and told the Count about me. He came down to hear me and liked me. Three days later I went into the studio with Count Basie for RCA."

During the early 1950s, Mr. Google Eyes was hot as a firecracker. "It seemed like everything I cut was sellin'. I had four releases on four different labels in one month — Columbia, RCA, Lee's and Domino. See, they would pay cash up front with no royalties. I also cut for Savoy, with Johnny Otis' Orchestra. "By the time I was 19, I had made a quarter of a million dollars!" exclaims Mr. G, still shaking his head.

But like all Cinderella stories, Mr. Google Eyes' was fast approaching midnight. "I wound up broke," he shrugs. "I partied. I had big cars. I remember Lubinsky [Savoy Records owner] would buy me five pairs of silk pajamas.

"I enjoyed it all. Fats and them didn't have no cars. Grown men that worked all their life didn't have no cars. I had a '49 Buick convertible. The seats were leopard skin, the rugs were leopard skin. Uncle Sam got that," laughs Mr. G. "Tax."

"I had a chauffeur and a valet, so what am I complaining about? Believe me, I thought it was never gonna end. Every time I had something to complain about, somebody would stick some money in my hand and say 'Go out and play.'"

While in Newark, Mr. G had struck up a friendly and a professional relationship with bandleader Johnny Otis. Johnny was doing A&R work for Don Robey's Duke/Peacock label, and was responsible for placing Mr. Google Eyes on the label. "Robey was a slick character. I made less money workin' for him than anybody. All he ever wanted to pay anybody was $25. I wrote a lot of stuff for him too. I wrote one of Johnny Ace's big hits, 'Please Forgive Me,' but I didn't see a nickel."

After Mr. G left Newark, he headed for greener pastures on the West Coast. "I was workin' for these mafia guys in Newark, Joe Cacuzzi and 'Blackie' Wells. They had the Crystal Club, and I was their only black entertainer — white band and all. I made a lot of money for them. My mother was out in California takin' care of my son, 'cause me and my old lady split up. So I went out to L.A. and worked in one of their clubs with Johnny Otis."

By 1960, Mr. G had made his way back to New Orleans and decided to stay awhile. He picked up a job hosting an all star revue at the Sho Bar on Bourbon Street. Mr. G became a regular attrac-

```
              Open House
                   AT
            Blue Eagle Club
              2026 FELICITY STREET
         ........................................
         Fri.-Sat., Nov. 29-30, 1963
               9 P.M. UNTIL ??
         ........................................
                ⋈ PRESENTING ⋈
                   Mr. G
                  AND HIS
                 All • Stars
                ∽ FEATURING ∽
           AWOOD JOHNSON on TROMBONE
             CANNONBALL on GUITAR
              SCHEKSNIDER on SAX
              ARTHUR VIENE on BASS
             HARRY NANCY on DRUMS
         ........................................
               FREE ADMISSION
```

tion at the popular after hours Bourbon Street nightery, until an incident occurred that not only changed his life, it almost took it.

"You see, back then if you were caught dead with a white girl, they'd kill you again. Segregation was heavy here in New Orleans. We could play the clubs but we could never sit at a table and have a drink. We had to go in the storeroom to do our drinkin'. I remember one night Lee Allen got beat up just for comin' out during a break to play the jukebox.

"I got hooked up with this white dancer at the Sho-Bar named Vicki. She cared for me, but we could never go nowhere, there was nowhere for us to go anyway. So we got closer and closer, and we wanted to see more of each other. So Vicki and I got an apartment on Orleans Street in the Quarter. It was convenient, right near Bourbon Street, and it wouldn't look out of place me goin' over there after work.

"Well Vicki was determined that me and her were gonna got out in public together. She had heard me talkin' about the Dew Drop, and she wanted to go there with me. She had this beautiful blonde hair. She dyed it black, and cut it off short. She started wearin' this Man Tan, to get her skin to look darker. She decided she was gonna be Creole.

"She kept buggin' me, and buggin' me about taking her to the Dew Drop, but I kept ignoring her. Finally, one night she talked me into takin' her after work. So I said okay, but I told her, if the police stop us don't make 'em mad. 'Cause she had a temper, and it was my ass they was gonna kick.

"So I got all dressed up — new suit, shoes, process, sharp — and met her after work at the Sho-Bar. Vicki called a United Cab, and that was a mistake, 'cause we don't take United Cabs, only white people did. The guy gave us a funny look and I didn't feel right about it right off. By the time we got to La Salle Street, I turned around and saw a police car followin' us. When we got out at the Dew Drop, they stopped us. See, the cab driver had radioed the police.

"They told me to go inside the club, and told Vicki to stay where she was 'cause they wanted to talk to her. I went inside for — it must have been 15 minutes. They kept on talkin' to her, and talkin' to her, so finally I came back outside. The police said to me, 'I thought we told you to stay inside.'

"I said, 'I just wanna know what's goin' on.'

"The policeman says, 'We're takin' you down to the precinct.'

"'What charge?'

"'Loitering,' he said.

"So they put us in the back. Vicki stuck to her story about being creole, and I didn't say a word. We got to the precinct and they just kept it up. Finally, Vicki just blew up. She started screamin' she could be with whoever she wanted, and go wherever the hell she wanted. She was just rantin' and ravin' and I still hadn't said anything. They had to get a bucket of water and throw it on her just to shut her up!

"So I went over to the precinct captain and said, "Look. You can book me for stealin' somethin', or you can book me for killin' somebody. But don't book me for bein' with that bitch.'

"She was just soakin' wet, and I was still lookin' sharp. They put her in a cab an' sent her home and took me in a little back room. The captain said to me, 'Look, if you bring any more white girls down here, I'm gonna lock you up, and make it hard on your ass.'

"They put me in a cab — I didn't have but $1.25 — and I went back to the Sho-Bar. By then the word had reached the Quarter about us gettin' busted. So the club owner gave me $25, and told me to get on home. I called my mom, and asked her if I could come spend the night over there. She had already heard too, and said, 'What you foolin' with white girls for?! They gonna kill you!

They're probably waitin' outside right now.'

"'I didn't want to, but I had to head back to the apartment. When I got there she was sittin' on the bed dryin' her hair. I said, 'Baby, we got to talk. I told you not to get the police riled up.'

"'Then she reached under the bed — I thought she dropped her brush — and pulled out a rifle and said, "If I can't have you, nobody can,' and shot me through the abdomen. I fell on the floor and she came up to me and stuck the gun to my head and said, 'You don't love me.'

"'I said, 'That's not true baby,' and turned my head and played dead. She ran out of the apartment with the rifle, and I got up and sat on the bed. I wasn't bleedin' too much, and it didn't really hurt yet. I thought, 'Jeez, G, what did you get yourself into?' See, they had just integrated the first school in New Orleans that very day, and they had people marchin' and carryin' on, and now here were us two livin' together!

"'Just then I heard this runnin' up the stairs an' this policeman come runnin' in, with his gun out yellin', 'Where the nigger at, where the nigger at?' I put my hands up and he asks me, 'Nigger, why you want to break in this woman's place for?'

"''Break in, hell I live here!'

"'So I reached in my pocket and gave him the keys and told him, 'Would a man break into a house if he had the door key, if he had his suits hangin' in the closet, if his picture was in a gold frame on the bar, if his shorts were dryin' in the bathroom?'

"'He looked around, put his gun down and said, 'Say you look kind of familiar.'

"''Yeah, I work down at the Sho-Bar.'

'Then another policeman come runnin' in with Vicki, with his gun out yellin', 'Where the nigger at! Where the nigger at!'

"'The other policeman said, 'Ah put that gun away, him and Lee Allen got more white women than you.'

"'When Vicki came in, she looked white as a ghost, 'cause she thought I was dead. The first policeman said 'I thought you told me he was a prowler.'

"'She looked down an' said, 'Yeah, he live here.'

"'Well, I was startin' to hurt, so they called an ambulance and took her away in her nightgown, in the squad car. They put me in the ambulance and they took 45 minutes to drive me half-a-mile, at four o'clock in the morning, to Charity Hospital! Red neck mother-fuckers stopped for a beer, and were pokin' me where I got shot, sayin' 'Don't it hurt nigger? Nigger, you oughta die.'

"By the time I got to Charity, my mother had already heard and was there waitin' for me. I thought I was gonna die for sure, if they didn't take me to the black hospital Flint Goodrich. But she thought I might not make it, so they operated on me just after I blacked out at Charity.

"When I woke up the next day, they had tubes in my nose, in my stomach, in my arm, they had me handcuffed to the bed, and they had a policeman on the door so I wouldn't get away!

"They had charged me with miscegenation [mixing of the races]. As it turned out I was the last person in New Orleans ever charged with it because they had already wiped it off the books. When I was in the bed recoverin' people were comin' in and lookin' at me sayin' "There's that nigger.' They just come in and said that shit to me.

"My lawyer got the miscegenation charge dropped, after he convinced the DA he could never get it to stick. After I got out of the hospital they tried to get me to press charges against Vicki. See, they wanted to make some kind of example of her. But I told 'em, 'Uh-uh. I played the game and I lost. She could never be anything to me anymore. So just drop it.' So they finally had to let her out of jail."

After this close call, Mr. G decided to put a hold on his entertaining career, and stayed as far away from Bourbon Street as possible. "I moved down here into the Ninth Ward, into a house my cousin owned near the Desire Projects, so I could get my strength back. Now Miss Elsie Montgomery, that had The Plum Room, took sick, and they put her out of her building. They were buyin' up all the buildings on Rampart and tearin' em down to make parkin' lots. She moved down the street to the Boogie Bee, but they made her get out of there too.

"All she knew was the barroom business. Cursed like a sailor, big woman — get drunk, man, sit at the bar with her pistol under the bar, and her wig sideways on her head! Fess used to work for her plenty. After I decided to stay clear of Bourbon Street, I told her I'd help her out, 'cause I needed something to do. We started lookin' for a place, and found the old Fan Tan, on Burgundy and Bienville. Back then [early Sixties], Burgundy on back was all black, but there were no black bars. That place was a trap, but we fixed it up. I'm the one who really put that building in shape. I went into the bar business and quit singin', except for that last record I cut with Allen [Toussaint] on Instant."

Like many of Mr. G's stories, a certain amount of color and controversy surrounds his last recording session. "We did 'Everything

Happens At Night' that was written by Victor Kirschman — the guy who owns the department store downtown. A lot of people don't know it, but he wrote some stuff for Ella Fitzgerald. Well this record could have done big things. Kirschman paid for the session, and said he was gonna pay for a full page ad in *Billboard* and *Cashbox*, but he froze on the deal just as it was takin' off. Toussaint says it was one of the best things he ever produced too, 'cause it had a big band on it."

It's been twenty years since Mr. G has set foot in a recording studio. "They tried to get me to come down; Allen called me, and Senator Jones [Hep' Me Records]. But it's like this, if I can't do it right, I just don't want to do it. There's just too many bad vibes out there between the musicians and Toussaint. I just don't want to get mixed up in that rat race. But if I can do it right I will... 'Cause I got some material."

Besides the bar business, Mr. G got into radio as well, becoming a deejay on WBOK, through the aid of Victor Kirschman, who bought time for his store. "I created this thing called 'The Man on the Street.' After awhile Jax and Regal Beer bought time too."

Mr. G kept his radio slot until the mid-Sixties when he became the regular emcee at the Dew Drop, which was experiencing its last hurrah as an entertainment spot. "The Dew Drop was a beautiful place, man," sighs Mr. G. "That place will never be replaced. But once Frank Pania got sick, things started goin' downhill, and then he died. That ended the music scene around there."

He also stayed in the bar business, having a hand in "Mr. G's" on North Robertson, and "The Green Parrot" on First and St. Thomas. But as Mr. G admits, "I just got tired of it; it was too hard a work."

Mr. G stayed close to the field of entertainment throughout the Seventies, pursuing a variety of activities. "I started the Mason's Strip scene. I worked there five years singin' and emceein'. Then I managed a few groups, Las Vegas Connection, Antoine Domino Jr., and Oliver and the Rockettes."

Since he started his political organization in the late Seventies, entertaining has had to take a back seat to helping the black community. In 1980 and 1981, he hosted the Contemporary Art Center's "Dew Drop Inn Revivals" that took place during the New Orleans Jazz and Heritage Festival. He still occasionally makes a gig as part of the "New Orleans Blues Revue," along with Earl King and Deacon John. His voice still remains as strong as ever, and he obviously still enjoys singing the blues.

Despite his contribution to the city's rhythm and blues development, he has been overlooked by musicologists, but it doesn't slight Mr. G in the least. "Look, anybody who was around then knows I was right in the middle of it, when the whole thing started."

DAVE BARTHOLOMEW
The Man Behind The Big Beat

Whether he likes it or not, Dave Bartholomew's name will forever be linked to Fats Domino. An extremely tall, dark and disarming man, when he tells you "I invented the big beat," he demands to be taken seriously.

If Dave Bartholomew were never to play another note, he could sit back and bask in the knowledge that he was very much responsible for shaping today's popular music. But he does still play, because he enjoys it, now pursuing his first love, Dixieland music. With a B.M.I. catalog that's probably as thick as the New Orleans city directory, he lives comfortably on the spectacular royalties it must generate.

"My catalog's got about 4,000 tunes," he says offhandedly. "Some of 'em just make a couple of cents, some make a few thousand." It's immediately apparent that numbers are extremely important to Bartholomew and that he often bases success and failure on them.

He has come to accept interviews and questions pretty much as part of his everyday procedure. He's not in the least bit surprised by one's knowledge of his early life. At times it seems as if he has a standard interview that he carries around in his head. Some of his answers are gruff and abrupt. Even though he can be polite and helpful, he doesn't go out of his way to supply information, and when questioned about one of his contemporaries, Bartholomew might simply reply, "Him? Oh he always was full of shit."

Dave Bartholomew was born December 24, 1920, and raised in Edgard, Louisiana, a tiny St. John the Baptist Parish town, nestled on the west bank of the Mississippi, just 30 miles upriver from New Orleans. Louis Bartholomew, Dave's father, was a Dixieland tuba player with Kid Harrison's and Willie Humphrey's jazz bands.

Louis had moved his family to New Orleans by the time Dave was ready for high school. "When my dad had a job, they would ride around on the back of trucks and play to advertise, that's how I got interested in playin'."

With marching bands popular in New Orleans, the youngster chose the trumpet so he could soon join right it. In high school he was lucky enough to be instructed by the same man who taught Louis Armstrong, Peter Davis.

"Mr. Davis played everything, and he use' to keep the bad kids off the streets by teachin' music."

Once Bartholomew gained enough confidence in his playing, he joined Marshall Lawrence's Brass Band in Reserve, Louisiana, located across the river from his home. From there he moved on to Toots Johnson's Band from Baton Rouge, and later to Claiborne Williams' Band, in the Bayou Lafourche town of Donaldsonville.

One of Bartholomew's most impressionable periods was his stint with Fats Pichon's Band between 1939 and 1941 on the S.S. Capitol, a Mississippi River steamboat. When Pichon left to work at the Absinthe House back in New Orleans, Bartholomew took over the band until he was drafted into the army the following year.

His stint in the army was very important for the development of his career and his music. While in the 196 AGF band, Bartholomew learned to write and arrange from Abraham Malone. His earliest records were influenced by his stint in the army, and he even blows a dead-on version of "Reveille," on Fats Domino's 1951 version of "Korea Blues."

When he came back home after the war, he formed his first band and quickly installed himself as the most popular band-leader in New Orleans. One of the first musicians that Bartholomew hired was saxophonist Red Tyler. Tyler recalls, "As far as jazz and rhythm and blues was concerned, Dave Bartholomew's Band was 'the' band in the city." Bartholomew's group made the rounds of the local clubs: The Greystone, Club Rocket, The Starlight, The Robin Hood, Al's Starlight and, of course, the Dew Drop.

By April of 1947, Bartholomew had installed Theard Johnson as the full-time vocalist with his orchestra, working single and occasionally backing up Smiley Lewis, Larry Darnell, Dotie Daniels or Patsy Valdeler for "Midnight Rambles" at the Gallo Theater. Such was Bartholomew's popularity that he began broadcasting a regular Sunday evening show for Dr. Daddy-O on WMRY, from the J&M Record Shop.

Dave's biggest, though friendly, competition came from Roy Brown and Paul Gayten, both of whom recorded for the Braun Brothers' DeLuxe label. It only made sense that the Brauns would look for Bartholomew next. "They were just walking around and going into clubs looking for talent," allows Bartholomew. "They told me they were interested in recording my band. So we went down to Cosimo's studio and cut."

The Brauns extensively recorded Bartholomew's Orchestra, with Dave exercising his vocal chords on the likes of "She's Got Great Big Eyes (And Great Big Thighs)" and "Bum Mae." They also stayed around the studio long enough to back a number of other DeLuxe artists. The Brauns feared a recording strike come 1948, and attempted to stockpile a number of masters by Bartholomew and other New Orleans artists, so a number of sessions took place.

The 1947 DeLuxe releases did poorly saleswise, but it never affected Bartholomew's local popularity. He could pick and choose his work. A number of other labels attempted to sign the bandleader, including Capitol, but Bartholomew wouldn't return to the J&M Studio until 1949, again for DeLuxe.

Bartholomew recorded "Gert Town Blues," a popular local tune about a rowdy New Orleans neighborhood located behind Dillard University, and the suggestive "Country Boy." " 'Country Boy' was the biggest thing I ever did on myself," says Bartholomew. "It did about a hundred thousand. But that was pretty good for 1949. I still get checks on it."

The band that Bartholomew carried during 1949 was one of his best, and deserves special mention for the role it would soon play. Its members were Ernest McLean, guitar; Clarence Hall, tenor sax; Red Tyler, tenor sax; Joe Harris, alto sax; Salvador "Bashful" Doucette, piano; Earl Palmer, drums; Theard Johnson, vocals; and of course Dave on trumpet and occasional vocals.

As fate would have it, Dave Bartholomew would soon meet the man who would change his life , while he was on the road pushing his DeLuxe hit: "I was working for Don Robey at his club over in Houston, the Bronze Peacock. Well we had been playing there for a couple of weeks when this guy walked into the club and introduced himself as Lew Chudd, from Imperial Records in L.A. He was sellin' records to Mexicans then, that's why he was in Texas. He said he was interested in starting to sell rhythm 'n' blues records, and he liked my band because we were doing a lot of original tunes. He said, 'How'd you like a job?' So in December of '49 we drew up the contracts."

Drummer Earl Palmer explains the sound the band had immediately preceding the Imperial recording contract. "The band didn't play very much R&B then because that really hadn't come in yet. We started playing blues with a funkier feel to it. We had a lot of quintet-type arrangements and ballads. I used to sing, Dave used to sing, and we had a fellow, Theard Johnson, who had a real good voice and sang ballads. Then came old 'pregnant eyes,' Tommy Ridgley. Tommy had a high-pitched thin voice; he was more of a blues singer."

Tommy Ridgley and Jewel King, a reedy-voiced New Orleans blues songstress, were first recorded for Imperial under the eye of Dave Bartholomew. But it was Jewel King, who occasionally sang with the group, who accounted for Bartholomew's first production hit, "$3 \times 7 = 21$."

Not surprisingly, these earlier sessions lacked the drive and distinctiveness that Bartholomew's later productions would flaunt. In contrast, these sides had a jazzy uptown blues approach, sounding more West Coast (the Lew Chudd touch?) than anything else. The sound didn't have the "live" feel of later records, partially due to the primitive recording equipment at the J&M Studio. Chudd in fact threatened to pull Dave out of New Orleans because he didn't like the muddied sound of Cosimo's studio.

While he was in New Orleans setting up the first sessions, during December of 1949, Chudd was also interested in finding more talent for the label. "I'd heard about this guy who was supposed to play pretty good boogie woogie piano down at the Hideaway

Fats Domino

Club," recalls Bartholomew. "It was a Friday night, and I wasn't working, so Lew and I went down there. That was the first time we heard Fats Domino. He was singing this tune 'The Junker's Blues,' and Lew really liked it. So at the intermission I introduced Fats to Lew Chudd, and that's how everything got started."

It is at this point that fact mixes with fantasy in the ongoing Bartholomew-Domino-Chudd saga. Earl Palmer claims that Fats asked to sit in with Bartholomew's band at Al's Starlight Inn, which was in Fats' neighborhood. Bartholomew said "no," and it was Palmer, who would run the band at intermission, that let Fats first sit in. Whatever the case, Fats would soon be whisked into the studio by Bartholomew and Chudd.

Fats, who sounded unbelievably young at the time, was backed by Bartholomew's band, and eight sides were recorded, including "The Fat Man." In contrast to the Ridgley-King sides, Fats' session blended jump-blues with Dixieland, for a unique hybrid that would become the trademark of both Bartholomew and New Orleans rhythm and blues productions. Bartholomew's production hand was much more evident on Fats. He toned down "The Junker's Blues" lyrics to perfectly suit Domino, and demanded the horn section uniformly play one beefy riff. Although Domino's rippling right hand would take the break two-thirds of the way through, as opposed to later records characterized by Herb Hardesty or Lee Allen's braying tenor sax, "The Fat Man" was clearly a prelude of things to come.

An unabashed perfectionist, Bartholomew still wasn't satisfied with Domino's initial effort: "Fats' piano was too loud and it didn't fit right. But there was nothing we could do 'cause we were workin' with just one track. It was a mistake, but we sent the record out anyway."

Domino's first pairing was "Detroit City" and "The Fat Man." Originally it was the Bartholomew-Domino-penned "Detroit City" that was picked for the A side of the release, but by January of 1950 it was already apparent that "The Fat Man" — mistakes and all — was the public's choice. The *Louisiana Weekly* commented, "Fats Domino, recorder of that big jukebox sensation, 'The Fat Man Blues,' is becoming nationally famous. The chubby-faced little fellow set them on their ears at Lloyd's Place 1/24, with Dave Bartholomew backing." Further down the page they also noted, "Dave Bartholomew has just been released from his DeLuxe contract, he's gonna wax some of that real gone stuff for Imperial."

With both "The Fat Man" and Jewel King's "3x7= 21" riding the national R&B charts, Chudd arranged a national tour, featuring the two tunes, with Bartholomew's band, that included stops in Las Vegas, Oklahoma, Kansas City, Los Angeles and the rest of the West Coast. Bartholomew, who was in charge of the project, had headaches right from the start. First, the headliner, Jewel King, backed out of the tour because her husband/bandleader, Jack Scott, wouldn't let her go on the road without his band. Then just as they were about to leave, no one could find the bashful Domino! Fats had never left New Orleans before, and it took three days of cajoling to budge him. The tour helped to boost the sales of "The Fat Man" — and Domino's confidence.

Bartholomew must have been anxious, though, to get back home to reassume his new Imperial Record's responsibilities, which were to tie him closer to the recording studio. Though Domino would become the real jewel in the Imperial crown, Bartholomew busied himself recording other New Orleans artists throughout the early Fifties. Archibald, Jesse Allen, Fats Mathews, Country Jim and Smiley Lewis waxed sides on Imperial or its Colony/Post subsidiaries during his early Imperial years.

It's only when discussing Smiley Lewis that Bartholomew will drop his reserve — even if just slightly: "Smiley used to live in the same neighborhood as my father, and they were pretty good friends. When I got in the position of where I could choose who I wanted to record, I told him I wanted to cut some records on him.

"Smiley was what I'd call a bad luck singer. He never made an awful lot of money — oh maybe twenty to twenty-five thousand. But everybody else was makin' hundreds of thousands. We did about three or four hundred thousand on 'I Hear You Knockin', but Gale Storm picked it up and did a million. Smiley just couldn't get a hit."

Fats became Imperial's biggest seller throughout the early 1950s. Most notable were: "Everynight About This Time," in 1951; "Goin' Home," which became the first Domino-Bartholomew effort to become a #1 national R&B hit in 1952; and "Goin' To The River," in 1953. The Bartholomew production style was taking shape, and Domino was its ticket to success. New Orleans dee-jay Dr. Daddy-O probably sums up the situation best when he says, "Dave was shrewd, cool and gifted. He was a maestro when it came to arranging a session. Dave found the talent he needed in Fats. But Fats fooled him too. There was more talent there than what Dave originally thought, and Dave was able to mold it to sell millions of records."

"We were actually searching for a sound in those days," stresses Bartholomew. "I never wanted to get things too complicated. It had to be simple so people could understand it right away. It had to be the kind of thing that a seven-year-old kid could start whistlin'. I just kept it simple.

"I always felt Fats was a country and western singer because he didn't sing from the bottom. Fats played triplets at the piano; he got it from a guy called Little Willie Littlefield out in California. That was Fats' style; so once he started, he couldn't leave it, 'cause that's what the people wanted to hear."

With Bartholomew spending virtually every waking minute in the studio, or attending to his Imperial duties, his career as a performer was sacrificed, as he had to limit his live appearances. Besides his Imperial obligations, he also produced some early Shirley and Lee sessions for Aladdin, and was responsible for their first hit, "I'm Gone." He also produced Lloyd Price's "Lawdy Miss Clawdy," for Specialty, and, when the urge arose, even recorded some of his own light-hearted material. Although his own recordings lacked the commercial appeal of some of his artists, Bartholomew's version of "Shrimps and Gumbo," "Another Mule," "Country Gal," and the social commentary "The Monkey Speaks His Mind," were

New Orleans rhythm and blues classics. His jazzy "My Ding-A-Ling," which curiously appeared on King in 1951, would become a massive hit over two decades later for Chuck Berry.

It was Fats' waxing of "Ain't That A Shame" in 1955 that would spell success in no uncertain terms for the duo. Even though Bartholomew would in no way change Domino's basic style, the shy rhythm and blues singer suddenly appealed to the rock and roll record buying public. Even though "Ain't That A Shame" would only dent the Hot 100 for a single week, it opened the door for a mind-boggling string of hits that would span nearly a decade.

The years 1956 and 1957 were incredible years for the duo. No less than seventeen Domino sides cracked *Billboard's* Hot 100, with "I'm Walkin'," "Blue Monday," and "Blueberry Hill" breaking into the Top Ten. "I had a good feeling about 'I'm Walkin'," says Bartholomew. But I didn't think "Blueberry Hill" was hittin' on shit! It was Fats' idea to do it. It took all day to record it, and it still didn't sound right. Lew Chudd put it out, 'cause he didn't have anything else to put out on Fats. I said, 'No, don't put that thing out. It's no damn good.' So he calls me back two weeks later and says, 'Dave, from now on, cut nothin' but no-good records. We just sold three million.' "

Bartholomew's productions from this era were noted for their clean, catchy quality of musicianship — and their startling sales. Bartholomew still revels in his glory. "I could turn on the radio and hear five or ten records that I produced playing at once. I was burnin' up, makin' all kinds of money, almost a million dollars a year!"

Although he won't allow more than, "Uncle Sam got his share too," it appears that the IRS took Dave and Fats to the cleaners in the late 1950s. It's evident that when Bartholomew states, "at one time I used to hate to hear my music," it was because most of the royalties that were being generated were going into the pocket of Uncle Sam.

The gravy days for Bartholomew and Domino continued through the late 1950s, into the early 1960s. It's easy to understand why Bartholomew would say, "I honestly thought it would never end."

The year 1959 produced two back-to-back Top Ten hits, "I Want To Walk You Home" and "Be My Guest." While Fats' basic style was never tampered with, Bartholomew was keen enough to gauge the public's taste, adding the occasional female chorus or string section, taking some of the bite out of Fats' rhythm and blues approach. "We started using strings in them when we started using multi-tracks. I wrote the arrangements 'cause I wanted to keep it as commercial as possible." The marriage of the New Orleans string section and Fats' triplet piano is best evidenced on Fats' last Top Ten hit, "Walkin' To New Orleans," in 1960.

During the early Sixties, Bartholomew continued trying his hand at producing other Imperial artists. He had a taste of national success with Frankie Ford, Bernadine Washington, and Earl King, while Smiley Lewis, Huey Smith, Robert Parker, Chris Kenner, Ford (Snooks) Eaglin, and Wardell and the Sultans enjoyed varying degrees of local success.

Fats continued to account for a constant string of mid-range national hits for Imperial up until 1963, but he never really got another giant hit. Nevertheless, the quality of his releases was superb. Among his later hits, "I Hear You Knockin'," "Dance With Mr. Domino," and his definitive version of "Jambalaya" merit comparison with any of his earlier work.

Like other independent record companies, Chudd was finding the going increasingly tough. Distributors often neglected to pay their accounts, and the cost of sessions, advertising and materials forever escalated. In 1963 Chudd sold out, precisely at the right time, to Liberty Records. Fats Domino, in turn, went his own way and decided to sign with ABC-Paramount for a deal that reportedly guaranteed $50,000 per year over five years.

Bartholomew, who stayed intensely loyal to Lew Chudd during their Imperial Records association, is still discerningly remorseful about the label's sale. "Lew got what he wanted," sighs Bartholomew. "But I still think he got out of it a little early. We had some *very* big successes, but then the Beatles came in, and we sort of got lost on the way. We probably couldn't have sold any more records, though we wanted to."

Domino's sound suffered under the auspices of ABC, and they never could duplicate the Bartholomew-Domino team, in terms of sound or sales. "I had hundreds of offers after Imperial," says Bartholomew, "Hollywood, New York, the West Coast. But I wanted to stay near home. I spent too much damn time in the studio; it took too much out of my life. I just wanted to take it easy for awhile."

Bartholomew proved to be as shrewd in business as he was in the studio. He invested his royalties wisely and bought a number of apartment buildings during the '60s. Musically, he still maintained a band, picking and choosing occasional jobs. The old record bug was still with him though, and he started his own label, Broadmoor, in 1967, even luring Fats into the studio for two releases. But "nothing serious," he assures. Bartholomew only stuck his nose in the studio as a hobby, clearly aware he could never recapture the past. As the Sixties wore into the Seventies, Bartholomew continued his laid back approach to music, content to sit back and collect his B.M.I. checks. His most ambitious projects were national and international tours with Fats Domino, as their relationship has remained intact over all these years. "With Fats I'm followin' my livelihood around. That's all my material out there," he points out.

In 1981 Bartholomew released his own Dixieland album. "I've always stayed interested in Dixieland, even when we cut all those hits. It's just what I like to play. It's between that and swinging jazz."

The question inevitably arises, "Will Dave Bartholomew ever get back into the studio on the serious level he once was?" "Never!" he declares. "I spent so many years in the studio, I don't think I'd like to do that again. I might produce a few things but I'll never work in the studio again seven days a week like we used to. I just wanna have fun playin' music now."

Part Three:

THE RECORD MEN

The big four, as far as record labels are concerned in New Orleans, were Minit, Imperial, Ace, and Specialty. Throughout the Fifties and well into the Sixties, they were able to dominate the New Orleans rhythm and blues recording industry. Because of promotion and distribution, being contracted to one of the above usually insured exceptional sales, and — if you were lucky — national chart placement. While the monetary return from these companies might have been questionable, the esteem they generated their artists insured plenty of live work and exposure.

Other large independent record companies like Chess, Atlantic, Fire and Amy, made inroads into New Orleans with some national and local success. But their forays were infrequent, and they never stayed long enough to establish a foothold. Even some of the giant companies — Decca, Columbia, Mercury and R.C.A. — took a stab at New Orleans, but with marginal success.

Not all of New Orleans rhythm and blues performers were lucky enough to sign with a major national label. Often they recorded for small backroom record labels: Watch, Frisco, Hot Line, Rip, Ron, Sho-Biz, Hep' Me, Scram and so on. Even Fats Domino recorded for the tiny Broadmoor label during the Sixties when he couldn't secure a major recording contract.

The first record company representatives that worked out of New Orleans were invariably outsiders. They were shrewd enough to ascertain the untapped musical potential of the city, and took advantage of it, to their economic benefit. It wasn't until the Sixties that New Orleans-based record companies tried to reverse the trend, but by then it was too late.

The record men were luminous characters. To survive they had to be cunning, bold, intelligent, and, at the same time, lucky. For them, taking chances was part of their everyday routine. In the highly competitive New Orleans record business, the difference between success and failure was often merely being in the right place at the right time.

Success for the record men in the New Orleans rhythm and blues-cum-rock and roll record business meant that the public had to hear their product, and then go out and buy it. To get it heard they had to have a rapport with the radio stations and the disc-jockeys.

The disc-jockeys were an important link in the New Orleans musical chain. Groovy Gus, Pappa Stoppa, Ernie the Whip, Sputnick Shelly, Dr. Daddy-O, Okey Dokey, Jack the Cat — the names of the New Orleans disc-jockeys were deliberately as colorful as those of the artists they played: Professor Longhair, Mr. Google Eyes and Guitar Slim. Broadcasting to a potential audience of almost a million listeners, the disc-jockeys could exert enough influence to make or break a record, therefore insuring the artist's ever-increasing importance to the record industry.

Some stations went over to almost total rhythm and blues broadcasting in the late Forties, like WJMR. Other stations featured rhythm and blues music, interspersed with their regular programming, like WWEZ. Stations WBOK and WNNR switched to total R&B broadcasting in the mid-Fifties. Even the "white" stations played R&B records as part of their rock and roll programming.

Through the record men, and the disc-jockeys, New Orleans rhythm and blues would thrive for two decades.

COSIMO MATASSA
New Orleans' Recording Giant

To say that Cosimo Matassa is one of the chief figures responsible for creating New Orleans rhythm and blues is really just barely underlining the fact. Virtually every R&B record made in New Orleans between the late Forties and the early Seventies was engineered by Cosimo Matassa, and recorded in one of his four studios.

"Cosimo was just it," recalls singer/guitarist Earl King. "When those cats from out of town came here to record, they came to see Cosimo. They literally had guys lined up around the block tryin' to get an audition for days. It was like a lineup to get into a theatre."

Still closely involved in music as an engineer and an executive, Matassa,—everyone calls him Coz—remains one of the most helpful and enthusiastic people you can talk to. He still revels in the New Orleans "glory days" when his studio was the mecca for scores of recording artists and the catalyst for the R&B sound of New Orleans.

Originally Cosimo had no lofty musical ambitions. "I backed into the record business," he explains. "Right place right time. I never was drafted during WWII; I expected to be, but they were sending guys home before I got called. I was going to school to study chemistry, but when I found out what a chemist was, I changed my mind.

"When the war was over, I was looking for an opportunity to start a business. I had a partner, and we bought an old grocery store on the corner of North Rampart and Dumaine Street. It was intended just to be an appliance store. We thought with the war being over, people would have a lot of money to spend and that an appliance store would be a good idea.

"My father had a bunch of juke boxes, so as a side line we started selling the old records off the boxes to make some extra money. After not too long, we started getting a lot of people coming in asking us about new records. There really weren't too many stores around that sold records back then."

Cosimo was quick to realize he had a good thing going and that there was a demand for a good record shop in New Orleans. Since he was selling more 78s than waffle irons or Mixmasters, he and his partner phased out the appliance end of the business and began building up one of the city's most popular record stores—the J&M Music Shop.

"We had the jump on the rest of the record shops in town," he laughs. "At the time, a lot of the best blues and jazz records were coming out of the West Coast, so I had this friend of mine who was a Pullman porter on the Sunset Limited. Every time he'd go out to Los Angeles, he'd bring back copies of the latest records from the West Coast. If I thought one was pretty good, next time he'd go back to the Coast I'd get him to bring back two or three hundred."

The J&M Music Shop continued to prosper until 1946, when it became apparent to Cosimo that there were no outlets for recording music in New Orleans. "There was a studio in the Godchaux Buiding on Canal Street, the National Radio Recording Studio," he continues. "It was run by two engineers from WWL Radio. They did air checks and acetates, but not really much recording of music. It seemed to me that a recording outlet for a city with so much music in it was a good idea. I had attended technical school during the war, so I decided to try and open a studio.

"I bought a brand new Duo-Press disc cutter and set it up in one of the building's back rooms and opened the 'J&M Recording Service.' We cut direct to disc on that machine. That means we recorded the actual master right there in the booth. If we had a bad take of a song that meant that we had to throw the acetate away and start over. The acetate was a big thick plastic disc that the stylus cut into. You had to brush the plastic away as it cut into the disc."

Business at the J&M Recording Service was slow at first as it was confined to private recordings of glee clubs, school groups and other similar projects. The first major companies to employ the studio were RCA and Decca who occasionally recorded dixieland jazz in New Orleans.

The year 1947 turned out to be the major turning point as far as Cosimo's recording business and the music industry in New Orleans were concerned. With no home-based record labels, New Orleans was fair game for the rising wave of independent record companies springing up after the War that were more than willing to take advantage of New Orleans' rich musical climate.

"Deluxe Records from Linden, New Jersey, was really the first company that came down here to record blues," explains Cosimo.

Coz, 1984

"Dave Braun looked around town and brought Dave Bartholomew, Paul Gayten and Annie Laurie in to record early in 1947. I remember we charged them $15 an hour plus materials."

Deluxe's initial New Orleans session proved to be fruitful, racking up a hit with the Paul Gayten ballad "True." Although pleased with the initial success, and hoping for more recording business to come his way, not even Cosimo was prepared for what was about to happen.

Deluxe returned to New Orleans late in 1947 for a massive recording session that was intended to stockpile sides for the impending musician's union strike (the 1948 Petrola ban). Among those recorded included Fats Pichon, Pleasant Joseph, Smiley Lewis, Al Russell and Papa Celestin. But, most importantly, Deluxe recorded national hits by Annie Laurie ("Since I Feel For You"), Dave Bartholomew ("Country Boy"), and Roy Brown's innovative hit ("Good Rockin' Tonight"). It wasn't long before other independent record companies began using the New Orleans studio looking for what some called the "Cosimo Sound."

Many were surprised when they first laid eyes on the primitive J&M recording studio. Even by 1940s' standards, "It wasn't exactly a state-of-the-art studio," points out Cosimo. "The studio on Rampart Street was about sixteen feet by nineteen feet. Most of that area was occupied by a grand piano. Believe it or not, I recorded a 17-piece orchestra in there. I never had any trouble with sound separation. Oh, it got pretty crowded in there, but it was just a matter of sticking the microphone in the right place and setting the group up around it. I would go in the studio and listen to the group and then try to duplicate the sound in the studio inside the booth."

In 1949, the first tape machines became commercially available, and Cosimo bought one of the first in the South. "I bought one of the early Ampeg units," he continues. "They said it was a portable, but it weighed over 300 lbs., and it came in two cases. It was an excellent machine—the 600 model. We had four microphones then instead of just one, but we still just had one track. I had Altec 21B condenser mikes; they looked like baseball bats with a microphone on the end. They all came into the booth through a four-input mixer, I never did have a control board. I think the first session we did on tape was Fats Domino doing "The Fat Man" for Imperial.

Considering the technically primitive conditions under which Cosimo was forced to work, it is amazing how full and driving the sound is on the early recordings that came out of his studio, particularly the early Imperial releases by Fats Domino, Archibald, Jewel King and Tommy Ridgley. The pianos were crisp, the horns weren't muddied and the vocals ran clear. "I always tried to capture the dynamics of a live performance," stresses Cosimo. "These guys were doing these songs on their gigs and that was the sound that I was trying to get. We didn't have any gimmicks—no overdubbing, no reverb—nothing. If Lee Allen had to blow a sax solo, he'd have to move up to the mike or someone would literally have to pick up the microphone and move it in front of him. Those guys played with a lot of excitement; and I felt if I couldn't put it in the groove, people weren't going to move."

"Coz was the master of one track," confirms Earl King. "He could get things pretty mellowed out with just that one track. The acoustics in his first studio were really good. He had a real good balance. The only problem I felt he had was sometimes the bass wouldn't come out the way you heard it in the studio. You couldn't get that real solid bass. But it didn't matter to a lot of companies that came from out of town. Their emphasis was on piano and drums. They really didn't care about the bass."

Tommy Ridgley, who recorded his earliest Imperial hits at J&M, outlines a typical session: "There was always plenty of food and booze around, and everybody was pretty loose. Coz would move the microphones around and then go back in the booth. I remember the booth was so small only two people could fit inside. If things didn't sound right, he'd come back out and move the microphones around until he got it. Then he'd go back in the booth with Dave Bartholomew. Usually we'd get started real quick because we'd always have those songs rehearsed. Usually we'd be done in two or three takes. They did things a lot faster back then. A session was four tunes, which usually took a couple of hours."

However, as Cosimo is quick to point out, not all of his recording sessions were so easy. He recalls Guitar Slim making over sixty takes of some songs before he got things right. Even Fats Domino wasn't that easy to record, as Cosimo reveals. "Fats wasn't exactly a real joy to record. Oh, he was really a nice guy and all that, and let me tell you he was real creative. But sometimes Fats lost sight of the fact we were trying to make a record. Sometimes he'd stop in the middle of a good take and ask, 'Hey, how do I sound?' It was incredible.

"We had some problems with Professor Longhair too, not because he was hard to record, but because he was used to playing upright pianos. He liked to kick the front of the uprights and the grand didn't have a front, and it made him uncomfortable. So when he came in to record, we'd nail a board to the front of the piano so he'd have something to kick."

As the Fifties progressed, Cosimo only became busier and busier as labels like Chess, Aladdin, Atlantic, Savoy and Specialty all came from different parts of the country in search of Cosimo's expertise. "I practically lived in that place," says Cosimo. "We'd start at 9 o'clock in the morning, and sometimes wouldn't get out until midnight. We never charged overtime, and that would go on seven days a week.

"We didn't have a sense of creating history, we were just having fun and doing something that we enjoyed. We were paying the rent and buying groceries, that was all that was important to us at the time. We really hadn't opened our eyes to the realities of the business."

"Coz was one of the boys," adds Tommy Ridgley. "We were all a closely-knit bunch of guys. When we had a break, we'd go over to Buster Holmes' Restaurant because it was just behind the studio, and it was the cheapest place in town to eat. You'd always see plenty of musicians hangin' around Buster's; there was always a chance they'd need another trumpet or guitar player, and there would surely be somebody over there to fill in."

Eventually, the recording business outgrew the record retailing business, and the shop was discontinued in the early Fifties. Cosimo foresaw a need for more studio space if his business was to continue growing. "We just outgrew that old studio," he says. "It was real small to start out with, but having that store in the front made it inconvenient, because you had to come through it to get into the studio. It got to be a hassle at night running out of the booth to unlock the door all the time.

"There was a guy upstairs that ran a bookie joint. That didn't bother me, but the police were always around, and one night they raided the guy and tore the phones out of the wall. That kind of stuff tended to become distracting. I got a good offer from a real estate guy and sold the building. That was in 1955.

"I had my eye on a building at 523 Governor Nicholls Street that was being used as a cold storage warehouse near the French Market. I bought it and built a small studio in there with a couple of three-track recorders. That was really the first time we got to do any kind of overdubbing. I also bought an EMT reverb plate, which I felt really enhanced the sound of our recordings.

"We didn't stay in the building at 523 very long because I had a chance to buy a bigger building next door at 525 Governor Nicholls. That's where we put the first really big studio. It was a cold storage building also, but it had parking in the back, which is real important in the Quarter. That studio really sounded alive. I've always liked the sound you get out of a big room the best.

"This was in the days before you could air condition a big room. So in the summer I'd buy a couple of tons of ice and put it on a plastic sheet in the driveway next to the studio. I'd put big window fans behind the ice and blow the air in through the windows a couple of hours before the sessions. It cooled the place down pretty good in the summer, but of course the humidity went up considerably. That bothered the musicians that played string instruments because they always had to check their tuning."

Two of the most successful out-of-town recording artists that employed Cosimo's facility were "Big" Joe Turner, who recorded for Atlantic, and Little Richard, who was on Specialty. "Atlantic was almost forced to record Big Joe here," points out Cosimo. "I think he lived here for some time, and he was always performing somewhere along the Gulf Coast. Sometimes Ahmet Ertegun and Jerry Wexler came down for the sessions, but a lot of times Big Joe would just go in the studio and record himself. Big Joe was one of

J&M Recording Studios
838 N. RAMPART ST. NEW ORLEANS 16, LA.

Our Work No. _____
Date _____ 19 ___
Their Order No. _____
Time Called _____
Time Dismissed _____
Total Studio Time _____

Supervised By _____
Mixed By _____
Recorded By   2 x 5 6
Description _____

Artist(s): LLOYD PRICE

MASTER OR I.D. NUMBER	TITLE	PGM TIME	PITCH AND/OR SPEED	COMMENT
1	CANDY	2:05	15	
2 x 3	"			Hold
4	"	2:03		2 pic chick
5 - 6 - 7	"	2:24		
8 - 9 - 10 - 11 - 12 - 13		2:20		DC 7(?)
- 14 x 15		2:20		"
16 -		2:19		" (1)
Take 1 2	BREAKING MY HEART	2:32		
2		2:26		
3 - 4 - 5		2:25		

those guys who sang so powerfully and had a real emotional sound that really struck a nerve when you listened to him.

"I'm not a real stickler on details, but I recall the Little Richard sessions vividly. They were always real high energy just because Richard was that kind of guy. Bumps Blackwell would come to town to produce those sessions for Art Rupe at Specialty. Rupe had a nickname, Pappy, and Bumps would always be saying, 'One more for Pappy, Richard.'

"We always had about two or three good takes on those Little Richards songs. Everybody wanted to get the best take they could, for Bumps because he was a perfectionist, and for Richard because he had the 'Queen of the hill' attitude. They always thought they could do better, so a lot of times those sessions were long and drawn out."

Cosimo also points out that quite often the original studio sound was "doctored" once the session tapes reached the prospective record companies. "A lot of times the tapes were sped up before they were mastered," points out Cosimo, "particularly Fats' and Richard's. The tape machines didn't have the variable speed capabilities at the time, so what they'd do on the West Coast is add a layer of tape to the capstan on the head of the tape machine. Then they'd add or subtract until they got the desired sound.

"They'd speed the tapes up to get a brighter sound and maybe to make them a little faster for the kids, but it also made it impossible for another record company to 'cover' a song note for note, because to do that you'd have to play in the cracks of the piano. Sometimes they'd edit them or add a chorus but they didn't really change them too much. There was a real good engineer on the West Coast who did the tape transfers for Aladdin, Imperial and Specialty. His name was Barry Robyn, and he always got a real bright sound.

"I learned a trick from a piano tuner that made my piano sound brighter on records. I 'cheated' on the treble end of the keys. I had them tuned just a bit higher than normal so that the instrument would stand out more. I guess that was the only real secret I had."

Cosimo also expanded his interest into the personal management aspect of the music industry. In 1954 he was briefly involved in managing the Spiders, a successful New Orleans vocal group led by the Carbo brothers, Chuck and Chic. The group had been recorded by Cosimo for Imperial, and he worked with the group for a couple of years during their stay with the label.

Cosimo was also instrumental in discovering the teen idol Jimmy Clanton in 1957. The 17-year-old singer from Baton Rouge, Louisiana, brought his group, the Rockets, to Cosimo's studio to book $25 worth of studio time to make a demo record. Cosimo saw the promise in Clanton and brought him to the attention of Johnny Vincent at Ace Records. Initially, Vincent couldn't see the appeal of Clanton, but Cosimo eventually convinced him to sign and record the teenager. Clanton's premier disc, "I Trusted You" (backed by the Rockets), flopped badly, but not so for the follow-up, "Just A Dream," penned by Clanton. Using Mac Rebenack on guitar, and Allen Toussaint on piano, the record skyrocketed to number 4 in the Hot 100 during 1958, eventually selling nearly two million copies and becoming Ace's biggest hit ever.

With Clanton, Ace had a bona fide teenage idol in the image of Elvis, Fabian, and Ricky Nelson. The only difference was that Cosimo made sure that Clanton's sound (at least in the beginning) didn't stray too far from the hard-driving R&B sound of New Orleans. Clanton even starred in a movie, *Go Jimmy Go*, and toured the entire country headlining Allen Freed's rock 'n' roll caravan shows.

"Jimmy's really the only artist that I ever got personally involved with," recalls Cosimo. "I helped out with the production of some of his records, picking musicians and songs. I even went out on the road with him when I could get away from the studio. I spent a lot of time and money trying to develop his career. Then he got called into the army and my contract expired. After that we went in different directions for better or worse. I wasn't too keen on getting too involved in personal management after that."

In 1958, with the aid of Johnny Vincent, Cosimo took the plunge into the swirling waters of the independent record business, founding the Rex label, which became a subsidiary of Ace. The label became a launching pad for several up-and-coming local artists that Cosimo saw potential in. "Rex was really just a local thing," he explains. "I named it after the city's most popular carnival krewe. We did some different stuff on Lee Dorsey, the Emeralds, Earl King and Chuck Carbo. In fact, we had the first Mac Rebennack record, "Storm Warning."

Cosimo explains the reasoning behind forming his own label. "I saw these guys come from out of town and cut all these guys around New Orleans. Except for maybe Fats and Dave Bartholomew, it didn't seem like anybody around here made any money. I didn't feel like the Atlantics and the Specialties had given back what they had taken. I've always maintained that the city needed a strong local label to push the New Orleans talent. In fact, if somebody would have opened a studio right across the street from me, I don't think I'd have been mad. I wish there would have been half a dozen, because then maybe we would have developed an industry here."

It was basically this lack of selfishness which drove Cosimo on to greater success, but sadly also to failure. By 1963, many of the independents had begun to desert the city. Fire, Ace and Fury labels, all of which relied heavily on New Orleans talent, went belly up. Instant had become temporarily inactive after the record distribution business in New Orleans collapsed. But when Lew Chudd sold Imperial to Liberty Records, it didn't take a genius to realize the writing was on the wall as far as the music industry in New Orleans was concerned. Coupled with the advent of the Beatles and the Motown sound, the New Orleans R&B record industry, which had earlier seemed nearly invincible, was, by 1964, perilously close to disaster.

With most of the major independents out of the picture, the spoils of the New Orleans R&B talent was left to the abundance of local labels that sprung up like weeds around town. Cosimo realized that individually none of the companies had much of a

115

Robert "Barefootin'" Parker

chance for success. They couldn't promote, and the old bugaboo, distribution, held them back. With this in mind, Cosimo stepped out of the studio and founded Dover Records. The object behind Dover was to band all of the tiny labels together in a cooperative venture that would help the production and distribution of New Orleans records.

"A lot of local record companies would try to lease out sides to the big companies," explains Cosimo. "That was about the only shot they had at getting any kind of a hit outside of New Orleans. But it looked to me like that made it worse business than before. I felt if we had to take the risk of cutting sessions, then we should get the profits, not the big companies.

"I formed a label called Dover that leased and bought masters. When we formed Dover we had about forty New Orleans labels involved. We worked out deals to get distributed nationally, which was the best thing we could do. We also licensed the company internationally. I opened a record pressing plant with six presses called Superior Plastics. It looked like we were really going to get things going in New Orleans again."

On paper, Cosimo's theory should have worked. Right off the bat, Dover distributed a big hit on the NOLA label, "Barefootin'," by Robert Parker in the spring of 1966. With a national hit, and plenty of strong-selling regional records, including Curley Moore's "Soul Train," Willie Tee's "Teasin' You" (leased to Atlantic), Robert Parker's "Tip Toe," and Smokey Johnson's "It Ain't My Fault!" all around things looked good. Cosimo had moved yet again to another vacant warehouse at 748 Camp Street, which Cosimo aptly called Jazz City.

The massive hit that Dover so eagerly sought surfaced in early 1967, with Aaron Neville's bluesy "Tell It Like It Is," which was released on the Parlo label. The record topped the national R&B charts and peaked at number two in *Billboard's* Hot 100. But instead of spelling success for the company, it actually proved to be too big a hit and literally ruined the promise that the New Orleans record industry had held.

"I lost my ass on it," admits Cosimo, "but I have to blame the banks for it. We were just under capitalized. There wasn't a bank in the city that didn't dread the sight of me coming in the door. Hell, in Nashville you can borrow money on a song, but not New Orleans. Looking back on the situation, we just overextended ourselves. I just didn't know enough about the manufacturing end of the music business. I sunk everything I owned into the studio and the pressing plant. We had all our money spread out with records, and the distributors wouldn't pay us on time. On top of that, I had a lot of companies owing me thousands of dollars on studio time, whether it was cash or from advances on records. I had lots of money out there, but it wasn't coming in fast enough. I had all these people I owed money to, including the government, and I just couldn't hold them off any longer. I was too old-fashioned to declare bankruptcy, so finally the IRS just closed the studio and seized all of the equipment. I was hamstrung without the studio. They eventually sold everything at a sheriff's auction. I can't tell you how much it hurts to see everything you worked for and own get sold off for a fraction of its value."

Such a failure might have embittered some men and made them throw in the towel, but Cosimo wasn't ready for retirement just yet, and he pitched in to help get Sea-Saint Studio going and helped them engineer sessions. Throughout the late Seventies he could be found either engineering sessions or dabbling with a small eight-track studio he built in a garage near the Industrial Canal.

As the Eighties have progressed, Cosimo helped to head up (along with Marshall Sehorn) Jefferson Jazz, a corporation that has been busy buying up masters they hope to issue at some point in the future. At present they are marketing an Elvis Presley album, which was recorded at the Louisiana Hayride, and a six-LP boxed set of Louisiana music, commemorating the 1984 World's Fair. Most of Cosimo's days are spent in his office/warehouse, scrambling around organizing various album packages.

Cosimo still feels strongly about New Orleans' musical potential even though he admits, "I've pretty much seen it come and go. But there's still a lot of talent in New Orleans that's being ignored. That's one of the reasons I've stayed involved in the music business this long.

"We're a lot smarter about the business now, and I hope we can finally build up some kind of music industry here in New Orleans. Hopefully we'll get lucky one of these days and cut another hit. This time we'll be ready."

DR. DADDY-O
New Orleans' First Black Radio Personality

On the front page of the May 29, 1949 edition of the *Louisiana Weekly*, one of the headlines read in bold print:
"Doctor Daddy-O" (sic), Vernon Winslow to become the first colored disc jockey in New Orleans, on WWEZ. His show is to be called 'Jivin' With Jax.'"

Of course the gigantic step towards racial equality was immediately apparent. But at that time there was no way to determine the far-reaching effect that the first "colored" disc jockey would have on the music in New Orleans.

To this day Dr. Daddy-O is a household word throughout the black community of New Orleans. His name has been synonymous with black music for well over three decades on radio, and recently television.

When you visit his sprawling Gentilly bungalow, however, you are greeted by Vernon Winslow, a delicately featured man with a curious smile, dressed casually but fastidiously. One needs to plan ahead if he needs more than a few moments of Winslow's time. His schedule demands that he rise each weekday at 2 AM, in order to prepare for his 4 AM gospel program on WYLD. Most of the rest of his time is taken up with organizing his newest project, New Orleans' first regularly scheduled gospel music television program.

Now in his early sixties, Dr. Daddy-O is aware of the revered niche he has carved for himself in New Orleans. His words are well chosen and he is precise when he is questioned. It becomes immediately apparent he is a virtual Pandora's box of information, when he is quizzed about the formative years of New Orleans rhythm and blues.

Originally from Dayton, Ohio, he is an advertising design graduate from the Chicago Institute of Art. He came to New Orleans via Atlanta, to fill a vacancy at Dillard University in 1938. It wasn't until a decade after his arrival that Vernon Winslow's career in radio began. "They had a jazz program on WJBW," he recalls. "They played King Cole, Duke Ellington, Billy Eckstine. I got interested in the show and one night I called up and said to the guy on the air, 'Hey, you know, for a white guy, you really know jazz. I like you.'

"He said, 'You must be a negro. Look, I'm going to the New Orleans *Item* next week as a writer, and I want to write about you people. I'm fascinated by what you guys do — why you wear these zoot suits, and talk jive. I want to meet ya.'

"I said, 'Sure, I'll meet you.' So we met and talked. He said, 'You know, you ought to be an announcer, you're a pretty smart guy.'

"I told him, 'Well I'd like to handle jazz.' That was all that came out of that, but it put the idea in my head.

"So about a year later I started writing letters around to radio stations, just for kicks, saying, 'I think I can handle your negro market, because the population is so high, and they might identify with your advertisers, and have more of an impact than it does now.'

"I got a letter back from WWL that said they were sorry, they were anticipating black programming but it was years off. But WJMR called me and said that they got my letter, and were interested in talking to me, and were certain we could work something out. They said come on down.

"See, they didn't know if I was white or black, but they assumed I was white from talking to me on the phone, because I didn't sound like most of the blacks in New Orleans.

"So I went down to the Jung Hotel, walked into the front door and up to the studio. Had they known I was black I could have been thrown in jail. I saw the man whom I'd spoken to on the phone and said, 'Hello, my name is Winslow.'

"He looked at me once, he looked at me twice, and said, 'Hey, sit down, I wanna talk to you.' And we talked quite awhile 'till finally he said, 'By the way, are you a nigger?' (Winslow's olive skin and straight hair allowed him to "passe blanche.")

"I said, 'I'm a negro, yes.'

"'We can't do that,' he said. 'Naw, they'd shoot us if we put a nigger on the air. But I'll tell you what. If you write a script for a show you can train one of our announcers. We want somebody that can talk that language. Besides, niggers don't want to be announcers.'"

So the ambitious Vernon Winslow was to start from scratch, organizing a daily program that would be aimed at New Orleans' black population. But he was to instruct one of the regular white announcers on how to speak like a hip Negro! Not only that, Winslow had to buy records to play, and go out into the street and

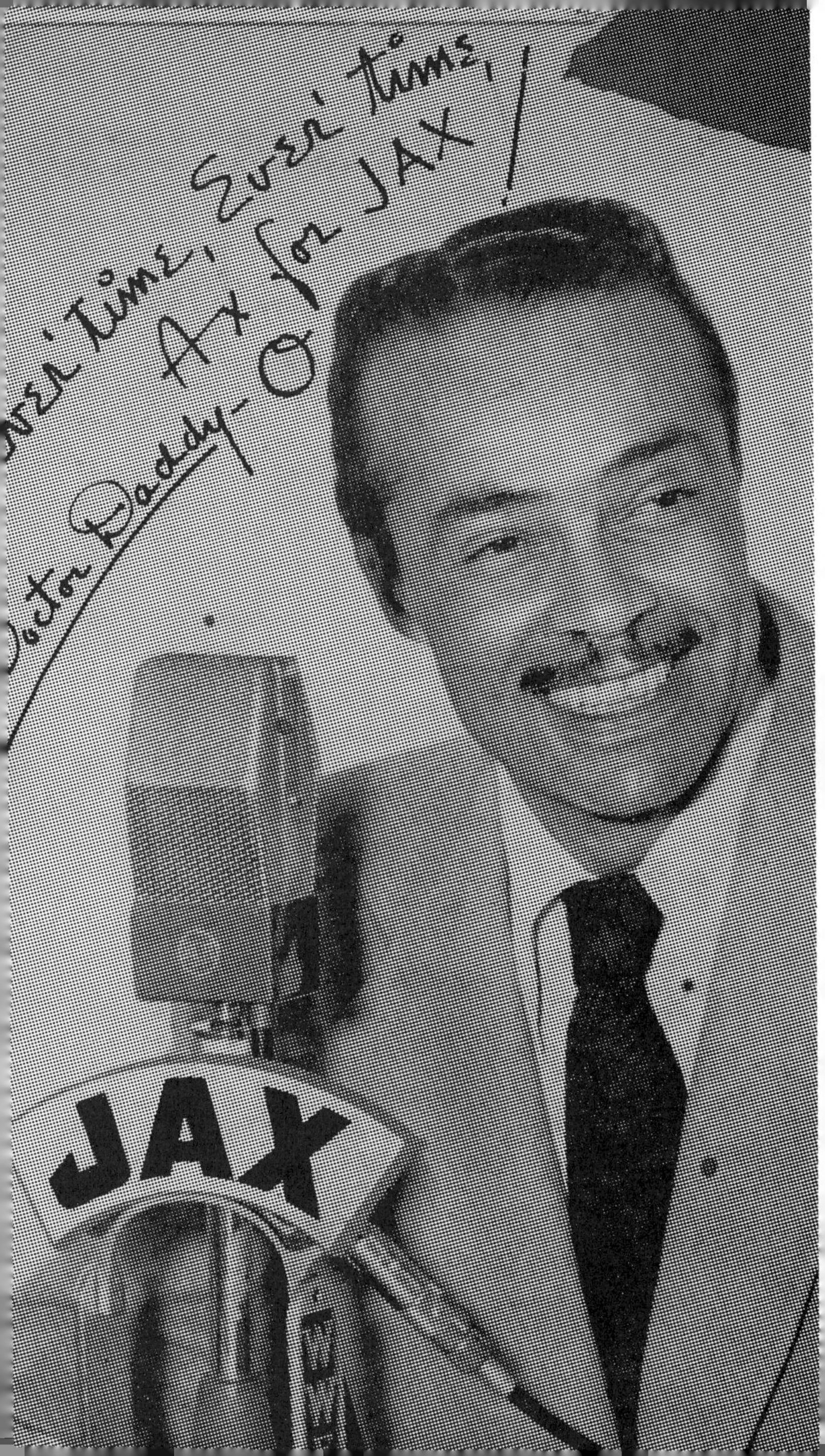

ver' time, Ever' time,
Ax for JAX!
Doctor Daddy-O
JAX

listen "to the cats in the street." Winslow also was responsible for inventing a colorful alias for the masquerading announcer and came up with the unforgettable "Poppa Stoppa."

"Poppa Stoppa came out of that rhyme rap that the people in the street were using. That's what the ghetto produced, they were trying to mystify outsiders. It became a unique identity, and they were proud of it. So I began writing my script in that language — 'Look at your gold tooth in a telephone booth, Ruth,' 'Wham bam thank you man' — I had a penchant for alliteration.

"So I would coach the white announcer who would read my script and I'd say, 'No, no, a black person doesn't talk that way, it's like this.'"

Winslow went along with WJMR's charade for a few months. All went well until one night when the white announcer left the microphone for a few minutes and Vernon Winslow did the unthinkable. He read part of his own script over the air. The station owner's reaction was typical for 1948 standards.

"They kicked me out!" says Winslow increduously with a sense of injury that 35 years has done little to abate. "There was nothing I could do. I couldn't sue, they only had one black lawyer in town and he couldn't even plead your case in front of a judge. So what the hell, I thought, I'll just stay at Dillard."

The station kept the Poppa Stoppa identity and used it for several announcers before the current Poppa Stoppa, Clarence Heyman, assumed the title. It looked as if Winslow lost on all counts. But he would come back to satisfy his grudge, becoming bigger and better than ever.

"About six months later I got a telegram saying, 'If you are the one who wrote the scripts for the Poppa Stoppa show, our advertising agency would like to talk to you about setting up a career as our advertising consultant.' It just blew my mind! Apparently the Fitzgerald Advertising Firm and the Jackson Brewing Company had heard the Poppa Stoppa show, and it was just what they were looking for. They had just completed a study about the black population's market potential, and they just went wild. So I went down to Fitzgerald's and they said give us a name. Forget about Poppa Stoppa, give us something just as catchy. We know you can write, just get your voice tested and write us some scripts and think of a name.

"'Doc' was a name you called everybody then — 'hey doc,' you got a match?' 'Hey doc can I buy you a drink!' Then the term came out 'daddy-o,' I'd heard Louis Jordan use it at the Auditorium. I put the two together and they went for it."

Winslow is quick to point out, "I wasn't a radio announcer at first, I was an advertising consultant for the Jax Brewing Company. That was just part of my job, it was something to make the black population proud and to associate with Jax Beer.

"With a three million dollar a year contract, the Fitzgerald Advertising Company could move into any station and say, 'We want to buy one hour. Give him an engineer and we'll set everything else up and supply the black announcer.'"

The first "Jivin' With Jax" radio program, hosted by the new Dr. Daddy-O, was aired on WWEZ every Sunday. As expected the impact was colossal. "Dr. Daddy-O was it, man," recalls Mr. Google Eyes. "When he came on you didn't see a soul in the street, they would all be crowded around the radio."

Initially the first few "Jive, Jam and Gumbo" programs as they were called were broadcast from the studios of the old New Orleans Hotel until they were moved to Cosimo Matassa's J&M Studio, where Dr. Daddy-O was joined by Dave Bartholomew's Band for a live broadcast. "Hell, they had to bring him up the freight elevator at the hotel," says Cosimo. "I didn't think that was right, so I said, 'Look, we've got all the facilities down here. Why not do it from here? That way it let everybody off the hook.'"

"Those live broadcasts really set off the Dr. Daddy-O impact. You couldn't get within three blocks of the studio when we were broadcasting," says Mr. Google Eyes.

Dr. Daddy-O's presence set off shockwaves in the local radio broadcasting industry, sending other stations scrambling for a piece of Dr. Daddy-O's action. Suddenly there was a horde of Dr. Daddy-O sound alikes on the air with equally colorful names: Ernie the Whip, Jack the Cat, Okey-Dokey and even a Momma Stoppa. "Everybody was trying to beat Dr. Daddy-O," laughs Winslow. "My ratings were just stupendous."

Jax also arranged for Dr. Daddy-O to write his own column, "Boogie Beat," an entertainment report, in the *Louisiana Weekly*. "Jax covered every angle of promotion. They asked me if I could do a column, and they offered it to the *Weekly* free. They told 'em 'Look, he'll be moving through the bars and he can pick up all the news.' So it was great for everybody."

Record companies took note of Dr. Daddy-O too, and inadvertently the introduction of black disc jockeys would soon change the trends in material they would record. "It had been Nat King Cole, the Ink Spots, and the Mills Brothers, but most black people didn't listen to that. About the blackest thing out there was Louis Jordan. It seemed like Roy Brown's 'Good Rockin' Tonight' was the first instance where New Orleans felt there was such a thing as black music.

"'Good Rockin' Tonight' was our ace, we would just play it loud and long. You see the white stations would never play that. People — both white and black — began to realize that I was the one who played that racy black music. It was nothing to back up the record and play it two-three times in twenty minutes.'

Suddenly this harder, more authentic brand of black music had another outlet besides the jukebox at the corner tavern. The independent record companies were quick to capitalize on it. Besides coming here to find talent, New Orleans was one of the only places they could actually get their records played over the air.

"We had to play New Orleans records," emphasized Dr. Daddy-O, "there was just no other way. We played whatever was available, as fast as they could get 'em to us."

Going into the clubs at night as Dr. Daddy-O, Winslow perceived a change there, too. "Most of the clubs had a lot of the out-of-town acts that came to New Orleans as part of the circuit, Cecil Gant, Wynonie Harris, Jimmy Liggins, Buddy Johnston. It seemed like when Paul Gayten and Annie Laurie had 'Since I Fell For You,' and started working at The Robin Hood, it was like the beginning of a brand new day here. It made people know that there was talent in New Orleans, and they started coming out to see it.

"You could go out to see Dave Bartholomew, Roy Brown, Larry Darnel, Tommy Ridgley and Fats get their chance, and then the record companies would hear 'em. The night spots really had a lot to do with who was recorded. If somebody got to play the Dew Drop, you can bet one of the record companies was going to talk to them.

"Those were really exciting days. I sensed that something was happening, just from going through the clubs and talking to people. Things were just happening so fast, it seemed like magic."

In looking back on the period Winslow felt it was the partnership of Dave Bartholomew and Fats Domino that brought the New Orleans sound to a national level. "Fats broke it," states Dr. Daddy-O, "he's the one that led the pack. People all over the country associated Fats with the New Orleans style of music. Dave was able to sense just what he needed, and Fats was gifted enough to bring it out to the public."

Without choosing favorites, Winslow recalls that he was extremely impressed by Professor Longhair, Smiley Lewis and Jack Dupree. "Those guys were worth a million dollars. It's too bad we didn't know it then."

Besides being in the constant public eye, Winslow was responsible for preparing sales reports for Jax and attending corporate meetings for the brewery and the Fitzgerald Agency. "My wife tells me she hardly knew me," he shrugs.

One of his other projects for Jax was to prepare short "featurette" films that were shown at black theatres. Winslow recalls filming Fats, Roy Brown, Smiley Lewis, Paul Gayten and Annie Laurie as part of a series of New Orleans music during the early 1950s. Although he is unsure of just where they might be today, the idea of this rare footage in some long forgotten drawer boggles the mind!

"It seemed like it would just never end," continues Winslow. "After Fats everyone was getting into the action. The flow just kept up. People like Guitar Slim, Shirley and Lee, Earl King, Huey Smith; every time you turned around there was a new face from New Orleans with a hot record."

Winslow says that the payola scandals of the 1950s never affected him or any of the rhythm and blues stations. "It never hit the black stations. We heard of it and saw it, but we just didn't have the kilowatt power that the white stations had. I know we broke a lot of New Orleans records that maybe went national because we played the hell out of 'em, but I took pride in that, I felt like it was part of my contribution to the city."

The Dr. Daddy-O/Jax Beer relationship remained intact until 1957. "Falstaff just killed us with their Brooklyn Dodger promotion. That just knocked us out of the market. I'd gone just about as far as I could go with Jax, so we mutually split up. They kept my voice on the Jax commercials, but I accepted an offer to be a station manager at a station in Detroit."

Winslow stayed in Detroit until 1961, and returned to New Orleans, where he assumed his duties at Dillard's art department again, and reentered the field of black radio, but with a different emphasis. Dr. Daddy-O signed on as the late night gospel music disc jockey at WNNR, a position he holds today.

Why this about-face? "Well, my grandmother used to tell me, 'You can't enter the kingdom of heaven unless you've been saved.' I never listened to her at the time but it started to work on me. The sincerity of the ministers and gospel performers impressed me. I got a good feeling out of gospel music. One night I was walking past the Two Winged Temple and heard the music coming out and I said to myself, 'that's what I want to do.'"

Winslow never had any problem being accepted by church people after spending so many years spinning "racy black music." "When I was out in the clubs I never was one of the crowd, I was just part of it," he is quick to point out. "I had to relate to two different types of people. Church people are forgiving. If they realize that you're sincere they'll accept you."

Just as Vernon Winslow made in-roads as Dr. Daddy-O in black radio, he is doing the same thirty years later in television. "There's still that same excitement now I felt when I first got behind the radio microphone. It's just like when I played that first Roy Brown record. I knew something was gonna happen then."

JOHNNY VINCENT
The Ace Records Man

The roller-coaster-like chronicle of Ace Records closely parallels the rise and fall of the classic New Orleans rhythm and blues period. Even if its home office was located in Jackson, Mississippi, effectively, Ace, on Baronne Street, was New Orleans' first local record company.

Ace's catalog boasted such New Orleans rhythm and blues performers as Huey "Piano" Smith, Earl King, Bobby Marchan, James Booker, Red Tyler and Mac Rebennack. Ace grew from humble circumstances into one of the nation's largest independent record companies before an ill-fated merger with Vee Jay Records sank both companies in a sea of red ink.

The man behind Ace Records was Johnny Vincent Imbragulio, known to the record world as Johnny Vincent. An aggressive, cigar-chomping, Italian-American businessman, Vincent is reminiscent of a Southern version of Edward G. Robinson. He still lives in Jackson, and, depending on the mood he's in, is still in, or out, of the record business. He still owns a building on Capital Street, the main drag of Jackson, where he can usually be found. The bottom floor of the two-story building currently serves as his makeshift office. But it has also served as a studio, a record store, a newsstand, a nightclub, a warehouse, a Chinese restaurant, a Texas barbeque and a cafeteria, all under Vincent's direction. Upstairs, his attic is still piled full of records he hauled back from New Orleans in the early Sixties, after his distributorship went belly-up. Through the years, most of the best records have been sifted out by collectors, but there's still plenty enough stuff to keep one searching for days.

Vincent is always in the company of a fat cigar, or a "seegar" as he refers to them, and a new way of making money. But he still enjoys talking about the days when Johnny Vincent was one of the kingpins of the record business. Although sometimes prone to "exaggerations," and withholding information, Vincent is still sincere in his appreciation of music. He is one of the key figures in the development of New Orleans rhythm and blues-cum-rock and roll. Few people are as qualified as Vincent to chart the music's history.

Born in Laurel, Mississippi, Vincent started to work for a jukebox operator after high school, changing records and collecting change, just prior to World War II. After Johnny got out of the service, he bought ten Rockola jukeboxes and went into business for himself in his home town.

"When I took records off the box," begins Vincent, in his rich Mississippi drawl, "I noticed that they were good sellers, especially the blues records. So I opened up a lil' old record shop in downtown Laurel.

"I got married in 1947, and thought I'd like to do better than just the jukebox business. So I went to New Orleans, and got a job with William B. Allen. He had just opened Music Sales of New Orleans, which was a big independent record distributor. I used to sell 78s all in Mississippi, Alabama and Florida.

"When I came to Jackson, I noticed there was just one record shop, down on Farish Street, that sold to all the jukebox operators for a radius of one hundred and fifty miles. So I had a chance to buy it and keep my job with Music Sales too."

Vincent was keenly aware of public trends, and how he could cash in on them. "I noticed I couldn't keep blues records in the shop. I couldn't get 'em from the distributor fast enough. So I decided I'd get into the field of cuttin' blues records, and started the Champion label. Back then there was blues singers on just about every corner in Jackson, so I had no trouble findin' people to record."

Of Vincent's early Champion releases, Arthur "Big Boy" Crudup was the best known artist. But nothing that Vincent released on Champion sold more than a few hundred copies around the Jackson record shop.

One day in 1951, Dick Sturgil, from Music Sales of New Orleans, brought the owner of Specialty Records, Art Rupe, to Jackson to meet Vincent. Rupe admired Vincent's hustle and offered him a job with his label that evening over dinner in the Heidelburg Hotel. Vincent sold his shop and agreed to help promote, distribute, and search for talent for the Los Angeles-based label, with his territory being the deep South.

"I worked for Specialty, two years night and day," declares Vincent. "I'd go to record shops and buy every record that was a hit. I'd go back to my room at night and play it over, and over, to find out what made that record a hit."

Vincent turned out to be a valuable addition to the Specialty staff, bringing Earl King, Frankie Lee Sims, Li'l Millet, and The

Johnny Vincent, 1981

Five Notes to the label during 1953. While in New Orleans, Johnny Vincent used to frequent clubs like the Tiajuana and the Dew Drop looking for talent for Specialty, where it was often assumed he was a dope pusher! On a tip from Frank Pania, the Dew Drop's proprietor, Vincent became interested in Guitar Slim. "I went over to Doc's (Doc Augustine's Novelty Shop on Dryades), where Slim use' to rehearse at. Huey Smith and Earl King would be in there too. Slim was just a fantastic performer. Nobody could outperform him."

After signing with Specialty, Vincent produced Slim's first session for the label, which he claims took over ten hours to complete. Vincent mailed the session off to Art Rupe, who commented, "That's the worst piece of shit I ever heard in my life!" Rupe eventually consented to release two sides from the session, but if it didn't sell, Vincent would be out in the street. Luckily for Vincent,

Slim's "The Things That I Used To Do" went on to be the biggest-selling rhythm and blues record of 1954.

Vincent stayed with Specialty until 1955, when he was "laid off" as part of a budget cutback by Art Rupe. Dave Bartholomew recalls being in the studio when Rupe called to give Vincent his walking papers.

Vincent bounced back in a hurry, though, returning to work for Music Sales. New Orleans' rhythm and blues talent hadn't been fully exploited, as he relates: "I went into New Orleans, and ran into Eddie Bo, Al Collins and Bobby Marchan. I asked Cosimo about recording them, and he said, 'Okay.' So we went right in.

"I took the masters up to Buster Williams' Plastic Products, in Memphis, to get pressed. I ran into Les Bihari (a co-owner of Modern/R.P.M. Records), and we were trying to think up a name for the label. We went into a drugstore, and I bought a comb that was made by a company called Ace. I figured Ace would be the first name on everybody's bookkeeping lists, and the first on the list to write checks. So that's what we called it."

Musically, Ace's initial releases were mediocre, and sales were poor. In desperation, Vincent even attempted to cut hillbilly music, but with no success. "I was gettin' low on money," admits Johnny. "While I was in New Orleans, I went to see Earl King and Huey Smith, and I told 'em, 'Look, I haven't got much money, but if you guys want to make a record, I know a lady in Jackson[Lillian McMurry], who has a studio and will let us use it cheap!'

"So we all drove up to Jackson, and Earl cut 'Those Lonely, Lonely Nights,' with Huey on piano. I had some dubs of the session, and let some of my territories hear it. Some of the shops started calling New Orleans and said they wanted some records. So when I got back, Dick Sturgil said, 'We're gettin' calls on that Earl King dub you got out there. Man, I could use two thousand.' So I went ahead and pressed it, and it went on to sell eighty thousand. But it wasn't as big as it could'a been, 'cause Johnny 'Guitar' Watson covered it, and made a real hit out of it."

Vincent was able to build Ace, using the revenues from "Those Lonely, Lonely Nights" as a foundation. Ace later had some regional hits with Frankie Lee Sims, Mercy Baby, Bobby Marchan and Earl King again. But Huey Smith would turn out to be the first national Ace hit maker. It was Huey "Piano" Smith's "Rockin' Pneumonia and the Boogie Woogie Flu," that sent Ace Records into the Hot 100 for the first time. "All of a sudden it seemed like everything we cut was magic," exclaims Vincent. "Huey came back with 'Don't You Just Know It,' then Jimmy Clanton had 'Just A Dream,' and it seemed like everything we cut was going into the Top Ten."

Huey Smith's national hits made Vincent interested in recording other New Orleans rhythm and blues artists. Besides continuing to record Earl King and Bobby Marchan — with Huey's Clowns, Vincent also recorded other talented New Orleanians. Roland Cook, Dave Dixon, Little James Booker, Eddie Bo, Joe and Ann, Alvin "Red" Tyler, The Supremes and Joe Tex (really from Baton Rouge, but who was living in New Orleans) were among the New Orleans people recorded.

"I wanted to keep that New Orleans beat," emphasized Vincent. "We had a unique sound. Ace's records weren't like anybody else's. I'd go into the studio and even watch Dave Bartholomew cut records, and there was no comparison. I didn't want to make records like anybody else. The most important thing about a record is not the artist, it's the sound. A guy's got to feel what he's singin' or playin', or it's not gonna be worth a damn. If you don't like the sound, how are you gonna like the artist? People won't buy the record.

"I didn't even care if the band was playing a wrong note or was out of tune [perfectly illustrated by Earl King's 'Those Lonely, Lonely Nights'] just as long as there was feelin' in it. I'd get in the studio with these guys at Cosimo's and ask the musicians what they thought of the damn stuff they were cuttin'.

"I wanted to make sure there was a beat on my records. I figured if you could dance to it, or sing along to it on the radio, that's what was important. It had to have a simple beat. Simplicity is what I tried to get out of my musicians."

It was hard to argue with his reasoning. Vincent cut some of the greatest New Orleans records during the late Fifties and had widespread commercial success. But even with New Orleans rhythm and blues keeping the coffers at Ace Records full, Vincent had higher aspirations.

"We went out and found some white artists," says Vincent. "Jimmy Clanton, Frankie Ford, Ike Clanton and Roland Stone recorded for us. I wanted to diversify into all fields. When rockabilly was hittin', we cut Mickey Gilley, Hershel Almond, and Narvel Felts. When the teenie-boppers were going crazy over Elvis, we decided we were gonna get into that market too. The major companies ignored us, so I tried to specialize in certain areas where they couldn't."

One of the white artists that Vincent was instrumental in discovering in the late Fifties was Mac Rebennack, who would go onto worldwide acclaim as Dr. John. "Mac use' to bum around the studio all the time with Huey," recalls Vincent. "He was one of the greatest little prospects as a producer and a writer, even at the age of sixteen."

Vincent gave Rebennack a free hand around the studio as he wrote material, produced and performed on a number of Ace releases. "Mac stayed around people like Huey and Professor Longhair," continued Vincent. "He stayed with 'em, and got a lot of ideas from 'em. Talk about a writer, he could make guys like Neil Diamond and Sedaka look sick! Back then, he could write five songs a week for different artists."

Besides the high quality of his rhythm and blues records, Vincent had interesting methods of marketing his label as he reveals: "We couldn't afford to pay all the deejays the way the big companies did. So we had to come up with some other ideas.

"From Specialty, I got to know there were breaking points for a record, and I'd try to work those areas. Places like Eunice and Opelousas could bleed a record into New Orleans and force the New Orleans stations to play it. New Orleans, in turn, was a big national breaking point. Hell, in New York they were always looking at what New Orleans was playing.

"Man you wouldn't believe the things we use' to do to create a hit. I can remember hiring li'l girls to write up as many as 1,500 postcard requests an' send 'em to WLAC (Nashville), 'cause that was a powerful station. I'd stick 'em in the mail when I was travelin' around the country. You had to get a record exposed anyway you could."

By the late Fifties, though, Vincent was straying from his basic simplistic philosophy. He was shying away from the basic rhythm and blues sound and recording an increasing number of his white artists in commercial surroundings. The result was a decline in the general quality of Ace's releases — and a drop in sales. Most importantly, he lost some of the artists that supplied his driving R&B sounds. Earl King, Huey Smith and Frankie Ford, who were supplying the biting sounds, departed for greener pastures at Imperial Records. Basically, all three left Vincent over disagreements over royalties, or, rather, lack of them.

Huey Smith is still trying to get what he claims Vincent owed him — some twenty years later. When confronted with these accusations, Vincent vehemently denies he withheld royalties from Huey, or any other artist. "Hell, those are all damn lies!" he seethes. "I bought Huey a house and paid the note. I bought him three cars and opened him up a club here in Jackson. Shit, when he went to Imperial, I stopped payin' the notes and he lost everything."

By the early Sixties, only Jimmy Clanton was producing hits on Ace, and Vincent was falling into a financial hole. Not only were his records not selling, his distributorship was in the red; and an investment he made in a department store lost $60,000. Vincent took on some business partners; Joe Ruffino, Cosimo Matassa and Joe Caronna bought into the label. But this only served to further confuse the direction of Ace Records.

Finally, Vincent saw a way out by signing a promotion and distribution agreement with Chicago's Vee Jay label in 1962. Vincent was certain the deal would solve all his problems. The agreement specified that he would be responsible for supplying records in the volume he felt necessary. Vee Jay, in turn, was to take care of all aspects of distribution and promotion. The agreement was heralded as a symbolic step for independent record companies. At the time Vincent commented, "I can see great things coming out of all this." Sadly, it wasn't to be.

"It was the biggest mistake I ever made in my life," admits Vincent. "The Vee Jay deal was a disaster. I didn't want to make the deal, but their lawyer, Paul Marshall, told me what a great deal it would be. They were a hot company; they had Jimmy Reed, John Lee Hooker, Jerry Butler, the Four Seasons and even the Beatles later. You see they were a black company, and they were trying to get into the white market. They saw that I had crossed records over and that I could help them. Paul Marshall sold me a bill of goods that assured me that if I went with Vee Jay, I'd be a wealthy man the rest of my life. So I merged with them.

"Well I probably got three checks. After that I took such a bath it was unbelievable. I had to accept all their records back from my distributors. The distributors owed me for Ace records, but wouldn't pay me because Vee Jay owed them money.

"Our first record was a monster though, 'Venus In Blue Jeans' [Jimmy Clanton]. Vee Jay owed us a lot of money on the session, and said they were gonna pay us out of the royalties. I imagine the record sold close to a million, but Vee Jay said it only sold three hundred thousand. I started checkin' and found out the record did over two hundred thousand just in the Cleveland area. That shit really hurt us.

"I couldn't get my money from them. They owed over a million dollars, and they wouldn't live up to their end of the deal."

Vincent pulled out of the agreement by late 1963. He tried to rebuild, but it was already too late. By 1964 both Ace and Vee Jay were forced to declare bankruptcy. Vincent leased out some old Huey Smith tracks to Constellation the following year, but, effectively, he was out of the record business.

Since Ace went under, Vincent has dabbled in the record business from time to time. He has repackaged some of his Ace material and even recorded some new groups that caught his ear. His other investments in the restaurant and the nightclub business have also gone the way of Ace Records — out of business.

Overseas interest in the Ace catalog has put some money in his pocket, through leasing agreements. But many people in the record industry feel Vincent isn't using his catalog to its fullest potential. "He's sittin' on a million dollars," comments one record executive. However the disarray of Vincent's files and masters would discourage the most ardent researcher or investor. While Johnny will tell you in one breath he's going to straighten out his business, in the next he'll tell you he's going to record the next Bruce Springsteen.

"You've got to understand," says Vincent. "New Orleans will never be like it was in the Fifties and Sixties. I remember seeing six out of the top ten records come out of New Orleans. Those days are gone. The local stations don't get behind the New Orleans artists. I mean to tell you it's pathetic that a city of over one million people can't get any hit records. You still have good artists and writers, but they're just sitting there because there's no record scene anymore.

"New Orleans use' to mean hit records. New Orleans is where Professor Longhair, Huey Smith and Fats Domino came from. What if Nashville did the same to its inheritance to country music? Well they couldn't, 'cause the people wouldn't let 'em. It's like an endangered species. If something doesn't happen real soon, the music's gonna die, and there'll be nothing left."

JOE BANASHAK
The Record Man

Chances are that if you have ever listened to, and/or bought a New Orleans rhythm and blues record, somewhere along the line Joe Banashak probably had something to do with it — as a powerful independent record distributor, as an influential record label entrepreneur, and most recently as a coordinator of reissue recordings. Banashak has come full circle, riding the New Orleans musical bandwagon during the boom years of the Fifties and early Sixties, staying on until the late Seventies, when the ride was over for everyone. But most recently he has become active on a "part time" basis, making many of his priceless masters available once again to the record-buying public.

Besides often being credited as the person who afforded Allen Toussaint's talent to blossom, Banashak's myriad record labels produced some of New Orleans' most memorable musical moments. Banashak was responsible for recording people like Irma Thomas, Ernie K-Doe, Aaron Neville, Benny Spellman, Jessie Hill, The Showmen, and Chris Kenner. But just mentioning these names really only scratches the surface. Even the discerning record collector must be amazed at the depth of the catalog that appeared on the dozen or so labels Banashak was responsible for initiating. Had not his doors been open, the world might never have heard from the likes of such lesser known artists as Diamond Joe, Boogie Jake, Lee Bates, the Hueys, Roger and Gypsies, Willie Harper, the Stokes, Sam Alcorn, the Del Royals and Eldridge Holmes, to name but a few.

Joe Banashak was born on February 15, 1923 in Baltimore, Maryland, where he first encountered black music. He developed an ongoing taste for jazz, bebop and big band music, which he readily purchased on 78's and on occasion went to see live. After returning from a three-year stint in the military during World War II, he saw the record business as "a way to make my fortune."

"I had worked for a distributor doing sales in Baltimore which sparked my interest in the record business. They handled many independent labels like Sonora and Sterling, and then they picked up Capitol. I married a girl from Texas, and we decided to move to

Houston, because at the time things were really starting to explode there. I looked at it as an adventure. We just had a new baby, and my wife's father sent enough money for us to pay all our bills in Baltimore so we could leave clean.

"I tried to get into the record business in Houston right away, but nothing was available. All the record business in Texas was based in Dallas at the time, so I sold paper products for about a year to make a living. Then Capitol decided to let a guy from Houston open up a branch office so I got a job there. This was when Capitol had just come out with 'Nature Boy,' by Nat 'King' Cole, which was a big hit. But the people I worked for weren't very aggressive. They were just interested in selling to jukebox people so they just ordered minimum amounts. I got tired of not being able to supply records to my accounts, so I quit.

"Then I started looking around, and I met up with Bob Dunbar, who owned an independent record business, Dunbar Distributors. He had just started selling something new in the record business, the 10″ lp. Well he hired me because I'd had experience selling them back East and with the Capitol line in Houston. When I started, my commission was 2¢ a selection, which worked out to 20¢ a record. That was a lot of money back then, in fact it was more than the artist was getting. After a couple of weeks though I had made so much money that Dunbar came to me and said, 'Wait a minute, Joe, we have to work something else out.' So we worked out another arrangement. But what was really important was that I really got a taste of the independent record business which I felt was the grass roots of the industry.

"Then in 1949, they promoted me and moved me to New Orleans. Dunbar bought a company here called Gramaphone Enterprises, at 602 Baronne Street, that was basically a classical record distributor. Their owner was Everett DeGoyer Jr. Dunbar didn't know much about the classics back in Houston, so that's where my experience at Capitol helped, because I had a classical background. They sent me here to be the manager."

The move to New Orleans intensified Banashak's commitment to the independent record industry. "At the time there were a lot of people distributing records in New Orleans. There was Delta Music, William B. Allen that handled Mercury, Mel Malory had Capitol, there was Carmen's Records, and A-1 Distributors, which I ended up owning. This was before there was a One Stop. There was a lot of competition, but I think it was good because the stores and the records got more attention. We had to know our product

Joe Banashak, 1945

better because the buyers from the shops and the jukebox operators would come to us to buy records.

"We had the Aladdin, Imperial and Swingtime labels, so we were selling records by Fats, Amos Milburn, Lowell Fulson and Ray Charles. That was my real introduction to rhythm and blues. We sold a lot of R&B records here.

"There used to be a place on South Rampart Street, Jiles — I think they repair televisions now. We used to sell 300-400 78s on each new release to them a week. Rampart Street was full of record shops. There was the Be Bop Shop that Al Young owned, Frank's Record Shop that was owned by Frank Mancuso — he sold to a lot of jukebox operations — and Johnny's Music House. There was a Woolworth's and a McCrory's at 1037 Rampart Street that sold a lot of records too.

"Radio was important for selling records then. We used to give samples to people like Jack the Cat and Poppa Stoppa. That's when it became important to promote our products. You see when I started working for Capitol we used to play records for disc jockeys and they would pick out what they wanted to buy. So you really had to know your product and hustle in those days."

But besides the fierce, and oftentimes cutthroat, competition of

137

the New Orleans record business, Banashak was soon entranced by the local sound that abound in the clubs. "Like everyone else, I rushed down to the French Quarter and listened to Dixieland, because that's all there was there. But then I started going around and listening to some other local rhythm and blues music. I remember sitting there and listening to it and saying to myself, 'This is so catchy, so melodic. This stuff can really go places.'

"I started going down to the J&M Studio where Cosimo recorded a lot of the things I sold. I got to meet Fats and Dave Bartholomew, and I just fell in love with that music at that point. I had already started to think about the music crossing over, because I was in the studio when Fats cut 'Going To The River,' and I thought, 'Gee, that's the kind of thing that can go pop.' Regrettably I didn't get into the manufacturing end of the business at the time, because I probably would have made a lot of money. But I knew then that something was going to happen, if it wasn't Fats, it was going to be someone else."

To Banashak's dismay, however, his brief infatuation with New Orleans was interrupted when he was transferred back to the Houston office in 1952. "I was really angry that they transferred me back. I was doing a good job here and I liked New Orleans. But they wanted to get me back to the home office. So I packed up and went back. In a few months DeGoyer just quit. He just locked the doors.

"Well I got despondent about the business because I felt like I was left high and dry. So I went to work on the road for Lew Chudd at Imperial, doing promoting, checking on sales and on our distributors throughout the entire country. I think Lew hired me out of appreciation because I found him two artists that he made a lot of money with, 'Slim' Whitman and Dave Bartholomew.

"I had heard 'Slim' Whitman in Austin, Texas when he didn't have a recording contract, and I knew there was a big demand for his type of songs. First I called Eddie Mesner at Aladdin Records, collect, but he wouldn't accept my call. Then I called Lew. I told him about 'Slim' Whitman and said that Capitol was interested in signing him. Well later that week I read in *Billboard* that he signed with Imperial.

"Now I didn't introduce Dave to Lew Chudd, but there was a period of time where they had become distant and angry, and Dave started doing sessions for other people. So when Dave had finished 'Lawdy Miss Claudy' for Specialty, he brought it in and played it for me. Well I knew right away that that was a tune meant for Fats'

**Jack The Cat and Jackie The Kitten
New Orleans Deejays mid 1950's**

[author's note: Fats in fact plays piano on the session]. So I called up Lew Chudd and said, 'Lew, I want you to hear this record that Dave did on a new artist called Lloyd Price. Man it's gonna be a hit.'

"Lew listened and said, 'Look, can you arrange for me and Dave to get together and talk. I'd like to talk to him and get some business straight.' So three days later he was in my office talking to Dave and I was doing the listening. They cemented a relationship that day that guaranteed the success of Imperial Records for many years."

Banashak stayed only two months with Chudd's powerful label because the rigors of travel were taking too much of a toll on his personal life. But he did establish an important contact which would serve him later on. "I was supposed to be on the road for a week and then off for a week. But the first time I was out for eight weeks in a row. When I'd call in to Lew, he'd send me off to someplace else and say 'You can go home after next week.' Another week would go by, and the same thing would happen again. I couldn't go on like that because I had little kids. So finally I had to call Lew and tell him that I had to quit."

In the interim, Banashak returned to Houston and worked with his father-in-law as a plumbing contractor and later as the Houston sales manager for the Admiral Corporation. But it wasn't too very long until Banashak was back in the record business, in a position he wanted to be in.

"In 1955 the guy that owned A-1 in New Orleans came to see me. They had opened another branch in Oklahoma City and Dick Sturgil wanted to move there and have me run the New Orleans operation with a buyout option. He thought I was a good competitor when I worked for Gramaphone Enterprises and felt I could help him. In the meantime A-1 had picked up all the strong independent R&B labels like Atlantic, Imperial and Specialty.

"Well I said no at the time because I was quite successful out of the record business. At Admiral I had a company car, an expense account, a brand new house — I didn't want to go through the hassle of moving again and starting over.

"A year later Dick came back again, and the offer was so much better that I decided to go back. So in January of 1957, I took over A-1 Distributors at 628 Baronne Street. There were about four other companies that distributed independents, but A-1 had all the labels that counted.

"It was a big company then; I had sixteen people working under me. I had an office, warehouse people, and a bunch of salesmen out on the road. In fact I had Joe Ruffino (who later owned the Ric and Ron labels) and Johnny Vincent (who owned Ace Records) working for me.

"We distributed Ace Records at A-1. Johnny was cold when I came over, he wasn't making any money. As a favor to Johnny, I paid him right away for his records so he'd have some money in his pocket to make more records or for him to live off of. This went on for awhile.

"Back then I had a jukebox guy come by and every week he would buy two or three copies of Johnny's record, "Walkin' With Frankie" by Frankie Lee Sims. So we asked him why he kept buying that record, and he said, 'Every place I put the record it spins the meters.' So I took the record down to Okey Dokey (James W. Smith), but he said, 'I'm not gonna play anything by Johnny Vincent.' So I said, 'Look, don't look at it as Johnny's record, you know that I sell it.' So he started playing it and it took off. That's when Johnny started making a little bit of money.

"We carried Ace right up until he had this thing with Huey Smith, 'Rockin' Pneumonia.' Then Johnny opened up his own distributorship, Southern Distributors, with Joe Ruffino, Cosimo and

Joe Caronna across the street."

It wasn't long before Banashak got the bug himself and decided to try his hand at making his own records too. "I used to go out of town to a lot of record conventions. One night I was at one and I was talking to Dave Kapp, who owned Kapp Records. He considered his label a mini-major when comparing himself to all those little record manufacturers in the Brill Building or 1650 Broadway in New York. He was saying that all those guys do is throw $750 against the wall and hope they come up with a hit. I said to myself, 'Is that all, $750? That's the initial investment?' So I kept thinking about that when I got back to New Orleans.

"The first record I did was in 1958 with Wayne Shuler. He was working for me as a salesman, and he had found this artist in South Louisiana, Elton Anderson. We started the Trey label. Wayne's father of course is Eddie, and we did the session over in the Goldband Studio in Lake Charles. So we put out this record, 'Shed So Many Tears.' It started doing pretty good, around 10,000-12,000 around here, and Mercury wanted it. Well I didn't want to sell it to them because one of the reasons I wanted to start making records was because I didn't want people from elsewhere to make all the money like they had been.

"It ended up that I gave everything to Wayne Shuler and he leased the record to Mercury (and Vin as well). We had a problem about whether to do the sessions union or non-union. I wanted to do it right and have union sessions because it either had to be one or another. Wayne didn't. So I decided to start something else."

After the aborted Trey deal, Banashak and New Orleans disc jockey Larry McKinley struck a deal in January of 1958 which turned out to be much more profitable than anyone could have foreseen.

"I had known Larry McKinley from my days at Gramaphone Enterprises in '49, when Larry had a show at WMRY. He was just getting started in radio then, I guess he was 18 or 19, he wasn't really that significant. When I came back in '57 he was the program director at the station, and he used to come by the office to pick up records and stuff.

"Larry was probably the hottest jock in the city at the time; Larry could break a record. Believe this or not, there was a period of time that Atlantic Records almost went out of business, they were cold. I was probably their best customer because I was in a heavy blues area. Honestly, they would call me on the phone all the time and thank me for buying their records. At the time Atlantic had six different dubs of a Ray Charles record, and they asked me if I liked the one they sent. You see they were sending different dubs around to see which one would get the most reaction and that would be the one they would go with. I talked to Larry about it and I explained that he had the only copy of that particular dub. Well it so happened that right after I gave the dub to Larry, I had to go to a record convention in Chicago. Well the day after I got there I got a call from my wife, she was at the office and said that people were screaming for this record that Larry was playing. Well I was gone three days and I already had a back order of 25,000 records! Of course Jerry Wexler and Armet Ertegun were at this convention and they jumped for leaps and bounds when they heard that.

"To make a long story short the record was 'What'd I Say,' and that was the record that Atlantic decided to go with, just on the strength of Larry playing it. That's how powerful a jock that Larry was then.

"Larry and I began developing a relationship beyond the distributor - disc jockey arrangement. One day I said to him, 'How about starting a label together?' Well, he seemed to think it would be a good idea because he was managing K-Doe and looking for a record deal. But I said, 'I'm not gonna give it to you, you've got to put up the money on your own.' So we both put up $650. That was enough to cover the cost of a session and getting 1,000 records pressed.

"Since I had A-1 Distributors I had an advantage. I could sell A-1, one thousand records, and A-1 could issue a check to our label immediately so we'd be able to have some capital to do something else.

"Of course I knew that Larry was going to play the records, which was the most important thing about selling records. We had a great all around deal going I thought."

Banashak's first release curiously wasn't a product of New Orleans, but a downhome Baton Rouge blues item, in the tradition of the best Excello titles cut by J.D. Miller during the Fifties.

"Our new arrangement started when this guy, Matthew Jacobs, came down from Baton Rouge. He had a tape with 'Early In The Morning Blues' and 'Bad Luck and Trouble' on it. It was a real lowdown blues and he called himself Boogie Jake. Well I wanted to release it, but we didn't have a name for the label.

"At the time the disc jockeys were always looking for a one-minute record so they could play more commercials. I was driving down Airline Highway one day, and I passed this restaurant called 'Meal a Minit;' there used to be a chain of them here. So I saw this sign that said 'Minit.' So I thought, 'Well if the disc jockeys are looking for minute record, I'll give them a 'Minit' record. So I took the spelling, M-I-N-I-T, from the 'Meal A Minit' sign, and that's how we called it Minit Records.

"Boogie Jake's record (Minit 601/2) turned out to be such a big local success that it got the attention of Leonard Chess in Chicago. It sold 16-20,000, which is a big blues record. Chess wanted to carry it nationally, so I gave it to him. Chess could have had the whole Minit line if they would have sent me a royalty statement. But they never even sent a statement, and that was a big record in the blues areas like Mississippi and Georgia. We were getting the record played in the South, but Leonard Chess wanted to get it played in Detroit and Chicago. Apparently the stations wouldn't play it because of the name 'Boogie.' I guess there was some kind of nasty connotation.

"On his next record (Minit 608) we used the name Matthew Jacobs to try and get some national play, but that was a big mistake. We should have stayed with Boogie Jake. I think we destroyed the artist. We could have had more records under the name Boogie Jake and they'd have sold."

143

Minit's next offering was the desultory "What Is Life" by Nolan Pitts, a member of Boogie Jake's group, which was a dud. But once Banashak began concentrating on New Orleans artists, the tables soon turned.

"We wanted to have an audition to find some local talent. So Larry McKinley arranged to have it at the WYLD studio. That was in January of 1960. The night of the audition we had Benny Spellman come by; Jessie Hill brought this raggedy tape of what turned out to be 'Ooh-Poo-Pah-Doo;' Wilbert Smith, a singer who went by the name of Lee Diamond; and Irma Thomas came with her husband. Aaron Neville came to the audition and Joseph Arrington, who of course is Joe Tex. There was a singer named Allen Orange that came by with a piano player that backed him up. His name was Allen Toussaint. That was the first time I met Allen.

"As it turned out, Allen backed up some of the other singers who didn't have an accompanist. I remember that when we were going home that night, Allen said to Larry McKinley, 'Don't forget to call me if you do any sessions.'

"That night we accepted Jessie Hill, Benny Spellman, Irma Thomas, Joe Tex, Allen Orange, Aaron Neville and a vocal group called the Del-Royals. I mean all these people came out of one audition. Now K-Doe wasn't part of the audition because Larry McKinley was already managing him, but we accepted him too.

"We didn't sign anybody that night, we just said come on down to the office the next day. Well we lost Irma Thomas; Tommy Ridgley took her to see Joe Ruffino, because he was recording for Ruffino. When Ruffino found out that I was going to sign her he grabbed her right away. You see I had fired Joe Ruffino and there was some animosity between the two of us. Losing Irma at the time was a big disappointment, but we signed everybody else. We signed Joe Tex too, even though he had a commitment to Johnny Vincent over at Ace. I didn't know how secure his commitment was. But right after I signed him I got a call from a guy in Baton Rouge (Tex's home town) and he sent me a copy of a contract he had on Joe Tex. Then I got a call from Leonard Chess, and he had a contract on him. So I didn't want any legal hassles; I just tore my contract up. I guess he resolved his problems with Johnny though, because his next record came out on Ace."

Although Banashak would have massive national, not to mention local, success with his new roster of then-unknown talent, the real catch at this historic audition turned out to be the quiet pianist Allen Toussaint. "I had already talked to Harold Battiste about arranging and producing some sessions before I even got started, but he was with Specialty at the time. So then Larry and I had a talk and I asked him if he'd like Allen to be our arranger and producer. So that's how Allen came to be in charge of our sessions.

"Allen completely directed the recordings. He wrote most of the songs and made sure the musicians played the way the arrangements were written. Sometimes he'd change things when a singer or musician couldn't hit a certain note, but he was in full charge at the sessions. Sometimes I'd come to him with an idea, but if he didn't like it that was it. I had complete confidence in him.

"Allen was paid double the union scale for arranging and being the leader of the session. It was $107 when we got started and of course he got writer's royalties too. The other musicians got $55 each and the background singers $30 each. That was for a complete session which was four tunes."

Toussaint's first production for Minit was K-Doe's "Make You Love Me" b/w "There's A Will There's A Way." The record heralded a new era of New Orleans rhythm and blues. Minit's future productions would be characterized by a sound that was more energetic and bouncier than earlier New Orleans productions. It would be a sound that would become instantly recognizable, and sell millions of records.

"That very first record on K-Doe, 'There's A Will There's A Way,' did real well locally, and it got some action around Memphis. It sold in the neighborhood of 10,000, which was real encouraging. We kind of stalled after that for a little while. I leased a session by this white guy, Doyle Templet, that did nothing, and Benny Spellman's first release 'Life Is Too Short,' that didn't happen."

At this point in time, early 1960, Lew Chudd of Imperial Records came back into the picture, offering to distribute the Minit Line nationally. Since distribution has always been the biggest problem small labels face, Banashak viewed Chudd's offer as the way to solve all of Minit's problems and maybe put it on the map with the other major independents. Although Minit's biggest hits were on the immediate horizon, as things turned out, the deal with Chudd would have its mixed blessings.

"When we started Minit, I didn't know everything about the manufacturing end of the record business. But Lew Chudd presented such a sweet-sounding deal that I could see all that money in the bank. I saw it as learning the business from an aspect that I didn't know before. Producing, manufacturing, buying masters — I had never done that. I went for the deal because I saw it as a learn-

145

ing experience. Because let's face it, Lew Chudd really knew the record business.

"Imperial was supposed to pick up the distribution and promotion of the Minit line. We were all supposed to participate equally, Larry, Lew Chudd and myself. Allen worked strictly on a royalty basis. Imperial was supposed to pick up the cost of all the sessions, but of course in the end all that was charged back to Minit."

The Minit-Imperial arrangement started off with a real bang with Minit's next release, the uproarious "Ooh Poo Pah Doo" by Jessie Hill. "Jessie had this raggedy demo of 'Ooh Poo Pah Doo' that he told me he'd taken around to a bunch of people. Well, we got it down in the studio and it really sounded good.

" 'Ooh Poo Pah Doo' began to get quite popular around New Orleans — it might have done 10,000. But that was without any effort from our One Stop. By then One Stop had complete control over the music operators, and they weren't helping it; they might have ordered just twenty-five. So I realized I'd have to take things into my own hands.

"It seems like there's always been a lot of jealousy in the local record business. As soon as I started having a measure of success, a lot of people started backing away. Even people that could profit from the situation themselves.

"One night I stayed late with a couple of people from the office and we staged a phony 'long distance' phone call to the One-Stop, at 340 South Rampart. I had one of the secretaries say she was calling from California and ask, 'I'm looking for a company that produced a record called "Poo Do Poo," or something.' Then another guy got on the phone and said people had been calling from all over looking for this record and then we hung up.

"Five minutes later Joe Assunto called and said 'Hey man, I got this call from California about your record.' Everything was straight after that, and I really think the One Stop grew with 'Ooh Poo Pah Doo' because they really got it going after that."

"Ooh Poo Pah Doo" really gave Minit a strong leg to stand on. It nearly topped the national R&B charts, rising to #3 for 11 weeks, which would have been enough to please everyone. But it fulfilled the dream of every R&B record man by "crossing over," eventually jetting to #28 in the Hot 100 during its 16-week stay in the 1960 charts. Banashak estimates that during the peak of the record's popularity it sold 500,000, during a three-month period.

"Ooh Poo Pah Doo" and its follow-up, "Whip It On Me," gave the fledgling label a strong leg to stand on and provided enough working capital to finance its other recording projects. Minit followed with a national R&B hit by Aaron Neville with "Over You" and good regional records with Ernie K-Doe's "Hello My Lover," Lee Diamond's "It Won't Be Me," and Roy Montrell's instrumental "Mudd." But it would be K-Doe that provided Minit's biggest hit of all in the spring of 1961, with the novelty smash, "Mother-In-Law."

"I knew 'Mother-In-Law' was gonna go right off. It was an immediate local hit, it went straight to #1 white and black. It was a natural because of all the mother-in-law jokes that were going around. I found out from the dealers that people who normally didn't buy any records were buying the record because they wanted to play it for their mother-in-law.

"When the record went gold, there was a picture in the *Billboard* of Lew Chudd giving the award to a jock on the West Coast in appreciation for breaking the record. That disturbed me because it was the New Orleans jocks that really broke 'Mother-In-Law.' They (the New Orleans jocks) got upset because they weren't given the credit, and it created some bad feelings for me."

It soon became evident that the deal between Chudd and Banashak wasn't going exactly the way Banashak had envisioned it. "Lew Chudd didn't fulfill any of his promises. He was supposed to teach us the fundamentals of the record business. But, as soon as we started showing some kind of success, he started to retreat.

"A lot of records could have made it bigger, but they didn't because they weren't promoted. Sometimes records will break on their own so all they need is a kick in the rump to make them do better. I thought Aaron Neville's 'Over You' should have done much better than it did. It broke in New Orleans, San Francisco, Baltimore and Philadelphia, and those were the key markets that showed me how well a record was doing.

"Looking back on the situation today, I realize Lew Chudd was jealous of our success. At the time Imperial was cold, Fats wasn't selling and neither was Ricky (Nelson). Chudd would just take out small ads in the trades and tack us on as an afterthought. He actually ran ads that said 'Imperial is cold.' I think he wanted to be the only guy that was successful and making money. He really enjoyed controlling other people's destinies."

It wasn't long after that another business opportunity arose for Banashak that would eventually take precedence over the Minit-Imperial arrangement. "Irving Smith came to me and said he wanted to start a label called Valiant, he named it after the car, and he asked me if I had any talent he could 'borrow.'

"Irving ran one of the busiest record shops on St. Charles Avenue next to the Pontchartrain Hotel; it's still there. I referred 'Red' Tyler to him as an arranger, and he asked me if I would steer any extra talent his way. Then he came to me and said he wanted to form a partnership. He said, 'I don't have time to do all this. You run it and I'll put up the money.' But I really don't think his father wanted musicians hanging around the record shop.

"We had a couple of things by Joel Moore and Errol Dee, but they didn't do too much. Then we put out the Lee Dorsey record 'Lover of Lovers.' It went big around here and we leased it to ABC. Irving liked that because he liked to run up to New York. We were supposed to have the next Lee Dorsey record, but we got shafted by Bobby Robinson and Marshall Sehorn (Fire and Fury Records) on it.

"I talked Irving into signing Chris Kenner and that's when we had to change the name of the label. We put 'I Like It Like That,' out on Chris on Valiant, but we got a letter from a label in California that was already using the name 'Valiant.' So we had to change it. I thought of the name Instant. The dee jays were always looking for an 'instant' hit, so I thought of Instant Records. The purpose of going on with Instant was to learn about the record business for myself. Larry McKinley was originally part of Instant. He didn't invest any money in it; but I felt Larry was important, so I made a gift of giving him part of the label."

McKinley's financial involvement in Minit and Instant soon after came to a premature halt. The payola scandal that rocked the record industry was at its height, and although payola was common knowledge within the New Orleans music industry during the Fifties, a popular disc jockey with a substantial interest in a record company would be open to federal scrutiny. "Larry was compelled to drop out of the record business because of the payola controversy. We tried to keep things hidden by keeping his shares in his wife's name. Finally his boss confronted him because I think he'd been tipped off by one of our competitors, so he had to sell out.'

"When 'I Like It Like That' really started to move, Liberty and Roulette tried to pick it up. I told them the deal was $10,000 up front. They thought that was high, but I had already sold that much so I knew that's what it was worth. When Lew Chudd found out about the record, he called me and said, 'Hey, what's going on?' He was just shocked. I told him, 'Hey you aren't doing what you promised to do, so I'm gonna try and do something on my own.' I even offered him the same deal I offered Roulette and Liberty, but I never heard anything back from him.

"It was a great beginning for the label; we sold half a million in three or four months. It was a great experience; we had a lot of money coming in. Eventually we only lost three percent from distributors that didn't pay; some even paid in advance and sent the money to the pressing plant."

Musically, Instant's sessions were also put in the hands of Allen Toussaint, who suddenly was one of the hottest producers in the country. "I really couldn't give Allen enough of the credit. I can remember in 1961 that at one time Allen was involved in seven records that were in the charts during one month. A lot of people think Allen had a piece of Instant and Minit, but it's not true. We paid him a flat royalty. By today's standards it wasn't much, but back then he had the best deal going. I got mad at him when he did those records for Barbara George ['I Know'] and Lee Dorsey ['Ya Ya']. He said, 'Well I just wanted to do them.' I said, 'Okay, but I won't pay you any percentage. I'll hire you just like those guys.' So he laid off doing arrangements for others. I gave Allen more than anybody else got, and I didn't try to take his songs like other producers would do to other artists."

Banashak is quick to point out that, contrary to popular belief, he was still very much involved in the affairs of Minit even after the initial success with Instant, though it's true his relationship with Lew Chudd was deteriorating. Minit continued its string of hits throughout 1961 and well into 1962. K-Doe followed his #1 hit with other national chart successes; "Te-Ta-Te-Ta-Ta," "I Cried My Last Tear," "A Certain Girl," and "Popeye Joe."

The Showmen, a vocal group from Washington, D.C., had a national hit in late 1961 with "It Will Stand," a record that reached #61 during its twelve weeks in *Billboard's* Hot 100, and which reentered the charts on Imperial in 1964. "They had auditioned a tape so that's how they came to record on Minit. I sent Allen up there to produce a session, but it turned out terrible. But when we brought them down here to record, things turned out pretty good and we got a hit."

Another big record was the two-sided hit "Lipstick Traces" b/w "Fortune Teller" by Benny Spellman, which rose to #80 nationally during the summer of 1962. "I really expected bigger things from Benny. He was by far the most popular rhythm and blues artist in New Orleans. He always was working even when nobody else could find a job. And he had those teenagers mesmerized, they just loved him. He would throw boogers at them and they'd still eat him up!

"He was a great guy, always willing to help out. He would sing backup vocals when he wasn't scheduled for his own session. I remember breaking a fight up between him and K-Doe, because they were arguing over who was responsible for making 'Mother-In-Law' a hit. But most of the time things were professional. At first we had two and then three tracks, so the background singers would sit in the back and get picked up by the vocal mike. Benny and Willie Harper did a lot of background singing and we also used Irma Thomas and some other female singers."

Local hits were also waxed by Irma, who had some big regional hits with "Cry On," "I Done Got Over It," "Ruler of My Heart" and "It's Raining," among others.

"I didn't want to sign Irma because I felt she broke her word by signing with Ruffino. I guess her contract expired with Ruffino because Allen came to me one day and said he wanted to work with her so I gave in. At first I tried to get Irving Smith to sign her but he took too long and I signed her to Minit. I don't know why some of those records didn't chart because they sold really well, especially 'It's Raining.' Maybe Lew Chudd held back on it."

Another big record was Eskew Reeder's "Green Door," which Banashak feels should have gone national. "I really got aggravated after 'Green Door.' It started breaking in all the key markets but Lew Chudd did nothing to push it. I had distributors calling me from all over the country about the record but there was nothing I could do."

Meanwhile, things on Instant had slowed down after starting with the bang "I Like It Like That" made. James Rivers had a nice instrumental, "Just A Closer Walk With Thee," and Al Reed had a couple of pleasant releases, "Magic Carpet" and "One-Eyed Monster." So too did Mr. G (Joe August) with "Everything Happens At Night," but which permaturely ran aground.

Chris Kenner again produced Instant's next hit, "Something You Got," which was a big Popeye dance record around New Orleans in 1962, selling in the neighborhood of 30,000. Another good local record was produced by a Toussaint discovery, street hustler Raymond Lewis, who made the much-remembered "I'm Gonna Put Some Hurt On You," and also Johnny Meyers' "Wonderful Girl."

Next to Kenner, however, Instant's hottest property at the time was Art Neville, whose biggest record was the haunting "All These Things," in 1962. "I bought Art Neville's contract from Specialty.

He had already cut 'All These Things' for them. I bought the session and all of Art's advances. I'd always thought 'All These Things' was a good country song, but that wasn't really proved until much later. We did a lot of sales around here and got some covers."

Banashak also formed ALON Records in the spring of 1961, which was a sister label to Instant. "That was pretty much Allen's label. But that's not what ALON stood for, though; it was NOLA (New Orleans, Louisiana) spelled backwards. It was kind of a short-lived thing, because Allen went in the service before it got to doing anything. We did have a good seller with Willie Harper (former Del Royal) who had 'Power of Love.' We had some nice things by Al Fayard and Eldridge Holmes, but really that was just local."

All seemed to be going rosy for almost everyone involved in New Orleans' record industry in 1961 and 1962 when no less than sixty of the city's R&B singles charted in *Billboard's* Hot 100. But then, in 1963, New Orleans's purple patch came to an abrupt, and disasterous halt.

"Everything in New Orleans fell apart in April of 1963," recalls Banashak. "Henry Hildebrand and Ken Eliot — Jack the Cat — got a promise from Leonard Chess (owner of Chess Records) that he would back them in a distributorship. Well I had the Chess line and I sold a lot of their records. So I confronted Leonard Chess and I said, 'Look. If you're gonna finance a new distributor, I'm not gonna pay my bill. You're gonna have to hassle me for the money.' Well he denied and denied it. Hildebrand got somebody else to back him and he still eventually started All South Distributors. But Jack the Cat was out of the deal; he didn't have the contacts to get any hot labels.

"At the time there was an unconscious collusion among all the New Orleans distributors that they weren't going to take any labels that sold to Stan's (Stan's Records in Shreveport) at the same price that we paid. In those days Stan's wasn't a distributor. He was a big One Stop, but he was getting the same price so he was becoming competitive with us and undercutting our prices. Everybody agreed not to take the labels that charged Stan the same price as us, even Hildebrand said 'No' at first, and he didn't have any good labels. But when the labels started looking to get around the situation, Hildebrand said, 'Yes, I'll buy at your price,' and he started grabbing all the hot labels. Then instantly the rest of us distributors were dogs.

"So, in the meantime, Allen Toussaint gets called up into the service, which means there won't be any new product for awhile. On top of that, I didn't know it at the time, but Lew Chudd was looking to sell out, and then Chess did start his own distributorship, Delta, with Paul Glass out of Chicago. That took a considerable number of labels from me. When the labels started leaving, my cash started getting short because my accounts were slow paying the bills. You see when the labels start moving, and you don't have a new record out as an incentive to pay the bill, accounts are slow paying. Things just started to snowball.

"I talked to my lawyer, and he recommended that A-1 file for bankruptcy. Well I shouldn't have listened to him, but I did. Two weeks after I filed the papers we got a check for $18,000, and that would have held us over. In the end I settled all the bank business by selling my own personal telephone stock on the pretext that I could make a bank loan and reestablish the distributorship. But when I went to the bank to apply for a loan, the bank said they couldn't loan me any money because I just had a bankruptcy!"

As a result, all of A-1's assets were sold at an auction to the top bidder, Cosimo Matassa, who picked up everything at a fraction of its worth. He immediately got his money out by selling all of the records to Sammy Teritto, who owned a record shop in Gretna that catered to record collectors.

"I was cold then, all my labels were fading, Allen was still in the service, so I was bouncing around from producer to producer. Since I wasn't having any hits, I decided to just get out of the record business. I started pulling weeds and cutting grass at home to get my mind back in order. The thing that really bugged me was my pride. The money didn't mean a thing to me because I didn't have anything as a kid. But to have gained so much and then to see it all blow away. I was just angry that in this part of the country we weren't smart enough for the invaders. We gave into their whims and it cost us. In fact it cost me more than $125,000."

Banashak's sojourn from the record industry lasted only a few months, until Atlantic Records expressed interest in a record Banashak had issued much earlier, Chris Kenner's "Land of 1,000 Dances." The record only sold moderately well in New Orleans upon its issue, but after nearly a year it surprisingly began selling in the Midwest. Banashak wanted to lease the record to Atlantic, but his partner Irving Smith disagreed with the idea. So rather than provoke a situation, Smith agreed to sell his percentage of Instant, in return for removing the responsibility of past, present and future debts incurred by Instant. It was a big gamble for Banashak, but it turned out for the better when the record turned into a substantial hit later in the year.

"After 'Land of A Thousand Dances,' a number of good things started happening; and I started to get interested in the business again. I started releasing some of my old masters to try and get something going. I didn't have anything big, but between that and some of the publishing royalties that were coming in, I was able to sustain things. I didn't have an office then, I had a telephone and a desk in the living room of my house and I operated from there.

"Then the Goodman brothers, Benny Goodman's brothers, had a big publishing firm. They called me and said they were interested in buying the copyright to 'I Like It Like That.' That made me think that something is happening somewhere that I don't know about. So I started borrowing the *Billboard* and the *Cashbox* from my friends and do some studying again. I found out that 'I Like It Like That' was the flip side of a big record that had come out in Europe. It wasn't the hit, but you still draw a lot of royalties being on the other side. So I started drawing royalties on that song.

"I got in touch with Allen, who was still in the service at Fort Hood, Texas. Allen was really interested in music at the time, so I arranged to meet him in Houston so we could sit down and talk. As it turned out, Allen wasn't getting any royalties on the material he had written under the name Naomi Neville. I put in a call to BMI and they said they had a lot of money set aside, but they didn't know who Naomi Neville was, or where she lived. I got them to send Allen a check right away and that really rejuvenated him. He started coming up with ideas and he was interested in recording again."

Toussaint also had Al Hirt cover an instrumental he had recorded on his RCA album *Java*. The tune became an international hit for the New Orleans trumpeter, and meant more royalties down the line for Toussaint.

"Allen had a small group over at the base called the Stokes. 'Java' was in the charts, and I asked Allen to write some more catchy instrumentals in the same style. He said, 'Man I can write those any day of the week.' So I said, 'Do it, then.'

"We did 'Whipped Cream' first over in Houston. It started to happen, but then Herb Alpert covered it and killed our record. But that didn't matter, because I had the publishing on it. Irving Smith was the one responsible for introducing 'Whipped Cream' to Herb Alpert. Some of the other Stokes' singles did well, too. 'The Fat Cat' did well in Detroit and so did 'Young Man, Old Man.' The other made it around New Orleans, and we got a couple of other covers."

When Toussaint returned from the service in 1965, he found the record scene in New Orleans in a depressed state. Imperial was sold, along with Minit; Ace folded; and most of the other major independents had fallen by the wayside or no longer were interested in what New Orleans had to offer musically. For awhile, he continued producing material for Banashak, including Al Fayard's "Doin' Sumpin'," and Eldridge Holmes' "Emperor Jones," but nothing got started outside the city. The closest thing to a national record in 1965 was Benny Spellman's "Word Game" on ALON, which was leased to Atlantic, but narrowly missed the charts.

Not long after, Toussaint was to abruptly end his association with Banashak and begin a new partnership with Marshall Sehorn. "I was deeply hurt when Allen left. I gave him his start and I treated him with respect and fairness. When Allen was in the service, I hired a lawyer to get his royalties for 'Java,' and I didn't even have the publishing. It took over a year, but when he got back to New Orleans, there was a check for $16,000 waiting for him. Allen was still under contract when he left, but I felt like if that's what he wanted, I wasn't gonna make a fuss. But I found out that Marshall had been going behind my back to get Allen to jump. I really felt like I'd been stabbed in the back."

Losing Toussaint was a major blow to Banashak, but he had no choice but to carry on with the business at hand — making and selling new records. "I started a new label, Seven B, that stood for seven Banashaks, in 1966. Originally it was going to be a label on which I issued masters that I had bought. The first thing I had was a record by a white kid, Phil Dana, but it didn't do anything. Then I got a master from Earl Stanley's group, 'Pass The Hatchet' [issued by Roger & the Gypsies] that did real well locally.

"I was listening to this thing ['Pass The Hatchet'] at Cosimo's Studio, and Eddie Bo was around and offered to help me out with it. Eddie Bo did all the shouting and clapping on the record; that was overdubbed. 'Pass The Hatchet' would have been a bigger thing, but the Watts Riots broke out just as it was taking off, and that killed it.

"I made a foreign licensing deal with London Records - Burlington Music, in England, for product and copyrights. They advanced me $40,000 and then I decided to really get back into it and get some offices.

"I rented an office upstairs at 715 Camp Street, I guess you might say right in the wino district. Ordinarily I'd have never picked Camp Street, but Cosimo had purchased a building across the street and then put in a new studio. I assumed that maybe that section of Camp would become a record row. The rents were cheap, and I thought it would be a good place for small companies. Sehorn looked there, but eventually he moved to St. Philip Street.

"I really started releasing a lot of records. I was trying to get something going locally and to supply product as part of my London Records deal. That's why I started putting out my own stuff on Seven B. I only put one album out and it wasn't until 1969. *The Solid Gold* thing with all the different artists. [*Solid Gold* was Instant's only lp and featured some of Banashak's biggest successes on the Instant, ALON and Seven B labels.] It was my thinking that, for the dollar, there was a greater return from singles. There was a minimal investment and a greater return.

"Eddie Bo started to do some producing for me, but his stuff just didn't sound right. We had a little noise with some of the Oliver Morgan stuff he did, but I always felt that there was something that didn't fit, or was out of tune on everything Eddie Bo produced. I tried to tell him, but he just laughed. I leased one of his records to Capitol ["Lover and a Friend"], and he produced Skip Easterling's 'The Grass Looks Greener,' a thing by the Bobby Williams Group, 'Boogaloo Mardi Gras.'"

Eddie Bo was responsible though for a few palatable records among the many sides he produced and recorded on Instant, Seven B and Busy B — yet another subsidiary in Banashak's growing myriad of labels. Bo's "Fence of Love" and "Horse With The Freeze" (credited to a nonexistent Roy Ward) are worth citing as are the occasional sides by Oliver Morgan and "Little" Eddie Lang.

Throughout the mid-Sixties, Banashak's labels — which now included Polytex, IMA, Tune Kel, Flower Power, AIR (which was supposed to stand for A-1 Records, but the printer made a mistake on the label), Local, and Channel One — were a source of good local music, some of which sold quite well around New Orleans. "It was my idea to get a lot of product on the market, hoping that something would catch on and sell. That's the way I did business at that time."

One of Banashak's more memorable records from the period was a surprisingly primitive blues item (for 1965) "A Thing You Gotta Face" b/w "Ain't Broke Ain't Hungry," by Polka Dot Slim. Slim's real name was Vince Monroe, and he had earlier recorded for J.D. Miller in Crowley under his real name and under the moniker "Mr. Calhoun." "There was still a good market for blues records in the South. That particular record did well in Georgia, Mississippi, and even Ohio. Sax Kari found the guy. He recorded both sides at his house with a portable tape recorder. Sax kept trying to get him to come back and do a real session at a studio, but it just didn't happen."

Sax Kari, up until his association with Banashak, had been a successful jazz/blues recording artist for nearly two decades. "I had bought Sax's records back in the Forties when I lived in Baltimore. One day when I was working at Gramaphone Enterprises, a dee jay brought Sax by to meet me. When he left he said, "Look, I just got in town and I don't have any money or a place to stay." So I gave him $50 and didn't see him again for a long time. When I got things going with Instant, he stopped by to visit again. He didn't have much going at the time so we sat down and talked. I think he started recording and producing for me as a way of saying 'thanks' for helping him out when he was in a jam. We ended up having a little bit of success with him too.

"Sax Kari immediately had a big record with a bouncy instrumental called 'Ludwig.' One of the studio musicians wrote that,

SEVEN B

White Cliffs Pub
BMI — 2:42

7001
165-162

"PASS THE HATCHET"
(Part II)
(R. Leon, Jr., R. Theriot
E. Oropeza)
ROGER & THE GYPSIES
7001

and Sax cut it. I remember that there was an animated character in Kolb's Restaurant [on St. Charles Avenue, near Canal St.] called 'Ludwig' and that's what inspired the tune. Clyde Kerr Jr. was playing trumpet on it and I put it out on the Tune-Kel label. That was more or less a label for Sax's stuff. Tune-Kel was also the name of one of the publishing companies that Irving Smith started.

"The record took off in New Orleans and Atlantic leased it nationally. In the meantime Al Hirt covered the song, and that killed it. I was kind of mad at Atlantic because I felt they dragged their feet on Sax's record. I think we had a better version, but they were afraid of Hirt's record."

Sax produced a number of other fine sides on Tune-Kel, including those by Al White's Highlighters, Sonny Jones, Tammy McKnight, and Bobby Camel. He also was responsible for one of Chris Kenner's better post-Toussaint releases, "Wind the Clock," which appeared on Instant.

"Sax was a good guy. All business. It's too bad that he didn't have the ear for what was hitting right at the moment. He's a guy with a lot of talent. Last I heard he was selling used cars in Miami."

Another of Banashak's finds was R&B and rock 'n roll veteran Huey "Piano" Smith, who began recording for Instant in 1967.

"Huey had a partner at the time, Carlton Picou, and they had a small label called Pitty Pat. They had this record called 'It Do Me Good' [by the Pitty Pats] that they were trying to lease. Huey came in the office one day and said he had taken it all over, but every label said they didn't want it because it sounded too much like New Orleans. I said, 'Good. I'll put it out and sell it here.' It turned out to be a real big local record. The girl that sang on in only did that one record. She got superstitious about something and wouldn't sing anymore.

"I really admired Huey because he was a hard worker and had a lot of good ideas. One day we were in the studio and Huey wanted to record something right there. Well we didn't have a band, so Huey asked if there were any tracks around that he could work with. I had this track Chris Kenner had out which did nothing ['Stretch My Hand To You']. Huey took it and wrote 'Coo Coo Over You' which became a good local record by the Hueys. Little Buck sang the lead on that record.

"Huey produced lots of sessions that I thought a lot of. We did 'Sophisticated Sissy' by Curley Moore, which was a big record around town. We did some things with Little Buck, but he went over to Houston and signed with Don Robey before we could really get anything going on him. Huey brought Larry Darnell in and we did a record on him ['Son of A Son of A Slave' b/w 'Stomp Down Soul']. I thought we might be able to do something with him, but he left town before we could get anything started."

Huey Smith's biggest production hit turned out to be the funky "Hoochie Koochie Man" by the "blue-eyed soul brother" Skip Easterling. A soulful singer/pianist hailing from Slidell, Louisiana, Easterling had a long and productive local recording career. "I had first recorded Skip back in 1964 — I guess he was 14 at the time — on ALON. Of course Allen produced those things: We had 'Sugar Blocks' and 'Wishing Well.' They didn't exactly set the world on fire, but Skip had a lot of talent, and he was a great artist to work with. I tried to release a lot of records on him to try and get him going."

Easterling didn't really hit big until "Hoochie Coochie Man" in 1971, which was a phenomenal hit in New Orleans. Even when New Orleanian Jean Knight had the number one record in the national soul charts with "Mr. Big Stuff," it only made it to #2 in New Orleans, because Easterling's record stood in its way. Easterling also became a popular attraction at black soul clubs around the state after "Hoochie Koochie Man."

By the early 1970s, Banashak had reestablished himself in his business to the point where "my kids tried to convince me to buy a Rolls Royce. I was having enough hits around town to keep covering the cost of sessions and putting new records out. I got the distribution business built up again, I was handling Vee Jay, International, Audio Fidelity, Roulette, and a few budget lines. I was even having some success overseas with my stuff."

But by 1972, Banashak was getting disillusioned with the record business. After Huey Smith left music and became a Jehovah's Witness, there was a drastic drop in the quality of production. Banashak put his sessions in the hands of the likes of Tex Liuzza, Isaac Bolden, Kent Morgan and even himself when the situation arose.

Banashak himself had generally grown tired of the record business. "I had a spiritual rebirth and accepted God back into my life. I began to look around and ask myself just what was I doing. I used to go out to the race track and gamble and live it up. Sometimes I'd take a jock out — I thought it was good public relations. Finally one night at a session we were getting nothing done. The musicians were drinking and smoking weed. Finally I just said to myself, 'I don't need this. I have to get out of here.' I just couldn't tolerate being around that kind of environment if I was going to be sincere to my beliefs. I had to get out of the business. There was no two ways about it.

"I moved out of Camp Street in January of 1978. I remember taking all the sleeves off my records so I could sell them for scrap. I moved all of my records and most of my files across the street to Cosimo's Studio. But when the sheriff auctioned off all of Cosimo's equipment at the bankruptcy sale, they just put most of my stuff out on the sidewalk to be picked up by the garbage men."

Banashak sought solace in the scriptures and he survived by doing odd jobs like plumbing and small house renovations, with no immediate interest about getting back into the record business. That was until 1980, when Banashak was approached by Cajun record man Floyd Soileau. Soileau had established a record pressing plant in Ville Platte, Louisiana, and convinced Banashak to reissue many of the masters that were piled inside Banashak's house.

Today Banashak, still a devout reborn Christian, has over a dozen albums in his "Bandy" catalog, collecting some of the finest examples of New Orleans R&B, with many more planned for the future.

"Floyd is really the one that's responsible for getting me back into the record business. I really had no interest in it at all at first. I'm starting to get the bug back, but not to the extent of recording anything new. I still work during the day and try to keep up with records at night. I'd like to get to the stage where I could maybe get a mini-computer and make a living just by putting out albums, but that won't be for awhile. I've realized that if I don't put these things out again somebody else is going to pirate them, and they already have.

"I'm looking at putting out records as leaving a legacy, something to show my grandchildren even when I'm gone. But I think that I put a lot of good music out, and I think everybody should get a chance to hear it again."

MARSHALL SEHORN
The Mind Behind The Music

New Orleans' longest and most successful musical partnership is that between Allen Toussaint and Marshall Sehorn. Besides a long string of hit records, the duo has built a modern studio, created a successful publishing firm, run a number of independent labels, and, most importantly, focused worldwide attention on the New Orleans music community.

While the reserved Toussaint has taken care of the musical side of the partnership, the vociferous Sehorn manages the business affairs at Sansu's Clematis Street offices. As Sehorn explains in his thick Carolina accent, "It don't matter how good ya' sound, it don't mean a thang if ye ain't got no money behind ya!"

A hard man to tie down, Sehorn is constantly attending to music business. If he's not haggling over the phone to try and close a deal, he's flying off someplace to promote the latest Sansu recording session.

A seasoned veteran of the music business, Sehorn's involvement in rhythm and blues goes back over twenty-five years. "I'd be lyin' if I said I grew up on black music," begins Sehorn. "I cut my teeth on rockabilly, which is really a bunch of country boys tryin' to sound black. We used to ride around all night listening to John R and Hossman, over WLAC; they were always playin' blues."

Like most other teenagers interested in music, Sehorn joined a high school band. Hailing from Concord, North Carolina, the group stayed busy during the summer playing the Carolina beach circuit. It was the summer after his last year of college that Sehorn decided he'd try to get into the business aspect of the music.

In fact, he recalls the exact instant. "It was the day after Labor Day 1957. I was sittin' on the back porch of a house in Myrtle Beach with some guys in the band. The day after Labor Day Myrtle Beach is deserted, and we were tryin' to figure out what to do. One of the guys in the band said to me, 'Why don't you go back to

Concord and be a teacher? You can't sing, and you sure can't play guitar worth a damn.' So the band split up and everybody went home but me."

With those words of encouragement, Sehorn promptly took a job with a construction crew in Myrtle Beach. After a month though, Sehorn took his savings and left for New York's "Tin Pan Alley" to look for work. "I knocked on doors, but I didn't have any luck. I wasn't so much looking for a job in the music business as I was looking for someone to tell me what the hell to do."

Sehorn's initial trip to the Big Apple proved to be fruitless. He returned to the Carolinas, only to save enough money to try again. In the spring of 1958 he got his first break. When he returned to New York, he managed to get MGM's Morty Craft interested in an Indian singer from South Carolina named Tommy Rowe (not the artist of "Dizzy" fame).

"Morty got me a room in a hotel and gave me some advice about the music business. He told me to go back to North Carolina and hit on some people locally for a job. I tried, but I couldn't even get to first base back home."

Sehorn couldn't get his wheels turning until he befriended Bobby Robinson, owner of Fire and Fury Records, at a record convention in Miami. "I presented myself as a disc jockey. I told everybody I met that I was working on some acts, as well as being a dee-jay too. So Bobby said if I ever got to New York to look him up. Little did he know I'd be up there in a week.

"I told Bobby I needed a job, and I knew I could do it. So we sat down and made an arrangement. I supplied my own car, I made $50 a week and got $50 expense money. In return I'd be his promo-promotion man in the South.

"You see, this was 1958; there was no such thing as black record salesmen, or promotion men. Whether people want to admit it or not, it took a lot of balls for a white man to work for an all black record company and travel the south saying 'Hey, I work for Fire and Fury Records'."

Besides promoting Fire and Fury, Sehorn also kept his eye out for talent, as the tiny independent label was trying to stay one step ahead of the pack. His first find was Wilbert Harrison, who was to turn in one of the biggest records of all time.

"I got Wilbert out of Charlotte, North Carolina," recalls Sehorn. "He was singin' with a group called the Calypso Five at The Seltzer Club. When he did this song 'Kansas City,' the whole place started jumpin'. I got on the phone right away to Bobby. I had never heard

"Big Hugh Baby" and Marshall Sehorn, 1959

of Wilbert, but Bobby had heard his records on DeLuxe and Savoy.

"I told Bobby, 'I swear I got a hit record.'

"Bobby told me to come in because he had a sales meeting, and to bring Wilbert in, and maybe we could do something with him.

"We drove in, and Bobby was having a gospel session out at Beltone Studio. We had about fifteen minutes of studio time left and went through 'Kansas City' about three or four times. Wilbert just sat down at the piano and ran through it, so the band could get the changes right.

"We (Fire) were broke at the time, and I had to send Wilbert home with my own money. We didn't even have any money to pay the phone bill, and I was sleeping on Bobby's couch over at his record shop on 125th Street. We went on the road with about ten demos to get the response from the disc jockeys. The record was such an overnight smash that before we could even get back, the record had already broken in Cleveland. Chess was in the studio with Rocky Olsen cutting a cover. And we hadn't even pressed it yet!

"When we got back, there must have been fifty telegrams sayin' send me 10,000, send me 5,000. All we had to do was take the telegrams to the processing plant and show them. We were really afraid of being covered more than we were."

Such was the impact of "Kansas City" that it inspired a host of cover versions. Little Richard (Specialty), Rocky Olsen (Chess), and Hank Ballard (King) all made the Hot 100 with the same song in in 1959. Wilbert's version won out though, rising to #1 on the R&B and pop charts, partly due to Dick Clark's airing it on American Bandstand.

Things weren't particularly rosy, even for a company with a four million seller on its hands. Savoy Records produced an exclusive contract on Harrison blocking a follow-up release. Leiber and Stoller also claimed they owned the song. Sehorn claims the whole mess could have been avoided if they had put a publisher on the song on its initial release, and offered a token payment to Savoy in the beginning. (Savoy was paid $60,000 in the resulting settlement.) Sehorn estimates that to date "Kansas City" has sold in the neighborhood of ten million records. Not a bad start for a Carolina country boy.

After "Kansas City," Sehorn and Robinson went on an incredible tear, knocking out hits like Buster Brown's "Fanny Mae," "Mojo Hand," by Lightnin' Hopkins; "Every Beat Of My Heart," by Gladys Knight; "I Need Your Lovin'," by Don Gardner; "There's Something On Your Mind," by Bobby Marchan; and "Soul Twist" by King Curtis, to name but a few.

During 1960, Sehorn visited New Orleans and was introduced to Allen Toussaint. "The first time I came down here was when we cut 'Something On Your Mind,' on Bobby Marchan. I came back to cut 'The Booty Green,' and I got Allen to play on the session. Then in 1961 I got him to work on Lee Dorsey's 'Ya-Ya.'

"Allen was under contract to Minit, and Joe Banashak wouldn't let him work the session. Allen rehearsed Lee, and got it down on tape. Then Harold Batiste wrote the arrangement from it. Next thing, we drilled Marcel Richardson all night, so he could sound just like Allen.

"After that I kept coming down here on business and to cut Lee. That's when I really started gettin' close to Allen," says Sehorn.

By early 1963, Robinson's labels were in financial difficulty. One of Robinson's silent partners, Fats Lewis, pulled out of the operation just as a major deal with ABC was about to consummate. Consequently, Fire and Fury folded, and Sehorn and Robinson went their separate ways.

Sehorn still credits Robinson with showing him the ropes of the record business. "I really respect Bobby Robinson; he has the best set of ears in the business. He can recognize a hit in the rough and develop it. That's the greatest talent in the record business."

Sadly, little of the Fire/Fury catalog is available and is likely to remain so. Most of the unreleased material has just disappeared. "Gone forever," shrugs Sehorn. The remaining catalog is the subject of a legal battle between teacher and pupil. "We don't really fight," smiles Sehorn, "we just argue."

Once he was on his own, Marshall decided to try his luck with his own company, naturally called Sehorn Records, in association with ex-Vee Jay rep Ewart Abner. Sehorn Records had a mild hit with Wilbert Harrison's "Near To You" when Abner talked him into consolidating with Constellation/Dart Records for his next Lee Dorsey release.

In the meantine, Abner changed course in mid-stream by deciding to go back to Vee Jay. Likewise Sehorn split, forming a partnership with Jake Freedman of Southland Record Distribution of Atlanta.

Sehorn's next move was to head for New Orleans and run Lee Dorsey and Toussaint into the studio and see what he could come up with. "I came down and cut 'Ride Your Pony,' 'Work, Work, Work,' 'The Kitty Cat Song,' and 'Shortnin' Bread,' on Lee."

Just as Sehorn was arranging for the release of the Dorsey sides, Freedman's wife called with the bad news her husband was ill. He died soon after, so Sehorn had to hit the streets with the Dorsey sides.

He managed to interest Amy/Bell Records, who released "Ride Your Pony," which rode its way to #28 nationally during its nine-week stay in the charts. Sehorn took over Dorsey's management and was approached by the Apollo Theatre (ironically located next to the old Fire and Fury headquarters) about booking Lee. Sehorn and Dorsey brought Toussaint to lead the band, and while they were in New York, the partnership between Sehorn and Toussaint was struck.

"Allen and I went to dinner and talked about starting some sort of deal. Allen had some offers from Motown and the West Coast, but he told me his convictions were in New Orleans, and that's where he wanted to stay."

Consequently Sehorn moved to New Orleans where the newly-formed Sansu Enterprises started the Tou-Sea, Deesu and Sansu labels, recording most of the available R&B talent in town. The duo set up offices on St. Philip Street, utilizing Cosimo's newly relocated

Jazz City Studio. They continued to have national success with Lee Dorsey, which they still leased to Amy. Releases on their own labels scored well enough around New Orleans, but other than Betty Harris' "Near To You," they couldn't crack the national charts.

Nevertheless, it is unlikely that such New Orleans singers as Ernie K-Doe, Eldridge Holmes, Willie West, Diamond Joe and Curley Moore would have recorded in the late Sixties and early Seventies without Sehorn's aid.

The biggest find that sehorn and Toussaint made was the Meters, one of New Orleans premier instrumental funk groups. "Allen saw them playin' in a club in the Quarter. He knew Art real good, and we called them in to do some work as a rhythm section. Then we thought we'd try and cut a few instrumental sides on them. We did 'Cissy Strut,' and 'Sophisticated Sissy,' and I took them up to New York to see if I could get somebody interested. Well, at first nobody was, and I was real frustrated because that had never happened to me before.

"I couldn't get Amy/Bell interested in it because they were p.o.'d at me for not signing an exclusive contract with them. I mean I had practically given up. Finally, I took the tapes to Tommy Sands at Josie Records. I practically had to give 'em away, 'cause I needed the money and didn't want to go home empty handed. Finally I leased it to him for $500 and a small royalty."

The Meters surprised everyone making the Hot 100 with their first four singles in 1969. Their ear-catching bouncy rhythms helped to refocus national, and later international, attention on the New Orleans' sound, and the two men behind it, Allen Toussaint and Marshall Sehorn.

With a slightly altered style, the Meters remained one of the few bright spots on the New Orleans musical horizon throughout the Seventies. After switching to Warner Brothers, the group released half-a-dozen albums. Their raucous union with George Landry—Big Chief Jolly—resulted in the highly acclaimed *Wild Tchoupitoulas* album. The Meters' funky, second line backing was the perfect springboard for the traditional street chants of the Mardi Gras Indians. The album provided one of the decades' musical high points for New Orleans.

By 1973, Sehorn and Toussaint had organized enough investors to open the ultra-modern Sea-Saint Recording Studio. It didn't take long for the Clematis Street studio to become one of the country's trendier locations, largely due to Toussaint's lofty reputation as a producer and writer. While Toussaint garnered public acclaim,

Sehorn stayed busy behind the scenes, cementing a deal with Warner Brothers, who agreed to utilize the studio for a number of their artists and to release material recorded and produced by Toussaint. The studio hosted sessions as varied as Paul McCartney's Wings and Albert King. Local sessions still took place, but Sea-Saint's emphasis was on luring out-of-town businesses who would buy large blocks of time from the studio, a very profitable situation for a recording studio.

Sehorn is aware of recent criticism accusing him and Toussaint of abandoning the local artists, instead, trying only to attain maximum profits. "There's a lot of prejudice in this town about me and Allen," says Sehorn matter-of-factly. "A lot of it is jealousy, but frankly, the salt and pepper situation has had a lot to do with it. Sure it's also helped us. When it was popular to be black, Allen took the shit for me, and vice versa. Anytime somebody gets ahead, there's gonna be somebody trying to bring them down.

"My note on this place is $20,000 a month, even if I don't cut one session. To make something happen, you've got to make some money, and in our case that means going out and hustling.

"I read where the Meters said I beat them out of thousands of dollars. How I built my house on the lake, and Allen bought a Rolls Royce with money we owe them. Shee-it! When the Meters left me they owed me $120,000. Warner Brothers gave them money for them to go out on the road and for studio time. But that money came out of my royalties.

"I had one of them come in here with a gun wanting money one day. These records that we lease overseas—these guys think they sell millions. They only sell between five and ten thousand. Hell that's not big money."

The incentive that inspired a young Sehorn to peddle records out of the back seat of his car still possesses him today. Never one to stand too long on past accomplishments, of late Sehorn has been working feverishly on restructuring Sansu Enterprises. Among his latest projects is the building of a record pressing and tape duplicating plant in Slidell. He also hopes to present a mid-line reissue label called Jefferson Jazz. Even though the Warner Brothers deal was never renegotiated, he's still constantly busy, buying, selling and leasing masters.

Other plans at Sea-Saint include some video projects and lots of sessions. But with a different emphasis. "Every record company that depends on hit records today is running in the red," says Sehorn. "There's too much money involved in trying for a hit. The law of averages is only one chance in fifty you'll ever hear any noise. We're still gonna make records, but we're not gonna go overboard on production."

Even though the future looks bright for Sansu, Sehorn doesn't exactly feel the same way about music in New Orleans. "We're really losing the traditional jazz and rhythm and blues sound. I'll be surprised if it's still around in 1990," says Sehorn bluntly.

"If you look at blues and Dixieland jazz today, we're losing our best players, and there's nobody there to take their place. The young kids just aren't there playing it any more. There's nobody out there creating the impact of a Professor Longhair or an Allen Toussaint. Allen said it best when he said, "the young black kids look down on rhythm and blues today. They think it's old, and they just don't want to listen to it any more. I just hope that doesn't happen."

Part Four:

NEW ORLEANS BLUES

*"Going down to New Orleans,
Going to go down on Rampart Street;
'Till I find my pretty baby,
I'm gonna ask ever soul I meet.*

(Charles Brown, Venice Music-BMI)

New Orleans is commonly referred to as "The Jazz City"—mostly by tourists and out-of-town visitors. Its place in jazz history of course is reinforced by its brass bands, its barrelhouse pianists and because of the fabled Storyville district—often credited as being the actual birthplace of jazz.

Although jazz is strongly rooted in the blues tradition, curiously there has been little blues recording activity in New Orleans. Of the recordings made by the major companies during the 1920s and 1930s, the majority were of dixieland groups and gospel choirs and quartets. Richard "Rabbit" Brown is the only "country" blues artist of any merit that recorded and lived in the city. Other New Orleans blues artists of major importance, like "Champion" Jack Dupree and Lonnie Johnson, left the city early in their careers to record in Chicago, New York, Cincinnati and even Europe.

Even so the blues has always had a special place in New Orleans. Jelly Roll Morton once commented: "Back in 1901 and 1902, we had a lot of great blues players that didn't know nothing but the blues . . . They'd sit on a piano stool and beat out some of the damnedest blues you ever heard in your life. There's always been the blues in New Orleans."

But even though New Orleans has often been the subject of blues recordings, it never developed the identifiable blues tradition that Chicago, Memphis, and even nearby Baton Rouge were to enjoy. Not surprisingly, all of these blues centers had powerful home-based record companies that took advantage of their city's blues activity, thereby documenting and helping to develop an identifiable blues style.

Times have always been tough in black New Orleans, but life slowly began to improve after World War II. Nightclubs and taverns that featured live blues began to open, and the juke box became extremely popular. In this environment the blues thrives. Blues piano players like Sullivan Rock, Tuts Washington, Drive 'Em Down, Robert Bertrand and Kid Stormy Weather ruled the rough and tumble joints of Rampart Street, a veritable blues breeding ground.

When the independents swooped down on New Orleans they picked and chose whatever blues talent was available. But while the New Orleans rhythm and blues tradition rapidly took a direction, the real down home blues never developed an identifiable style. Instead, blues became a mosaic of various styles. Individuality has always been the trademark of bluesmen in New Orleans.

BILL WEBB
"They Call Me Boogie Bill"

The term "country blues" quite often brings to mind pictures of endless cotton fields, and ancient black men flailing at old beat-up guitars in front of weather-beaten shacks. Many people would be surprised to know that one of the finest exponents of this rapidly fading art form lives right in New Orleans. He's relatively young, in good health, and he still sounds phenomenal. His name is "Boogie" Bill Webb.

Bill Webb—"they calls me Boogie Bill"—lives in a small house next to the Industrial Canal, deep in the Ninth Ward. Now 58, Boogie Bill is a warm, intelligent man who is quick to make one feel welcome. Immediately after a visitor is seated in his living room, Boogie Bill will plug his vintage Fender Telecaster into one of the amplifiers that crowds his house, and launch into an impromptu blues history course. Tommy Johnson, John Lee Hooker, Muddy Waters and even Z.Z. Hill—Boogie Bill can play them all while interjecting his own songs, too.

It was in fact the great country blues artist Tommy Johnson who spurred Boogie Bill into taking up the guitar. Johnson was a most influential singer/guitarist from Crystal Springs, Mississippi, whose style was widely copied. Between 1928 and 1930, Johnson recorded eleven magnificent sides, including the popular "Big Road Blues." "If it hadn't been for the 'Big Road Blues,' I wouldn't be playin' this here mess today," Boogie Bill says matter-of-factly, pausing between songs.

"See, my momma used to give fish suppers, and she'd send for him to come on down to play here in New Orleans. They was kids together back in Jackson. Fact I was born in Jackson, but raised up here. He never did teach me nothin' but when I was a kid I would sit and listen to him play. The peoples always did like Tommy Johnson's playin'. My momma used to make as much as $35 some nights, which was a heap of money in those days.

"I didn't have no guitar then, cause I was too young. So when I was about eight years old, my cousin made me a guitar out of a cigar box. It had two strings on it, made out of screen wire. For the bass string you wrapped two pieces of wire together. I kind of got a sound out of it though," he winks.

"Then I went to six strings, when my momma got me a real guitar. But I still couldn't play it until this fellow Roosvelt Holts (a blues singer/guitarist from Bogalusa, Louisiana) come to stay at my Momma's house. She used to get him to play at her suppers too, but he got in some kind of trouble back home, and he stayed with us a couple of weeks. Roosvelt straightened me out. He told me, ' You ain't never gonna play nuthin', 'cause you got the guitar tuned wrong.' He showed me how to tune up the guitar right."

After learning the rudiments of the instrument from Holts, Boogie Bill's appetite for the guitar became insatiable, as he began learning from records and from watching other guitar players. As he grew older his time was divided between Jackson and New Orleans. Consequently his influences were indeed diverse as Boogie Bill explains: "I knowed a lot of musicians in Jackson. Fact, one of my cousins was the great piano player Otis Spann, that played with Muddy Waters. I knew Coot Davis—he used to play with Little Brother Montgomery. He played on the radio, that must have been around 1939.

"Johnny Jones, too, he was a real good piano player. He played in Chicago with Jimmy Reed, Howlin' Wolf and Elmo James. Son and Stack Hill (string musicians from Jackson) too, they was terrific."

His New Orleans influences were just as varied: "I learned the 'Dooleyville Blues' from Bubba Brown who played with Cary Lee Simmons. He was a terrific guitar player! He showed me this boxcar chord (Bill plays a complicated walking pattern.) Yeah, that's what he called it."

While in Jackson during the late Forties, Boogie Bill won a talent contest, and was chosen to play in a motion picture, *The Jackson Jive*. "It weren't no full-length picture," points out Boogie Bill. "It was just thirty minutes. They had this fellow 'Bear Trap' in it. He was the most famous shoe-shiner in Jackson, he was always singin' 'Chattanooga Shoe Shine Boy,' down on Farish Street. They showed it in the picture shows before the feature."

Back in New Orleans in 1952, Boogie Bill befriended his old childhood pal Fats Domino, and Harrison Verret, Fat's brother-in-law and piano instructor, who also played guitar in Domino's first band. "I used to sit in for a couple of numbers with Fats, but I never was none of his guitar player," clarifies Boogie Bill.

"Now Harrison, he taught me a lot, he could play guitar, banjo, mandolin, piano and read music." Verret introduced Boogie Bill to

"Boogie" Bill Webb on Bourbon Street

Imperial Records' Dave Bartholomew, resulting in Boogie Bill's only commercial release. "Dave Bartholomew's the one that got me on Imperial," says Boogie Bill. "Fats didn't do too much for the rest of us. I guess he wanted to make all that money himself," he laughs.

In 1953, Boogie Bill Webb recorded four sides for Imperial Records. Two sides were released, "Bad Dog" and "I Ain't For It." Both sides were excellent country blues, with Boogie Bill being supported by only bass and drums—likely Frank Fields and Earl Palmer. "Bad Dog" was an exemplary country boogie, while the slower "I Ain't For It" was a superior rework of the Tampa Red standard.

"They didn't do too hot," says Boogie Bill softly. "In fact I never did see the record." Unfortunately for Boogie Bill, the demand for true downhome country blues was on the wane, as the suave city blues by the likes of Louis Jordan, Amos Milburn, and Fats Domino had replaced it.

After the ill-fated Imperial session Boogie Bill left New Orleans, spending five years in Chicago and Galensburg, Illinois, toiling with a series of laboring jobs. He didn't abandon the guitar though, as he played solo at a number of house parties, and sat in with groups whenever he could. "Chuck Berry, Jimmy Reed, John Lee Hooker and the great Muddy Waters—I played with all of them," says Boogie Bill proudly. "I was with all them real good guitar players."

Boogie Bill left Chicago around 1959, returning to New Orleans where he began working as a longshoreman. He continued to play around his house only occasionally venturing into a tavern or a neighborhood party to perform. "I never really was a professional musician," he is quick to point out. "There just ain't enough money in it, unless you're a genius."

Boogie Bill continued to write new songs and play them in his home, becoming a legend in his neighborhood, and later Europe, of all places! Boogie Bill explains the circumstances: "I met this fellow (Mississippi State folklorist) David Evans around 1968. It turned out he knew more about me and the blues than I did. He made a record on me here at the house, but I never did see it. (Boogie Bill is referring to *Roosvelt Holts and Friends*, Arhoolie 1057, where he performs on two tracks).

Evans also published a series of interviews in the British magazine *Blues Unlimited*. Not long after, European blues enthusiasts began making pilgrimages to Boogie Bill's doorstep. "Yeah they been in touch with me about fifteen years now. They been tryin' to get me to come over there. Fact, I was suppose to have gone years ago, but I never did take too much interest in it. I don't know why, I just figured I didn't know enough. They told me though if I ever had a notion to go just call 'em."

Finally in November 1982, Boogie Bill made his first European appearance at the Dutch Utreck Festival. Upon returning he was ecstatic. "They liked it! They really like those blues. They just kept clappin' their hands and makin' me come back out to play. I really enjoyed that!"

Despite his notoriety among European blues enthusiasts, Boogie Bill remains virtually unknown in New Orleans. Even though he is perhaps one of the greatest living exponents of country blues, he only recently began appearing at the New Orleans Jazz and Heritage Festival but never at a club in the city.

"Well, I guess it's my fault, really," he sighs, putting down his Telecaster. "I could have gone down to tell 'em, but I just never did.

"I guess it's like this boy Roy Byrd (Professor Longhair). He wasn't hittin' on nothin' until he went over the river (overseas). Then he started gettin' famous. None of his records ever got out of New Orleans. I guess that's the way it goes. I sure hope I don't have to wait 'til I'm a hundred."

Today Boogie Bill is retired, content to fish, repair an occasional lawnmower, and of course play his ever-present guitar. It's easy to sense from his attitude that he'd like nothing better than to get a second chance to prove his talent. On Sundays, he usually hosts a small get-together of harmonica and guitar players. Boogie Bill is much sought after by other guitar players, who even call him to tune their guitars over the phone! On Sundays the music lasts long into the evening, with the blues flowing all along the Industrial Canal. But as Boogie Bill's neighbor, Mr. G. explains: "It don't matter how loud, or how late they play, 'cause it sounds so good, nobody ever calls the police."

GUITAR SLIM
The Things That He Used To Do

"Now they call me Guitar Slim, baby,
And I'm come to play in your town;
Now if you don't like my music, baby,
I will not hang around!

I like my pocket full of money, baby,
And my whiskey, gin and wine;
I like to eat a country dinner, baby,
And I like to get my lovin' all the time.

Now they call me Guitar Slim, baby,
And I'm come to play in your town.
Now if I can't play my guitar, baby,
I'm still gonna jump and clown."

(© Venice Music — BMI)

Simply entitled "Guitar Slim," and recorded in 1955, the song conveys in the man's own words Guitar Slim's life and attitude. Earl King remembers seeing Guitar Slim at the peak of his all too short career:

"Gatemouth Brown, T-Bone Walker, Lowell Fulsom and Guitar Slim were all performing one night at the White Eagle in Opelousas, Louisiana. Slim was headlining because 'The Things I Used To Do' was a scorcher. They were all sitting in the dressing room and Guitar Slim walked up to 'em and said, 'Gentlemen, we got the greatest guitar players in the country assembled right here. But when I leave here tonight, ain't nobody gonna realize you even been here.' Well, they all laughed, but that's exactly what happened.

"Slim come out with his hair dyed blue, blue suit, blue pair of shoes. He had 350 feet of mike wire connected to his guitar, and a valet carrying him on his shoulders all through the crowd and out into the parking lot. Man, he was stopping cars driving down the highway. No one could outperform Slim. He was about the performanest man I've ever seen."

King's description coincides with that of mostly everyone else who saw Guitar Slim on stage or knew him personally. Though Slim has been dead for over two decades, his legend continues to grow. Even though his music has remained popular all these years, many details concerning his life are still shrouded in mystery, so much so that putting together a concise biography is like completing a complex jigsaw puzzle.

Guitar Slim was born Edward (Eddie) Jones, December 10, 1926, and is known to have had at least one sister. Even though Slim claimed in his Specialty biography that Greenwood, Mississippi was his birthplace, Hollandale, Mississippi has also been suggested. No matter, Slim was raised in the Greenwood area, a rural region of intense cotton production in the heart of the Mississippi Delta. Times were probably tough, and it's likely that Slim did his fair share in the fields, visiting Greenwood on weekends.

The first mention of Guitar Slim (he was six feet tall, 160 pounds, so he easily fit the colorful alias) in the *Louisiana Weekly* was during September, 1950. It stated: "New Orleans' newest gift to the show biz world is Guitar Slim, held over at the Dew Drop. The New Orleans blues sensation has made a terrific impact on blues fans in New Orleans. Acclaimed to be an exact carbon copy of Gatemouth Brown, the singing guitarist includes 'My Time Is Expensive,' 'Gatemouth Boogie,' and several other performances made popular by Brown."

The comparison between Guitar Slim and Gatemouth Brown is indeed apt; it is interesting to note that he would draw his greatest influence from the Texas guitar school, rather than the guitar players from his home state, Mississippi. "Gatemouth's 'Boogie Rambler' was Slim's theme," adds Earl King. "He listened to all of 'em and compiled bits of their style — Gatemouth, T-Bone, B.B. King. But he took a different approach, he had a lot of melodic overtones in his solos. He used to play a solo that had a marriage to the rest of the song, rather than just play something off the top of his head."

Earl also chafes when others suggest Slim was a poor instrumentalist and unable to even play without the aid of a capo, or as Slim referred to it, "a choker." "Slim tuned Standard, but he used that capo to get the effect of open strings. You can't do that without that choker. I've seen Slim play many a time without it. He just used it for effect."

Percy Stovall booked Slim during his early career. "I used to worry him sometimes and hide his choker. He'd be runnin' around

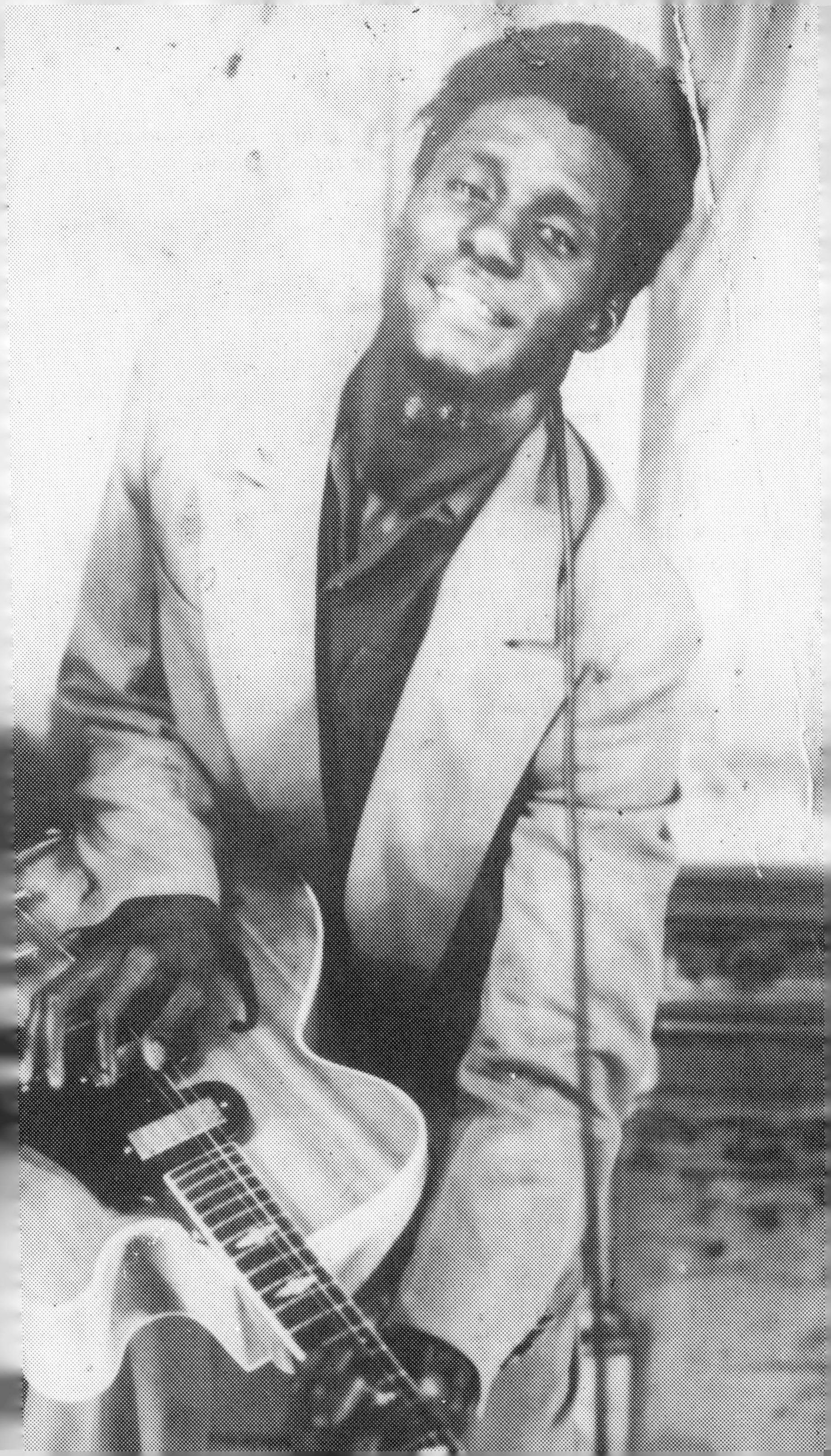

sayin' 'Stove, where's my choker at? I can't find my choker.' I'd say 'I ain't seen it, Slim,' and he'd be runnin' around tryin' to find it everywhere. Then just before he would go on, I'd pull it out of my pocket and hand it to him, and he'd say, 'Stove, I knew you had it all the time.' "

Stovall is the first to admit that Slim was his favorite artist, but also points out he had his share of headaches with him. "Man, he loved to drink," says Stovall, shaking his head. "If I didn't watch him all the time he'd miss his job. If he had a job over in Florida, I'd have to ration him. I'd make sure the valet gave him only a fifth of wine when he left New Orleans, another fifth in Biloxi, and one more by the time he got to Mobile. And don't nobody fool with Slim's wine or he'd be in trouble."

One of Stovall's favorite stories concerning his early days of booking Guitar Slim took place in Monroe, Louisiana. "Fats and Slim played a 'Battle of the Blues' at the Monroe Civic Auditorium. Man, the place was packed. Slim had told Fats before the show, 'Fats, I'm gonna run you offa that stage tonight.'

"So Slim went on first because Fats had hit records out. Slim just tore 'em up. The place was goin' wild. Slim walked off the stage with his guitar and went out the back door of the place and got in a car, still playing. Everybody wondered where Slim had went. When it came time for Fats to come on, Fats just told the people, 'Ain't gonna be no battle tonight. You just saw it.' So Fats just played his regular show."

By 1951, the record companies had been hearing about this wild guitar player in New Orleans. Imperial approached first, and Al Young produced four sides on Eddie Jones at the J&M Studio. The session was rather chaotic, originally producing "Bad Luck Is On Me," and "New Arrival," but the record sounded and sold poorly. Imperial wouldn't ask Slim back to the studio, but still issued the remainder of the session when Slim hit the big time, using his alias instead of Eddie Jones.

Slim's next record was a different story. Percy Stovall arranged a session with Jim Bullet in Nashville, producing the popular "Feelin' Sad," in 1952. David Lastie played sax on the tune and remembered the circumstances that surrounded the session: "We was working at the Kitty Cat Club in Nashville, and me, Huey, Little Eddie Lang, and Willie Nettles did the session with Slim. 'Feelin' Sad' was a good little record, it had a church sound to it. We worked pretty good off it."

When Slim came in off the road, he stayed upstairs at the Dew

Drop. "Slim liked to be where the action was," chuckles Earl. "In fact you knew Slim was back in town, 'cause early in the morning, around seven-eight o'clock, if he was tanked up, you'd hear them amps and P.A. going off. People'd be calling the police, 'cause you could hear Slim three blocks away! And here's Slim up in his room with his shorts on, goin' through his stage routine.

"And Slim's room was something else, man," laughs Earl. "If you went up there, there'd always be about seven or eight different women up there. He'd have his songs written with eyebrow pencil on pieces of paper tacked to the wall."

Earl also recalls that Slim bought the first Les Paul guitar in New Orleans. "Slim was playing one of those big hollow boxes like T-Bone had. But when the solid boxes came out he got one right away. Slim said the hollow boxes were too big, and they didn't give him enough room on the stage. He couldn't control the feedback that was comin' out of 'em. So he dealt with the Les Paul."

By 1953, Guitar Slim was one of the biggest draws on the Southern R&B club circuit. The responsibilities of managing and booking reverted to Slim's landlord, Frank Pania, who owned the Dew Drop, while Percy Stovall concentrated on building up a larger roster of performers. Pania also took it upon himself to find Slim a new band. He hired the Lloyd Lambert band from Hosea Hill's Sugar Bowl in Thibodaux, Louisiana. Hosea was a friend and business associate of Pania, and paired Slim with the band for a series of road dates. Lloyd Lambert claims that Pania was responsible for introducing Johnny Vincent, then a Specialty A&R man, to Slim. Vincent was impressed enough to convince his boss, Art Rupe, to sign Slim to a recording contract. Vincent recalls that "Slim was supposed to sign with Atlantic, but this was one artist I just had to get. He was fantastic. Slim wouldn't let anyone outperform him. I wouldn't let him out of my sight until he signed with Specialty."

On October 16, 1953, Slim entered the J&M Studio to record what was to be the biggest record of his career, "The Things I Used To Do." Backing Slim on the session were Gus Fontenette, Charles Burbank and Joe Tillman on saxes, Oscar Moore on drums, Lloyd Lambert on bass and Frank Mitchell on trumpet. Vincent claims he had to bail Ray Charles out of jail to arrange and play piano to complete the personnel.

When Vincent says, "Slim was hard to record," he has lots of support. Tales of Slim's recording sessions are many. Vincent claims that it took "all night" to record "The Things I Used To Do." Engineer Cosimo Matassa says "all day," and Lloyd

Lambert reports it took "two days." Nonetheless, the musicians were obviously gratified when it was over, because Ray Charles is clearly audible yelling "Yeah!" in relief in the last bars of the song.

Cosimo Matassa recalls, "We had a really good take of the song going. Slim played a particularly hot solo and just stopped. He turned around and said to the band, 'Gentlemen, did you hear that?' It just really moved him."

According to Earl King, the idea for the tune came to Slim in a dream. Slim related to King that in the dream he was confronted by a devil and an angel, both of whom held the lyrics to a song. Naturally, Slim chose the devil's song and it turned out to be "The Things I Used To Do."

Vincent sent the tapes of the session out to Rupe, who was less than impressed with the result. According to Vincent, "He told me it was the worst piece of shit he'd ever heard. He said, 'I'm gonna put it out, but if it don't sell, you start looking for a job.'"

The public disagreed with Rupe, to say the least. Immediately after its release, both *Billboard* and *Cashbox* made it the pick of the week. *Cashbox* commented, "a slow Southern blues rhythmically chanted by the blues shouter ... great vocal with the proper blues styling and this side is headed for sales ... top notch."

"The Things I Used To Do" stormed the charts. It topped the R&B charts for six solid weeks, and ended up the biggest selling R&B record of 1954. The record caught the imagination of the public: the lyrics, sung in Slim's impassioned gospel-like style, struck a chord in everybody's mind. For many, the real appeal of "The Things I Used To Do" was the novel guitar approach that Slim took, as Earl King explains: "Slim was gettin' a fuzz tone distortion way before anyone else. You didn't hear it again until people like Jimi Hendrix come along.

"Believe it or not, Slim never used an amplifier. He always used a P.A. set, never an amplifier. He was an overtone fanatic, and he had these tiny iron cone speakers and the sound would run through them speakers and I guess any vibration would create that sound, because Slim always played at peak volume. That's why it was hard to record him, because of the volume he was accustomed to playing — 'cause let's face it, if Slim was playing you could hear him a mile away."

Lloyd Lambert agreed that Slim played as loud as he could. "He had this tinny sound," says Lambert, "that he'd get by turning all the bass controls on his guitar and amplifier as low as they would go, and turn up his treble controls as high as they'd go."

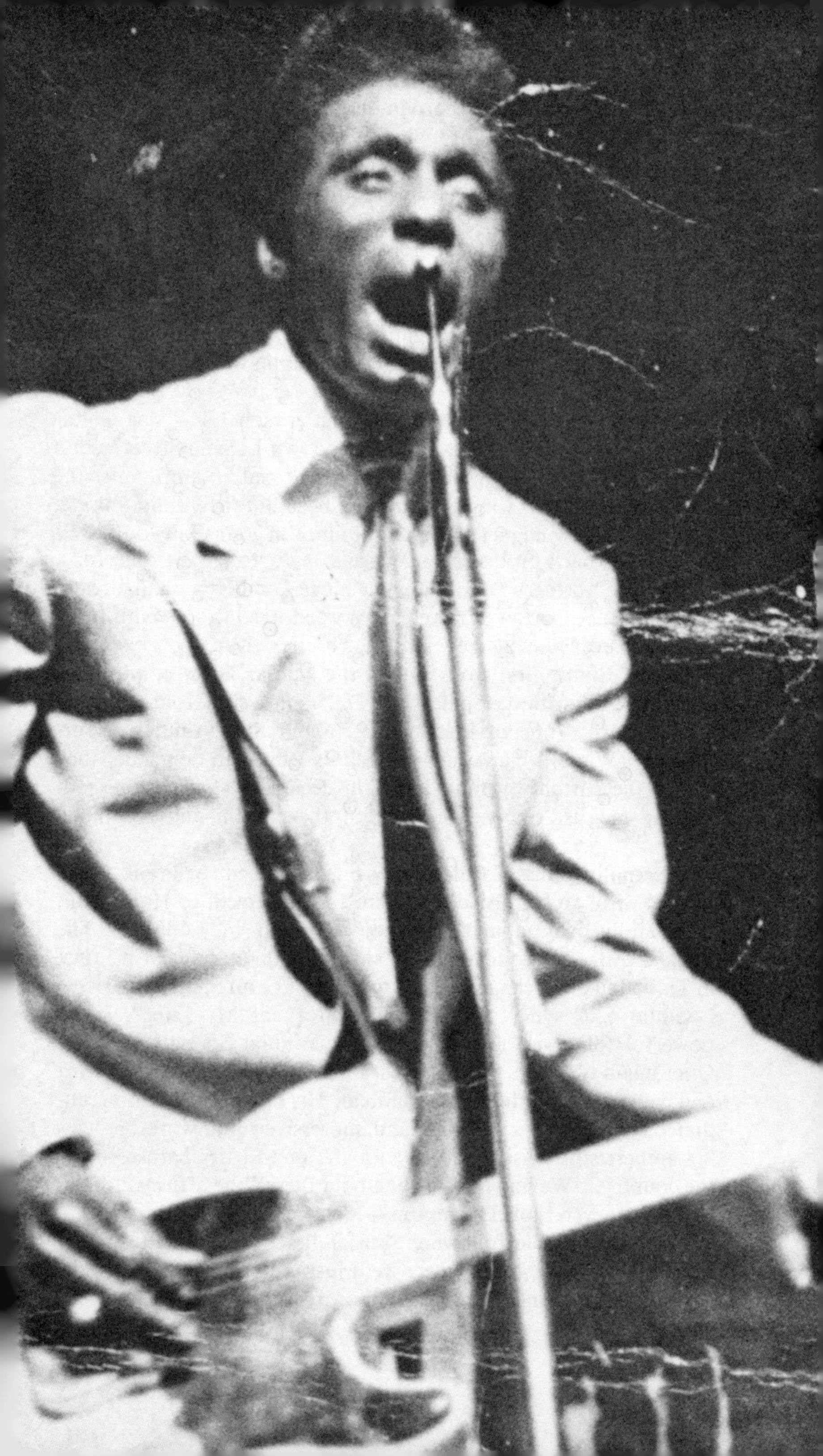

With the number one record in the country, Frank Pania booked a full itinerary for Slim through the South, and bought him a brand new Olds Rocket 88. Slim promptly got drunk one night and ran into a parked bulldozer, wrecking the car and ending up in the hospital. "Slim weren't too good a driver," laughs Lambert. "He didn't hurt himself too bad, the doctor just told him to take it easy for a month."

Pania decided to send Earl King out to impersonate Slim on a number of dates, and apparently got away with it. Even though King went along with the charade, he admits he was "scared to death."

"When I got back to town, the first person I saw was Guitar Slim," laughs Earl. "He was walking down LaSalle Street with a hospital gown on, a guitar under one arm and an amp under the other, yellin', 'Earl King, I heard you been out there imitatin' me. If you wreck my name I'm gonna sue and I'm gonna kill you!'"

Slim was back on his feet soon, and ready to hit the road for a tour of the northern theatre circuit. Since Lambert's band already had Lawrence Cotton on piano, Slim was forced to split with Huey Smith, an event which likely saddened both of them.

One of Slim's first stops was at the Apollo Theatre, where he shared the bill with the Spiders. Earl recounts a story told to him by Chuck Carbo (one of the Spiders), about Slim's initial performance: "When it came time for Slim's cameo to conclude, they closed the curtain on him, but Slim decided he wasn't finished. Instead he just stepped in front of the curtain and continued playing!"

Eventually Slim's popularity became too much for Frank Pania to deal with, so he turned over Slim's management to Hosea Hill, who ran his own popular nightspot in Thibodaux, Louisiana, The Sugar Bowl. Consequently, Slim spent a good amount of his time in Thibodaux, which nestles next to Bayou Lafourche.

Guitar Slim's next release, "The Story of My Life," was a powerful follow-up and came from his initial Specialty session. Once again *Cashbox* spotlighted it by giving it their weekly award and calling it "another powerful item. His mournful tale is accentuated by the chanter's stylings and impressive guitar work."

Lambert still relishes the days of the mid-Fifties barnstorming the country. "We had *the* best band out there," he affirms. "Fats, B.B. King, even Lionel Hampton — we could cut 'em all.

"We had trouble following Slim at first 'cause Slim'd always jump meter, but it got to where we'd just jump right with him and it would sound fine. Slim was a showman and a musician. He'd have purple suits, orange suits, green suits, with shoes and hair to match. He'd make motions and faces that would drive people berserk. You couldn't hardly get into the place when he was playing."

Earl King agreed: "You could play Slim at the Dew Drop and get a mob of people, and the next night play him in Shrewsbury [in adjacent Jefferson Parish] and get the same mob. Even the people who knew him to say 'Hi' to in the streets would think nothing of driving 100 miles to go see him that same night."

When the first Electric Fender basses came on the market, Slim wanted one for his band and talked Lambert into buying one. Although Lambert became one of the first electric bass players, Earl King says that it took a lot of convincing on Slim's part to prod him into buying the new bass.

"When he saw that B.B. King's band had one that was it. Slim wanted everything electric. If Slim would have had all the gadgetry that's out today it would be ridiculous. When the Cadillacs came out with all the gadgetry he was like a little kid. He just marvelled over that — seats moving, water shooting."

Slim stayed so busy that Specialty had to arrange to record while the group was touring. Lambert recalled that the second Specialty session took place at Chess Studios in Chicago, and produced Slim's next big seller, "Sufferin' Mind," in 1955, with Art Rupe flying in from L.A. to produce.

Rupe, however, took it upon himself to bury Slim's guitar way down in the mix, and even added a Hammond organ. The session lost a little of the New Orleans feel, but it was identifiable Slim just the same. His final Specialty session took place in early 1956, and was recorded out in Los Angeles, before he switched to the Atlantic/Atco label.

Even though Slim's record sales began dipping, he was still a top attraction. He and the band criss-crossed the country, playing to overflow houses. When he came in off the road he would spend the days in a lazy manner usually drinking with friends in the Dew Drop or in Thibodaux at the Sugar Bowl.

Atlantic recorded Slim both in New York and at Cosimo's, according to Lambert. There was little departure from the last Specialty sessions (although voices were occasionally added and the horn section beefed up) largely due to the strength of Lloyd Lambert's tight band. Atlantic must have been somewhat disappointed though in their attempts with Slim. They had visions of crossing his records into the teenage market on the same scale as Chess had done with Chuck Berry, but with little success. As it would turn out, his last Atco session in 1958 would produce the prophetically titled, "When There's No Way Out" and "If I Had

Frank Painia, 1950

My Life To Live Over."

Despite doctors' warnings about his heavy drinking, by 1958, Slim was really sick and getting weaker, so much so that he was unable to travel and was forced to stay in Thibodaux. "I wouldn't say he was a pretty good drinker," says Lambert. "He was the best! Slim just wouldn't take care of himself. He lived fast, different women every night. I'd try and tell him to eat good and get his rest, but he'd say, 'Lloyd, I live three days to y'all's one. The world don't owe me a thing when I'm gone.' "

Earl King gives some insight into the last days of Guitar Slim: "Slim got ruptured (from riding the guitar on stage) and I think that's what caused him to drink more than he ever had. Man, when he came in off that last tour, he almost had to wear a truss.

"I went over to visit him in Thibodaux when he was sick and he had empty 100 proof bottles laying all over his room. The doctor told him to stay off that hard liquor, but what are you gonna tell a guy who drinks a pint of gin and chases it with a fifth of black port every day?"

Strangely enough, Slim had quit drinking the last months of his life, according to some. "Slim was getting ready to go on another tour," continues Earl. "Slim sat in the Dew Drop one night and he was talking very straight and serious. He told me, 'Earl, all this liquor I been drinkin', all the wrong things I been thinkin', you know my body's been slowly sinkin'.' "

"That's when I went over and asked Hosea Hill, 'Is there somethin' wrong with Slim?' and he said, 'No, he's fine, he just got out of the hospital, and he's not even drinkin'. Why do you ask that?' I said, 'Cause Slim talks too straight tonight, he's not funny. He's never under the weather about anything.' That was the last time I saw him."

In February 1959, the group embarked on a tour of dances and nightclubs in New York State. "We went up to Rochester," recalls Lloyd Lambert, "and Slim came up to me and said, 'Lloyd, I'm tired, I don't think I can make it no more. Y'all got a good band, you can get another singer.'

"I said, 'Come on, Slim, you can make it. You just been with a broad or something.'

"He said, 'No, Lloyd, my time is up.' So we played the dance and when it came time for Slim to come on, he could only do part of the first song and couldn't finish.

"So we drove to Newark to play the next night, and Slim played the gig but he collapsed right after. One of the valets ran and got a doctor, and the doctor looked at Slim and said, 'Man, check this man into a hospital, he's really sick.'

"We were gonna stay in New York 'cause that's where our next date was. So we drove up to the Cecil Hotel, and I sent the valet across to take Slim to the doctor, while I checked into the hotel. When I got to the desk, there was a telephone call waitin' for me from the valet. He said, 'Lloyd, Slim's dead.' I didn't believe it 'cause I'd just seen him not more than five minutes before. We got in the station wagon and drove 'round the corner to the doctor's. But sure enough Slim was layin' up on the table gone."

Word on Slim's death was slow getting back to New Orleans. The *Louisiana Weekly* was a full week late in its announcement. "Somebody knocked up on my door and said 'Slim's dead,' " says Earl. "I said, 'Man, that can't be true. People like Slim don't die. They're still here when I'm gone.' "

"It wasn't liquor that killed him," specified Lambert. "The doctor said it was bronchial pneumonia. Today they might could have saved him, but all that drinking and hard living brought his resistance down."

Slim's body was kept in New York by authorities to see if drugs were involved in his death. Hosea Hill eventually paid the fare to fly Slim's body back to Thibodaux for a massive funeral at the Mt. Zion Baptist Church. Guitar Slim now lies in an unmarked grave

Guitar Slim Goes Home

NEW YORK — Guitar Slim, one of the last of the down home blues singers and guitarist, passed away last week. Slim, who was born with the name Eddie Jones, died in New York. He was buried in Thibodeaux, La., his home. Slim's first recordings were for the Imperial label, but his first hit was on Specialty, a tune called "Things I Used to Do" in 1953. His biggest hit was "The Story of My Life" for the same label. Slim went with Atco Records in 1956. His biggest hit for the label was "Down Thru The Years." Other tunes waxed by Slim for Atco included "It Hurts to Love Someone," "I Won't Mind at All," and "When There's No Way Out."

with his Les Paul, next to his benefactor, Hosea Hill.

So ended the all-too-short lifespan of the 32-year-old Guitar Slim. He is survived by several common law wives, and a number of children, one of whom plays guitar in the small clubs around New Orleans and who keeps Slim's name alive. Hardly a year has passed since his death when someone doesn't rerecord one of his songs. Earl King's 1982 version of Slim's anthem, "It Hurts To Love Someone" only reinforces the timelessness of his work.

Almost everyone is adamant about what would have happened if Slim were alive today. "He'd have been on the scale of a B.B. King or a Ray Charles," says Earl King. Lloyd Lambert states simply, "No question about it. Guitar Slim would have been the biggest."

EARL KING
Still Letting The Good Times Roll

Nowadays, New Orleans recording artist/songwriter/producer and historian Earl King can be found most often seated comfortably at the counter of the Tastee Donut Shop on the corner of Prytania and Louisiana Avenue. Surrounded by honeydips, a bursting briefcast that serves as a portable office and a miniature Earl King museum, and a cast of unusual regulars that "hang by the shop," Earl has been known to drink as many as twenty cups of coffee and spend as many as eight hours a day "conducting business" inside the establishment. Any conversation there with Earl is interrupted by numerous phone calls, messages being relayed to him via Liz, the counter girl, or someone recounting their day's fortunes at the Fair Grounds.

Earl isn't there at Tastee's to kill time or lament about past successes; always in the company of a note pad and tape recorder, he is constantly jotting down song ideas, plotting arrangements for impending studio dates or lining up gigs. "I get a lot of ideas from watching people come and go," points ou Earl. "I'm not much of a homebody. If I'm not going in the studio or on a gig, you can usually find me sitting here trying to get some ideas together."

Recently turned 50, Earl King is a contemporary of Fats Domino, Allen Toussaint and Guitar Slim. While Fats has become New Orleans' most successful recording artist; Toussaint is presently acknowledged as the city's most innovative and progressive writer-producer; and Guitar Slim has long been cited as New Orleans' most dynamic showman and top-ranked bluesman; Earl King embodies the brilliance of all three men, achieving renown in all phases of the music business.

A stocky man, usually clad in one of his matching safari suits, Earl King speaks with great care, measuring his words, making sure he is clearly understood at all times. When conversing with him, his sincerity is immediately apparent. He avoids the "pregnant ego" syndrome that other artists too often display. Anyone with the slightest interest in New Orleans music knows his importance, but Earl would never spell it out in so many words.

Earl King made his mark as a recording artist by waxing a couple of regional blues hits, "Mother's Love" and "Those Lonely, Lonely Nights," in the mid-Fifties. Although he continued his recording success well into the Sixties, Earl also left his mark as a writer and producer, accounting for scores of great records, some of which became national hits. Today his song catalog is most impressive, surpassed in New Orleans only by Toussaint's and Domino/Bartholomew's. His influence and direction in the recording studio is still sought out and his live performances can still excite even the most placid audience.

Born Earl Silas Johnson IV, February 7, 1934, he is the seventh and only living son of Ernestine Hampton and Earl Silas Johnson, III. He was raised in the Irish Channel, a largely interracial neighborhood, at 2834 Constance Street. Earl's father was a renowned blues pianist but died when his youngest son was just two, obviously before Earl could get to know much about him. However, septugenarian pianist Tuts Washington offers this insight on Earl Johnson, Sr. "Me and Earl's Pa come up together around Josephine and Claiborne. He was a good blues piano player with a good left hand. Sang all of Lonnie Johnson's tunes. We bummed in all the "tonks" up and down Rampart Street. He got sick and joined the spiritual church as a minister for awhile but he died young. He liked to live fast."

Earl's mother was a heavyset woman nicknamed "Big Chief" (the inspiration for the Professor Longhair tune), who began taking her son to the Antioch Baptist Church as a preschooler. Earl enjoyed singing in church so much that he started a street-corner gospel group with his best friend Robert Lockett. Earl describes himself as a "bug" as a youth and he developed a wide variety of childhood interests. But music always seemed to be his overriding influence and he often listened to Gatemouth Brown and T-Bone Walker records that blared from the jukeboxes of the corner bars.

"I paid my dues in church," explains Earl. "I didn't get a chance to shoot too many marbles as a kid, so when I got to be 14, I started looking in other musical directions. My mom never tried to hold me back, even though she was a devout church woman. She stayed low-keyed and accepted the change."

Being the inquisitive type, it didn't take him long to discover live music. "I guess I was barely a teenager when I heard Smiley Lewis and Tuts Washington playing in a place called Big Mary's at Fourth and Tchoupitoulas. I had no business being in there, but it was crowded inside and I just eased on in when I heard the music playing from the outside. My mother really cut into me because I

Earl King at 3 years old

stayed out real late that night, but I had to hear that music.

"After that I'd go around Sal's, at St. Thomas and St. James, and hear Smiley too. They had another guy that played in there that was a real kick, 'Hold That Note Sam.' I remember that particular joint because the smell of reefer was so thick; that place was a haven for reefer smokers.

"I was standing on the corner one day with my best friend John Davis. He was playing the guitar and I was dueting a few gospel songs, when this man came up to us and listened to us sing. After we were finished he said, 'You boys ought to be singing the blues because you could make a lot of money. Gospel music don't pay too much.'

"He said his name was Victor Augustine and that he had a shop on Dryades Street. He told us to drop by and see him sometime because he knew a lot of talent scouts and he might be able to get us recorded. He left us a calling card and walked on. John and I laughed because we didn't know what to think.

"A few days passed before we built up the nerve to check him out. When we went down to the address he gave us, there was a sign painted in the window that read 'House of Hope — Dr. Mighty the Voodoo Man.' When we walked in we heard a piano playing a boogie-woogie, but we almost got knocked down by the smell of burning incense. Inside he was selling mojos, candles, prophecies, incense wonder water, ointments and records. We saw Mr. Augustine and said, 'Well we're here to audition.'

"He was real friendly and said, 'Call me Doc. Everybody else does.' He introduced us to the piano player who turned out to be Huey Smith. We didn't get into too much right off because I didn't know too many songs. Huey gave me the words to a few boogies, so we went on from there. After that I started coming by Doc's regular."

Earl was 15 at the time and a student at Booker T. Washington High School. He began learning the rudiments of playing the guitar, so he and fellow student Roland Cook, a pianist, formed a trio with John Davis and began rehearsing at the "House of Hope." On Wednesday evening the group would enter the talent show at the Dew Drop, on LaSalle Street, and try to win the $5 first prize. Eventually Earl's group won the prize so often that they were disqualified, and had to move on to the talent show downtown at the Tiajuana, on South Saratoga.

"The Tiajuana introduced me to a new circle of ideas and ambitions. Back in the early Fifties the Tiajuana was a real scene. K-Doe, he was Ernest Kador then, would emcee the shows. I got to meet a lot of other local musicians that were in the same bag I was into. Spider Bocage [Eddie Bo], Billy Tate, Robert Parker, Charles Williams, Albert Scott, Ricardo Lopez, Big Willie Johnson and Lloyd Price. A lot of jocks like Ernie the Whip and Larry McKinley would be in there. Talent scouts too — Art Rupe [Specialty], Johnny Vincent [Specialty and later Ace] and Dave Bartholomew."

But the person who influenced Earl the most was the great Guitar Slim — Eddie Jones. "Guitar Slim will always be my greatest inspiration," admits Earl. "I met Slim at the Tiajuana. In fact, I thought Slim and Huey Smith were brothers because I used to see them together so much. I really got interested in the guitar after seeing Slim play in the Tiajuana.

"I didn't really get to know him personally until later during the Dew Drop era, but he took a liking to me because I used to listen to what he said. A lot of people didn't take Slim seriously because he was a jovial character, but I took him dead serious. The things he talked about in close quarters had a lot of depth. Like one time he told me, if you can ever help it, go on the stage from left to right, because people read from left to right, and the audience feels more comfortable that way.

"Slim gave me the idea to write lyrics from a psychological approach — saying things that people want to hear. Like, ''I'm gonna send you back to your mother, and I'm gonna go back to my family too.' I mean, that hits home. Slim also inspired me to contemplate a marriage between a song and its solo, instead of playing something at random."

King often visited the guitarist's room over the Dew Drop for "lessons," and he even bought his first electric guitar from Slim. "I owed Slim some money on that guitar," says Earl. "He caught me coming around the Dew Drop when they had the talent show and said, 'Earl, where's my money?' I said, 'Man, I don't have any money right now.'

"So Slim says, 'Well, I tell you what you're gonna do. You're gonna get on that talent show, and you're gonna win the money and give it to me, and that's that.' I told Slim, 'That's impossible because I don't have a guitar.' So Slim goes upstairs and gets his Les Paul-Gibson, and says, 'Now you ain't got no excuse.' Well I didn't win because they gave it to this guy who was touched in the head who liked to sing and everyone felt sorry for him, but Slim liked to have fell out dead he was so upset."

Before Earl could get around to waxing another record, his mentor, Guitar Slim, was hospitalized after a car wreck, just as his massive hit, "The Things That I Used To Do," was taking off. Slim had a full roster of dates booked by Frank Pania, the proprietor of the Dew Drop, but couldn't make them. Pania in turn talked Earl into impersonating "the star," until Slim could get out of the hospital. "I went out on the road with Slim's band, but it had never been pointed out to the promoters that I was a substitute. I was scared half to death even though I knew all of Slim's tunes. I got away with the charade because we were booked into places Slim hadn't played before. The first job I played was at the Magnolia Ballroom in Atlanta with Ray Charles as the opening act. I was terrified when I got on stage but when we kicked off with 'The Things That I Used To Do,' it was like a cannon going off. People started throwing money and I nearly got pulled off the bandstand."

When Earl got back to New Orleans after Slim had recuperated, he went back to playing with the Swans and rehearsing at Doc's "House of Hope." Earl had earlier run into "the apple man," Specialty Records talent scout/producer Johnny Vincent. "Johnny was the superstitious type," laughs Earl. "He took the saying 'an apple a day keeps the doctor away' one step further. He'd eat as many as a dozen apples a day. Johnny had got Slim with Specialty and Huey got him interested in a tune I had wrote called 'Mother's Love.' Johnny thought it reminded him of Slim, so he wanted me to cut it.

"I listened to Slim's philosophy about writing about things that were personal. That's how I came up with 'Mother's Love,' because the closest thing to somebody is there mother.

"I wanted to get a new guitar for the session, because this time I was gonna play one. I needed to get a co-signer because I was gonna buy it on time, so I got Frank Pania to sign and I got a Les Paul-Gibson.

"When the record came out I took a copy down to Frank Pania to say thanks. Frank went into his office and listened to it, then called A-1 Distributors and ordered 300 copies of it. He mailed them out to all his contacts. Within a month he started getting back some positive letters and he started booking me around Texas, Mississippi and Alabama."

Being so close to Guitar Slim's style did pose some problems as far as Earl establishing himself as an identifiable artist. "I heard that a lot of distributors were ordering Slim's records thinking they were getting 'Mother's Love.' I was in some places in Texas where they had 'Mother's Love' on the jukebox and it had Slim's name on the tag."

"Mother's Love" was big record in the Southern R&B market, establishing Earl as a strong New Orleans recording artist. Specialty brought Earl back to the studio twice more, and a total of four records were issued, all in 1954. Although he couldn't repeat the success of his initial sides, "Funny Face" and "Eatin' and Sleepin'" were particularly enjoyable. "My stuff caused a conflict of interest up at the company," explains Earl, referring to Specialty. "Slim was stark raving mad that I was so close to his sound and it posed some problems with promoting two artists that were so close. Well, I got wind that some politics were going on so I decided to try something else."

In one of Specialty's other political moves, Vincent was sacked by his boss Art Rupe in 1955. Vincent in turn started his own small label in his hometown, Jackson, Mississippi, and took a job with Music Sales in New Orleans as a salesman. "After Johnny got on his own he told me he could get my release from Specialty," recalls Earl. "He said, 'Why not cut some sides for me?' Johnny was hurting for money at the time, I think he had a record out on Eddie Bo but he wasn't selling anything. Johnny said Cosimo's studio was too expensive, but he could get some up in Jackson."

Earl King at the Autocrat Club

So Huey Smith, Earl, and now-bassist Roland Cook, made the five-hour drive up to Jackson, where Lillian McMurry's Trumpet Studio was located on Farrish Street. The session yielded Earl's biggest hit, the South Louisiana styled "Those Lonely, Lonely Nights." Although the record will never be considered a technical masterpiece — due to the primitive fidelity, and the fact both Huey's and Earl's instruments were badly in need of tuning — "Those Lonely, Lonely Nights" quickly caught the public's ear. It eventually sold in the neighborhood of 80,000 copies, just in the Texas-Louisiana-Mississippi R&B markets, providing Vincent with the hit he needed to keep his label going.

"I knew from my sales territories that you could sell a lot of good blues records in a small area," explains Johnny Vincent. "I knew Earl was a great writer because he had already come up with 'Mother's Love.' I was looking for a strong blues artist like a Guitar Slim or Muddy waters that could get me established in the South. Earl really came up with a lot of great ideas."

When Slim began touring with Lloyd Lambert's band in 1953, his former pianist Huey Smith stayed home in New Orleans. "Huey was very much hurt that he couldn't go on the road with Slim, but there was nothing Slim could do about it because Frank Pania [the owner of the Dew Drop] put the band together and they already had a piano player. So when Slim left, I went with Huey. Me, Huey, Willie Nettles and Roland Cook started playing the Moonlight Inn in Algiers. Cookie was playing bass now because Huey had the piano covered.

"Huey needed a vocalist, and he asked me to make the gig, because he'd heard me audition over by Doc's. The guy who owned the club wanted a guitar player and a singer, so Huey started showing me how to play some of the songs. I really couldn't play well enough to be on the bandstand so I just faked it. I turned the guitar down so low that you couldn't hear it and just concentrated on singing. After a few weeks I built my nerve up enough to play some. Huey would call the key out and I'd try to play 'em.

"Then I started listening to a lot of records — T-Bone Walker, Gatemouth, B.B. King. I started to feel that country-swing type blues that Gate was playing, like on 'Boogie Rambler'."

It was not long until Earl became "hungry for the wax" as he refers to it. During June 1953, Lee Magid of Savoy Records came in search of talent for his Newark-based label. Like many other aspiring musicians, Earl and Huey Smith headed down to Cosimo's for a prearranged audition. "It was a standard thing for writers and musicians to line up outside the studio once they knew a recording company was coming to town," he explains. It would be like the lineup to go see a movie like *The Ten Commandments*. Huey and I managed to get into the studio early that day. Lee Magid's technique was to listen, and if he liked you, he'd tell you to stand off to the side. If not, out the door you went. That was standard operating procedure."

"Earl passed the audition but was still not confident enough about his guitar playing to use it on a record. Both he and Huey wound up splitting a session, cutting "Have You Gone Crazy" and "Begging At Your Mercy," which were issued under the name Earl Johnson. Earl was supported by Huey on piano, Roland Cook on bass, Lee Allen on sax, and Charles "Hungry" Williams on drums. Both sides were reminiscent of Fats Domino and Lloyd Price's then popular styles, but Earl's voice sounds so youthful, it bears hardly any resemblance to his later work.

"They gave you ten bucks a side, I think that was some kind of union thing. Then they'd sign you to a half-cent artist royalty contract, which really wasn't too much even then. They just put the songs out and that was it. There was no kind of promotion. Right after that I started to audition for Specialty. I didn't wait around for Savoy, because the product didn't really impress me too much."

Around this period Earl joined a "jukebox band" called the Swans, that included Alvin Bailey, Lamon Scott, Buster Scott, Roland Cook, Junius Cannon, Melvin Stenette, Raymond Lewis and Ralph Willis. Earl recalls the band's primary function was to churn out the latest R&B hits for dances. The group's first job was at the Streamline Cafe in Lutcher, Louisiana, where the drunken crowd heckled and threatened the band for not knowing all their requests.

In Early 1954, Earl cut his first session for Specialty with Johnny Vincent supervising. The similarity to Guitar Slim is immediately apparent, as Earl has Slim's style right down to a tee on "Mother's Love." Just before the release of the first Specialty disc, Specialty's boss Art Rupe decided to credit the record as "King Earl," perhaps hoping that Earl would join the court of blues royalty a la B.B. King and Crown Prince Waterford. But the pressing plant accidentally flip-flopped the name and the record was released as being by Earl King.

"I was beginning to formulate a different style after 'Mother's Love,'"says Earl. "I had been around Eunice and Opelousas and I began to get a feel for that ballad sound that those people liked to hear. If you listen closely to 'Lonely, Lonely Nights,' you can hear that turn around right after the break. I wanted that to be my trademark and put it on all my records. I wanted people to associate that with me. Funny thing, right after the record came out, I ran into Guitar Slim. Slim said, 'Yeah Earl, that's where you stay. Right there. And don't go nowhere else!'

"That particular session was odd for a bunch of reasons. I remember the room that we cut in had mattress covering the ceiling and the walls. Huey got real made because the engineer told him to keep the volume down. You can really feel that anger when he hits the intro on the piano. Johnny ended up putting out the first take even though we knew we were all out of tune. We cut a bunch of takes of 'Lonely, Lonely Nights,' and it was pointed out to Johnny that we had better versions of it. But Johnny said, 'No let's put this one out — it's got a lot of feeling in it.'"

Earl cites Don Robey as the person responsible for making "Those Lonely, Lonely Nights" the success it was. Even though Robey was one of Vincent's competitors — he owned the Houston based Duke/Peacock labels — he also booked Earl occasionally through his Buffalo Booking Agency, along with his other artists. "Robey took some of Johnny's pressings and mailed them out to all of his deejays. Robey was a powerful cat, he had a lot of those jocks in his pocket. See, Johnny had a tendency of talking too much and making people mad. So the jocks wouldn't play his records. Robey was the one who really got the ball rolling."

Even though Johnny "Guitar" Watson subsequently covered the tune on RPM and outsold Earl's version, "Those Lonely, Lonely Nights" insured return trips to the studio and plenty of work. Robey often booked Earl with Gatemouth Brown and Edgar Blanchard throughout the South and Mid-West R&B circuit. For a few months, Earl teamed up with Smiley Lewis, who was hitting with "I Hear You Knockin'," for a series of engagements along the Gulf Coast.

Vincent chose to record Earl's second record at Houston's ACA Studio, with Edgar Blanchard's band backing. "Little Girl" b/w "My Love Is Strong" was technically an improvement, but didn't click like the first Ace release. Neither did "It Must Have Been Love" b/w "Take Me Back Home" which followed soon after.

Vincent realized he had to try something different, so he released the remaining two tracks from the Houston session on his subsidiary label, Vin, under the name "Handsome Earl!" "Johnny was just that type of guy," explains Earl. "It wasn't unusual for him to put two records out on you at the same time. He figured if you were hot you were hot. Now 'Handsome Earl,' that was part of Johnny trickinology. The distributors were telling him, 'Hey man, you got to bring us some new artists.' So Johnny would just invent them. He had a one-track mind."

Earl was able to assist his benefactor, Huey Smith, by hiring him on out-of-town dates, and he often played on Huey's early Ace recordings. Although at first listen Earl is nearly inaudible behind the piano, Earl is in fact supplying the percussive "chops" in the rhythm section, a trick he learned from Guitar Slim.

By 1956, Earl's sessions were being conducted back in New Orleans at Cosimo's Studio, often using the likes of James Booker, Lee Allen, 'Red' Tyler, and Charles Williams on sessions. Earl's records attained a more balanced, professional sound, although he didn't match the success of his first Ace disc, songs like "Well'O, Well'O, Well'O, Baby," "Weary Silent Night" and "Buddy It's Time To Go" were excellent records and sold reasonably in New Orleans.

"Earl was just a bitch of a writer," claims Johnny Vincent. "That's what impressed me about him. He was one of the best young writers in New Orleans. 'Mother's Love,' 'Ship On A Stormy

Sea,' 'Lonely, Lonely Nights' — those songs just knocked me out. Basically, I thought Earl was a real good act too. He was a good lookin' guy who had a lot of stage presence. When he played those dances down in Abbeville, Crowley, Lafayette, and Opelousas, the girls used to swoon right in the aisles.

"I thought Earl and Slim were basically the same kind of act. Slim was more dynamic on stage, but Earl, I thought, was a much better singer. We really only had one big hit — 'Lonely, Lonely Nights' — that did close to 100,000 but after that nothing more than 5,000. I wanted Earl to develop into an A&R man. He had a lot of great ideas and I felt he could become a good producer and he did do some really successful records later on."

However Earl was able to account for hits in another way, after developing an interest in arranging and producing. "From hanging around Cosimo's I began seeing what people like another way, after developing an interest in arranging and producing. "From hanging around Cosimo's I began seeing what people like Johnny and Dave Bartholomew were doing. Johnny really couldn't be considered a producer. His idea of producing was saying 'Put some shit into it.' So I started getting some ideas on my own.

"I never got credit for it, but I produced 'Just A Dream' for Jimmy Clanton. Johnny was brought by Cosimo from Baton Rouge, but Johnny just couldn't hear him. Johnny rejected 'Just A Dream.' He said, 'Naw, I just don't hear it.' But we put it out anyway and it was Ace's biggest record.

"Johnny really missed a lot of talent. I brought him Allen Toussaint and he rejected him right off. All he could hear was Huey Smith after Huey started hitting."

Earl wrote material for Clanton, including "Angel Face" and "My Love Is Strong." he also produced other Ace recording artists, including Roland Stone, Floyd Brown, Curley Moore and even Huey Smith. Earl eventually parted ways with Vincent — as did many other Ace artists in 1959. "Johnny was just going off the wall trying to run the distributorship and the record company. He just couldn't deal with the studio right. I won't even go into the royalties that he was paying — which were nil."

After leaving Ace, Imperial Record's Dave Bartholomew became interested in Earl's talents as a writer and a recording artist. Initially, Bartholomew liked a tune Earl played as a "sign off" on gigs, "Come On (Let The Good Times Roll)," and decided to sign him.

"I really enjoyed working with Earl," says Dave Bartholomew. "Earl was a hard worker. He had a lot of ideas and suggestions that were valuable. Earl could really write good, catchy songs. I still think there's time for Earl to make it real big. He's that talented. I've really got a lot of respect for Earl King."

"Joining Dave at Imperial really gave me a chance to go in a different, creative direction," says Earl. "A lot of things I wanted to do, Johnny wasn't interested in. Working with Imperial was a whole different scene. It was a real eye-opener working with Dave, he had an open ear to production and he listened to suggestions. It was a real learning experience. Dave knew how to do things that were appealing to the public and weren't too far in left field."

"Come On," Earl's initial Imperial release, began to take off around New Orleans, but was stalled when Johnny Vincent applied more of his "trickinology." Earl's last session for Vincent included a demo of "Come On," which was recorded in Biloxi during a period when Vincent and Cosimo had one of their periodic fallings out. When "Come On" started to make noise for Imperial, Vincent dug out his session and leased it to Cosimo's Rex label, which was distributed by Vincent! Although the Rex record was titled "Darling Honey, Angel Child," it still managed to keep Earl's current Imperial release from doing better.

Earl sidestepped Vincent's action and began composing new material, for himself and other artists. "Bobby Robinson and Marshall Sehorn came looking for something to follow "Ya-Ya" for Lee Dorsey. I came up with "Trick Bag" but Bobby said, 'No, too many words.' The second song was "Do-Re-Me," and he went for that. Then I came up with "Ixie Dixie Pixie Pie" and "One and One." That's what really got me into writing for other artists.

"Dave Bartholomew pointed it out to me that Lew Chudd said he didn't want me writing songs for other record companies, because there was enough people on Imperial for me to write for. That's what brought about 'He's Mine' by Bernadine Washington. that got me going in that direction."

With "Do-Re-Me" and "He's Mine" in the 1961 charts, Earl was an in-demand songwriter. Consequently he began spending more time around the studio and less time performing. "I really had my hands full writing," says Earl. "When you write something that sells, people start thinking you can pull a rabbit out of your hat and they start crowding you for material. I was sticking around the studio simply because I was so busy. Eight hours a day I was writing, seven days a week. Didn't have time for much gigging."

Earl even penned a couple of tunes for Imperial's top hitmaker, Fats Domino, "Hum Diddy Doo" and "Teenage Love." "It doesn't sound like it, but that was work. Fats worked real hard on those tunes. It was an all day thing when you rehearsed with him. Fats took them songs seriously."

Earl's own records continued to do well on a regional basis. His version of the Guitar Slim anthem "The Things That I Used To Do" was excellent, as was the dramatic "You're More To Me Than Gold," and the humorous "Mama & Papa." in 1962, Earl finally got back into the charts with "Trick Bag" b/w "Always A First Time," which rose to number 17 in the *Billboard* R&B charts. The popular "Trick Bag" was written in the best tradition of the Coasters and Huey Smith's humorous material on Ace. Earl feels the record likely would have nudged even higher, but Imperial's Lew Chudd held back on promotion because he was in the process of selling the label.

When Chudd finally did sell in 1963, he really pulled the rug out on Earl, and a number of other New Orleans artists. "We were just getting going when Imperial went down," laments Earl. "My hopes were really with Imperial. It really hurt New Orleans when they pulled out. I often wonder what would have happened if Chudd had hung on for a little while longer."

Rather than lick his wounds, or roll over and play dead, Earl bounced back and began concentrating on new projects. During the summer of 1963, Earl, Johnny Adams, Chris Kenner, George French, Smokey Johnson and Joe Jones piled into a station wagon and drove to Detroit to audition for Motown.

"Joe started and ended the Motown situation. He told us we had a guarantee of recording for them but when we got there, we found out different. In fact, if Clarence Paul and Berry Gordy hadn't been so knocked out by Smokey's drumming we might have been on our way home the day after we got there. But they heard Smokey and said be here at 7 a.m. tomorrow and be ready to cut.

"They got real interested in everybody: Johnny was gonna record, Chris and myself. Johnny got messed around, though, when Ruffino sent Gordy a telegram saying he was gonna sue Motown if he cut him. I put down a whole album and was getting ready to lay some stuff on Marvin Gaye.

"Well Joe Jones messed the whole deal up. He said he had a contract on all of us and that Motown had to pay him $10,000 before they could release anything. Of course he never did, but Gordy was just getting things off the ground and he wanted to avoid any legal hassles. So I've still got that album sitting out there in the can."

Undaunted, Earl returned to New Orleans to try to take advantage of the few opportunities that were left there. He wrote and produced a great deal of material for some of the smaller local labels. Among his biggest local successes were Dell Stewart's "Mr. Credit Man," on Watch; Danny White's "Loan Me Your Handkerchief," on Watch; Smokey Johnson's "It Ain't My Fault," on NOLA, and Johnny Adams' "Part Of Me," on Watch. Earl also penned Bobby and the Heavyweights' "Soul Train" (originally recorded by Curley Moore on Hot Line) and Willie Tee's "Teasin' You," which both were leased to Atlantic and became national hits in 1965.

Besides producing New Orleans artists, Earl served as the local A&R man (artist and representative) for Duke records. Earl supervised sessions by Buddy Ace, Bobby "Blue" Bland, Joe Hinton and Jr. Parker. Still, most of Earl's time in the mid-Sixties was spent writing and producing material for other New Orleans artists.

"We had a chance then to make a real turnaround here in New Orleans," explains Earl. "Wardell Quezergue and myself were doing a lot of great things for Watch and NOLA. When Cosimo formed Dover, I though we were out of the woods. Dover pulled all the small New Orleans labels together and gave us a chance to break things nationally. Finally we had promotion and distribution. But the jocks backed Cosimo against the wall; he couldn't afford to pay them, so they refused to play any of his records. Wham, everything from Dover went in the garbage can. So with no outlet to get records played we went under."

After Dover and NOLA crashed, New Orleans was pretty quiet musically. But rather than pulling up stakes, Earl decided to stay in New Orleans and weather the storm. "I could have moved, but I just didn't think about it. I had offers from Motown and Capital, but I didn't follow them up. I wrote a book about songwriting in 1969 and I concentrated on getting my catalog straightened out. You know I've got two song publishing companies, so I eased back for awhile."

In 1972, he did an album with Allen Toussaint that was intended for Atlantic. But rather than possibly turn Earl's career around, the deal fell through. A single, "Street Parade," was issued on Sea-Saint Studio's house labels, Kansu, which became a popular local Mardi Gras record, but it was small consolation for the hope Earl put in the project. When the album finally was released in 1981, it confirmed that Earl was still a talented artist to be reckoned with.

Other recordings from the Seventies included a live pairing on the 1976 New Orleans Jazz & Heritage Festival LP, and singles on

Earl King, Monterey Jazz Fest., 1980

Amy, Wand, Island, and Seminar. One album was recorded for Sam Charters' Sonet label (Sweden), but being cut in one day as it was, it was rushed and the results weren't always satisfying.

The late Seventies saw Earl back gigging regularly. Backed by a young white group, The Rhapsodizers, he appeared at many college niteries and annually at the Jazz Festival. Recording dates weren't as frequent as in past decades, but he was always willing to offer advice and encouragement. Many evenings found him staying late at Sea-Saint banging at the piano, trying to translate an idea into a song.

"My approach to songwriting is always try to get a title first. From a title you can get a refrain line and then try to compose my ideas at the piano; very rarely do I deal with the guitar, unless I'm writing something for myself.

"In my case, I get ideas from several sources, but my favorite is listening to other people's conversations. I prefer writing for a particular artist, that way you know about how an artist feels about things — what and what not to say. Some artists you can go across the board. You can write a good song and they can deliver it.

"I hear a lot of writers say how you have to wait for that creative urge, but I don't think it works that way. Sometimes you have to work yourself out of a rut. Not everything you write is always that great, a songwriter has to realize that. You might write 35 songs before you write a good one. I write a lot of songs that end up in the trash."

So Earl continues to perform and write new songs even though opportunities for lucrative engagements and recording opportunities have grown exceedingly scarce. Nonetheless Earl King remains cautiously optimistic. "It all comes back to New Orleans having an outlet," he concludes. "I go out and hear new groups all the time and we've still got so much talent here it's ridiculous. I still think that if we had a powerful radio station that played our records we could turn things around. That would make the record industry pay attention to New Orleans again. Right now the major labels have got all our radio stations tied up so much a new Orleans record doesn't have a chance. My last record, 'It Hurts To Love Someone,' never got played except on WWOZ and WTUL [both low-powered "public" FM stations], so it didn't sell. But I put it on about thirty jukeboxes and it moved the meter. That proves that people will listen to New Orleans records if we can just get them played."

Part Five:

WOMAN'S VIEWPOINT

New Orleans has always had a soft spot in its heart for its female vocalists. Not surprisingly, the history of female singers in New Orleans goes right back to one of the city's first national rhythm and blues hit records, "Since I Fell For You," in early 1947, by Annie Laurie.

Annie Laurie's string of great late Forties hits on DeLuxe paved the way for other New Orleans songstresses. By 1950, "Chubby" Newsome had scored with the rowdy "Hip Shakin' Mama," Erline Harris with "Jump and Shout," and Jewel King with the swinging "3 x 7 = 21," which even preceded Fats Domino recordings on Imperial.

Originally, female vocalists were furnished by the rhythm and blues orchestras and combos that flourished in the late Forties. These bands usually provided a blues shouter and a sultry songstress to suit the occasion. No band worthy of hearing was without a female vocalist. So naturally they warranted plenty of exposure when the record companies came looking for talent.

During the early Fifties the most distinctive and successful New Orleans female voice was undoubtedly Shirley Goodman, half the duet of Shirley and Lee, which provided some of the city's biggest selling records. Shirley and Lee's success also inspired other New Orleans duets, Sugar and Spice, and Joe and Ann.

The Fifties would also produce the powerful voice of Christine Kittrell, who is best known for "Sittin' And Drinkin'," and Bernadine Washington, who hit with Earl King's "He Mine." Out of the same rhythm-and-blues-cum-rock-and-roll era emerged Irma Thomas, whose roots were deep in the blues, but whose distinctive voice appealed to young audiences. Irma is one of the few New Orleans artists who has been able to adapt to soul and even disco music successfully.

Others that followed her path into the Sixties were Barbara George with "I Know," and Betty Harris with "Nearer To You." Three girls from New Orleans, The Dixi-Kups, even topped the *Billboard* Hot 100 in 1964 with "Chapel Of Love." While the above-mentioned were lucky enough to have national hits, other deserving singers like Tammy McKnight, Gerri Hall, Mary Jane Hooper and Tamy Lyn weren't, despite fine records.

New Orleans' Jean Knight has led the charge into the charts in the Seventies and the Eighties with "Mr. Big Stuff" and "You Got The Papers (But I Got The Man)," respectively. Rose Davis and Mathilda Jones have also waxed outstanding R&B singles in the past few years.

New Orleans' female singers can look back with pride upon their distinctive contribution to New Orleans rhythm and blues.

SHIRLEY GOODMAN
Sweetheart of The Blues

Shame on you if you didn't realize that it was Shirley Goodman of the classic Fifties rhythm and blues duet, Shirley and Lee ("I Feel Good" and "Let The Good Times Roll") who also recorded the 1974 massive disco hit, "Shame, Shame, Shame."

As the female side of the unforgettable "Sweethearts of the Blues" duo, Shirley and Lee burst onto the record scene in 1952 with the surprising hit, "I'm Gone." Other R&B hits followed: "Keep On" in 1953, "Feel So Good" in 1954, and "I'll Do It" in 1955. From that point on, Shirley and Lee records began crossing over into the previously staid pop charts. Suddenly the duo became the "Sweethearts of Rock and Roll," as they were embraced by the teenage record buyers of the era.

Shirley and Lee were tailor-made for the young record buyers of the Fifties. The perfect picture of innocence, Shirley and Lee participated in an ongoing vinyl love affair for most of the decade. While some criticized their records as being childish and repetitive, their music was undeniably classic New Orleans rhythm and blues-cum-rock 'n' roll. Their biggest sellers, recorded for the Aladdin label, always employed the cream of the city's session men, and their material was both clever and provocative.

The Shirley and Lee days aside, Shirley Goodman has led a checkered musical life. After the duet split, she moved to Los Angeles to raise a son and has only moved back to New Orleans in the last few years. She still possesses the child-like, high-pitched soprano and sweet demeanor you'd expect her to have after listening to her records. She no longer sings professionally, "semi-retired," she laughs, hinting that the last chapter of her life story has not been written.

Shirley Goodman was born in New Orleans June 19, 1936, the daughter of Lenore Goodman and Myrtle Goodman. She grew up in the Seventh Ward on North Villere, between St. Bernard and Annette streets. Although her parents had six children, they divorced and Shirley was raised by her grandmother.

"Grandmother was a church-going woman," begins Shirley. "All day Sunday we'd be singing. Morning service, Sunday school, afternoon service, evening service—I had my share of singing in the Baptist Church.

"I'd be singing all the time with my friends in the streets. My favorite then was Dinah Washington: she had a light and happy sound that appealed to me. She was the greatest singer I ever heard. Every time my mother would buy records I'd beg her to get a Dinah Washington record. I guess I was about seven, because I remember we had this wind-up record player—and I'd wind that thing up when I got home from school and learn all her records."

Shirley's appetite for singing grew to be insatiable, and it wasn't long until she made her first on-stage appearance at the tender age of nine. "My cousin Ruth Bethley was a singer, too. She used to take me down to the Palace Theatre, on Royal and Iberville, every Saturday at the vaudeville shows. Oh, we'd never miss a Saturday. There'd be Lollypop and Alma Parnell, Memphis Lewis [comedians] and lots of singers and dancers. They'd have amateur shows, too, I'll never forget them because if you were no good, they'd shoo 'em off the stage and people would throw rotten eggs and tomatoes!

"My cousin had a show down at the Palace and I begged her to let me sing, because I just knew I could. They called me up and I sang 'Hip Shakin' Mama'—can you imagine that song at that age! Everybody applauded, and from that day on I knew I was going to be a singer."

As it turned out, Shirley's ambitions materialized sooner than she could have hoped, while she was a freshman at Joseph S. Clark High at the ripe old age of 13½. "After school we'd all go over to this girl Evangeline's place, because she was the only one in the neighborhood who had a piano. There was about twenty of us and we'd sing and she'd play the piano. We came up with this song 'I'm Gone,' which just went on and on, we'd sing that for hours. We found out from my cousin where they made records, so we started going down to Cosimo's studio every night after school and we'd knock on the door and ask, 'Please mister, can we make a record!'"

"He'd always say, 'Look, you kids quit bugging me and go home.' But we kept coming back every night so finally he said, 'Bring me two dollars, and y'all can make a record.'

"We went out and did everything we could to make that two dollars. After a few weeks we finally got the money, and got all dressed up to go down to see Cosimo because we were going to make a record," she laughs. "So we went down and said, 'Here's our two dollars, we're ready to make a record.' Cosimo just shook

Shirley and Lee, early promo shot

his head and brought us into the studio. I don't know who was recording, but Cosimo told them, 'Look, let me record these kids and get 'em out of my hair!'

"Earl Palmer and Lee Allen were in the studio at the time and they helped us. Evangeline played the piano and we sang 'I'm Gone.' Cosimo pressed us a demo 78, with a little white sticker on it saying 'I'm Gone.' When he gave us that, we were the happiest bunch of kids you ever saw! We passed that record around and around — so everybody would get a couple of days to listen to it."

As luck would have it, Eddie Mesner, the owner of Los Angeles' Aladdin Records, was in town in 1950 to try to cut Lloyd Price, and look for talent. "Eddie and Cosimo were in the studio getting ready to record somebody," says Shirley. "They needed a tape, so Cosimo said, 'Let's use this old tape. It's just a bunch of kids who come in here to bug me every day.'

"Eddie said, 'What kids? Lemme hear it.' So Cosimo played it for him and Eddie went crazy over it. He said, 'Who's that? The one that's screaming!' — because I've always had this really high shrill voice. 'Where is she?' he asked Cosimo. 'Can you find her?'

"Cosimo said, 'Man, you don't want that?' Eddie said, 'Yeah, I do. We got to find her.' So Cosimo sent Dave [Bartholomew] and everybody out to try and find us. He looked for several days and when he did find us, we were scared to death. We thought we were in some kind of trouble—because here was this man looking for us who was trying to get rid of us just a few months before. We thought, don't believe those people, but we finally built up the nerve to go back down there. When I walked in the studio, Cosimo knew it was me right away, because I had this little high pitched voice. As soon as he heard me talking, he said, 'That's her, that's the one!'

"Eddie Mesner asked me if I'd like to make records, and I said, 'Yeah, sure. But you'll have to ask my grandmother.' Eddie said 'Okay.' But in the meantime he wanted to put a boy's voice with mine. He auditioned all the boys who were in the group. He came up with Lee [Leonard Lee] because he had a deep, bluesy voice, and he thought we contrasted. I had known Lee and his family all my life, so things worked out between us."

Being an avid church-goer, Shirley's grandmother proved to be a major stumbling block. She didn't want her granddaughter singing 'sinful music.' "She said, 'You're not going to make any records.' It took a long time to talk her into it. Lee's mother talked to her, Eddie's wife Reccie talked to her, I begged and pleaded and cried. But she still said 'No recording!' Finally Eddie went to her and gave her a thousand dollars, and all she had to do was sign a paper and let me go down to the studio and record. That was a lot of money in those days, some people didn't make a thousand dollars in a year. Well, that changed her mind, and she signed the contract."

Dave Bartholomew produced the first three Shirley and Lee releases, setting the pattern for all the records that would follow. "Lee and I never sang together in harmony because our voices were just so far apart," continues Shirley. "I'd sing a part, then he'd sing a part. Everybody was real helpful, because we were a little green. Dave would even hold my head up to the mike because I had a tendency to move my head and go off mike. It took a long time to get the first record out, though, because it took so long to get my grandmother to sign the contract, and then we couldn't come up with a B-side. Finally Dave wrote something and we did it and sent it out to Eddie."

The A-side, "I'm Gone," rose to #2 on the R&B charts in September 1952, and the "Sweethearts of the Blues" were on their way. "It was a hit overnight!" declares Shirley. "Eddie released it here first, and New Orleans just bought every copy they could, and I love 'em for it. Eddie called me a week after it came out and said, 'It looks like it's really gonna happen.'

"The Sweethearts of the Blues" on the road mid 1950's

"Then Circle Artists called and wanted to book us. Well, they had to go through the whole thing Eddie went through with Grandma, only worse. It was one thing making records, but it was another thing leaving school to go out on the road and be away from home and the church.

"They offered her $500 and she chased 'em out the door. So Joe Glaser from Circle asked Eddie what he should do. Eddie told him, 'I guarantee, if you give her $1000, she'll let her go. So she signed, as long as they made sure somebody would be on the road with me. They paid either her or my mother to travel with me right up until I got married.

"Before we left on the first tour, we did a show at the San Jacinto Club with Dave's [Bartholomew] band. I'll tell you I've never been in a place that was so packed. You couldn't get in if you wanted to. Big Mama Thornton was on the bill too, she was just starting with 'Hound Dog,' and came on before us! That was the only time I got a case of the nerves. Here was this woman who was so powerful and such a great singer and I thought 'Gee, I really have to go out there and perform.' But when I got out there everything fell together and the people really liked us. New Orleans was always good to us."

The combination of a crack New Orleans band and the novelty of such a youthful pairing (on their debut, Shirley was 15 and Lee was 16) caught the record buyers' attention. Shirley wholeheartedly agrees, 'Oh yes, there weren't any young performers back then except for Little Esther, who sang with Johnny Otis. People were interested because we were so young and glad we were getting a break."

The pattern of Shirley and Lee releases was set by "I'm Gone." They retained their initial popularity by working through all the possible facets of a boy-girl romance. Shirley and Lee never really sang as a duet, Lee usually offered the questions, and Shirley would answer in the perfect picture of sweetness and innocence. "Shirley, Come Back To Me" followed "I'm Gone," which was followed by "Shirley's Back," which in turn was followed by "Two Happy People," etc. Their early records rarely strayed from the 12-bar blues, or Louisiana ballad, structure.

"We tried to write the songs as an ongoing story. When we came in off the road, we'd go over to Lee's house and write another chapter. One day I'd be leaving, then I'd come back, then we'd get married, then we were feeling good. Eddie thought it was a real cute idea so it was his idea to call us the "Sweethearts of the Blues" (later to become the Sweethearts of Rock 'n' Roll); he thought if we were pictured as teenage lovers, it would make the teenagers buy our records, just to see what would happen next."

Many people were of the impression that Shirley and Lee were actually married. "No, no, no!" chirps Shirley. "People always thought that because we sang those songs about each other. We didn't have time for each other, to tell you the truth. I got married and so did Lee. We were real good friends, but that was all."

After Shirley's grandmother consented to Shirley's singing in public, Shirley and Lee took to the road, traveling virtually for the remainder of the Fifties.

"We played all theatres at first," recalls Shirley, "because we were too young to get into clubs that sold liquor. We never played a nightclub until 1955, at W.C. Handy's Club in St. Louis. But when we came on they had to stop serving drinks, and when we were through singing, we had to get out. Lee and I would present our show just like our records: we'd get real close and sing to each other. Then I'd tell Lee I was leaving and I'd have him dragging all over the floor. We had this thing where he'd turn to the band and throw some water on his face when the audience wasn't looking. He'd start singing, 'Shirley Come Back,' and it looked like he was

> **NOVEMBER 12, 1955**
>
> Thanks, fellas, for making...
> SHIRLEY AND LEE'S
> **FEEL SO GOOD**
> AL 3269
> a SMASH!
>
> ... and now you're on their new one..
> **LEE'S DREAM**
> and
> **I'LL DO IT**
> AL 3302
>
> ... and for Gene and Eunice
> **I GOTTA GO HOME**
> **HAVE YOU CHANGED YOUR MIND**
> AL 3305
>
> **Aladdin RECORDS**
> Beverly Hills, Calif.

crying. Well, the people just stood up and started screaming! One time we were in Canada with Elvis and he came running out of the dressing room to see if Lee was really in tears!"

When the duo left town, they carried with them an impressive roster of New Orleans talent as part of their band. Nat Perrillat, James Booker, Willie Nettles, Roland Cook, Huey "Piano" Smith, and Allen Toussaint all toured with Shirley and Lee. Such was the popularity of the duo that there were a number of couples on the road making a good living impersonating "The Sweethearts of the Blues."

"I walked into a club in California one night and they had a Shirley and Lee! We went into cities where they had Shirley and Lees playing the week before we got there. We actually caught a pair in Little Rock [they turned out to be the duo Sugar and Spice] but we never did anything. I felt sorry for them, so we just asked them to stop."

Shirley relates that once they were accustomed to the studio, most of the recording sessions were simple and rarely took more than one or two takes. "Lee and I would write the songs over at his house, and then we'd go down to Cosimo's. We'd sing it to them, and they'd play. Lee'd [Allen] say, 'Yeah, I'll play this, man.' Ford

[Clarence Ford] would say, 'O.K., I'll play this.' Then Earl [Palmer] would get a beat and Dude [bassist Frank Fields] would fall in. It was easy, it was like we were one big family. I even remember Fats chink-a-linking on a couple of numbers, because we all helped each other out.

"We didn't see Eddie Mesner too much, because he stayed in Los Angeles. He ran that whole company by himself, so I guess we didn't really have a producer, because Dave went with Imperial after the first few records. Eddie was real fair with us. We only got a one-and-a-half percent royalty, but that was standard back then. I guess they knew they could pay more, but we knew what we were getting into."

The year 1956 turned out to be the biggest year of all for Shirley and Lee, and they started it with a bang with their first release, "Let The Good Times Roll." "We had a kind of lull after 'Lee's Dream,'" continues Shirley. "We stopped touring and everything sort of got back to normal. We both went back to high school and lived like ordinary kids. Then 'Let The Good Times Roll' came out and that was a whole different story.

"We were on a show one night when this guy came up to the bandstand and said, 'Hey baby, let the good times roll!' I turned to Lee and said, 'Did you hear what he said?!' We thought this was a good idea for a song, so we went home and wrote our parts for it. We'd been strictly R&B up until then, but 'Let The Good Times Roll' went pop."

"Let The Good Times Roll" was a lot more than a subtly suggestive song. Shirley's nasal, little-girl voice continually expresses her desire to "rock all night long," while Lee guarantees Shirley he's got "what it takes to thrill your soul." Obviously they weren't singing about going to the high school sockhop!

"Feel So Good" followed "Let The Good Times Roll" right into the *Billboard* Hot 100, incorporating similar sexual overtones. The parents might not have liked it, but the teenagers sent Shirley and Lee's record sales into the millions.

"It was real exciting," says Shirley. "We had so much work, we only had one day off a month for a couple of years. We'd do a show, then get on the bus and drive to the next place. We did the Apollo, the Brooklyn Paramount, the Uptown—we practically played everywhere and with everybody.

"It was a lot tougher being on the road in the Fifties, because you couldn't stop just anywhere you wanted. We slept on the bus a lot of times and sent out for our food." Shirley also recalls playing in Little Rock during the riots in 1956. The riots spread to the show and the band was forced to abandon their instruments and luggage to escape the Little Rock auditorium in helicopters.

Shirley and Lee stayed on with Aladdin until it folded just before Eddie Mesner died. "Eddie gambled a lot," relates Shirley. "Everything just went over to Imperial—records, contracts and all."

Shirley's original hiatus at Imperial proved to be short, but not too sweet. "I could never get things together with Imperial. They recorded a couple of things on Lee by himself, but they wouldn't record me. So Lee got his release first and then I got mine."

Morty Kraft approached the pair about redoing "Let The Good Times Roll" on the Warwick label. "Morty brought us up to New York and they had a big band in the studio. I mean they had twenty-nine instruments there, and sheet music all over the place. I couldn't understand it because all the best things we ever did were simple. I thought that stuff just was terrible. My voice was so high I was out of it."

As poor as the Warwick sides sounded, three of the singles that were released from the album made the Hot 100 in 1960 and 1961. "I've Been Loved Before" rose as high as #88, the remake of "Let The Good Times Roll" made it to #48, and "Well-A-Well-A" halted at #77. When Kraft sold Warwick, Shirley and Lee were without a label until Imperial came back into the picture in 1961.

"Dave Bartholomew asked us to come in with Imperial again, I guess because we had done so many things with him." According to Shirley, seven singles were released and solo sessions of both her and Lee were recorded.

"We broke the team up around 1962," says Shirley in a whisper. It seems there were some bad feelings between the two former "Sweethearts of the Blues." They kept out of touch except for a rock 'n' roll revival show in New York in 1972, until Lee's death from a heart attack October 26, 1976. "Let's just say there were some words between us and leave it at that."

After the duo split, Shirley and her son moved to California. "I'd wanted to raise my son in California because it was clean and there was less prejudice than elsewhere. I wanted to raise him right, I was tired of giving him to someone else to take care of. I just stopped singing. I had royalties coming in still, so I didn't have to work right away."

When word got out that Shirley was living in Los Angeles, she began getting calls to do backup session work. Harold Battiste arranged for her to work on Jackie DeShannon and Sonny and Cher sessions. She also did some duets with Jessie Hill that Huey Meaux leased.

During 1968 and 1969, Shirley recorded for the Whizz label with "Brenton Wood" (Alfred Swift). "Kid Games and Nursery Rhymes," released by Shirley and Alfred, did quite well. Another release followed on the Double Shot label, "Snake In The Grass," credited to Shirley and Shep. "I don't know why record companies always wanted me to record with a man," speculates Shirley. "I guess because I'd always done it, or because my voice is so high they feel they have to balance it."

Session work followed with Tami Lynn, and even on the Rolling Stones' *Exile on Main Street*. Shirley can also be heard oohs and ahhs on Dr. John's *Gumbo* album, and accompanied him on his 1971 European tour.

After that, she faded even further from the public eye, taking a job as a girl Friday for Playboy Records. "Nobody knew who I was, I just wasn't interested in singing. I took the job mostly to stay busy.

"I was working the switchboard, and I had access to the Watts line. I'd call up all my old friends when it was free. That's how I got in touch with Sylvia Robinson [co-owner of All Platinum]. We met at the Apollo when I was with Lee and she was part of Mickey and Sylvia, and we'd been friends ever since. We hardly ever talked about recording, just checking on each other. One day she said she was working on a song and thought it would be good for me. I didn't pay it any mind until she called me and said she had a pre-paid reservation for me to fly to New Jersey [Englewood] and for me to come out and record the song. Well, I told her I couldn't just walk out on my job after everybody'd been so nice to me. I told her I'd call her back after I talked to my supervisor. I talked to my supervisor and told her I had a chance to make a record, and she got a replacement. So I got on the plane that night at ten o'clock.

"The next day Sylvia said, "Take it easy, Shirley, we'll cut it tomorrow.' I said, 'No, that lady was nice enough to let me off, the least I could do is be back on time,' because it was a pre-recorded track anyway, so we went to the studio that afternoon and that's the first time I heard 'Shame.' I heard it about four or five times and I said, 'Okay, let's do it.' Hank Ballard came in and we tried to get it together but it seemed like Hank couldn't get it.

"There was this guy around the studio, Jesus Alvarez, who was just clowning around and my voice just cracked him up. Sylvia called in and said, 'Hey, y'all sound good, why don't you try it together?' So we sang it. We did a couple of more takes but it seemed like it wasn't getting any better, so we took the first one.

"There was a disc jockey in New York that came in the studio that night and heard us. He got a pressing of the record, and the next night, as I flew back to California, he started playing 'Shame' on the radio. The studio got calls like they'd never had before. When I got home, they were already calling me to come back.

"They put it out without even a B-side. I cut it on a Wednesday, I was back to work on a Friday, and by the weekend it was a million seller."

"Shame, Shame, Shame," issued on Vibration Records, proved to be an instant world-wide hit. Cut in late November 1974, Shirley had already made three trips to Europe before Christmas. In retrospect, "Shame, Shame, Shame" must be considered among the earliest examples of what would be known as "disco music."

Vibration followed the single with a hastily produced album. Besides containing a mixed bag of material, it featured a horrendous cover that pictured Shirley pointing her finger at Richard Nixon! "Ugh!" comments Shirley. "I didn't like it. They wanted to get it out so fast, they used demos. We went to Europe and they put it out before we could finish it."

Shirley was amazed that people in Europe knew she was one half of Shirley and Lee. "Every place I went I had to do 'Let The Good Times Roll.' They knew everything about me, they had all my records, they knew who played on them, who engineered them, where they recorded them. I couldn't believe it."

But back in America it was a different story. "Nobody knew. I never was asked to do any of those old tunes. Nobody tied the two together, even when I came back to New Orleans."

Shirley toured off "Shame, Shame, Shame" until the middle of 1976. After that, she returned to California briefly, before moving to New York to be near the studio. "We were going to do a revelation record—between gospel and pop—but they never could get it together. I stayed around for about a year, and then just decided to come home in 1979."

Today, Shirley lives by herself in a comfortable shotgun, only a few blocks from where she grew up. Occasionally, she'll get requests to go back to the nightclubs to sing, but she always politely refuses, content to sing spirituals at home and in church. "Really, I just want to sing spirituals," she says firmly. "I've written a few hymns and I'd really be interested in maybe recording them. Gospel is what's in my heart now. I owe so much because I was protected for so long. That's why I think God gave me a talent, and I should give him a little back.

DOROTHY LABOSTRIE
New Orleans Songstress

Q uite often the forgotten spoke in the music industry's wheel is the songwriter. While a recording artist is constantly in the spotlight, a songwriter often stays in the shadows, with little notoriety. But while a recording artist has to keep hustling gigs, keep a band together and make ends meet, a songwriter—a good one anyway—just has to sit home, write music, and wait for the postman to deliver the royalty checks. That's oversimplifying things, but a talented songwriter will always be in demand, as long as there are people making music.

A name that quite often appears on writing credits on classic New Orleans R&B songs is D. Labostrie. Maybe not too many people notice, but D. Labostrie appears as writer or co-writer on such tunes as Little Richard's "Tutti-Fruitti," Johnny Adams' "I Won't Cry," Irma Thomas' "Don't Mess With My Man," and Li'l Millet's "Rich Woman."

For the most part, D. Labostrie has been a mystery. There are no records by a D. Labostrie, there's no D. Labostrie in the New Orleans telephone directory and there hasn't been a new song credited to D. Labostrie in nearly two decades. Well, who is D. Labostrie? From Johnny Adams we learn: "That's Dorothy. She lived in the same building I did. She's the one who started me singing R&B." Studio engineer Cosimo Matassa adds, "She was always around the studio trying to get people to do her songs. Whenever someone came from out of town to do a session she was there with an armful of songs." Irma Thomas offers, "Dorothy was a real character, really full of life. She wrote some beautiful songs that really hit home, but I haven't seen or heard from her in at least fifteen years."

No one else around town knew of her whereabouts either. Unlike other New Orleans R&B legends, she didn't hang out in a coffee shop, live in the projects, or drive a cab for a living. After calling every Labostrie in the phone book, the only clue I had to her whereabouts was from a woman who was married to a Labostrie. She said Dorothy Labostrie was her husband's niece, but had been in a serious car wreck and she thought she had moved to Kansas City many years ago.

It seemed that D. Labostrie had disappeared in the same fashion as a sheet of newspaper does, twisting and blowing down a dark and windy street. But suddenly, long after I'd abandoned my personal search, Dorothy Labostrie miraculously reappeared. She was back in New Orleans and wanted to be interviewed by the city's community FM station, WWOZ.

With the help of WWOZ's production manager Jerry Brock, I was able to arrange an interview, which if I'd had my way would have been as soon as I could load my cassette with tape and get across town. After a quick chat with the woman over the phone, it was arranged that we'd meet the next day.

I wasn't quite sure what to expect, but I was greeted by a spirited dark-skinned woman with Indian features, who was more than eager to tell her story. Not only was Ms. Labostrie waiting, but so too was a woman introduced to me as her personal secretary. So much for the poor-downtrodden songwriter theory!

Dorothy Labostrie was born May 18, 1928, in the small mining town of Rayland, Kentucky. Her father, Amos Labostrie, came from a New Orleans creole family, but moved north to find work not long after his second marriage. After a mining accident, the Labostries moved to Mobile, Alabama, while Dorothy was still a child.

Dorothy left Mobile in 1941 and headed for New Orleans for the first time to look for her father's relatives. "The first day I came to New Orleans I was out enjoying myself," she began. "I was sitting in a bar on Melpomene Street when this fellow came up and started to talk to me. I told him my circumstances and he asked me if I would like to see the city. Well, I said, 'sure.' I told him my name and he looked surprised and said, 'Do you know Amos Labostrie?' Well, when I told him that was my father, I came to find out he was my stepbrother, Mark. From there I found my father's sister and his cousins. I got to feel right at home in New Orleans."

Labostrie took a series of jobs around town, including working as a domestic and as a bartender. But she had higher ambitions for herself, although at the time, she didn't know exactly where to direct them. "I went out to a lot of clubs to hear music," she continues. "The Dew Drop, the Tiajuana, the Robin Hood, the Blue Eagle—all up and down Rampart Street. All your national celebrities stopped here like Amos Milburn, Bullmoose Jackson and Louis Jordan. But of course, there was a lot of great local musicians, too, like Paul Gayten, Larry Darnell and Roy Brown. I got to know just about everyone who was someone in New Orleans.

"Ever since I was in school I used to love to write poems and sing. I knew that I wanted to do something musically but I wasn't sure

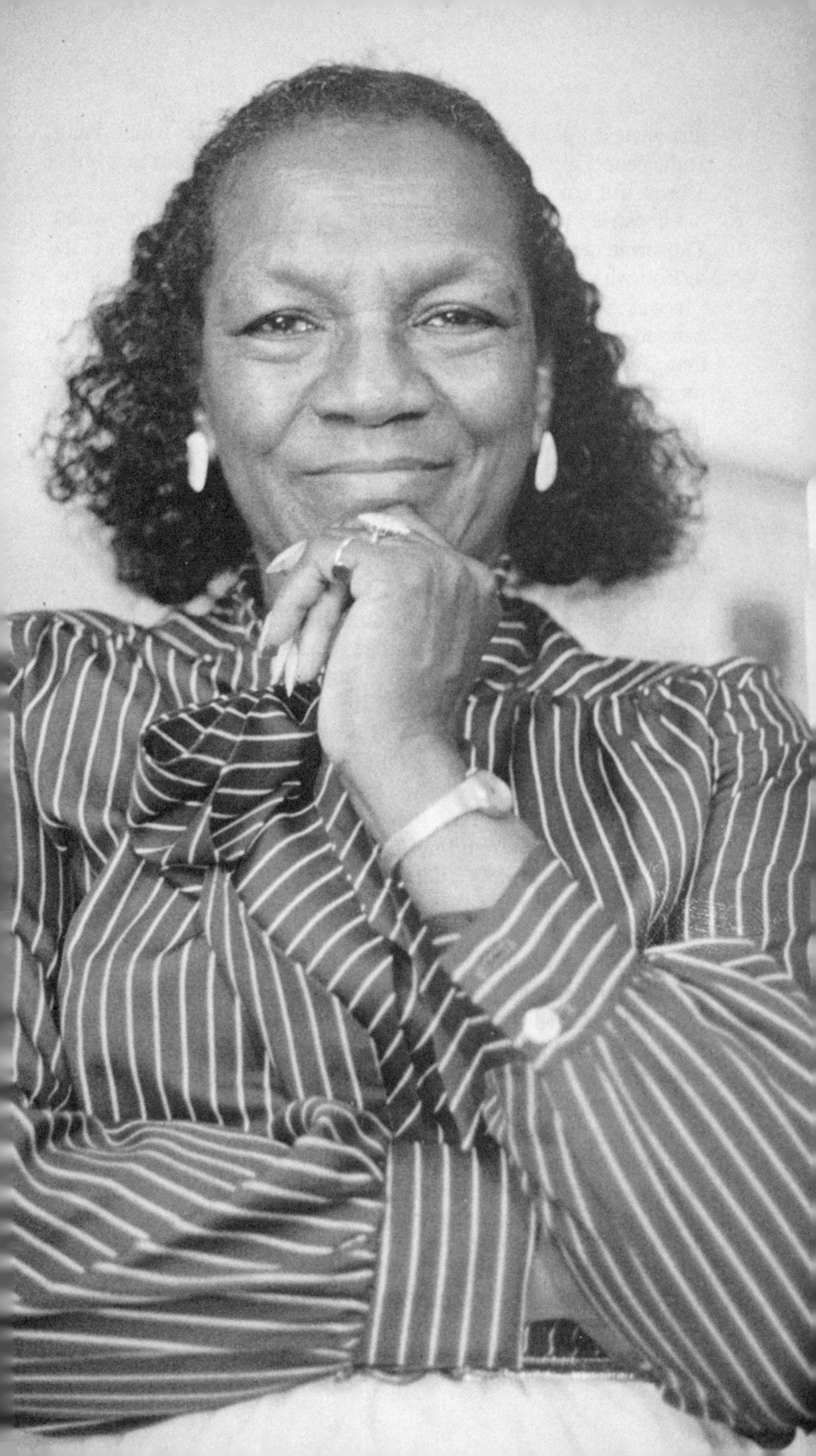

just what it was. I sang in church of course, but never with a band. Some people would think that's odd because I've been told that I have a beautiful voice."

Labostrie's break came when Specialty Records, from Hollywood, California, brought Little Richard to Cosimo's Studio for his first session with that label. "I'll never forget the date," says Labostrie. "It was September 3, 1955. I was listening to the radio and an announcement came on that immediately caught my attention. It said that Bumps Blackwell [Specialty's producer] was looking for songwriters. Well, as soon as I heard where he was gonna be, I decided I was gonna be a songwriter. I was working as a cook for a lady and I told her that I had to quit because I was going to write a hit record. Well, she probably thought I was crazy, but that's exactly what I did.

"I practically broke Cosimo's door down the next day. Little Richard was sitting at the piano and it was the first time I'd ever laid eyes on him. I just asked to hear his voice and I sat down and put 'Tutti Fruitti' down on paper in 15 minutes."

Although Little Richard has continually stated he in fact wrote the infamous rock 'n' roll classic, and has been bilked out of songwriter's royalties all these years, Labostrie just laughs at his claim. "Little Richard didn't write none of 'Tutti Fruitti,' " she says. "I'll tell you exactly how I came to write that. I used to live on Galvez Street and my girlfriend and I liked to go down to the drug store and buy ice cream. One day we went in and saw this new flavor, Tutti Fruitti. Right away I thought, 'Boy, that's a great idea for a song.' So I kept it in the back of my mind until I got to the studio that day. I also wrote the flip side of 'Tutti Fruitti,' 'I'm Just a Lonely Guy,' and a spiritual, 'Blessed Mother,' all in the same day."

Chart placements and *Billboard* and *Cashbox* reviews aside, "Tutti Fruitti" hit the record industry like an atomic bomb. Little Richard was suddenly the hottest thing in show business and took off on a torrid, but short lived, rock 'n' roll career. Being the writer of such an influential song, one would have expected Specialty to beat Labostrie's door down to get new material. But except for contributing the rousing "Rich Woman" for Li'l Millet, such was not the case.

"I wouldn't sell off the rights to my songs," points out Labostrie, explaining the situation. "Art Rupe was the owner of Specialty and he wanted to control everything. They wanted more songs, but they wanted to pay me a flat $500 for them. I knew better because the first check from BMI for 'Tutti Fruitti' was more than that.

"After that, the big companies like Chess, Atlantic and Imperial didn't want to deal with me. They knew I wouldn't sell out, so they didn't want to bother with me. But I just piled up material until I had another chance."

Her next opportunity, on a smaller scale, came in the form of Joe Ruffino, who looking for material for his local labels, Ric and Ron. "Ruffino had a number of great local artists," explains Labostrie. "I wrote songs for Tommy Ridgely, Chris Kenner, Johnny Adams and Irma Thomas. I'm proud to think that some of these great people are still performing today.

"The first time I had success with Ruffino was 'I Won't Cry' for Johnny Adams. At the time I was going out with a guy that I really liked, but he wanted to break up. I remember like it was just yesterday, we were sitting under a tree and I said, 'I know you're going to leave me, but I won't cry and I won't shed a tear.' Those words stuck in my mind and I used them in the song.

"I was living in an apartment at the time at 3418 South Robertson. I was waiting to get in the bathroom and I was in a hurry because I had to go to work. There was this guy from down the hall in there singing 'Precious Lord' and he was really something. It was Johnny Adams. He was working as a roofer at the time and singing in spiritual groups at nights. I asked him if he wanted to sing rock 'n' roll, but he said he couldn't because all his friends would get mad at him.

"Eventually I got him to sing a couple of lines from 'I Won't Cry,' and I knew it was just for him. I finally got him to come and talk to Ruffino and we talked him into doing the song. It came out great."

Labostrie was also responsible for supplying Irma Thomas' first hit, the bawdy "Don't Mess With My Man" in 1959. "That was kind of a bold song," she explains, "especially for 1959. I was looking for a young girl with a lot of spirit to sing it and when Irma came along she was just perfect. Irma was just 16 or 17 at the time, but believe me she had a voice."

Labostrie explained that the Ric and Ron sessions generally employed Edgar Blanchard's Gondoliers, with Lee Allen and Eddie Bo helping out on occasion. "Edgar was real talented and a guy that I don't think got enough credit. He was a great guitar player and real professional around the studio. He always was coming up with little ideas that were useful."

Eventually the relationship between Labostrie and Ruffino soured. Labostrie says that she was being cheated by Ruffino over writing royalties and claims that to this day she hasn't been paid a cent for "I Won't Cry" or "Don't Mess With My Man."

Labostrie continued to write material in the Sixties, eventually signing an agreement to write material for Cosimo Matassa's White Cliffs

Publishing Company. Although she wasn't to write another earth-shaker that compared with "Tutti Fruitti," she claims to have written "hundreds of songs," of which twenty-seven were recorded at least once.

"I get inspired to write songs from different sources," she explains. "I've written a lot of good songs just sitting on the bank fishing. I might hear somebody say something in a conversation that strikes me as interesting or I'll just see something that catches my eye. I don't play an instrument so I just try to sing the lyrics for my songs. I always keep a pad and pencil with me so I don't miss anything. I like to go out and listen to music, all types of music, and I get inspiration from that."

The last record that D. Labostrie's name appeared on was "Mickey Mouse Boarding House," Walter Washington's first single recorded for Al Scramuzza's Scram label in 1970. But a serious car accident and the death of her mother temporarily put her out of commission, and she eventually moved to New York where she lives today.

Although she is a devout member of the Church Of God In Christ, she doesn't disdain secular music and even went club-hopping to see Johnny Adams and Tommy Ridgely during her New Orleans sojourn. In fact she still writes "rock 'n' roll" songs and reveals she's penned a song called "Outer Space Woman," that's just waiting to be a hit!

She seems to be living quite comfortably on her writing royalties, which come in every few months. From the song "Tutti Fruitti" Labostrie claims she receives on the average of $5,000 every three to six months, although $30,000 was the size "of the last big one."

"A lot of people thought I was dead," she laughs, "but as you can see, I'm not. I'm really interested in writing spirituals now and that's what consumes most of my energy. I want to be a great evangelist and record gospel music. That's where I'm at now."

IRMA THOMAS
The Soul Queen of New Orleans

For nearly 25 years, Irma Thomas has been referred to as "The Soul Queen of New Orleans." For good reason too. For although she has experienced more than her fair share of setbacks, she's managed to bounce back each time, and to this day, with the possible exception of Fats Domino, she maintains one of the most diverse local followings of any New Orleans R&B performer. Young, old, black, white—Irma's appeal knows no age or racial barriers. Thousands of highschoolers who bought her records in the Sixties now crowd into local clubs, private dances and riverboat cruises to partake in Irma's unique brand of nostalgic indulgence.

"Anybody remember that F&B Patio? " she quizzes from the stage of the Riverboat President on a moonlight cruise. "Warren Easton? The Rockery? The Walnut Room? How about the Sands?" As Irma names off each bygone New Orleans hotspot, she is answered by a chorus of shouts and hand claps because it was probably one of these locations where they first discovered Irma's music. Today Irma still remains a solid live attraction, she still cuts records, she appears on television commercials and she even has her own fan club!

Now in her early 40s, Irma still could pass for someone 15 years younger. She now is able to leisurely spend her days shopping, bowling, or watching the soaps on TV, knowing her manager/husband, Emile Jackson, is taking care of her "business." Although they live in a comfortable bungalow in Eastern New Orleans, the only visible sign of Irma's success is a new white Mercedes with the "Mrs. J" tag parked next to the house.

But life hasn't always been so easy for Irma. "I was born in Ponchatoula, Louisiana, February 18, 1941," she begins, relaxing on the couch of her front room. "My real name is Irma Lee—real country. My parents' names were Percy and Vadar Lee. One of my earliest memories is singing on the front porch of our house in the country. We moved to New Orleans when I was about three, but when I got to the first grade, I stayed with my auntie in Greensburg, Louisiana, to help her take care of my nine cousins. I guess that's where I learned to take care of kids," laughs Irma, who has raised four of her own, and is still helping with a growing flock of grandchildren.

"After the 4th grade, I came back to live in New Orleans with my folks. We lived in a rooming house behind the Bell Motel on Melpomene Street. That's where I really got interested in music. The lounge in the motel had a jukebox, and I'd sneak off and listen to it every chance I'd get. I heard Clyde McPhatter and the Drifters, Joe Liggins, Lowell Fulsom and Annie Laurie. My favorite record then was 'Ida Red' by Percy Mayfield."

Irma got her basic singing training on Sundays when she accompanied her parents to marathon services at the Home Mission Baptist Church, where the whole family sang in the choir. She also recalls tuning in to the likes of Jack the Cat, Poppa Stoppa, Dr. Daddy-O and Okey Dokie, who then ruled the local airwaves.

"A lot of people don't remember the old Ritz Theatre," points out Irma. "It was on the corner of Felicity and Magnolia. They used to have Sunday afternoon vaudeville shows. I remember when I was 10 or 11, going to see a movie and a show. It was $1.50, which was kind of a lot of money back then, but it was a real good bargain. Besides the movie you'd see a fire eater, a magician, a snake dancer, a couple of comedians; and then they'd have groups like the Coasters and the Drifters on the bill too."

Irma's sixth grade teacher brought her to a talent show at the Carver Theatre on Orleans Street, where she won first prize for singing Nat King Cole's "Pretend." Later on in junior high, Irma began taking voice lessons, and she was chosen to record her class song with Henry Carbo (the brother of the Spiders' Chuck Carbo) at Cosimo Mattassa's J&M studio. But suddenly it seemed like Irma's life stopped at the age of 14, when she was forced to leave school because she was pregnant.

"A pregnant 14-year-old girl was a no-no," says Irma. "I was made an outcast. But it gave me the determination to try and make something out of my life and prove I wasn't a waste. The father's name was Eugene Jones. We had old-fashioned parents that insisted that we get married, but it was a marriage doomed from the beginning."

Irma took a job washing dishes at night for 50¢ an hour, while her mother took care of the baby. Irma's first marriage ended in less than a year and soon after she married a second time, to Andrew Thomas. She had two more children, and eventually took

a job working at the Pimlico Club, located on South Broad, near Washington Avenue. It was here that Irma got her first break, when she approached bandleader Tommy Ridgley, whose group, the Untouchables was installed as the house band on Wednesday evenings. Ridgley invited Irma, now just 18, to sing a few numbers with the band one Wednesday night. Although he liked what he heard, Irma's boss didn't, and she was promptly fired for neglecting her duties.

Ridgley was impressed enough to hire Irma as a vocalist, giving her a short cameo performing popular R&B tunes of the day, quite often from Miss Lavel's repertoire. Irma recalls that the first time she went out of town with Ridgley, she made just $1 when the Untouchables failed to show up for a dance in Waveland, Ms. Most often though, Irma didn't travel outside of New Orleans much because of her responsibilities to her growing family.

Irma got wind of a talent audition at WYLD in January of 1960, sponsored by Joe Banashak and Larry McKinley, who were getting the Minit label started. Irma attended the audition with her husband, but according to her, she was told, "Don't call us, we'll call you," which she took as a rejection. A few days later, Tommy Ridgley took her to see the man he recorded for, Joe Ruffino, who owned the Ron and Ric labels. Ridgley chorded the piano behind Irma for the audition, which took place in the back of the One Stop Record Shop on South Rampart Street.

"Joe Ruffino said he liked me and he was interested in making a record with me. Dorothy LaBostrie had given Joe a song, 'Don't Mess With My Man,' that he wanted to record. I went home and the next day we went into the studio. I was really so young then I couldn't grasp just how important a step that was at the time. I didn't even have sense enough to be scared."

"Don't Mess With My Man" b/w "Set Me Free" employed Eddie Bo as the arranger and used Cosimo Matassa's regular studio musicians. The rowdy shuffle "Don't Mess With My Man" couldn't help but be a hit. After doing well in the New Orleans charts, it eventually made it to #22 in the national R&B charts during the summer of 1959.

With a hot record out, Irma began getting calls for out-of-town work. Since Ridgley had more work than he could handle around town, Irma split with the Untouchables and joined Al White's band for dates as far away as South Carolina and Texas. "Al was doing the bookings," explains Irma." He would contact the clubs or a radio station and we'd drive to the gig.

"We all travelled in an old Mercury station wagon—five of us—clothes, instruments, amplifiers—everything. All one-nighters, we must have driven 100,000 miles and played every little town in the South. I remember playing this little club near an army base on the Georgia-Alabama border. I was singing that part about 'You can have my husband, but please don't mess with my man,' and this woman got up and yelled 'Yeah you right honey!' Well I guess she was sitting next to her husband, because he stood up and decked her right on the spot! That song stirred up a lot of people's feelings."

Irma still feels those early days on the road have been the key to her career's longevity. "There was something about that road, that chittlin' circuit, that matured you. You either grew up or regressed. There was no in between. You either had it or you didn't. And believe me, if you didn't have it, the audience let you have it! I've seen crowds throw bottles and fruit at performers they didn't like. It never happened to me, though; I guess I was just lucky.

"Entertainers today don't realize what we had to go through in the Fifties. I was making $50 a night, but sometimes the promoter would disappear with the money and nobody would get paid. And a black band couldn't just stop and eat at any restaurant or rest at a hotel. Most of the time we ate in the backseat of the station wagon. I lived on sardines and Stage Planks for years."

After "Don't Mess With My Man" cooled off, Ron released the similarly styled "A Good Man" trying to cash in the appeal of the initial release. The record didn't catch on nationally, but helped build Irma's local reputation. Irma refused to re-sign with Ron, claiming Ruffino underpaid her for her record royalties.

In 1961, Larry McKinley, who hadn't lost interest in the songstress, talked his partner Joe Banashak into signing with Minit. Being a distributor, and having his label nationally distributed by Imperial, meant Banashak was well aware of the large avid white teenage record-buying public for properly-presented black performers. Not only had Banashak sold a pile of Fats Domino's Imperial records to teenagers, but he was also in the charts himself with Jessie Hill and Ernie K-Doe. The gravy days were on the immediate horizon for New Orleans, and Irma was ready to give it her best shot.

Her first Minit release was the haunting ballad "Cry On," which was a dramatic change from her earlier blues-based recordings, with the production hand of Allen Toussaint very much evident. The record was a good regional seller, as it received good airplay from both the white and the R&B stations. Other local hits were forthcoming—"Too Soon To Know" and the uptempo "I Done Got Over It," penned by labelmate Ernie K-Doe, who also helped out on the vocal refrain. Irma had left Al White's group when she became pregnant again, staying close to home, singing weekends in the Dew Drop. Through Earl King, Irma was introduced to the famed New Orleans booking agent, Percy Stovall, who took over the reins of her career. "I had 'Cry On' in the local charts, and I told Stovall about the experience I'd had as an entertainer. He told me he'd see what he could do, and he started booking a few out-of-town dates.

"Stovall had his own little circuit. He always knew when to play and where. When the workers got paid after the fruit harvest in Florida, we'd play around Fort Walton and Pensacola. He knew where every club, armory and hall was that gave dances in the South. We had a little Christmas run we'd do down in South Louisiana after the sugarcane harvest. We'd play Paterson, New Iberia, St. Martinville, Opelousas and Crowley. Some of those places were just a few miles away, but we always had packed houses because at that time of the year those people had money and they liked to spend it.

"He would put a bunch of us out on the road at the same time. Earl King, Johnny Adams, Robert Parker, Chris Kenner—whoever had the hottest record at the time would be the headliner. Stovall was the kind of guy that would hold back some of your money until we got home. He used to say, 'I'm not gonna pay y'all now because I want you to have some money to take home to your family when you get home.'

"He was a shrewd businessman. When I went to him, he asked me how much I wanted to get paid. I said 'One hundred and twenty-five dollars a night.' That sounded good to me. He was still paying me that $125 when I had the #17 record in the country. Some people were getting $1,000 a night, but I didn't know it, so it didn't bother me.

"But Stovall taught me to put some of that money in the bank. He was strict, and I learned a lot about the business from him that I still use today. He didn't allow for any messing up. He emphasized being dependable and being on time. He said that was more important than being talented, and he was right!"

Irma's popularity grew with each successive Minit release. In 1963 she recorded two songs that New Orleans still remembers fondly, "It's Raining" b/w "I Did My Part" (Minit 653).

Although the record sold heavily in Louisiana and Mississippi, it just barely missed cracking the national R&B charts. Nonetheless, it probably represents the best of Irma Thomas' early Sixties work. Written and produced by the ubiquitous Allen Toussaint (under alias Naomi Neville), Irma gives one of her most memorable and soulful performances on the ballad "It's Raining," while the flip proved she was equally adept at handling a shuffle. "Funny thing about 'It's Raining.' I didn't think anything about it when it was cut. I had to relearn the song after it came out because everybody wanted to hear it. I guess I've sang 'It's Raining' more than any other song in my life.

"Allen Toussaint produced and arranged those early records. We had a nice little family then, and we'd help each other on sessions. Really just about everybody on Minit had some kind of hit: K-Doe, Aaron Neville, Jessie Hill and Benny Spellman. They sang background on a lot of my records, and I did the same on theirs. It didn't seem like work then! It was just a whole lot of fun to me."

Irma was lucky enough to get her records played by all the white radio stations in New Orleans, for which she credits former WNNR program director Ed Munez. "Ed started giving Tuesday night dances—sock hops—at Germania Hall on Bienville Street so the teenagers could hear local artists like Sugar Boy, Johnny Adams, K-Doe and Bobby Mitchell. Then we'd start getting calls for jobs at the Tulane frat houses on Broadway Street and all the high school dances. Some nights we'd be triple gigged. We'd play a record hop, a fraternity party, and then go play at a club like the Sands or the F&M Patio."

Irma was even chosen to take part in an ad campaign sponsored by Coca Cola. Her photo appeared in a number of regional magazines and newspapers, making her one of the first blacks to appear in advertising endorsing a major product.

Irma's final release on Minit was the moody "Ruler of My Heart," in late 1963. While the record was at the height of its local popularity, Otis Redding, who was working in New Orleans, was so impressed by the tune that he covered it with a slightly altered title as "Pain In My Heart." For Redding, the song became his first national hit and helped to springboard his all too short career.

In 1964, the option to Irma's Minit contract was purchased by Liberty Records, which bought out Lew Chudd's Imperial label and made Imperial one of its subsidiaries. Liberty brought Irma to Los Angeles to be produced by Eddie Ray. The initial West Coast session was immediately fruitful, yielding her biggest national record of all "Wish Someone Would Care" b/w "Breakaway," which ironically ranks as one of her biggest New Orleans hits.

A stirring ballad, "Wish Someone Would Care" was one of the few songs penned by Irma herself. "I was really at a low point when I wrote that," she explains. "I was just looking back at life. I was a 14-year-old mother, I had three kids by the time I was 17, and I was on my second marriage. At the time, I was breaking up with my husband because he was giving me a hard time about being on stage. It was a song from my heart, that's probably why it sold so well; I really wanted someone to care, to stand behind me and care."

Irma toured extensively after "Wish Someone Would Care." Besides all of the major American soul music palaces, her travels eventually took her to England, where she appeared in a number of clubs.

As far as records were concerned, 1964 proved to be the biggest year of all. Besides "Wish Someone Would Care"—which rose to #17 during its 12 weeks in Billboard's Hot 100—its follow-up "Anyone Who Knows What Love Is" likewise charted nationally. Ironically, the flip of "Anyone Who Knows What Love Is," the blues ballad "Time Is On My Side," was covered by the Rolling Stones and turned into an international hit. Contrary to what some people believe, Irma shows no bitterness towards the Rolling Stones' success. "That's just the music business," she says.

As the year drew to a close, Irma had two more records in the Hot 100, "Times Have Changed" and "He's My Guy," both penned by an emerging performer/songwriter Van McCoy. Imperial released an album entitled "Wish Someone Would Care," which mostly included standard R&B tunes.

After Irma's initial success, Liberty decided to record her back in New Orleans with her old cohort Allen Toussaint producing a number of fine singles that were eventually collected on the "Take A Look" album. Although there were a number of fine performances, including "Teasing But Your Pleasing" and "Wait, Wait, Wait," Irma couldn't sneak another record into the charts. The kids that bought her records in 1964 instead spent their allowance on the latest Beatles and Dave Clark Five records. Imperial decided to try once more, and even went as far as to bring James Brown in to produce "It's A Man's World," which was a disaster. This time when her option came up, her contract was not renewed, and she wouldn't record again until Chess came into the picture.

In the meantime, Irma formed her own booking agency with her "old man" Victor Dispenza, and started working what she calls "the college circuit." "We started to play at a lot of sororities and fraternities all over the South. We played at 25 out of the 27 fraternities at the University of Alabama. During rush week the fraternities would try to outdo each other to try and get rushees. I remember playing on the same block one night in Tuscaloosa with James Brown, Ernie K-Doe, Hot Nuts, and Hank Ballard and the Midnighters. It's hard to believe but true.

"Those kids used to get so drunk at those dances. The worst thing that ever happened to me was at Ole Miss. One night everybody really got carried away and they were jumping on top of one another. This one fellow was really stoned and he fell into the microphone stand and knocked my front teeth out! I stopped using the microphone stand after that."

When Chess signed Irma in 1967, they brought her to the trendy Muscle Shoals Studio to record, and it looked like she would once again be back in the national spotlight. But sadly it wasn't to be.

"Chess was gonna do big things for me," explains Irma. "But they had a thing where they wanted to lock their artists up. They wanted to control my life, and I wasn't gonna go for that. They were working directly with the Walden Booking Agency, who wanted to take 25% off the top.

"Since I wouldn't go along with their plans, they wouldn't promote my records. They just sat on them. I did 3 or 4 singles for Chess, but they didn't do anything. It's too bad, because I really liked that Muscle Shoals sound."

Irma's Chess releases are somewhat overlooked but still topnotch. She managed a mild hit with "Good Things Don't Come Easy" and also a powerful version of Otis Redding's "Good To Me," which slipped into the national R&B chart at #42 in February of 1968. "I guess I was getting even for 'Pain In My Heart,' " she laughs.

In comparison to Etta James and Laura Lee, who also recorded on Chess at Muscle Shoals during the same period, Irma's records were every bit as good. But while the James and Lee discs—with better promotion—hit the charts, Irma returned to New Orleans to continue hustling one nighters.

After the Chess disappointment, Irma's career hit a downward stretch. The local recording scene was on the ropes, and none of the bigger labels wanted to take a chance with Irma. Club work was slowing up too, as the "guitar bands" were now in vogue, forcing many of the R&B groups to fight for the few scraps that were left.

"We were carrying a smaller band," recalls Irma. "Sometimes just a rhythm section. We couldn't work too much in New Orleans, pretty much on the Gulf Coast in Mississippi and Florida. But when Hurricane Camille came along, it wiped out all the little work we did have. In fact it destroyed some of the clubs that we had booked. So the band disbanded and I decided to move to California. I figured if I had to start all over again, I might as well try California because I had some relatives out there."

In Los Angeles it was back to square one for Irma. She was no longer "the soul queen" but just another good vocalist trying to make it. "I got a job as a clerk in a Montgomery Ward store. On the weekends I worked in some of the black clubs around town with pickup bands.

"I got to sing down in Sacramento and in the Bay area because there were a lot of people from Louisiana out there. But really I was just accepted as a good entertainer. I couldn't do any of the songs I was known for like 'It's Raining.' I pretty much had to stick to the Top 40."

Irma did run into some other transplanted New Orleanians in California, such as Harold Battiste, Dr. John and Shirley

Goodman; and Tammi Lynn, who turned her onto some studio work. Eventually, Irma was introduced to producer Jerry Williams, who was also a colorful entertainer, recording under the alias "Swamp Dog." "He was one weird dude, but he knew how to take care of business. We had a small West Coast hit on his own Fungus label, 'Coming From Behind.' "

Williams also produced an album that was to be issued on Atlantic-Cotillion, but only one single was issued. When the deal didn't work out the way Williams felt it should, he got the masters back and released the excellent "In Between Tears" album on Fungus. He also produced one other single in the early Seventies, the bawdy "Woman's Viewpoint" on the Roker label.

Periodically Irma had returned to New Orleans to appear at the New Orleans Jazz Festival, but in 1974, she decided to return home and stay. New Orleans hadn't forgotten her, and she again became as popular as she had been in the early Sixties, working once more with Tommy Ridgley.

In 1975, Irma married landscape gardener Emile Jackson who began forming a permanent band for Irma and booking her jobs. She also signed a recording contract with Sansu Records, which, as far as Irma was concerned, proved to be fruitless. "Marshall (Sehorn) and Allen (Toussaint) didn't even call me in to pick out material. The only thing they recorded was the stuff I sang out at the Jazz Fest in 1976, and they tricked me into that. I didn't know I was even being recorded. As far as I'm concerned that Jazz Fest album (on Island) and that album on Charly ('Hip Shakin' Mama') are a no-no. I didn't sign anything, and you bet I'll never see a dime out of it."

In 1977, Irma was approached by John Fred, who produced the "Soul Queen of New Orleans" album, which appeared on Floyd Soileau's Maison de Soul label. The album, which was recorded in one day in Baton Rouge, was a pleasant assortment of many of her hit tunes from the Sixties. Although it didn't set the world on fire, she did have a record back in the catalog and "at least I get a little royalty check once a year," she says.

Irma's latest album, the contemporary *Safe With Me,* was recorded in 1980 for Cyril Vetter's Baton Rouge-based RCS label. After much initial attention, sales of the disc fell short of what was anticipated. "I've been real lucky getting local airplay. WTIX and WNOE (white AM stations) played "Safe With Me," but the black stations wouldn't touch it.

"I really admire RCS, they wanted a good album and they

covered the globe to get one. We went to New York and Chicago to finish it up, but promotion-wise, I guess they just had their head someplace else. I can't knock 'em though, it just didn't work. I guess disco was just on the way out, and maybe my public just doesn't want me doing disco.

"At this point I've come to the conclusion I'll never have another national hit. You've just got to have big bucks. It's been my luck to be with a small company that can't promote, or a big company that won't promote. I honestly don't know what to record anymore. You can't live in the past, but basically that's what I've been living on. But I guess you can't knock a successful thing."

Recently Irma has found a new medium to showcase her talent—local television commercials. Most any night of the week she's plugging Gulf States Gold Exchange or endorsing a New Orleans burglar bar company. She even gets requests to sing the themes from her commercials at her engagements!

Today Irma works almost every weekend with her crack band, The Entertainers. Irma's enthusiasm and energy is still immediately contagious, and no Irma Thomas show sports an empty dance floor, although she admits it's not always easy.

"Sometimes I get onstage and people just sit there dumbfounded. I know what they're thinking: 'She must be 50. What's she doing up there dressed like that for?' Sometimes I have to stop the show and say, 'Y'all must be used to the way I look by now, why don't you just have some fun.' "

Irma attributes most of her present success to her husband, Emile Jackson. "I can relax now knowing all I have to worry about is the singing. Emile takes care of all the business. He fires and hires all the musicians. He bawls me out if I give a half-assed show. If I get up on stage and don't give an hour of Irma Thomas, I get two or three hours of Emile Jackson! But it's paid off. We get more and more bookings all the time and I think the people really get their money's worth when they come out to see us. The band's great too; we rehearse twice a week.

So what does the future hold for Irma Thomas? "Oh, I guess I'll just keep singing and hopefully do a few more commercials maybe.

"When I'm 60 you know what I'd really like to do? I'd like to think I'll still be worthwhile enough for some fancy hotel to hire me to sing in their cocktail lounge. Can't you just picture me with some old grey-headed man playing piano with me singing 'It's Raining'?"

Part Six:

THE SECOND LINE

In New Orleans, the term "second line" refers to the rag-tag group of revelers that forms behind the main procession of a jazz funeral. While they aren't intended to be the main focus of attention, the "second line" is very much a part of, and certainly adds color to, the jazz funeral proceedings.

"When you say second line," points out blues-shouter Mr. Google Eyes, "that's the only way to go. That's the last party you can give anybody. There's nobody cryin' over you. You could be nobody your whole life, but at least they take you out right."

"Second line" might also be an apt term when referring to the lesser known rhythm and blues artists in New Orleans. For every performer who became well known through hit records, scores remained unknown, unappreciated, and unsuspected. As record companies mushroomed during the Fifties and Sixties, a surprisingly large number of "minor" New Orleans artists did, in fact, record. Their music was good, some of it *very* good, and it was worth the risk of recording. Unfortunately, many didn't sell records in sufficient enough quantities to sustain their careers.

For many of the "second line" artists, the only way for them to get a break was on the small labels, and hope they could generate enough local interest so that a major record company might take a chance on leasing their material, and finance further recording sessions. Such was the case of Lee Dorsey, Johnny Adams and King Floyd. But while a handful succeeded, hundreds didn't. New Orleans is cluttered with "casualties" of the New Orleans rhythm and blues recording boom.

But while they might not have had success in terms of record sales, they made things a lot more interesting and exciting. They provided a solid foundation for music to develop. The "second line" artists are extremely important in the overview of New Orleans rhythm and blues.

LEE ALLEN
Cookin' with Mr. Lee

Lee Allen, now 56, possesses that modest dignity and charm found in so many musicians from the early days of New Orleans' rhythm and blues. Best known for the countless number of sessions he played on in New Orleans during the Fifties, he has since been recognized as one of the foremost tenor saxophonists in the music business. His work has spanned over three decades, playing on hit records by the likes of Paul Gayten, Fats Domino, Shirley and Lee, Little Richard (that's his out-of-control tenor on "Tutti Frutti"), Dr. John, The Stray Cats and most recently the Blasters. In between he even managed to squeeze in a couple of his own hits. Lee Allen is as responsible as anyone in New Orleans for putting the "rhythm" in rhythm and blues and the "rock" into rock 'n roll.

Lee Allen was born in Pittsburg, Kansas, on July 2, 1926, but moved to Denver with his mother after his father died, when he was just a year old. Lee became interested in the tenor saxophone in his early teens along with Dale Graham, Paul Quinashay and Joe Gibbs, who all went on to work at one time or another with Count Basie. Upon completion of high school, Lee was offered a music and athletic scholarship to New Orleans' Xavier University in 1943 where he was to letter in track, basketball and football.

Once in New Orleans' rich musical climate, Lee made himself right at home. "I was playing with some big bands on campus, Don Raymond and Sidney Desmond. I started working off campus one night a week on weekends when I could slip off. Played around the Dew Drop mostly, the Robin Hood and the Tiajuana too. I didn't have any trouble getting in clubs and getting to know musicians. There were no strangers; everyone was like family.

"I used to like to listen to other saxophone players back then like Louis Jordan, Illinois Jacquet, Lester Young, Ben Webster and Gene Ammons—I really liked his style. I really copied my tone around Coleman Hawkins, I always loved his sound."

Allen never did get to graduate from Xavier, because his studies were interrupted first by the death of his mother, and his continuing musical aspirations. By October 1947, Lee was a regular member of the Annie Laurie/Paul Gayten band, which was using Jackson Avenue's Robin Hood Club as its home base. Although Lee doesn't recall the first time he stepped into the J&M studio, it was likely with the Laurie-Gayten duo, who started the whole New Orleans rhythm and blues ball rolling earlier in the year with their hit waxing of Gayten's "True."

Lee was quick to cite Al Young, a generally unsung figure, as one of the primary proponents of early New Orleans R&B. "Al Young was a fight promoter who branched into recording and promoting shows. Al had a record shop [the Bop Shop on North Rampart Street near Cosimo Matassa's J&M Studio]. He opened some doors here for the local blacks who wanted to make some records. He really got things started for Paul Gayten and Dave Bartholomew. He was getting stuff for one label from Dave [Imperial] and for another from Paul [Deluxe]."

After quitting school, Lee married while continuing his musical career which really began to mushroom in the late Forties. "There weren't too many sessions just then. I was mostly playing with Paul Gayten and Annie Laurie around town. I didn't like to travel too much. Oh, we might go to Vicksburg, Jackson or Baton Rouge, but I liked to stay around New Orleans."

Eventually through recording and playing with Gayten, Lee was invited to play on other sessions produced by Dave Bartholomew. "I'd been knowing Dave since the mid Forties. He didn't have his own band then, because he was still in service. He'd just come in a club with his horn and his G.I. issues on and play. He got a band together after he got out of the service and I played in it from time to time but not as a regular member. Dave and I took a liking to one another. I guess the first thing we worked on was an Earl Williams session. Dave and I worked well with each other so we just got a little group together to work in the studio."

The basic "studio band" that worked out of J&M Studio during the early Fifties was Lee Allen and Alvin "Red" Tyler, tenor sax; Frank Fields, bass; Earl Palmer, drums; Ernest Mclean, guitar, and depending on if a piano was called for, either Edward Franks or Salvador Doucet.

With this talented unit at his disposal, Bartholomew was able to shape a distinctive New Orleans' sound to the records he was producing, best typified by Fats Domino and Smiley Lewis on Imperial Records and Shirley and Lee on Aladdin.

"The money wasn't great for side musicians then. We got $35 a session and we worked a lot of hours. A session was 4 tunes then.

Sometimes we'd work all day and half the night. We had some rough sessions too.

"It seemed like once Fats got a few big hits that the record companies from New York and California started coming here to use the band and the studio. We played behind Joe Turner, Ray Charles, Little Richard. The records kept being hits and they kept flying down here.

"I didn't try to play differently behind each individual, I played the way I felt. I got my message from the singer and stayed close to the melody line of the song. I never tried to change my playing for different artists.

"We stayed pretty busy around that studio, but like I said I never was too much on travelling because I was raising a family and had a house on Mandeville Street over by the Falstaff Brewery. The only time we really went on the road was a mid-west tour with Fats and Professor Longhair and that was some trip. None of the club owners wanted Professor Longhair to play their piano because he would kick holes in the bottom keeping time. That was his thing."

The list of artists Lee Allen accompanied on record is practically endless. Besides the previously mentioned, his tenor sax also graced sides by Huey "Piano" Smith, Lloyd Price, Guitar Slim, Amos Milburn, Charles Brown, "Frogman" Henry and the Spiders to name but a few. By 1956, Aladdin Records' Eddie Mesner approached Lee about making a record on his own. The result was Aladdin 3354, "Shimmy"/"Rockin' at Cosimo's," both blistering instrumentals that hardly warranted its poor sales.

In 1957, Lee was signed on with Al Silver's New York R&B label Herald/Ember, producing singles on Tommy Ridgley, Joe Jones, Ernie Kador. At Silver's suggestion Lee also recorded his own instrumental session which was to have surprising results. A Bill Doggett-inspired "Walkin' With Mr. Lee" (Ember 1027) entered *Billboard's* Hot 100 early in 1958 rising as high as number 54 during its eleven-week visit to the charts.

"I'd been working some dates with Fats Domino and we used to close the show with an instrumental. I'd come up with this riff that everybody liked and this guy from New York [Al Silver] suggested I cut it. After I did, he went back to New York and called me after a couple of weeks and said 'Lee you got a hit!' Sure enough I had a hit with my first record. I got my own band together and went on the road for three years. I had Jack Willis on trumpet, Placide Adams on drums, Curtis Nichols piano, Bill Jones on guitar—who by the way went on to play with Stevie Wonder—and Frog Joseph

Lee Allen, late 1950's

on bass. I was the youngest guy in the band. It was a lot of responsibility but it was a great experience. We had a number one hit on *American Bandstand* for something like six weeks. I played the Apollo, the Howard, all in the Carolinas and Florida, all up into Canada."

Lee managed to sneak one other instrumental, "Tic Tock" (Ember 1039) into the national charts for one week during October of 1958. Even though Lee couldn't duplicate the success of "Walkin' With Mr. Lee," Ember thought enough of his work to release an album aptly titled "Walkin' With Mr. Lee," which now changes hands among collectors for as much as $100, according to Lee.

After the public's interest in his hit subsided, Lee returned to New Orleans and joined Fats Domino's band in 1961. Although he still was present on a few isolated recording sessions, things had definitely changed on New Orleans' recording scene. The hard-edged R&B sound that typified the city's sound of the Fifties was being replaced by a softer "pop R&B" sound that was being penned primarily by Allen Toussaint for a new roster of up-and-coming performers. Consequently, booming sax solos gave way to less dramatic instrumentation.

Lee remained the backbone of Fats' dramatic horn section until 1965 when the strain of constant travelling dissolved his family and he decided to pull up stakes and move to Los Angeles. In many ways Lee's departure was typical of the direction of the overall trend of New Orleans up-and-down musical fortunes. The demise of the independent record labels had New Orleans' recording activity at a standstill, and Lee was just one of the scores of musicians who headed for the greener pastures of New York and Los Angeles.

"I had an offer to go to the West Coast when Earl Palmer left in 1959 with Aladdin Records, but I didn't want to go at the time. I always loved Los Angeles because it's wide open and beautiful, and because I love to play golf! I got a job working in an aeronautics factory but I was still playing music as much as five nights a week. You know how it is, sometimes you got to do something else to get by, it doesn't matter who you are.

"I ran into Clifford Scott who was Bill Doggett's saxophone player on 'Honky Tonk.' He had a lot of work so when he'd get an overflow, he'd call me. I had an organ trio, so we started getting around and things just sort of snowballed. You know your name just starts getting around. We played one place steady for two years. I made a few sessions, but other than the stuff with Dr. John, it wasn't really too much to speak of."

During the mid-Seventies Lee returned to Fats Domino's band, touring extensively throughout the United States and a number of times in Europe. After the 1980 Fats Domino tour concluded, Lee suddenly found himself being the key figure in the resurgence of rhythm and blues among the young rock 'n rollers, primarily through his work with the Blasters.

"I used to help the kids out in the Blasters [Phil and Dave Allen] about 13 years ago. They wanted to play Jimmy Reed and Joe Turner songs and I showed 'em how the changes went. We've stayed friends pretty much ever since. They were going into the studio to do an album [*The Blasters* on Stash] and Phil asked me to help out. After we cut the album it started to take off and I started to help out on gigs once in awhile. One-nighters aren't exactly my cup of tea, but a trip back to New Orleans is like a holiday back home because I get to talk to my old friends like Dave [Bartholomew] and Shirley [Goodman].

"I recently did sessions with Diz and the Doormen in Europe and the Stray Cats too. It seems like a lot of younger listeners are now interested in the old music and musicians. It really gratifies me to see people like Lowell Fulsom and Big Joe Turner out there playing again. I love to help guys out like that anyway I can."

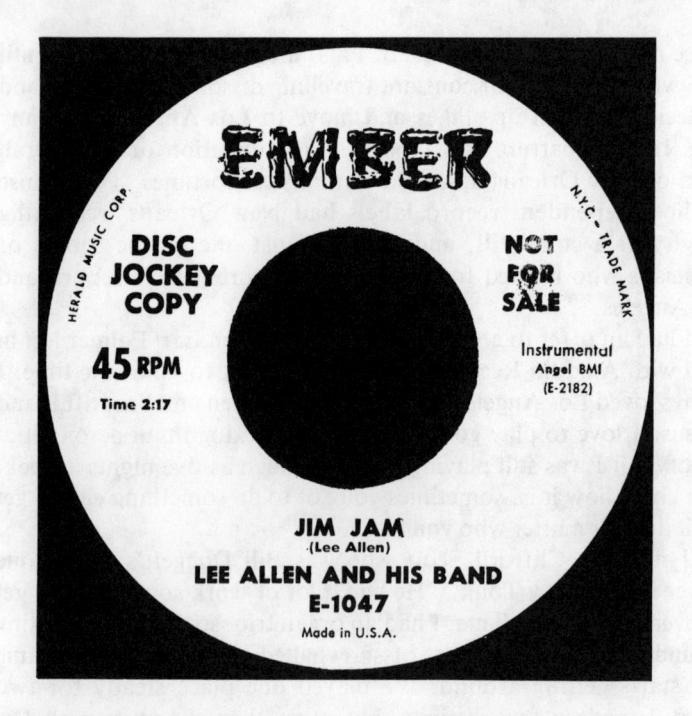

Lee Allen's mastery of his instrument has been documented by three generations of music lovers. It might be easy for him to coast on his reputation but Lee has no such intention. "A lot of people might laugh, but I'd love to do a gospel album. I really think I could do a good job. I've got a few other things I've been working on that might make a good R&B album too. Maybe when all the excitement with the Blasters dies down I'll get a five-piece band together and work on some new material. It doesn't work if you just stand put. I'm always looking for something new."

SMILEY LEWIS
I Hear You Knockin'

It's sad to think that New Orleans' greatest blues shouter missed out on the last decade's resurgence in New Orleans rhythm and blues. Smiley Lewis possessed the strongest and most identifiable voice in the business. Even though he recorded scores of great records, Smiley just couldn't get that hit that would propel him to stardom. But thankfully he left us a legacy of nearly two decades' worth of some of the most consistent and enjoyable performances ever to be put on wax.

Unfortunately, no researcher got to Smiley before he died. As a result, most of what we know about him is secondhand, and a number of misconceptions about his life have been propagated since his death in 1966.

Smiley's real name was Overton Amos Lemons, and, according to his first wife, Leona Robinson Kelly, he was born July 5, 1913 in DeQuincy, Louisiana, a small town in Calcasieu Parish near Texas. Due to incorrect information supplied by Smiley's second wife, Dorothy Estes from Smiley's death certificate, it had been commonly accepted that he was born July 5, 1920 in Union, Louisiana, but that is certainly not true.

Although Leona knew little about his childhood, Smiley's sister-in-law, Thelma Lemons, who still lives in DeQuincy, sheds some light on his youth. Smiley was the second of three sons born to Jeffrey Lemons and his wife, possibly Lily Mae Lemons. His oldest brother, Jeffrey Jr. "favored Smiley strongly." Jeffrey Jr. married Thelma and settled in DeQuincy, where he lived until his death in 1957. The youngest brother, Odelius, eventually moved to Chicago. It is possible that Smiley's mother died early in life, because Thelma recalls the family living in West Lake, Louisiana, a small town near Lakes Charles, where the Lemons brothers were raised by a stepmother. Jeff Lemons Sr. supported his family by "working common labor" according to Thelma.

It is possible that young Overton might have been sent to New Orleans to be reared when he was ten years old, or, possibly, he might have run away from home. Leona recalls Smiley telling her "he was part raised by a white family that lived in Frontatown

[Irish Channel.]" She also adds, "When Lewis was laying in the Charity Hospital (just prior to his death) an older white lady who was in another ward came to visit him and called Lewis 'my baby.' Lewis said that that was the lady who raised him when he came to New Orleans."

As a teen, Smiley was apt to be exposed to much of New Orleans' musical heritage, and he eventually chose the guitar as his first musical instrument. During the Mid-1930s, Smiley joined trumpeter Thomas Jefferson's band, which also included Tuts Washington on piano and Edward "Noon" Johnson on "bazooka horn." The group played at Beck's Restaurant and Bar, The Court of the Two Sisters and the Gypsy Tea Room on weekends. The band's uniforms were red frock coats and tall beaver hats (toppers)!

Smiley played guitar and acted as the group's vocalist. Tuts Washington recalls, "Lewis always was a good entertainer. He sang the blues and all of them sentimental numbers. He would walk off the bandstand and sing to the people in the audience. See, Lewis had a voice so strong he could sing over the band, and that was before we had microphones."

During the day Smiley hustled odd jobs, and he drove a truck off and on for the Janecke Barge Company. After the Thomas Jefferson band dissolved, Smiley worked spot jobs with "Noon" Johnson and guitarist Walter "Papoose" Nelson Sr. (alias Captain Midnight). Often the trio would play for tips on Bourbon Street or try to convince a club owner to let them sing a couple of tunes inside in return for a dollar or two. According to Leona, Smiley often returned "with a guitar full of change."

In the summer of 1938, Smiley met 20-year-old Leona Robinson, who lived with her mother on Thalia Street, and who collected insurance for a living. "I was coming home from church on a Saturday when I met Lewis," recalls Leona, who still lives just a few blocks from her former residence. "I stopped to talk to a lady named Beatrice who was having a supper that evening. Lewis came by with another guitar player and they stopped to say hello. They seemed like nice fellows so I asked Beatrice 'Why don't you invite them to stop by this evening!' So she did and they played for the supper. He was a very friendly person, I'd guess you'd have to say it was love at first sight."

Leona recalls that Overton was already calling himself Smiley Lewis when they met and that he never said how he assumed the alias. But she did comment "he sure did smile a lot." However, he

Smiley Lewis, 1957

was most likely dubbed Smiley because he had no front teeth! He later got a bridge once he could afford it but the name remained. The Lewis moniker might have been adopted from the white family that raised him, or he might have used the name as a way to hide his past. Then again it might just have sounded better than his real name—Smiley Lemons!?!

Smiley and Leona were wed in November 1938, and the couple stayed with the bride's mother in a small house on the corner of Thalia and South Tonti streets. Life continued pretty much as one would have expected for the newlyweds. Leona recalls this period of Smiley's life. "Lewis didn't want me working, he wanted me at home. He didn't have a regular job but he always supported us. Today you'd call it hustling. He drove freight, worked on the river and did odd jobs. Some nights he'd play music and bring home some money, but he didn't have what you'd call a band.

"When Lewis and I met he was ever so slight. He didn't get stout until after we got married. Lord, how he loved to eat my cooking. He liked red beans, gumbo and greens. Lewis was a good cook, too. He loved to hunt and fish, and he'd cook rabbit or fish for supper.

"Sometimes Lewis would go to church with my mother and me.

He loved to sing hymns and one time he entered a singing contest at church. Of course he won. He liked to go the baseball games. I recall him taking me to Pelican Stadium to see Jackie Robinson play once."

By 1940 music was still a pleasant sideline to bring in a little extra money. He continued to freelance, singing and playing for whatever he could pocket on Bourbon Street, in the company of "Noon" Johnson. Smiley avoided serving in World War II, perhaps because he was the sole supporter of his family, which had grown by one with the addition of a daughter, Viola, in November 1941.

Around this time Tuts Washington was playing at a number of different clubs on Rampart Street and recalls Smiley stopping by the Kotton Club often to visit. "Lewis was shoeing horses in those days," says Washington. "He was living Uptown then and he'd stop in to see me on his way home from the French Quarter. He was always telling me, 'Come on Tuts. Let's you and me get a little aggregation together and make some money.' "

"Well, things were dead around here because the war was going on. So I took a job playing with Kid Ernest (clarinetist Ernest Mollier) and his brother Pat up in Bunkie, Louisiana at the Boogie Woogie Club. Well, the man at the club liked us but said he wanted a singer, too. I told them boys about Smiley, but they didn't want to hire him because he had a reputation for having a big head. I begged those boys to hire him and finally they did. We stayed up around Bunkie and Marksville for the best part of a year."

Even Leona brought the family up to Bunkie in 1942 or '43 (they now had a new son, too) for a couple of months. When Smiley returned to New Orleans from Bunkie, the house on Thalia had been razed by the city to make way for a federal housing project, and his household had moved into the Lafitte Projects on Orleans Avenue.

By the end of the war things began picking up in New Orleans - many clubs reopened and there was work once again for musicians. The Kid Ernest band broke up, but Tuts and Smiley teamed up with drummer Herman Seale to form a blues trio.

"We had the hottest trio in town," boasts Tuts. "Nobody could touch us. We played all through the French Quarter and down Bourbon Street. The El Morocco, the Cat in the Fiddle, The Dog House and the Moulin Rouge."

The group's popularity was such that in 1947 David Braun invited the trio to record for Deluxe Records, looking for them to follow in the successful footsteps of Paul Gayten and Annie Laurie.

Smiley's first sides were "Turn On Your Volume Baby" and "Here Comes Smiley," issued on Deluxe 3099. Both songs were written by Leo Franks; as Tuts recalls he was a white bartender in the French Quarter who gave the songs to Smiley. "Here Comes Smiley" was especially well suited to his booming voice. In it he sings:

> *Here comes Smiley,*
>   *I hope you let him in.*
> *Here comes Smiley,*
>   *Please take a chance on him.*
> *Well I ain't from no where,*
>   *And no places have I been.*

Bassist Papa John replaced Seale on the session and Tuts plays some especially dramatic boogie woogie piano.

The record did poorly in other markets, but well enough locally to insure plenty of club work. Tuts still fondly recalls visiting his aunt's bar and hearing himself blaring from the juke box. Deluxe's catalog lists Smiley's second release as "Love Is Like A Gamble" b/w "Swimming Blues," #3108. But, since a copy of the record has yet to surface, it can be safely assumed the record was never issued, perhaps due to the poor showing of the debut disc.

Even though Deluxe requested no more recordings, the trio stayed busy most nights of the week playing their usual haunts. Smiley even travelled as far away as Texas, and on the way stopped in to visit with his older brother Jeff and his wife Thelma (Leona recalls Smiley's father died before she met him in 1938 and that he attended his funeral, which probably took place in West Lake) Smiley also made some cameo appearances with Dave Bartholomew's Orchestra at the Dew Drop Inn, billing himself as "the drifting blues singer." The trio also had a regular spot at the Cinq Sou Hall, a club next to the Dew Drop, for a few months.

By March 1950, Dave Bartholomew had already begun recording local talent for the Imperial label, with instructions from Imperial's president Lew Chudd to develop new artists. "I grew up in the same neighborhood as Smiley," recalls Bartholomew. "He used to sing on the front porch of his house, and I used to say to myself, 'If I ever get a chance to help him I will.' So I got in the position to record Smiley with Imperial and I did. He was a real good blues singer, and back in those days that's what was selling."

Smiley's first Imperial release was "Te-Na-Na" b/w "Lowdown," with the trio being augumented by Bartholomew's horn section. "Te-Na-Na" became a good regional seller almost immediately, partly due to the effort of local deejay Dr. Daddy-O.

"Smiley had cut 'Tee-Na-Na' down at Cosimo's," recalls Dr. Daddy-O. "He brought me the acetate disc of the song the next day and asked me to play it, because the owner of the Club Desire promised to hire him if he had a record played on the radio. So I played it and I started getting a lot of calls on it."

"I'm the one who gave Lewis the words to that 'Te-Na-Na,' assures Tuts Washington. "That's a song that the boys used to sing up in the penitentiary. But Lewis and me was the first ones to put it out."

A catchy barrelhouse-type blues, "Te-Na-Na" made Smiley an overnight sensation. Melvin Cade, a New Orleans promoter, began booking one-nighters out of town for Smiley—whose "trio" had grown with the addition of Joe Harris on sax, Albert Fernandez on trumpet, bassist James Prevost and Buddy Williams replacing Herman Seale on drums, who was soon to die from diabetes.

A May 1950 issue of the *Louisiana Weekly* reported: "That 'Te-Na-Na Man' Smiley Lewis, whose recent recording 'Te-Na-Na' has caused a fervor on the local jukeboxes, returns from a three-week run of Texas and Mississippi niteries, May 30 at the Lincoln Theatre." Later that summer Smiley also took part in a widely publicized "Battle of the Blues" show with Roy Brown and Mr. Google Eyes at the San Jacinto Club on N. Villere Street.

"Man, we played nearly every place you can name" says Tuts "and making top money, too. Oklahoma, Texas, Tennessee, Florida, Georgia—we played everywhere. We had two station wagons, one was Lewis' the other was Melvin's. Sometimes we'd drive 500 miles a night to get to a job. Fats [Domino] was playing behind us in those days. Anyone who booked us had to book Fats after we left. We was playing a 'Battle of the Blues' at the Bijou Theatre in Nashrille with Joe Turner, Lowell Fulsom and Gatemouth Brown when a boy came in and told us Melvin Cade got killed in a car wreck bringing Fats up to the joint where we was playing. Everybody in the band cried that night because Melvin was a good man."

Even though "Te-Na-Na" failed to chart nationally, Imperial was keen on issuing more sides by Smiley to follow up their initial success. Imperial quickly issued the remaining tracks from their first session "Slide Me Down" b/w "Growing Old" (Imperial

5072) but without nearly the amount of success as "Te-Na Na."

In April 1950, Smiley returned to the studio to record "If You Ever Loved A Woman" b/w "Dirty People" (Imperial 5102) and "Where Were You" and "My Baby" which appeared on an Imperial subsidiary label, Colony 110. Even though these releases didn't become big sellers, they were excellent examples of New Orleans' developing R&B style. Smiley shouts some spirited lyrics, with the New Orleans horns and Tuts' rollicking boogie woogie piano all in top form.

Smiley didn't return to the studio again until a year later. Again he couldn't repeat the sensation of his initial hit, even though "Bea's Boogie" and "Where Were You" were just as satisfying. But despite the lack of national success, Smiley's records sold in large enough quantities in the South to make him a popular attraction and to keep Imperial interested in recording more sessions.

The strain of one-nighters caused personality conflicts and began to wear the band down, as Tuts Washington relates: "Lewis got ornery and big headed. Everywhere we went he was behind a gang of women running around and drinking. He threw me out of his car in Nashville over a woman one night and made me walk back to the hotel. Another night we was crossing the River [Mississippi] on a ferry and he said he was gonna kick my ass. I told him 'If you try, I'll take this knife and juke you in your big fat belly and throw you in the river.' Well, if Herman wouldn't have jumped in between us, we probably would have killed each other. But hell, I didn't need that; if it hadn't of been for me, Lewis would still have been shoeing horses."

But Tuts is quick to add "I can't fault him as an entertainer. He was the best singer we had around here, and he could sing them sentimental tunes like 'Someday You'll Want Me' just as good as the blues. Some people called him the black Bing Crosby. Lewis could imitate Amos and Andy on the bandstand, and you'd have to look twice to really believe it was him and not the radio playing."

Imperial's patience finally paid off when the pleading "The Bells Are Ringing" (Imperial 5194) snuck into the national R&B charts for two weeks at #10 in September, 1952. Unfortunately, the impact of Smiley's hit was overshadowed in Imperial's eyes by a larger hit, "Goin' Home," by Fats Domino, which had risen to #1 in the R&B charts earlier in the year.

Smiley and Tuts soon after split company after having words. According to Tuts, "Once he got his name out there he wanted to boss everybody and you couldn't tell him nothing. I told him,

'Lewis, I was playing long before I knew you. I don't need you.' So that's when Dave Bartholomew grabbed him. He tried to get me back in the band later on when his records stopped selling, but I had had enough of Smiley Lewis.''

With "The Bells Are Ringing" still selling strongly, Smiley was once again hot property, and Dave Bartholomew brought him back into the studio. For the rest of his days on Imperial, Smiley would use the regular session men, which included Charles "Hungry" Williams or Earl Palmer on drums, Frank Fields on bass, and a variable combination of Lee Allen, "Red" Tyler, Herb Hardesty, Clarence Hall or Meyer Kennedy on saxophones. Bartholomew dispensed with Smiley's guitar (his playing is spotlighted only on "Sad Life" and "My Baby Was Right" on his earlier releases) using Ernest McLean instead, despite claims by many that he was indeed a fine instrumentalist.

"Smiley was a good guitar player," recalls Earl King. "I don't know why Dave wouldn't record his guitar. Smiley had the kind of style that was instantly identifiable as soon as you stepped in the door. I really liked it.''

Tuts Washington adds, "He was really coming around with his playing. I recall he played a Fender. I was learning him some of the chords from the piano and he was making them fine. I tell you Lewis could do something with a guitar that I never saw before in my life. When it came time for him to take a solo, he would put a pick up under the strings, lay the guitar next to his amplifier and it would keep on playing. Then he'd get down off the bandstand and grab some old gal and start dancing. Some nights he'd do that for ten, maybe fifteen minutes before he came back and started playing again.''

Once again, Smiley couldn't find an immediate hit to follow up "The Bells Are Ringing." Surely this must have frustrated all parties involved, especially with Imperial label mate/rival Fats Domino's star beginning to shine brighter and brighter. But, in trying, Smiley and Bartholomew were to give us some of the most satisfying R&B recordings of the early Fifties.

Bartholomew began recording Smiley in a variety of styles. "It's So Peaceful" (Imperial 5208) tried to recapture the flavor of "The Bells," while the flip, "Gumbo Blues," was a classic New Orleans blues with Tuts Washington's ringing piano (here for the last time on Smiley's records) leading the proceedings. The Toppers were brought in to provide the background vocals on "Big Mamou" and the latin-tinged "Little Fernandez." Meanwhile, "Caldonia's

Party," penned by Bartholomew, was an attempt to mimic Louis Jordan's style and also signalled the increased dependency on Bartholomew's own material.

"Blue Monday," which borrowed its rhythm from "Caldonia's Party," did quite well locally in early 1954 for Smiley, but it wouldn't really become a big hit until Fats Domino covered it two years later. Other highlights included "Jailbird," That Certain Door," "The Rocks," "Play Girl," and "Down The Road," all of which sold in sufficient quantities to insure Imperial's continued interest, even if they missed the charts.

By 1955, R&B records started to infiltrate the pop charts with increasing frequency. Many white teenagers were beginning to listen to black radio stations and buy R&B records. Smiley started the year off right in the thick of things with "I Hear You Knockin'," which jumped into the national R&B charts, rising to the lofty heights of #2, and becoming his biggest seller ever. Kicked off with Huey Smith's characteristic piano intro, Smiley tells his woman in no uncertain terms, "I hear you knockin', but you can't come in!" But, once again, some of Smiley's thunder was stolen when Gale Storm's insipid cover version rose to #2 on *Billboard's* Hot 100, and even later when Fats successfully covered it in 1961.

With New Orleans R&B records beginning to dominate the black airwaves and jukeboxes, tunes like "Ain't That A Shame," "Feel So Good," and "Tutti Frutti" were defining a new musical era. As an arch-exponent of this style of music, Smiley should have cleaned up. But regrettably, such was not the case.

With "I Hear You Knockin' " riding high in the charts, Smiley and Earl King teamed up for a number of shows along the Gulf Coast. "We both had hits," recalls Earl. "I had just cut 'Lonely, Lonely Nights' and Smiley had 'I Hear You Knockin'.' The two of us worked as a package kind of like Jr. Parker and Bobby Bland's 'Blues Consolidated' thing. But Smiley got this new booking agent that told him he'd make a lot more money on his own, so he split. It's too bad, because the guy dropped Smiley when he couldn't get another big record."

Milton Batiste, who now leads the world famous Olympia Brass Band, played trumpet with Smiley during the mid-Fifties; he offers this insight into his character: "Smiley was kinda strict. He was an all right guy, but he didn't go for no bullshittin'. He mostly liked to stay off by himself and avoid any humbug.

"I met Smiley at the Dew Drop. I was just 19 or 20 when I went on the road with him. I never did get to record with him, I was one of the workhorses. Lee Allen, Earl Palmer and that bunch did the recording with him."

Batiste recalls that besides himself, the "Smiley Lewis Band" included: Nat Perrillat, sax; Charles Conners, drums; Edwin Mare, second guitar; and, occasionally, Huey Smith on piano.

Smiley bought himself a blue, two-toned 1955 Cadillac (with his name embossed on its doors in gold letters) that he polished up to looking-glass condition. It was a band rule that no one smoke or eat in Smiley's Cadillac, and he often insisted that band members remove their shoes before entering it!

"Smiley was a great performer," says Batiste. "He sang from the heart. When he grabbed the microphone, everybody stopped what they were doing and listened. Smiley got his drive from the drummer. He was real strict with the drummer.

"He was a real flashy dresser," continued Batiste. "Always clean. Shiny shoes at all times. Even if he was wearing a pair of dungarees around the house, they'd be pressed to a point. He must have had dozens of suits."

"Smiley could drink too, man. Drank straight gin by the fifth. One time him and Papa Lightfoot (singer/harmonica player George Lightfoot) got in a hell of a fight. We were up in Tennessee, and before the show those two were drinking that gin and throwing dice. Papa Lightfoot was winning, and Smiley wasn't too happy about that. Smiley started calling Papa Lightfoot "tangle eye" (Lightfoot was cross-eyed). So Papa Lightfoot took Smiley's money and sat in the front seat of his car and started eating a ham sandwich! Well, that was worse than taking Smiley's money. Next thing you know they were rolling in the snow beating the hell out of each other. It took the whole band to pull them apart. But, we did the show, and everybody was friends at the end of the night."

Smiley just couldn't get another national hit, even though Imperial afforded him every opportunity. Maybe he was just too bluesy, or too powerful, to catch the ears of younger record buyers. Regardless, Smiley's late Fifties output is now looked upon as classic examples of New Orleans rhythm and blues. The Imperial catalog is just littered with stunning sides by Smiley.

Records like "Go On Fool," "Queen of Hearts," "Hook, Line and Sinker," "Shame, Shame, Shame," and "Down Yonder We Go Balling," surely deserved to be bigger hits than they were.

Dave Bartholomew summed up the situation by saying, "We just couldn't get Smiley started. He always had the best material. His records would sell great all around New Orleans, but we just couldn't break him nationally like everyone else. It was a frustrating situation."

Smiley's frustrations were compounded by the fact that other artists were taking his material and having hits. Besides the beforementioned covers of "I Hear You Knockin' " by Gale Storm and Fats Domino, even Elvis Presley got into the act, sterilizing the lyrics of "One Night" and riding it to #4 nationally in 1958. "He had a few harsh words about people taking his numbers," recalls Milton Batiste.

"He had to be frustrated," speculates Hazel Lemons Bells, one of his daughters. "I couldn't understand how Fats could make a hit out of 'Blue Monday' and my father couldn't. He had some bad things to say about Dave [Bartholomew], but him and Fats were friends. I remember going to Fats' house where Fats had a bar that was covered with hundreds of silver dollars, and we were living in the Lafitte Projects."

It was also during this period that Smiley's domestic life began to split at the seams. Although Tuts Washington claims Smiley abandoned his wife and children for another woman, his first wife still speaks warmly about their relationship. "He just said that he was a musician and lived a different life. We wasn't angry with each other. He was proud of his children (4 girls and 2 boys) and he always sent money to support them, even when he was on the road. He'd come around at Christmas and bring presents every year. I thought maybe we'd get back together, but we finally divorced around 1960."

By the late Fifties, Imperial's Lew Chudd was reevaluating his label's position in the record industry and its commitment to New Orleans. Chudd had a gold mine in Ricky Nelson, but, of his New Orleans artists, only Fats Domino was selling sufficient amounts of records to keep Chudd's interest. To Imperial's credit they did try a Smiley Lewis album, *I Hear You Knockin'* (Imperial 9141), but after 1957, Smiley's sessions grew farther apart. Material-wise, his records began to suffer, as it seemed that Fats was getting better songs to record.

Still, there were a number of gems among Smiley's later Imperial releases, the best being "Bad Luck Blues" and "Rootin' and Tootin'." His final session for Imperial in September 1960 produced excellent versions of "Stormy Monday" and "Tell Me Who." But his contract wasn't renewed after a prolific ten-year stay on the label.

Most people recall that Smiley was pretty much down on his luck throughout the Sixties. He no longer carried a band, as most of his work consisted of spot jobs around New Orleans. He often opened for up-and-comers Irma Thomas and Ernie K-Doe at Germania Hall on Bienville Street. He also occasionally played the Sands on Jefferson Highway, where it is remembered that he used to load his equipment on the Jefferson Parish bus at the end of the night.

Smiley had taken up with another woman, Dorothy Estes, a nurse who lived over Ruthie's Record Shop at 4628 Freret Street. While this researcher has been unable to track the woman down, by all reports she was a fine lady, who even was instrumental in placing Smiley's first wife on the welfare role after Smiley's death.

Recordwise, Smiley waxed the spirited "Tore Up" and "I'm Coming Down With The Blues" for Okeh in 1961, which was reminiscent of the glory days on Imperial. But, once again, it didn't catch on, and it was his sole release on the label.

Dot issued a single in 1964, Cecil Gant's "I Wonder," but it met with the same reaction saleswise as so many of his other releases. Sadly, the many years of hard living and hard drinking were catching up with Smiley. He would enter the studio only once more, in December 1965, with Allen Toussaint producing a dispirited remake of "The Bells Are Ringing" on the Loma label. Smiley's once booming voice was so weak and strained, he couldn't even muster a B side, leaving Toussaint to cover with a bouncy instrumental.

Soon after, Smiley entered Charity Hospital a very sick man. "They had a benefit up in the hospital for him so they could get blood for him," recalls Tuts. "Smiley called me and asked me to come up and play a party, for people to donate blood the day before his operation. I hadn't seen him in a long time, but I could see that the cancer was eating him up. He tried to play with us but could barely hold his guitar. I walked Lewis up and down the hall, and he had his arm around me and his eyes got full of water. He said, 'Tuts, you taught me all I know. If I'd have listened to you, I'd still be doing all right today.'

"I went up to the hospital to visit him often," recalls his first wife, Leona. "He said 'I knew you wouldn't forget me, my dear.' He was in a lot of pain and he knew he was going to die. He was baptized up in Charity before he died."

After the operation, he was sent home, where Dorothy Estes did the best to make him comfortable. The March 19, 1966, issue of the *Louisiana Weekly* revealed Smiley's plight, and asked his friends to visit him and "drop by some of that green stuff."

Earl King remembers passing Smiley on Freret Street not long after he got out of Charity Hospital, and would have kept on walking had Smiley not stopped him. "He couldn't have weighed 100 pounds (he had as many as 240 pounds on his 5'2" frame)," says Earl. "I couldn't even recognize his voice."

Smiley's friends hadn't forgotten him, though, and a giant benefit show was organized by Benny Spellman and Dave Bartholomew, which was to be held October 10, 1966, at La Ray's Club on Dryades Street. Included on the bill were Porky Jones, Sugar Boy Crawford, Earl King, Bea Booker, Curley Moore and Johnny Adams. Tragically, Smiley couldn't live long enough to reap the benefits, as he succumbed to stomach cancer at home on October 7, 1966, leaving a widow, Dorothy Estes Lemons, whom he apparently married on his death bed.

A large funeral was held at the Denis Rhodes Mortuary, on Louisiana Avenue, with a number of musicians present. According to the death certificate, Smiley was buried in the St. James A.M.E. cemetery in Convent, Louisiana, but there is no such cemetery in that river-parish town. Smiley's daughter Viola claims that her father was buried in the Estes family vault in Eunice, Louisiana, which coincides with a similar story told by Tuts Washington and Bobby Mitchell. As for the rest of the inaccuracies on the death certificate, it is this author's guess that whoever filled out the death certificate might have misconstrued Eunice for Union, given by a grief-stricken Ms. Estes, who provided the information. As for the inaccuracies of his birthdate and place of birth, it could be possible that Ms. Estes thought Smiley was a younger man, and she could have just guessed at his place of birth. Perhaps Dorothy Estes was born in Convent and claimed Smiley was also, to in some way re-enforce their relationship to others. Whatever the case, we'll never know until the mysterious Ms. Estes is located.

In the years that have followed since his death, nearly all of Smiley's material has been reissued in one form or another, primarily on English labels. The timelessness of his material has been demonstrated over and over by young, white rock 'n' roll groups who have revived his material. One wonders what Smiley would have thought when Dave Edmunds nearly topped the charts with "I Hear You Knockin' " in 1970.

In terms of records release, Smiley Lewis was one of New Orleans' most prolifie R&B artists of the Fifties. Given the high quality of his material, we can only look with puzzlement at his lack of commercial success. For a proud man like Smiley, surely this disappointment, which he was forced to accept, was as painful as the cancer which eventually felled him.

"Smiley's situation was just one of those great cosmic mysteries that we'll never know about," says Earl King. "He just didn't get the breaks. But if he were alive today, he'd still be out there trying even if there wasn't a dime in it for him. That's just the kind of guy that Smiley was."

JAMES CRAWFORD
"Sugar Boy"

One of the more mysterious figures who surfaced during the classic 1950s era of New Orleans rhythm and blues was the legendary "Sugar Boy." Perhaps best known for his explosive Carnival record "Jock-A-Mo," not only were Sugar Boy's other records great, but his bands, The Chapaka Shaweez, The Cane Cutters and the Sugar Lumps, graduated some of the city's best musicians. Included in their ranks were Billy Tate, Irving Bannister, Snooks Eaglin, Frank Fields, David Lastie, Big Boy Myles, Warren Myles and Smokey Johnson, to name but a few. To this day, many New Orleans musicians still claim that Sugar Boy was the best singer, and carried the best band in the city until the early Sixties. Unfortunately, his career as an R&B artist ended prematurely after he was permanently injured, and nearly killed, by an overzealous police officer in Monroe, Louisiana.

Since the incident, Sugar Boy has abandoned rhythm and blues, instead finding solace as a member of an Uptown Baptist church. He now lives in a comfortably appointed house, and during his leisure moments he enjoys listening to his surprisingly large jazz record collection. His only lasting concession to his injury is a slightly slurred speech pattern when he tries to speak quickly and a golf-ball-sized bite out of his hair line. Although he is a devoted church goer, he still enjoys recalling the "old days," and although he doesn't spell it out in so many words, he is exceedingly proud of his career as an R&B artist, and rightly so.

Sugar Boy's real name is James Crawford, Jr. He was born October 12, 1934, the only child of Mary and James Crawford, and grew up in the Uptown section of New Orleans on LaSalle Street, between Thalia and Clio Streets.

"It was fun growing up in that neighborhood," says Sugar Boy. "I went to school, played football and stuff with the kids in the street. I wasn't into hot footing though, I never involved myself in gangs or humbugging. I really looked forward to going to church on Sundays because I enjoyed the singing. Sometimes when my folks couldn't take me, they would dress me up and wait at the gate for someone on their way to church. There were always nice people who wanted to take a little boy to church."

Although Sugar Boy's parents didn't have a piano, he learned the rudiments of the instrument in elementary school. "There was a lady in the neighborhood, Gladys Deveau, who had a piano at her house and she would let us kids come in and play and sing along. I can't say that I listened to anybody in particular when I learned to play. I never took lessons, I would just try to find what I wanted to play on the piano."

Once Sugar Boy entered Booker T. Washington High School, he received his first formal musical training. "I selected instrumental music as a course. I couldn't play piano in the school band so I played drums during my freshman year. After my first year, the trombone section of the band graduated and the music teacher asked if anyone wanted to take their place. So I volunteered and learned to play during the summer before my sophomore year. Trombone was really my best instrument."

Sugar Boy's interest in music spread beyond his school band involvement, as he joined some of his classmates at Mrs. Deveau's house to rehearse blues and spiritual tunes. "We had a little band, nothing real organized at first. I was back playing piano, because the regular guy didn't show up one night. The other guys were 'Big Boy' Myles, Warren Myles, Nolan Blackwell, Irving Bannister and Alfred Bernard—just a bunch of youngsters having fun.

"I guess someone had heard us rehearsing and told Dr. Daddy-O to check us out. He liked us and invited us to play on his Saturday morning radio show between 11:45 and noon. The band didn't have a name at first, but we had an instrumental that was our theme song, 'Chapaka Shawee.' We didn't even know what it meant, it was just a Creole word we heard in the street." [Roughly translated "we aren't raccoons."] "Dr. Daddy-O had a column in the *Louisiana Weekly* and he wrote, 'You ought to listen to those Chapake Shawee youngsters every Saturday.' So the name stuck.

"People started calling the station and asking for us wanting to hire us. Dr. Daddy-O booked our first job at the Shadowland Club on Washington Avenue around 1952. We were all still in school so we just could play on weekends."

The Chapaka Shawee developed a good local following, and it wasn't long before the record companies got wind of the group. Dr. Daddy-O approached Dave Bartholomew, who was then briefly doing some production for Hollywood's Aladdin Record label on behalf of the group and a deal was struck. In November of 1952, the group cut their first and last session, "One Sunday Morning"

Front: Sugar Boy, Jake Myles
Back: Alfred Bernard, Eric Warner, "Big Boy" Myles
Nolan Blackwell, Irving Bannister

and "No One To Love Me" under the guise of "The Sha-Weez." The record failed to catch on, but "No One To Love Me" has since gained a legendary reputation for its rarity and for Sugar Boy's weeping monologue.

"There were a lot of other bands out there, but we were the first band of youngsters. I guess they signed us because they thought the teenagers would associate with us."

Despite the disappointment of the Aladdin record, the popularity of the group grew, boosted by their weekly broadcasts. The Chapaka Shawee's itinerary grew to include the Tiajuana, the Dew Drop, the Joy Lounge in Gretna, and some out of town dates booked by Frank Pania. By 1953, the group's personnel evolved to also include Eric Warner on drums and David Lastie on sax.

"We had a hell of a band," recalls Lastie. "Sugar Boy loved to play. Man, when I was hooked up with Sugar Boy, we were working five, sometimes six, nights a week. He had a friendly way with people and everybody liked the way he sang and played."

When Leonard Chess, owner of the Chicago-based Chess and Checker record labels, came to town in 1953 to promote his latest releases, he overheard the group rehearsing one evening at the WMRY studio which was located in the Louisiana Life Insurance building on Dryades Street. "Leonard came in and asked us to play something original. He told us he wanted to tape a couple of numbers for an audition. After we finished he gave us $5 and said he might have a surprise for us. We went and bought red beans down at Papa Joe's and didn't think any more about it.

"About a month later I was back in the studio and a disc jockey, Ernie the Whip, said he had something to show me. Well, Leonard had released "I Don't Know What I'll Do' with my name on it and the 'Cane Cutters.' I'd always been called Sugar Boy since I was a kid but the 'Cane Cutters,' that was Leonard's idea.

"I wasn't mad, just surprised because we hadn't signed a contract. You see, I never took this thing seriously. We were teenagers still living at home with our parents. Having a record out was more for the glory. If we played a job then and got $5 a man, we were on top of the world."

Although the primitive fidelity of "I Don't Know What I'll Do" b/w "Overboard" might have adversely affected national sales, the record was a modest hit in New Orleans and confirmed Chess' hunch about Sugar Boy and his group. Subsequently, Sugar Boy inked a recording contract and his next session was scheduled for Cosimo's Studio in early 1954. His group, which adapted The Cane Cutters as their name, now featured "Snooks" Eaglin on guitar, and bassist Frank Fields, a regular New Orleans studio musician.

The session yielded Sugar Boy's biggest record, "Jock-A-Mo" b/w "You, You, You." Propelled by Snooks' slashing, distorted guitar and Eric Warner's riveting second-line drum pattern, "Jock-A-Mo" was among the first records to capture the "Carnival Sound" and sold heavily in New Orleans during the Mardi Gras season of 1954.

" 'Jock-A-mo' came from two songs that I used to hear the Indians sing," recalls Sugar Boy. "I put that together with the other musicians. We used to see the Indians a lot because we lived near the Battlefield (Claiborne and Poydras Streets). I never was interested in being an Indian, because to tell you the truth I was afraid of them. Back then they used to carry real hatchets that they decorated. On Mardi Gras Day they'd be running around the neighborhood singing and shouting. If they ran into another tribe that they didn't like, somebody was gonna get hurt."

Even though "Jock-A-Mo" was immediately established as a Carnival standard in New Orleans, it continued to sell nationally throughout 1954. *Cashbox* made it a "pick of the week," calling it "A happy sounding ditty with a calypso beat . . . moves with such an exciting beat the listener is caught and infected. Lending to the general excitement is a torrid horn in the break."

"When 'Jock-A-Mo' was out, Leonard Chess called me and said that a deejay in New York, 'Hound Dog' Lorentez, was interested in booking some dates up there. So he sent me my ticket and I went. I played the Copa Cabana, the Copa Casino—a lot of places. That's when I realized there was a lot of money to be made."

Sugar Boy's success whetted Chess' appetite enough to try his hand with other New Orleans artists, and other members of the Cane Cutters. Although their sides weren't issued until twenty years later, "Big Boy" Myles, "Snooks" Eaglin and "Slim" (Sylvester) Saunders were also recorded at Sugar Boy's sessions. "We really recorded a lot of stuff down at Cosimo's that was never released," recalls Sugar Boy. "Leonard Chess would call and arrange for us to go to the studio and record. I can't say that anyone was a producer, because we played those songs just the way we did on the bandstand. We just cut them and they were sent to Chicago where he would pick what would come out."

Sugar Boy's next Checker release, "No More Heartaches" b/w "I Bowed On My Knees," proved to be his last release on that label. Whether Sugar Boy was dropped because Chess' distributors weren't shifting his records in sufficient quantities, or Chess had his hands full with his other blues artists, is open to speculation.

By late 1954, Sugar Boy and the Came Cutters had been installed as a regular attraction at the Carousel Club, a white nightspot in West Baton Rouge. Bandmembers Ernest Holland, Batman Rankin, Billy Tate, Smokey Johnson, David Lastie and "Big Boy" Myles had all relocated there.

Sugar Boy's stints at the Carousel lasted for two years until 1956, when he returned to New Orleans to be near the recording studio. "Dave Bartholomew told me that he would record me for Imperial when I left Chess. Dave was I guess what you'd call an A&R man. He ran the whole show. I didn't get to use my band when I did those records for Imperial because Dave had his own group of musicians down there: Frank Fields, Lee Allen, Red Tyler and Edward Franks. I didn't play piano on all those records. It didn't bother me. I thought my best work was on Imperial.

"The first thing we did was 'Morning Star' which sold quite well around here. It was based on the same melody as 'I Don't Know What I'll Do.' I wrote that tune in Franklin, Tennessee, when we were on the road. We were way out in the country and it was real early in the morning. I just sat down at the piano and the words came into my head. I know Dave Bartholomew got his name down as co-writer, but if you look at any of those records on Imperial by Fats or Smiley, he got his name on there. That's just the way they operated in those days."

Sugar Boy's Imperial output, which included four singles, was excellent. Besides the ever popular "Morning Star," there was an excellent cover of Pee Wee Crayton's ballad, "I Need Your Love," and the smooth "You Gave Me Love." Sugar Boy's best performance was saved for the torrid "She's Got A Wobble (When She Walks)" where Sugar Boy sings his praise to his "big fat mama that's 55 in the waist, and 65 in the hips!"

All of Sugar Boy's records sold well around New Orleans and the Deep South. But by 1958 when Imperial began concentrating on Ricky Nelson and their younger white artists, Sugar Boy and most of Imperial's other black New Orleans artists got lost in the shuffle.

Not being signed to a recording contract didn't seem to affect Sugar Boy's popularity. "We were playing around New Orleans rather than in New Orleans then. Our territory was pretty much from Texas over to Georgia, with dances, nightclubs, and parties around the countryside. A lot of proms and colleges, too . . . Tulane, LSU, Georgia, Ole Miss—sometimes we'd get tickets to go to the football games, too."

Sugar Boy's next record was cut in 1959 for Sam Montalbano, who owned the Motel label in Baton Rouge. "That's when I cut 'Danny Boy.' I drove to Baton Rouge to rehearse with a white band from LSU, but we cut it down here at Cosimo's in the French Quarter. They put it out at Christmas time with 'White Christmas' on the other side, but it seemed like everybody liked "Danny Boy" the best. So after Christmas they put it out again with another song on the flip ["Round and Round"]."

Sugar Boy's next stop, record-wise, was on Johnny Vincent's Ace label in 1961, where he recut "I Don't Know What To Do" as "I Cried" and "Have A Little Mercy." The record didn't sell perhaps due to distribution problems. "I just did that one record under my own name but we cut an album with Jimmy Clanton, *Teenage Millionaire,* that was also a soundtrack for a movie. Johnny Vincent just had Clanton sing over my track."

Not long after, Sugar Boy's career, and nearly his life, came to an abrupt end. "It was in '63 when everybody was upset because of the freedom marches. We were driving to a job and the police pulled us over in Monroe, Louisiana. They said I was drunk and speeding. The police pulled me out of the car and hit me with a

ACE RECORDS

Arc Pub., Co. Inc., BMI

625
94-243

"I CRIED"
(Crawford)
SUGAR BOY CRAWFORD

pistol. They knocked a hole in my head and I ended up in the hospital in Monroe for three weeks before I was transferred back home.

"I was paralyzed for about a year; I was just like an infant. I had a blood clot on the brain, I couldn't hear, I couldn't see or walk. I was almost dead. They had to operate on me to put a plate in my head. I came back gradually but I had to be constantly watched for two years. The first time I looked at a piano, I knew what it was, but I didn't remember how to play it."

The "Jim Crow Justice" of Monroe eventually pinned a drunken driving charge on Sugar Boy, in an attempt to justify the brutal incident. Amazingly, the faith Sugar Boy has in God doesn't allow him to be bitter or cast the blame on anyone. "I just got caught on the bad end of a deal," he shrugs.

Sugar Boy did attempt a brief comeback, but since 1969 he has confined his singing to spirituals in church. "As far as being a human being I'm about back to normal. But as far as singing and playing I never reached the potential I had before I got hurt. After I gave up music I went to trade school to learn a job skill. I learned how to be a building engineer and take care of boilers. That's what I do today; I've had the same job now for around eight years. I found it more pleasing than being out there in that rat race.

"I've got nothing against rhythm and blues, I still like to listen to it myself. I mean show me a person who doesn't like music and I'll show you a person who is an idiot. But being a church person I have to object to the environment that rhythm and blues is presented in. I just feel like I don't want to be a part of it so I'm happy just to stay away from it.

"Even when I played music, I'd always get up early on Sunday morning to go to church, even if we played until 2 or 3 o'clock the night before. I still think my voice sounds pretty good; in fact if somebody was interested in me doing a spiritual record I'd do it without a second thought."

Sugar Boy is slightly taken aback by the renewed interest in his style of music. He was completely unaware that a two-record set of his Chess material was reissued until former Cane Cutter, David Lastie, brought him one. Sugar Boy possesses only one copy of his records. "I was really surprised that anyone would be interested in those old records. I still like to listen to them. I think they were just as good as anybody else's."

JOHNNY ADAMS
The Tan Canary

*"You know it's hard, loving another man's girlfriend,
You can't see her when you want to — you've got to see her
   when you can.
You may be fighting a losing battle,
But you'll have so much fun trying to win."*

— "Losing Battle"

*"That old sun just went down,
   and here I am again — with all of my friends.
That old Miller sign keeps on flashing
   and the jukebox keeps on playing — 'Together Again.'
I tried all I could, but there's no getting over you.
Since you left me, I live my whole life at night."*

— "I Live My Whole Life At Night"

Johnny Adams stands at the end of Dorothy's Medallion Lounge's bar, staring at a tall glass of Coke, chewing on a stick of Trident, lighting up yet another Kool. His slight frame is impeccably tucked into an expensive, custom-made, burgundy, double-breasted silk suit, complemented by a high-collared starched shirt, with matching grey shoes, tie and decorative handkerchief. The jukebox churns out an unending series of black top-40 hits which keep the go-go dancers, who perform in a barred cage next to the band's area, moving. Well after midnight the first member of his backup group, "The Solar System," ambles in with his bass under his arm and nods to Johnny.

"Where the hell is Walter?" says Johnny, inquiring about Walter Washington, his guitarist of five years. The bassist shrugs and Johnny looks at his watch, swearing lightly. A few middle-aged men sporting wide brimmed hats and layers of gold chains spot Johnny as they come through the door and exchange pleasantries and handshakes. Dorothy, the proprietress, a fiftyish woman with a blond bouffant wig and a number of gaudy gold medallions around her neck, flashes Johnny a stern look and takes a drink order from the men who have just entered. Finally, after another 45 minutes, Walter and the drummer arrive and head for the bandstand. Walter, now in his early forties, offers a broken-toothed innocent smile and mumbles something about car trouble. Dorothy confronts Johnny and Walter, pointing at her watch and informing them if they start this late again they'd be looking for another regular job.

Walter shuffles off to the bandstand with the look of a child who had just received a scolding, while Johnny remains impassive. He's seen it happen too many times. "If he couldn't play so damn well, I'd have gotten somebody else to take his place years ago," he mutters.

Finally, the jukebox is mercifully shut off at 1:30 a.m. Walter welcomes everyone to Dorothy's over a crackling microphone and then begins playing a chaotic jazz instrumental. The number ends without even a trace of applause. Walter checks his tuning and the bass player leads off with a recent funk pattern which Walter tries, unsuccessfully, to follow. The song ends in shambles after nearly five minutes, and even Johnny winces at its conclusion. "It looks like one of those nights," he offers, reaching for another Kool.

Walter begins playing the familiar riff to "Honky Tonk," which finally brings a reaction from the smoky room's patrons. One couple gets up to dance in the aisle next to the go-go dancers' cage, amidst shouts from the audience of "shake it!" The song concludes and Walter moves to the microphone and begins singing "Just My Imagination." The P.A. begins an insistent crackling and squeeling, but Walter tries to ignore it and finish the song. For the next five minutes he wrestles with the microphone and adjusts the dials on the P.A.'s amplifier. Johnny just shakes his head and orders another Coke. Walter finally gets the problem under control and breaks into the next tune, "The Things I Used To Do," as if nothing had happened.

After nearly half-a-dozen R&B covers by the band, Johnny disappears for a few moments and returns with a microphone and a long length of microphone chord. He waits at the far end of the bar while Walter breaks into the familiar introduction riff and announces that it's finally "star time." The audience focuses its attention on the tiny bandstand as Johnny squeezes between a couple of tables and reaches over to plug his microphone into the P.A. He grinds out his cigarette into a nearby ashtray and spreads his legs, as if seeking support. Johnny pauses just a moment, staring towards the ceiling as if looking for divine inspiration as the

Johnny Adams, 1960

band begins to play. Walter concludes a staccato guitar passage and Johnny leans back to wail, "Hell yes I cheated/even though it was wrong..." It's 2:30 on a Sunday morning and Johnny Adams has just gone to work.

Now in his early fifties, Johnny has spent most of his life singing in the tiny, windowless lounges around New Orleans and the rickety roadhouses of South Louisiana. His scores of singles, and occasional albums, have drawn critical acclaim from all corners of the globe. In Europe he has been cited as "soul music's finest singer," and in America as "one of the greatest voices of the age." But in the streets of his hometown New Orleans, Johnny is known as "The Tan Canary" (a tag he was given in the early Seventies by dee jay "Tex" Stevens), esteemed by musicians for his unerring ear, taste and imagination, loved by club and concert audiences for his always engaging performances.

"Johnny Adams has always been my all-time favorite singer," says recording engineer Cosimo Matassa, who has literally heard and seen them all from the control booth of his studios. "There are plenty of great singers in New Orleans, but for the most part, they have to choose songs to fit the style of their voice. But Johnny Adams can sing any song and make it sound great. I would have to say that Johnny Adams is one of the greatest singers of all time."

Johnny lives with his mother in the Lafitte Housing Projects, on Claiborne Avenue, underneath the I-10 overpass. Even though Johnny estimates he has waxed nearly 100 singles, and half-a-dozen albums, he would be hard pressed to find one inside his apartment. His front room is crowded with a menagerie of guitar amplifiers, ghetto blasters, jazz LPs (minus their covers), guitars and a broken turntable. Outside, the din from the passing traffic makes it all but impossible to keep up a conversation at normal level. Johnny slumps into a vinyl couch and attempts to stretch the weariness from his bones. It's early in the afternoon, but Johnny has just woken up.

Even though on the bandstand he looked 10 to 15 years younger than his age, every one of his 52 years is etched on his tired face as he clears some space for his visitor to sit down. He's wearing a Banlon jersey over a cotton undershirt and a pair of silver grey pants that look as if they were once one-half of an expensive suit. He slides on a pair of dark glasses that hide his "bad" left eye, and leans forward to explain how his last job went. Johnny Adams, perhaps America's greatest soul singer, finally begins to look like he'll live out the day.

While other stars in New Orleans have burned far brighter, few have burned longer than Johnny's. It still seems that there's always a new Johnny Adams record on the jukebox, and even though they never seem to garner the radio airplay that they perhaps deserve, the records keep Johnny's name in the public's eye and ears. There's always someone who wants Johnny Adams to sing.

Lathan John Adams was born January 5, 1932, and raised in the Hollygrove section of New Orleans, a neighborhood in the upper Carrollton section of the city that hugs the Jefferson Parish line. Johnny spent his youth as most any child, playing in the streets and absorbing New Orleans' bountiful musical heritage. He attended the Lawrence Dunbar primary school but never attended high school. Instead he found a job hauling sod out of the Barataria marsh to help support his mother, Rosetta Howard Adams. Religion was a big part of the Adams' household, and Johnny found himself in church most Sundays. It was while singing in the choir that his voice was first noticed and he was encouraged by his mother to "serve the Lord" with his gift.

Johnny joined his first gospel quartet in the early Fifties, The Soul Revivers, which sang at a number of local churches and on gospel music programs. It was with the Soul Revivers that Johnny developed his swooping vocal style (which ranges from a gutteral low C to a stratospheric high C), and he was soon appointed the group's lead vocalist. Johnny recalls the group cutting acetate discs at Cosimo's J&M Studio, but none of the sides were ever issued commercially, and according to Johnny have long since been lost.

Johnny bounced around to other quartets, and even had a spell with the great Bessie Griffin and her Soul Consolators. "Oh I really enjoyed singing gospel," confides Johnny. "There was this feeling of inner satisfaction that you don't always get from singing R&B. The people that come out to hear gospel are there to hear you sing. Most of the people at my gigs now are out to have a good time, not necessarily to listen to music. Listening to me sing is secondary to partying."

By 1959, Johnny had a steady string of work, performing at churches and small auditoriums with quartets throughout the South. At the time he happened to be living in Uptown New Orleans, in the same apartment building as the legendary songwriter, Dorothy Labostrie. Labostrie's credits then included Little Richard's "Tutti Frutti," Irma Thomas' "You Can Have My Husband," and Lil' Milet's "Rich Woman." Labostrie had just penned a song called "I Won't Cry," which Joe Ruffino at Ric Records was interested in recording. Labostrie knew that Johnny was a talented singer and approached him with the idea of recording the song.

At first Johnny spurned the idea. "You see, I've always been the type of guy who when he does something, he does it all the way. I wasn't the type of guy who was gonna record a blues song and then go out there and sing gospel the rest of the time. I didn't think that was right. It took a long time to make up my mind to cut R&B."

Eventually, though, Labostrie and Ruffino convinced Johnny to record the song, and from then on Johnny decided to go "straight ahead R&B." Produced by a youthful Mac Rebennack, "I Won't Cry" was a powerful blues ballad that became a strong regional seller, primarily due to Johnny's soaring, operatic, gospel-influenced singing. "I guess it did pretty well," speculates Johnny. "Ruffino wasn't the type of guy who paid you much more than a few dollars to go in the studio, but I started gettin' a lot of calls for work. I took that as a sign of encouragement."

Topping the local R&B charts in 1959, "I Won't Cry " remains one of Johnny's most requested numbers to this day. He even re-recorded it more than a decade later and scored a minor national hit with it as well. While the record was still popular, Johnny fell under the wing of talent-merchant Percy Stovall, who began booking Johnny throughout the circuit of clubs and auditoriums he had established. Johnny was often teamed with Chris Kenner, Earl King and Irma Thomas for dates throughout the Gulf South, with Edgar Blanchard's or Robert Parker's band providing the musical accompaniment.

The blues ballad "I Won't Cry" set the standard for most of Johnny's followups on the Ric label. Employing the Edgar Blanchard band on sessions, Johnny waxed similarly styled songs like "Nowhere To Go," "Teach Me To Forget," "Closer To You," and the churchlike "Life Is A Struggle," written by Chris Kenner. The arrangements on Johnny's early records were usually kept tastefully simple, as Johnny's voice was allowed rightfully to dominate the performances. Johnny's releases were alternately arranged by Rebennack or Eddie Bo, who both penned most of Johnny's early material. Quite often the song writing credits to Johnny's songs were split with disc jockey Larry McKinley as an incentive to spin the records on the air.

It was Mac Rebennack who wrote and produced Johnny's first national record, "Losing Battle," which rose to #27 in the R&B charts five weeks in the summer of 1962. A haunting ballad that told a tale of a backdoor romance, "Losing Battle" never brought Johnny anything in the way of a royalty, but, as Johnny puts it, "It kept my name out there. I was freelancing back then. I didn't have a band, I just sang with whoever the club owner could get. Sometimes I had some terrible bands, but that was the only way I could see to get by. I'd get on a Greyhound bus and ride off to gigs, like the White Eagle in Opelousas, or the Paradise in Baton Rouge. I'd go play all the hole-in-the-wall joints for next to nothing. But it was steady. I could go back to any of those clubs if I needed work. I made enough to get by."

Johnny Adams continued to have a string of local records on Ric, when through the intercession of his label-mate Joe Jones, he began looking for brighter horizons. Johnny, Joe Jones, Earl King, Smokey Johnson and George French took it upon themselves to drive all the way to Detroit, Michigan and audition for Berry Gordy at Motown Records. Gordy was extremely impressed with Johnny's voice and was ready to sign him to a Motown contract until fate stepped in. Earl King continues the story: "I was sitting in the studio with Mickey Stevenson (a Motown producer) thinking, 'This is it for Johnny. This is gonna break the cookie wide open for him.' Then right while Johnny's in the studio singing, a telegram

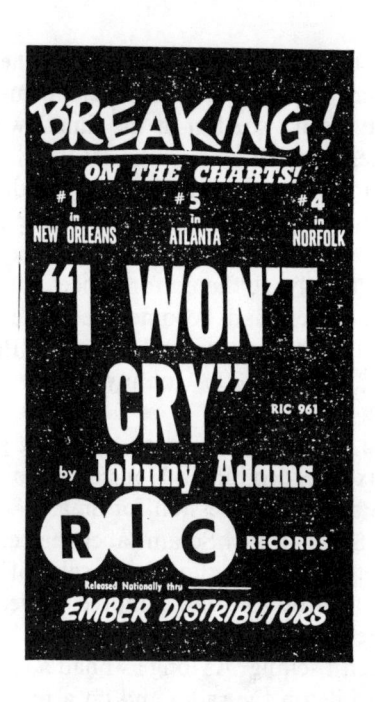

> **BREAKING!**
> ON THE CHARTS!
> #1 in NEW ORLEANS #5 in ATLANTA #4 in NORFOLK
> **"I WON'T CRY"** RIC 961
> by Johnny Adams
> **RIC** RECORDS
> Released Nationally thru
> **EMBER DISTRIBUTORS**

came from Ruffino in New Orleans. It said, "If you try to do anything with Johnny Adams I'm gonna sue.' So Motown dropped Johnny like a hot potato. Today they might have tried to work out a deal but they were just getting off the ground in those days, and Berry Gordy was paranoid about getting into legal hassles."

The episode haunts Johnny to this day. "I guess everybody tries to get back what they put into something," he reflects. "I had a contract with Ruffino, but to tell you the truth, I don't even know if it was valid. Still I don't think that if you see a good think happening to another person you should cut it off, just because you feel like you're being left out. I really believe I could have gone somewhere if Ruffino would have just co-operated with the major record companies. But he had it in his mind that his company was gonna be the biggest thing in the country and that everybody else could go to hell."

Johnny stayed on with Ric until Ruffino died in 1963, when his contract was "assumed" by the newly-formed Watch label. Watch Records was owned and operated by Ruffino's brother-in-law, Joe Assunton (who also ran the local One Stop) and Henry Hildebrand (who owned the newly-formed All South Record Distributors). "At the time I was just ignorant about contracts and legal matters," claims Johnny. "I just automatically assumed that they owned my contract and that what they told me was true. I came to find out later though that that wasn't so. But at the time I was just interested in getting another record out."

Johnny's early Watch sides were given the big production job — oftentimes complete with awkward strings and giant chorus accompaniment — by producer/arranger Wardell Quezergue. But Johnny still managed to salvage the performances with his by now breathtaking falsetto, which had become the trademark on his records. His best Watch record was undoubtedly "Part of Me," penned by Earl King, that really let Johnny stretch out his vocal chords.

From that point on, Johnny went on an unending path of label hopping. Huey Meaux recorded him in Houston for his Pacemaker label, Harold Battiste arranged a session for Smash, and Eddie Bo did a session for Al Scramuzza's Scram label that came close to being leased by Roulette. But even though the sales of these singles were sometimes only as little as a few hundred copies, as Johnny continually emphasizes, "They kept my name out there. I didn't care really if they weren't selling. As long as I had a record out that got played once in awhile on the radio and on a few jukeboxes, I could work off of that. When the records stop coming, so do the calls for work."

Johnny spent most of the mid-Sixties working weekends around New Orleans, or as before, taking a Greyhound to one of the clubs out on the "Sugarcane Circuit." Johnny still didn't have a big enough name to draw big performance guarantees, so he took a job working behind the counter at Joe's One Stop Record Shop to bring in a few extra dollars, and to kill some days between gigs.

Watch Records came back into the picture in 1968, when Johnny waxed a tune recorded earlier by Englishman Englebert Humperdink, "Release Me." Once again, Wardell Quezergue arranged the record, which turned into a soulful demonstration of Johnny's vocal gymnastics. The record immediately took off in New Orleans and began receiving outside attention from other record companies. Hildebrand spoke to Nashville recordman Shelby Singleton on behalf of Johnny and the record. Singleton in turn leased the record for his new SSS label and purchased Johnny's Watch contract outright.

"Release Me" immediately jumped into the national R&B charts for SSS, rising to a respectable position of #34 around Christmas of 1968. But it really surprised everyone by slipping into the Hot 100, rising to #84, during a brief three week stay.

The record's success inspired Singleton to bring Johnny to Nashville and produce his future session. The premier Nashville session yielded Johnny's biggest record of all time, the plaintive country ballad "Reconsider Me." The blend of Johnny's operatic voice and the Nashville arrangement, complete with a steel guitar, was the perfect blend of country and soul. "Reconsider Me" made it to #8 in the R&B charts in the summer of 1969, and to #28 in the Hot 100. The combination of these first two SSS hits was to signal a new, country-based approach for Johnny's future releases, which Singleton saw as a way of putting records in two separate markets.

"We had a beautiful thing going," says Johnny wistfully. "They really made sure everybody did a good job. All I had to do was go there and sing. We cut a lot of stuff, even stuff that was never issued. They had some great writers up in Nashville, like Margaret Lewis and Myra Smith (who penned a number of Johnny's SSS records, including "Reconsider Me"). It was really fun being around the studio in those days."

After the success of his SSS singles, Johnny's booking was handled by Universal Attractions Inc., who sent him on a few jobs along the East and West Coast. But, according to Johnny, even with a couple of successful records out, things didn't change all that much. "Sure I had a few good paydays, and I made a little bit of money off the records, but things weren't really that different from before. I went to a few different places, but it got to be a hassle staying out on the road for so long. Sometimes you'd work on a promise for three nights and the promoter would split with your money and you'd be stranded in Athens, Georgia or someplace. I bought a new car in 1970, but that's about all I had to show for it. I just kept on with my same routine."

Johnny closed out 1969 with another moderate hit, "I Can't Be All Bad," another Lewis-Smith composition which also did well in the R&B charts. The following year saw the release of the excellent *Heart and Soul* Album, and one last national record, the remake of "I Won't Cry," which made it to #41 in the R&B charts during the summer.

Johnny left SSS for a short time in 1972, and completed a session for Atlantic Records that resulted in two singles, "I'll Carry You" and "I Wish It Would Rain;" but the relationship soon soured. "I cut those records for Brad Scapiro in Miami," explains Johnny. "I didn't think 'I'll Carry You' was too bad, but those were pre-recorded tracks, and I couldn't get into those songs. Atlantic wouldn't get behind those records. They just put 'em out and that was it. I had two releases, but it was too long between records. Everytime I'd call Atlantic to find out what was going on, they'd brush me off. I had to get a record out there, so I had to look for another deal."

Johnny returned to SSS, but couldn't repeat the success of his earlier national hits. Nevertheless, Singleton continued to record Johnny in Nashville and at Playground Studios in Valparaso, Florida, where the excellent "Something Worth Leaving For" was done in 1973. Singleton recorded Johnny until 1974, when he became disillusioned with all of his black artists and suspended the SSS label to concentrate on developing his country acts.

"It disappointed the hell out of me," says Johnny, referring to Singleton's decision. "It was the kind of situation where you trust a man with your heart and soul and then you get let down. I had no idea I was going to get dropped. When Singleton bailed out he didn't even call or write to let me know what was happening. I had to read about it in the *Billboard*."

Johnny persisted, however, continuing to grind out the one-nighters using pickup bands for out-of-town work and sitting in with a number of combos at practically every black nightspot featuring live entertainment in New Orleans. But without a new record, the calls grew increasingly far apart. "You really are only as hot as your last record," points out Johnny.

"I guess I could have gone out to Los Angeles or to New York, but I've always had a steady thing going here. I might have really made it big, but I didn't want to starve to death trying. I've been up to Chicago, but it's not like here. Sure, they got a lot of record companies, but you can only find work maybe one night a week — and you really have to hustle to do that. And shit it's cold up there. I mean if the money is really good, I'll get up and go, but I'm really comfortable in New Orleans. I'm just not crazy about being gone all the time."

By 1976, Johnny was back in the studio recording for Senator Jones, a gruff, no-nonsense record producer who has owned a series of small local labels. Jones was able to record Johnny practically at will for his JB's label, as he had carte blanche to use Marshall Sehorn's Sea-Saint Studio in exchange for leasing rights and a percentage of the sales of his records. This once again allowed Johnny to have a steady stream of singles. Even though Johnny received little or no compensation for the records, he is far from being bitter. "Like I said, the money is in the gigs, not in the

Johnny Adams, 1970

records."

Most of the JB's singles were mediocre run-throughs of old soul standards. Still, Marshall Sehorn managed to persuade Chelsea Records to collect them on an album, *Stand By Me*. It did poorly, however, and Chelsea requested no more material.

Johnny and Senator Jones kept plugging though, and the quality of the singles improved with each new release. In 1978, the duo decided to try country again and recorded "After All The Good Is Gone," an old Conway Twitty tune. The single, which was issued on Hep Me did quite well regionally (50,000 according to Senator Jones), and it aroused the curiosity of Ariola Records, who signed Johnny to an album deal which was produced by Senator Jones and arranged by Wardell Quezergue and Isaac Bolden. The album represented some of Johnny's best contemporary work, also yielding a moderately successful R&B single, "Selfish," which was a hit around New Orleans. But even though the album received critical acclaim on both sides of the ocean, it fulfilled no one's commercial expectations. It was deleted after just a year on the market.

Ariola requested Johnny to attempt some disco-oriented material, which he wasn't too crazy about recording. "Trash," he blurts. "They wanted me to cut trash after we were selling R&B. So we tried to cut some trash, but it came out too good! They didn't want it."

As the Seventies drew to a close, Johnny maintained his regular routine working his circuit of small clubs, but now with a fine band led by Walter "Wolfman" Washington.

Walter Washington has spent over 25 years backing other artists and leading his own combos in the same circle of small clubs that booked Johnny. Walter had played behind Johnny as early as 1968, but the duo never teamed up on a regular basis until nearly a decade later. "Walter is definitely the most soulful guitarist that's ever played behind me," says Johnny. "He can feel everything that I sing. Walter has the soul to let me step out. I really get my drive from his playing. He's just always there at the right time. That's a hard thing to find in a guitarist. Even when he's bad, he still sounds good."

Along with Washington in tow, Johnny continued to cut records for Senator Jones' label and it seemed like every few months a new single was played on the local soul stations or appeared on the jukeboxes. In 1980, his pleading version of "Hell Yes I Cheated" was leased to Nashville's Paid label and just missed breaking into the national soul charts.

Occasionally, Johnny began performing in a few of the white, Uptown clubs like Tipitina's and the Maple Leaf, which exposed his music to a new audience. In 1982 he made his first trip to Europe, where he was warmly received by the audience at the Amsterdam Jazz Festival. "I like playing for the kids," points out Johnny. "They really come out to listen, not just to have a good time and to raise hell."

Senator Jones continued to release singles, but there was an audible loss in quality as Johnny began singing over prerecorded tracks that were sent from Nashville. By the spring of 1983, Johnny was approached by Rounder Records, which was interested in recording an R&B album employing Walter Washington and the rest of Johnny's working band. Johnny had come to an agreement with Rounder, but Marshall Sehorn produced a contract that was allegedly signed by Johnny Adams (Johnny claims he signed no such agreement) which had him under contract to Senator Jones, and Sehorn, until December of that year. Johnny was visibly disappointed, but used the extra time to rehearse new material and whip the band into shape for the session.

As the recording session approached, Johnny admitted, "I've put more work into doing this album than anything else I've done. I guess I'm not getting any younger, and this might be my last chance at getting something to go national. The trend is starting to come around to R&B again and I want to stay in that bag."

And truly he had worked hard. Johnny had sorted through dozens of tapes and records, trying to come up with about 15 songs that were suited to his taste and style. Johnny and Walter spent many evenings working on arrangements to songs that they felt positive about recording.

For the session, Johnny maintained his basic working band. Besides Walter on guitar, the group featured Darrel Francis, bass; Wilbert Arnold, drums; and George "Geege" Jackson Jr., congas and percussion. Augmenting the group were journeyman saxophonist Alvin Red Tyler, trumpet player Terry Tullos, Craig Wroten on piano, and Bill Samuel, who played saxophone and who wrote the horn charts. Johnny hoped to cut all the tunes "live" (without vocal overdubbing) to capture the feeling of a more powerful R&B record. He felt his most recent singles, which had been prerecorded tracks, weren't as good as they could have been had they been recorded with a studio band.

For the most part, recording sessions aren't pleasant affairs. They're long, boring, frustrating and they all too often fray one's nerves. Johnny Adams' session was no exception. Rounder's producer, Scott Billington, had flown from New England to oversee the session. Billington and Johnny had cemented a positive relationship through hours of long distance phone calls and a couple of in-person meetings prior to the session.

For three evenings in December 1983, Johnny, Walter, and the rest of the musicians were camped inside the comfortable Ultra-Sonic Studio on Washington Avenue across from Xavier University. Contrary to his stylish stage attire, Johnny had a knit cap pulled over his natural, a buttondown sweater covering an old polo shirt and mismatching slacks.

From the beginning, Johnny seemed somewhat frustrated as he stationed himself behind the microphone, with the lyrics before him on a music stand. Billington sat himself in the sound booth next to the engineer, hanging on each word Johnny sang. The band had obviously done their homework and accounted for few retakes. Johnny however seemed tired and strained. He seemed incapable of reaching his patented falsetto; his usually smooth vocals were clipped, and his phrasing seemed awkward. Most songs were completed with an unsatisfied grunt from Johnny or a mild cuss word. After the playback from each song, he listened attentively, frowning and shaking his head, while listening to his voice. It became obvious that Johnny would have to recut the vocals for most of the songs. Like an overtrained runner, Johnny seemed incapable of mustering the energy to reach his true potential.

A new song had been added to the session at the 11th hour, a strong ballad, "From The Heart," penned by renowned tunesmith Doc Pomus. The song seemed a natural for Johnny, but he feigned dislike and seemed unwilling, or unable, to negotiate its simple changes. Finally, after a number of attempts, an "acceptable" version of the song was down on tape, which was to conclude the session.

After three long nights, over a dozen songs were completed. But Johnny and Billington weren't satisfied with all of the vocals, and they arranged another session the next evening with Johnny just singing over the multi-tracked tapes.

Johnny seemed far more at ease with just a couple of familiar faces in the studio. With the lights turned low, Johnny seemed more relaxed, but still the rigors of the three-day session — backed by a weekend of gigs — had still taken its toll on Johnny's vocal chords.

The following day, Billington returned to New England with the tapes for the album, which was to be entitled *From The Heart*. "It's a good album," said Billington at the time. "But," he also conceded, "it's not as good as it could be. Johnny might have just overworked himself getting ready to do the album."

While listening to the tapes back in Boston, Billington called Johnny and asked about the possibility of returning to the studio once more, by himself, and recutting some of the vocals once again. Johnny agreed, and this time wisely took a few nights off to give his vocal chords a much-needed rest. When he returned to the studio, one week later, he reapproached the songs with added vigor and enthusiasm, knocking off half a dozen songs in just two hours.

"I think the album will sound really good," he reflects. "It's different because I helped pick the tunes and decided to sing them my own way. I could really feel these numbers and to me that's more important than hitting all those high falsettos. I can't say if there's a hit on there or not, that's up to the jocks and the public, but even if there is, I'll still have to go back to work. That's the only thing I know."

BOBBY MITCHELL
I'm Gonna Be A Wheel Someday

Considering the high quality of material Bobby Mitchell recorded during the 1950s and early 1960s, one questions just why he never had a national hit. Bobby Mitchell's records proved to be steady rhythm and blues sellers, though from the time he started recording for Imperial in 1953 until his last session a decade later on Rip Records, Bobby managed only one minor national hit, in 1956, with "Try Rock and Roll."

Bobby Mitchell remains a particularly important singer in the overall scheme of New Orleans rhythm and blues. His distinct tenor, backed by the cream of the New Orleans session men, was featured on some of the city's finest rhythm and blues records from the 1950s. Even though Bobby Mitchell couldn't get a hit on Imperial, in terms of numbers, his sixteen single releases rank him behind only Fats Domino and Smiley Lewis among New Orleans' Imperial artists.

Today Bobby Mitchell still lives in his native Algiers, just across the river from New Orleans. He makes a comfortable living as an L.S.U. medical school pathologist. He still sings at the occasional "Oldies Show," but for health reasons, he has to be selective. Bobby remains proud of his accomplishments as a rhythm and blues singer, and of his contribution to the development of the city's music. He is one of the few New Orleans R&B singers who actually possesses copies of his own records, and he spends much of his spare time listening to his extensive record collection.

One of seventeen children, Bobby was born August 16, 1935. "I lived out on the river batture," says Bobby, referring to the raised houses that once lined the Algiers portion of the Mississippi River. "Fishin' was our livin', and I helped out with that. I cut wood and sold it before school, 'cause I was the second oldest and had to help out. My great-aunt helped raise me, and she always told me, 'Look, I want you to be a man. I don't want you out there stealin', 'cause you know how to work.' So when I was about ten, I got a job making deliveries for a liquor store. I used to sing for kicks around the liquor store. People started givin' me nickels and tellin' me 'Hey Bobby, you sound great, why don't you try to do something singing?' Well I was strictly a religious kid; I wasn't interested in singing. I wanted to work and make something of myself."

But it was hard to stay away from music too long as Bobby was to find. "I started playing football at L.B. Landry High, but I wound up getting hurt and had to figure out something else to do. So the music teacher, Miss Margie Dickerson, talked me into taking music.

"During the summer vacation in 1950 a bunch of us guys got together and started a group, and we called it the Toppers. All the guys in the group went to Landry — Lloyd Bellaire, Frank Bocage, Gabriel Fleming, Joseph Butler and me. We all were singing, but I guess I was the leader.

"When we got back to school we would always be rehearsing and getting ready for a talent show. One of the teachers at Landry, Mr. Neilly, made a tape of us at a talent show, and he took it to Dr. Daddy-O. Well he liked it enough to play it over WMRY. One of the tunes was 'One Friday Morning,' that I wrote, and Dave Bartholomew heard the tape and liked the song. Mr. Neilly came back and told us, and we were pretty excited about the whole thing."

Bobby recalls meeting Dave Bartholomew on Carnival Day in 1952, where Dave's band was playing, and he told Bobby to come around to the studio some time when they had more time to talk. The next week Bobby skipped classes to go down to Cosimo's studio to talk to Bartholomew. "He said he liked the tape, and asked if we had any more material. Well, Lloyd Bellaire did most of the writing, so we were straight there. Dave said to bring the group down to the studio at night and he'd work with us. After a month or so, he taped us and sent it off to Lew Chudd."

Apparently, Chudd was interested in just Bobby and not the group. But when Bobby balked at the idea of excluding his friends, Bobby Mitchell and the Toppers were all signed to Imperial Records in 1953.

In singing with Imperial, the 16-year-old was joining a roster of some pretty heavy New Orleans talent that already included Fats Domino, Jewel King, Little Sonny Jones, Smiley Lewis, Tommy Ridgley, Archibald, Billy Tate and Fats Mathews. "I didn't really care to be on Imperial," says Bobby. "They had so many guys on the label. But I was a young guy and I felt like this was my break. The first thing we did was 'I'm Cryin' ' and 'Rack 'Em Back.' "

While their initial release did little saleswise, the performances were positively electric. With the regular Imperial session men backing the Toppers, the A-side "I'm Crying" is an exemplary blues ballad with Lee Allen contributing one of his more mournful sax breaks. But the best is saved for the rousing "Rack 'Em Back." Set off with Gabriel Fleming's rock solid piano, the youthful group manages to capture the carnival flavor, reminiscent of Longhair's "Go To The Mardi Gras."

Their first record did cause a stir around Landry, as the entire group was expelled from school because some of the teachers felt they were neglecting their book work. Finally the boys were reinstated when the principal signed as their guardian, but warned them, "I don't want you getting the big head!"

It was the group's third release, "Baby's Gone," another blues ballad roughly based on "I'm Crying," that made the New Orleans charts and went a long way to establish the young group. "That's the one that brought us out. We were really just singin' for fun 'til then. But the group started getting offers to work, and we got a check for $500 from Imperial Records. I said, 'Man this is all right!'"

Bobby explained how local radio helped them in New Orleans during the 1950s: "Disc jockeys were more heavy on local talent at that time. We had people like Ernie the Whip, Okie Dokey, Dr. Daddy-O, Poppa Stoppa, and Jack the Cat. Those guys pushed a lot of local records. At first I had trouble 'cause I was young, and a lot of people didn't want to listen to a young guy like me. But Poppa Stoppa used to advise me on all my records. So 'Baby's Gone' had just come out and he said, 'Let's make this a hit.' He told me to take the record over to Jack the Cat and tell him, 'Poppa Stoppa sent me.' They broke it, and that's how I got known. They used to break a lot of New Orleans records nationally in those days."

The group couldn't follow up their first hit though, largely due to the overworking of the "I'm Crying"—"Baby's Gone" theme. Lloyd Bellaire continued to write the group's material for the most part with Dave Bartholomew trying some of his own tunes to try to make something happen. The Toppers were never recorded in the tradition of most 1950s doo wop groups. It seemed that Bartholomew just couldn't get the handle on recording vocal groups. The Toppers' role was largely confined to shouting out the title to the song at the most opportune time, in what sounded like the remotest part of Cosimo's studio, while Bobby's tenor dominated. Besides their own recordings, they also backed up Smiley Lewis on occasion.

The Toppers split up in 1954, with some of the group going off to college and some into the service. Bobby and Gabriel Fleming would form the "King Toppers," and Bellaire would resurface fifteen years later as a member of the Watts 103rd Street Band, penning the hit "Express Yourself."

Although the Toppers' name would appear on Bobby's records until 1956, after 1954 he was a solo recording artist as far as Imperial Records was concerned.

"We couldn't do shit with vocal groups," admits Dave Bartholomew. "Bobby was a pretty good little singer, so I gave him some songs to do. He had a few minor things, but he never did get any hits." Dave, Bobby, and Robert Montgomery ("a boy from Gretna") penned Bobby's next notable record, the fondly remembered "Nothing Sweet As You," written for Bobby's mother.

By the time 1956 rolled around, the rock and roll craze was in full swing. Imperial had already had success with Fats Domino records crossing over into the teenage market. With Bobby being a young and established singer, Bartholomew thought he'd try to make him appeal to young white record buyers too. Since rock and roll was now a stock phrase, Bartholomew thought he'd use it in the title of Bobby's first release without the Toppers, "Try Rock and Roll."

"The idea was to get on the rock and roll beat and get myself established in the rock and roll field. Dave said, 'Let's get down to

> **SHIPWRECK DANCE**
>
> FRIDAY, MARCH 14, 1958
>
> F & M PATIO — 400 LYONS STREET
>
> *Featuring*
>
> **BOBBY MITCHELL**
> AND
> **THE TOPPERS**
>
> 8 p.m. to 12 p.m.   Donation............$1.75 couple

business and get out of that doo-wee (doo-wop) bag.' I did 'Try Rock and Roll,' and that brought me up to the public as a new and different artist."

"Try Rock and Roll" turned out to be Bobby's only nationally-charted record, as it spent two weeks in *Billboard's* R&B charts in March of 1956, rising to #14. (At the time, *Billboard* was listing 15 records in their "Best Selling Rhythm Singles" chart).

Bobby had established himself as a strong regional artist, working steadily around New Orleans, and as far away as Lake Charles. His releases "I Try So Hard" and "Got My Fingers Crossed" were exceptional bluesy numbers, but didn't cross over, or sell in the big way Imperial hoped.

As things turned out, 1957 was also a successful year. Bobby did a fine version of "You Always Hurt The One You Love," which later inspired his high school classmate, Clarence "Frogman" Henry's 1961 hit. But it was Bobby's next release that would also become a big seller and a song that would most often be associated with him.

"I met a kid in Baton Rouge that was singin' hillbilly — Roy Hayes. He had this song 'I'm Gonna Be A Wheel Someday,' that me and Dave got interested in. But it took me a long time before I felt comfortable enough to cut it. Paul Gayten's wife was my homeroom teacher and she and Paul talked me into trying to record it. She said, 'Why don't you try it? Maybe you'll be a wheel someday.' So I went in and cut it with Paul Gayten.''

"I'm Gonna Be A Wheel" was about as close as any black singer came to rockabilly, largely due to Charles "Hungry" Williams' lopping drums and guitarist Justin Adams' clear single note picking. "Hell we tried everything else, why not try hillbilly," remarks Dave Bartholomew.

Although the record never cracked the Hot 100, it was a big enough hit to earn him a spot on American Bandstand. Bobby also signed on to perform with the likes of Nappy Brown, Chuck Willis, Chuck Berry and Ruth Brown in a number of rock and roll caravan shows.

Bobby clearly still relishes these days, and can go to great lengths describing the places he's performed and "the celebrities" he befriended during his barnstorming days.

The gravy days weren't to last much longer for Bobby, despite his brush with success. By 1958, Imperial was changing the image of its operations. Rather than strictly pursue the R&B market, they were experiencing success in the national charts with the likes of Slim Whitman and Rick Nelson. Of course Fats Domino would remain on the label because of his universal appeal, but Imperial cut back on its "fringe" rhythm and blues artists. Bobby was to have one more release for Imperial during 1958, with the driving, stop-time "64 Hours," but they let his contract expire soon after.

Bobby still remains frustrated by the way he was handled by Imperial. "Truthfully, I never was satisfied with Imperial Records. I think I could have been stronger than any other artist out there. I wasn't really satisfied with a lot of the material I was given, but I was a young guy and didn't really have a choice.

"They had Fats and Ricky Nelson; those guys got the recognition, but we local artists didn't. People like me and Smiley worked so hard, and other people got the credit. If Smiley were here today he'd tell you the same. I don't think Imperial appreciated us."

After Bobby was dropped by Imperial he made a handful of singles for some small New Orleans labels, the best being "You're Doing Me Wrong" on Ron and "I Done Got Over" on Sho-Biz, a rework of Guitar Slim's classic.

Bobby was astute enough to realize that without a major label behind him he would be doomed to the life of a second-rate R&B singer, working for what amounted to scraps. Wisely, Bobby had

Bobby Mitchell with Bobby Reno on left, mid 1960's

retained his interest in schooling and entered Tulane University in 1962. Bobby studied radio engineering, before moving over to Charity Hospital to work. There he studied to be an x-ray technician before entering the field of pathology.

Bobby's musical semi-retirement was interrupted in 1963, when Imperial strangely became interested in him again, releasing four sides. One, a belated answer to his 1957 hit "I Don't Want To Be A Wheel No More," which perhaps summed up his feelings towards recording. He bowed out as a recording artist later that year with an excellent gospel-tinged "Walking in Circles" on Rip, that was produced by Eddie Bo.

After that Bobby concentrated on raising his family of eight and furthering his career in the field of medicine. The only jobs he was making singing were some oldies dances with Tommy Ridgley's band. Bobby began to work in the pathology department at LSU Med School in the late Sixties where he remains today. "I'm involved with research, we do a lot of electronic work, broadcasting autopsies from the morgue. I prepare experiments for the first and second-year pathology students."

Since the late Sixties Bobby's records became sought-after items among R&B record collectors, especially overseas. In the late 1970s he was approached by Jonas Bernholm—a Swedish R&B enthusiast who started his own reissue label—about repackaging some of his old sides. The album has done exceptionally well both here and abroad. Bobby himself has claimed to have sold over 1,000 copies at his "oldies but goodies" gigs and out at his annual Jazz Festival appearance.

The album, aptly titled *I'm Gonna Be A Wheel Someday* sparked a renewed interest in Bobby and his work around New Orleans; and Bobby clearly still basks in his minor celebrity status. Sadly his health has held him back from taking full advantage of his renewed notoriety. An accident at home rendered him nearly blind in one eye when a hammer fell from a ceiling he was repairing. In 1981 he suffered kidney failure, and he now depends on dialysis treatments three times a week.

But Bobby has dealt with these frustrations accordingly, trying to work around his handicaps. He's had to keep his singing engagements to a bare minimum—usually making the Jazz Fest and a couple of spot jobs during Carnival—and has shortened his hours at LSU.

"What are you gonna do?" speculates Bobby. "I've had a great career in two totally different worlds. I've really enjoyed both."

Part Seven:

THE HIT MAKERS

It's almost impossible to talk about New Orleans rhythm and blues without speaking in terms of commercial success. New Orleans has been responsible for hit records ever since the first independent record company visited the city. Just the term New Orleans R&B conjures up visions of: Roy Brown rocking the house to the accompaniment of a jumping band; Fats Domino turning sideways from the piano and singing into the microphone in that instantly recognizable rich Creole voice; or a frantic Ernie K-Doe singing to a rock and roll beat. The fantasy is indeed appealing.

In popular music, success is gauged in terms of sales figures. The music business constantly keeps its nose in the charts, looking for new trends. Between the years 1950 and 1970, New Orleans had a commanding position as one of the largest sellers of single records in the United States. In the neighborhood of two-hundred-and-fifty New Orleans singles graced the national R&B and pop charts during these two decades.

Just as it is impossible to assign specific reasons for the success or failure of a record or an artist, it is impossible to attribute New Orleans' commanding position as a source of hit records to any one factor.

New Orleans rhythm and blues did not acquire its distinctive identity overnight. Over the years, ballads, blues, and rhythm numbers have all done equally well. It's never been clear what the public has wanted from New Orleans, but there always was someone in the charts to tell them. A number of rhythm styles have been popular: 6/8 rock and roll piano triplets; Latin and rhumba tempos; 4/4 swinging second line drumming; riffing stop-time horn patterns. New Orleans rhythm and blues records have always had a little bit of everything.

It may have been the recording studios that gave New Orleans' records a distinctive flavor that appealed to the masses. Maybe a certain drummer or a sax player made a significant contribution or a specific producer was responsible for developing a hit sound. But as an overview it was all these factors combined and translated by the talents of a select group of individuals. The Hit Makers. These are their stories.

CHRIS KENNER:
Man of 1,000 Dances

What do Fats Domino, The Doors, Cannibal and the Headhunters, Junior Walker, Tom Jones, Wilson Pickett, Ike and Tina Turner, Major Lance, Paul Revere and the Raiders, the J. Geils Band and Patti Smith all have in common? Here's a clue:
> *You gotta know how to pony,*
> *Like Bony Morone.*
> *You gotta know how to twist,*
> *Goes like this.*
> *Mash potatoes,*
> *Do the alligator,*
> *Twist a twister,*
> *Like little sister.*
> *Then you get your yo-yo,*
> *Say hey, let's go-go.*

That's right. All the previously mentioned artists, plus a number of other major artists and lesser known ones, have recorded versions of one of the most recognizable rock 'n' roll songs of all time, "Land Of 1000 Dances," which was written and recorded originally by New Orleanian Chris Kenner. But Kenner was much more than a one-shot wonder. Besides having his material recorded by scores of other artists, he also managed to cut a few of his own hits. Kenner ranks next to Allen Toussaint and Bartholomew-Domino as a songwriter, yet his death a few years ago went virtually unnoticed and his work has largely been taken for granted.

Christopher Kenner was born on Christmas Day in 1929 in Kenner, Louisiana, a suburb of New Orleans in adjacent Jefferson Parish. Like many other R&B performers, Kenner began singing with his local church choir as a youth, and later with a gospel group, the Harmonizing Four.

After moving to New Orleans to work as a longshoreman, Kenner continued to sing in an informal gospel quartet with his brother, John Davis, and Earl King. Gospel singing would influence Kenner greatly, even after he made the switch to R&B in the late Fifties.

A squat, heavyset man of medium height, Kenner easily assumed his nickname, "Bear." Before turning to songwriting, Kenner had tried prize-fighting to pick up some extra money. "Chris had been trying a long time before he got a break," recalls Earl King. "Every time one of these record companies came to town Chris would be down at Cosimo's trying to audition. Johnny Vincent [Ace Records] was interested in a tune Chris had and he wanted someone else to cut it.

"Chris was always kind of a loner. He wasn't into the Dew Drop or the Tiajuana scene in those days. But you could always see him on the corner outside Sam's or the Dixie Belle on Rampart. See, Chris liked to oil—he liked to drink."

Kenner's first break came in 1957, when Baton Records, a New York R&B label, came here looking for talent. This time Kenner had made the grade and he cut the bluesy "Don't Pin That Charge On Me" and "Grandma's House." Despite the high quality of Kenner's performance, the record didn't sell and he continued working on the docks.

Not long after the Baton disappointment, Kenner approached Dave Bartholomew who was running Imperial Records in New Orleans. "Chris was always a person who didn't have a voice," Bartholomew told Rick Coleman and Terry Pattison in a radio interview. "Chris had been coming around for years. This day he said, 'I got something really good today.' I said, 'It better be, because I'm getting ready to go to lunch.' So he sang 'Sick and Tired,' and said, 'What do you think of that?' I said, 'You got it!' I didn't need no more. Sure enough, we recorded the tune and it was a very big tune for Chris."

According to Lee Bates, a fine soul singer in his own right and later a chauffeur for Kenner, there was considerable time between the actual recording of "Sick and Tired," and its release. "Chris was hauling sacks of sugar on the docks after he cut 'Sick and Tired,' " says Bates. "He was at his sister's house when the record first came on the radio. He didn't even know they were playing his record. His sister had to say, 'Chris, that's you on the radio!' He didn't even know himself! All of a sudden, bam. Chris is in a station wagon and we are working on the road."

Kenner's booking were done by Percy Stovall. "I always wondered why Chris had them hits," recalled Stovall just before his death. "He couldn't sing, he couldn't dance, he dressed raggedy—he just stood there. He didn't have any showmanship and he was drunk all the time.

"I put him on the road with the Dukes of Rhythm and I used to tell them to play loud, to cover him up. I never did book Chris back into the same place twice. I tried to get him to let Little Jessie Thomas take his place on the road, but he wouldn't have any part of it. I was in North Carolina once and I tried to tell him, 'Man, you got to please the people, you can't get away with that foolishness.' He would get so drunk he would forget the words to his song. They used to boo and throw bottles at him."

"Sick and Tired" proved to be a big local hit for Kenner in 1957. It inspired a version by Fats Domino the following year that became a substantial national chart buster. Nonetheless, Kenner would have only one more record on Imperial.

"Lew Chudd [owner of Imperial] said he couldn't handle him," continues Dave Bartholomew. "he said he didn't have a voice and he didn't think he was selling. One thing Chris had, he was a hell of a writer. And he was original. Lew Chudd dismissed him, but it turned out he was wrong because he stirred the world up a couple of times."

After receiving his release from Imperial, Kenner began making the rounds of the local independent labels. He stopped in to see Joe Banashak, who owned A-1 Distributors, the company that was getting Minit Records off the ground in 1959. Although Banashak felt most of his material sounded too much like "Sick and Tired," he expressed interest in recording a tune Kenner had down on a demo tape called "I Like It Like That." The project had to be scrapped for a time when the two couldn't come to contractual terms because Kenner apparently demanded an exorbitant 10¢ a record.

Eventually Kenner approached Wallace Davenport, who had a small label called Pontchartrain, and cut the rambunctious "Don't Make No Noise." Soon after, he had an isolated release on Joe Ruffino's Ron label "Rocket to the Moon," but neither sold like "Sick and Tired."

Later, in 1961, Kenner reapproached Banashak, who had since embarked on a new label called Valiant, with Irving Smith, the owner of a local record shop. This time the two came to an agreement and Kenner was dispatched to the studio with Allen Toussaint at the helm as arranger and producer. They cut "I Like It Like That," the tune Kenner had originally pitched to Banashak.

"Chris didn't happen until he got with Allen," says Earl King. "His stuff would turn a lot of people off. It took Allen to interpret what he meant. If you'd ever heard some of those tunes before they were cut they were nowhere near what the records were like.

"Chris kept the songs in his head. He got a lot of his ideas from Willie Mabon and Joe Turner. I think a lot of his songs sounded like Willie Mabon's style on 'I Don't Know.' His whole theme of writing was around Willie Mabon."

Just as the record peeled off the presses, Banashak and Smith were forced to change the name of their label when it was brought to their attention that a Valiant label was already in existence in California. Banashak knew that deejays were constantly looking for "instant" hits, so he decided to give them some—he named the label Instant Records, which would soon become one of the most influential and important R&B labels in New Orleans.

The name change hindered "I Like It Like That" initially, but after a few months of moderate sales, it spilled its exuberance over onto the national R&B charts and the pop charts soon after. When the smoke finally cleared, "I Like It Like That" sold one-half-million records during its seventeen-week climb to #2 in *Billboard's* Hot 100. Kenner appeared on Dick Clark's *American Bandstand* in June and his song was nominated for a prestigious Grammy Award. Quite a beginning for Kenner and a new record company.

Unfortunately, probably no one was more ill-suited to rock 'n' roll stardom than Chris Kenner. A kind but simple man, Kenner's drinking and spending sprees were legendary. Besides constantly frustrating promoters by missing gigs—not to mention forgetting the words to his songs—he just didn't behave in the manner befitting a person with the #2 record in the country.

"Chris was like Jimmy Reed," says Earl King, "If he was sober, it was abnormal. When Chris got his money, he put himself up in a hotel room. As long as he had his liquor, he would isolate himself from the public. If he had liquor and room service, that was his thing. He'd stay there until all the money was gone. When he was broke he was on the street and back to normal."

Lee Bates concurs. "Chris was a hotel man, he liked to stay up in a room. We had been with him in the morning when he had three or four thousand dollars and he'd be begging money for drinks that night. He'd give all his money to some woman in the projects.

"My job was to try and keep him sober. He never was too good on stage except when he wasn't drunk. Drink took over his mind and he lost a lot of gigs. Some nights I remember he couldn't even stand up to sing. But when Chris ate, I ate. He kept me alive. He was that kind of guy."

On the record front, Kenner's second Instant release, "Packin' Up," fell far short of the promise of his debut disc, selling poorly even in New Orleans. Not so though for his third Instant release, "Something You Got," which didn't hit nationally, but became one of the biggest local records of the Sixties.

" 'Something You Got' sold a lot of records here," recalls Instant's boss Joe Banashak. "I couldn't figure out why because I couldn't even give it away as close as Baton Rouge. Well, I asked K-Doe and Benny Spellman why the record was selling and they said, 'Don't you know, man? The kids are learning to dance the Popeye to 'Something You Got.' Well, I'll tell you how dances affected records: we sold 30,000 records and that was just in New Orleans off the Popeye."

Kenner had a couple of other releases on Instant in 1962, the gospel-flavored "Time" and "Let Me Show You How To Twist." The latter incorporated the "I Like It Like That" formula while trying to cash in on the latest dance craze. "Twist" and its flip, "Johnny Little" were a departure from most of Kenner's early releases in that both sides were penned by arranger Allen Toussaint (under the alias N. Neville).

"Allen had trouble writing for Chris," claims Banashak. "He took all these funny little breaths that only sounded good when they came out of Chris. I think Allen intimidated Chris a bit because of his talent. Chris would always be sober and on time for those sessions when Allen was around. You have to give Allen a lot of the credit for Chris' success because he really worked hard on those songs."

Later that year, Kenner wrote and recorded the song which would become synonymous with his name, "Land Of A 1000 Dances" (reworking an old spiritual, "Children Go Where I Send You") by interspersing verses about all the current dance trends. Whether he could handle it or not, rock 'n' roll immortality was on the immediate horizon. Curiously, nowhere on the record does Kenner say anything about a "land of a thousand dances," even though he does name twenty or thirty dnces. But a privileged listen to the master of the tune clears up the mystery. It contains a ten-second introduction that was omitted from the issued record. On it Kenner moans in true gospel fashion, "I'm gonna take you, baby, I'm gonna take you to a place. The name of the place is the land of a thousand dances," and then the band falls in. Later on Kenner even forgets a verse and manages to moan instead of sing at other appropriate moments.

"Chris kept the songs in his head," says Lee Bates, who observed a number of Kenner's sessions. "He didn't write down nothing. Chris would get behind the piano and moan and groan until he came up with an idea and then he was ready to cut."

At the start, "Land Of A 1000 Dances" failed to catch on, even in New Orleans. This was much to the chagrin of Joe Banashak, who suggested that Kenner try to get Fats Domino to record it for Fats' new label, ABC. On the advice of his lawyer, Charles Levy, Fats agreed to cover the tune in return for 50% of the song's publishing and writer's credit. Kenner was broke again and was only too happy to get some advance money. But if that wasn't enough, Kenner also cemented a similar deal with Fats for the rights to "Something You Got" and "Packin' Up."

Even Domino's cover failed to stir the ashes of Kenner's version, however, and "Dances" was considered all but dead. To make matters worse, A-1 filed for bankruptcy, putting the entire Instant label in limbo.

However, after more than a year, a strange thing happened to the record, as Joe Banashak picks up the story: 'Losing the distributorship was a real blow. I was completely out of the record business for a while. I started pulling weeds and cutting grass to relax my mind. Well, I got a call one day from a distributor in Chicago who wanted 2,000 copies of 'Land Of 1000 Dances,' and the record started happening there. Then Atlantic came to see me and they were interested in the record. I owed them some money and I needed some too, so I signed a deal. What I didn't know was that the pressing plant had an order for 15,000 the very next day. But it was too late, the record started breaking all over the country.

"Atlantic took the credit for making 'Land Of 1000 Dances' happen but it was already breaking without them. They had the single and I leased an album to them a little later. It was a good move for Chris. I was going through a dry period and it put him on an active label."

Kenner's version of "Dances" reached a respectable #77 during its seven-week stay in the charts, but really that was just the beginning. Kenner started gigging on the road again, often with tragicomic results. Percy Stovall recalled that there was more than one Chris Kenner imitator posing as our hero. Once he related, the real Chris Kenner had bottles and drinks thrown at him by an irate audience, when they felt that the authentic item was actually a fraud.

Rejuvenated by "Land Of A 1000 Dances," Banashak reactivated

Instant with a series of releases by local artists, including Kenner. "Come Back and See" and "What's Wrong With Life" were good tunes, but only scored around New Orleans.

Towards the end of 1963, Kenner, Johnny Adams, George French, Joe Jones, Eskew Reeder and Earl King were in Detroit auditioning for the Motown label. According to Earl King, Berry Gordy was set to sign Kenner, who was nearing the close of his Instant contract. "At the time, 'Land Of A 1000 Dances' was #1 in Detroit and it was scorching. Chris had a gig at the Greystone Ballroom with George French and Johnny Adams. When those guys got through, there was no response from the audience. But when Bear got up there, it was like a time bomb went off. He must have been sober that night because when he hit the stage, everybody in the place fell out screaming and hollering.

"That's the thing about a hit record, once it gets going, things snowball and there's not much you have to do. I think the reason why a lot of Motown groups put 'Land Of A 1000 Dances' on their albums was because it was such a hit in Detroit. Berry Gordy was all set to sign Chris, in fact they recorded some stuff, but Chris split a day before the rest of us and left Berry with the hotel bill to pay. I think that made him leery about Chris and nothing ever became of it."

Kenner eventually did get a premature release from Instant in 1964, engineered by Charles Levy, who was now also Kenner's legal counsel. Soon after, Kenner signed a songwriter's contract for Fats Domino. In return for writing material exclusively for Domino, Kenner received a $500 advance, and $20 a week for the 20-week duration of the contract, to be subtracted from his forthcoming royalties. On top of that, Fats would receive half of the writer's credit and, of course, half of the publishing money.

Although nothing much came of the Domino arrangement, quite suddenly, a number of covers of Kenner's tunes became national hits. In the summer of 1964, fellow New Orleanian Alvin Robinson had a #52 hit with "Something You Got." Then early the following year, a garage band from California, Cannibal and the Headhunters, scored a #30 hit with "Land Of A 1000 Dances," which was followed by the Dave Clark Five's rendering of "I Like It Like That," which notched in at #7. Not to be outdone, Wilson Pickett had his biggest record ever in 1966 with "Land Of A 1000 Dances," which climbed to #6.

As a result, Kenner was on the receiving end of a tremendous amount of BMI songwriters' royalties. "I think all that money was a shock," says Earl King. "I really think it did a number on his mind. A lot of people didn't think Chris was getting his money at all because every time you'd see him he was out on the streets looking like a bum—but that was Chris.

"Chris was the only guy that ever *owed* money to BMI. Every time I would see him, he'd ask me to type a letter to BMI to get an advance. And they would send it because they knew that money was coming in. Every few months they'd send him a check for three or four thousand dollars."

Eventually Kenner resigned with Banashak in 1965 after he failed to secure a better deal elsewhere, but he would have mixed results there. Banashak leased a session on Kenner to Uptown Records, which was produced by Allen Toussaint. Although "The Life Of My Baby" b/w "They Took My Money" was a catchy single, it failed to click. "Never Reach Perfection" and "What's Wrong With Life" later appeared on Instant and captured the spirit of earlier successes, but fell on deaf ears. So, too, did "She Can Dance" b/w "Anybody Here Seen My Baby."

After Toussaint left to form a partnership with Marshall Sehorn, Kenner's sessions were put in the hands of Eddie Bo and, later, Sax Kari. "As a recording artist, Chris lost his direction after Allen left," explains Banashak. "The more he tried, the worse he got. He drank too much at sessions and he had to squeeze lemons to make his voice sound better. He was always around the office borrowing money. Chris just couldn't get it together."

Kenner's song ideas were quickly evaporating as well, and his later Instant releases were often penned by others. Still, he managed a few good sides, including "I'm Lonely, Take Me," produced by Eddie Bo and "Wind The Clock," written and arranged by Sax Kari. There also was "Stretched My Hand To You" from 1967, which didn't do much nationally, but became a big local record as "Coo Coo Over You" by the Hueys on Instant.

Ironically, his 1968 Instant release of "Sad Mistake" would signal a screeching halt to Kenner's recording career. Not long after, Kenner was arraigned on a charge of statutory rape of a minor and began a three-year stretch in Angola. Lee Bates claims that the unfortunate incident involved the daughter of an ex-girlfriend and that Kenner was framed by the girl's daughter. However, Earl King, Joe Banashak and Percy Stovall all said that Kenner already had a similar charge pending, but that he'd had no money to bargain with the second time around, even though the shrewd Charles Levy was still his lawyer.

While Kenner was serving his time, he was joined by fellow New Orleanian James Booker, who had been sent up for possession of heroin in 1970. While in Angola, Kenner contacted the A.G.A.C. (Amaglamated Group of American Composers) to collect his composers royalties. According to Earl King, $21,000 was waiting for Kenner upon his release in 1972, but it was gone in less than two months.

Kenner attempted to put together the broken pieces of his career, enlisting the aid of Ike Favorite, confidant of Fats Domino, as manager. Things were slow in New Orleans, and gigs and recording deals were scarce. In 1974, he cut a session for Senator Jones which resulted in two terrible singles for the Hep' Me label. The following year he made his first and only appearance at the New Orleans Jazz Festival, but failed to turn many heads, including this author's.

When Quint Davis began booking R&B acts in 1976 at the 501 Club (later to become Tipitina's) Kenner often shared the bill with the likes of Professor Longhair and Earl King. Local producer Isaac Bolden was interested in recording new material on Kenner, and had gone as far as cutting some demos. However, Kenner's comeback never happened, as he died of an apparent cardiac arrest in January 1977.

"Last time I saw Chris was in the 501 Club," says Earl King. "He was dressed real nice in a black suit and a white shirt. He was sober that night because he sounded real good with us.

"Chris had started to hang down by the K&B on St. Charles and Louisiana, and all of a sudden he didn't show up any more, and people were asking about him. He was living in a rooming house on the corner of Dryades and Jackson, next to Bea Booker's house [Ms. Booker was a well-respected pianist]. She noticed his car hadn't moved for a few days and sent her husband over to check on him. He managed to get Chris door open, but the night latch was on and a terrible odor came out. They called the police and they broke down the door. Apparently, Chris had just come out of the shower and he fell on the bed. Chris had gained a lot of weight back and I think it put too much strain on his heart."

Details concerning Kenner's death and burial were kept hushed, without immediate notice in the locals papers, and no effort was made by Kenner's family to contact his friends. "It was quiet, extra quiet," agrees Lee Bates, who was deeply hurt by the circumstances. "Nobody said a word about a funeral, everything was secret. I don't even know where he was buried. I don't think that was right. Chris was a star and nothing was done for him."

"Funny thing," points out Earl King, "I really thought Chris might be turning things around. He had cut Levy loose as his lawyer and he was asking me about how to form a publishing company. He felt really bad about his son, Chris Kenner, Jr., being sent to Angola [Kenner's wife was also doing time for shooting a man in a bar] and he said he was going to start to change his ways."

Lee Bates, who considered himself Kenner's friend, eulogizes Kenner's career best by saying, "I was up and down with Chris two or three times. I was with him when he had to steal 36¢ to buy a plate of red beans at Sam's. Then the next thing you know he's driving around in a brand new car. Everytime he was down he'd say, 'Lee, next time I get back up again, I'm not gonna mess up no more.' But he always did the same thing. I guess things just happened too fast for Chris."

BOBBY MARCHAN
Is There Something On Your Mind?

Trying to piece together Bobby Marchan's life story is very much like trying to put together a very difficult jigsaw puzzle. Marchan has virtually ridden every trend in black music since the late Forties. He's cut city blues for Dot and Aladdin, vocal group rock 'n' roll for Ace, solo Sixties R&B for Fire, contemporary Memphis-type soul for Volt and Cameo, funk and bump records for Dial, and disco most recently for Sansu.

To make matters more difficult, Marchan is more interested in hyping his new group, "Higher Ground," than recalling details of his colorful career. It can be said Marchan is not a biographer's model subject.

Bobby Marchan is now in his early 50s. Most of the time he resembles neither his age nor his sex (please excuse this and any future puns). Marchan was raised in Youngstown, Ohio. As a youth he was interested in being an entertainer, and cites Larry Darnell as his earliest influence, particularly his version of "I'll Get Along Somehow."

As a teenager Marchan began working some of the clubs in his hometown as a drag comedian singer, and he became a regular attraction at the Club 77. Bobby remembers tours of twenty-four female impersonators going through Youngstown. [AUTHOR'S NOTE: Female impersonators have long been popular attractions in the field of black entertainment. Their origins date back to the touring medicine show days. In New Orleans, the Dew Drop Inn often had a female impersonator as the master of ceremonies, and impersonator shows are still popular (Marchan is proof of that). Also, a number of male singers are virtually indistinguishable from women on record—besides Bobby, one can cite Ted Taylor and Billy Wright.]

Bobby recalled how he made his way to New Orleans. "Everybody would come through town saying that New Orleans is where it's really happening. So around 1954, I had a troupe of about six female impersonators called 'The Powder Box Revue.' We were pretty good so we decided to try New Orleans.

"We worked some clubs on North Claiborne and also The

Tiajuana, where I met Huey Smith. That had to be around '54 or '55. Huey was working in the house band at the Tiajuana then."

Obviously New Orleans appealed to Bobby, as he has made it his home off and on since then. Marchan worked regularly in the clubs, still as a female impersonator, and lived on top of the Dew Drop Inn, where he often performed. He recalls seeing Guitar Slim, Ray Charles, Joe Turner, Sam Cooke, Little Willie John, and a host of other R&B stars around the Dew Drop.

His first trip to the studio was in 1954 for Aladdin. He cut "Just A Little Walk" b/w "Have Mercy" (Aladdin 3189). He then switched to Dot, a label out of Nashville. Both records were fine examples of city blues. But Marchan dismisses them. "Oh those? They were just records, they didn't do anything."

Next, Marchan found himself recording for Johnny Vincent's Ace label, using the alias Bobby Fields, probably because he was still under contract to Dot or Aladdin.

Marchan's next release on Ace was the first to make noise saleswise. Marchan recalls, "Huey had written this song (Chickee Wah-Wah) that we did over at Cosimo's. It started selling well in New Orleans and in the South. I was working in Baltimore when Huey came through with Shirley and Lee. Huey had just cut 'Rockin' Pneumonia,' and it was just hittin' the charts. So we got together and decided to get our own thing together and go back to New Orleans. Huey didn't have any money so I had to lend it to him; that's when I took over as leader of the Clowns. I could make more money leading the Clowns than working in drag, so I put that stuff away. The Clowns had some big hits and we travelled all over America with Frankie Avalon and Paul Anka."

Once Bobby took over the Clowns, the band took on a different style—many of the tunes were written with Bobby in mind as the lead vocalist. When quizzed on what records he participated on, he allowed, "Oh all of 'em, 'Don't You Just Know It,' 'Don't You Know Yockamo,' 'Havin' A Good Time,' 'High Blood Pressure,' lots of 'em."

Although he didn't write any material for the Clowns, Bobby said, "I did learn to write stuff by watching Huey." Marchan and Huey enjoyed over a dozen releases on Ace.

"I was with the Clowns from the beginning (1957) until I quit in 1960. I was the boss, Huey Smith stayed home with his wife and children. I took the group on the road, I paid the group off, and even sent Huey's wife the rest of the money. Not to Huey.

"Little James Booker played the piano on the road. He was so

Bobby Marchan, late 1960's

close to Huey we took him on the road and had a wonderful time. People thought I was Huey Smith! I had to tell them I was Bobby Marchan. Then they thought Booker was Huey Smith.

"Huey liked to stay around New Orleans—he enjoyed it. I guess he got tired being on the road with Shirley and Lee. So he said, 'Bobby you take the group.' Huey bought a brand new wagon, and I rehearsed the group and took 'em out. I did the hiring and firing.

"I hired Geri Hall, she sang with the Raelettes for a while. A boy named John ['Scarface' John] Williams, he's dead now, he could sing and clown a lot. I had Eugene, he couldn't sing but he sure could clown. He dyed his hair reddish green. I had Roosevelt Wright, who was one of the best bass singers in the country.

"A lot of companies tried to sign me, yes indeed. But I enjoyed being the overseer of The Clowns. I enjoyed those days. We were on the road all the time. I stayed with The Clowns until 'Something On Your Mind.' They called me from New York saying they were gonna pay me $1,500 a night. You know I was gonna go then.

"'Something On Your Mind' caused quite a stir. I tried to get Johnny Vincent to cut it but he wasn't interested in releasing it so I sold it to Bobby Robinson in New York of Fire Records. It was number one all over the country."

Actually, the record (Fire 1022) stayed on the *Billboard* Pop Record Chart for 11 weeks, peaking at number 31. All hell broke loose once the record was released. Not only was Bobby under contract to Ace still, but Marchan sold the master to two different companies: Fire, and Chess in Chicago. The end result was that Vincent sued Robinson, and Fire had to post $12,500 to continue releasing the hit.

None of this concerned our hero, though. "I left the Clowns and began working as a singer all over the country. I worked the Apollo in New York, The Regal in Chicago, The Howard in Washington, The Peacock in Atlanta, just about any city you can name. I toured with James Brown for 30 days."

"I was in heavy demand during the Sixties, 'cause I had all the hit records. I've always been a very good performer getting over and being able to execute. I was doing the shows in drag, just like I do now. See, I do this comedy thing in drag and I think the public should get more than just singin' all night. They should get something exciting for their money."

Fire accounted for an album, his only one, and a number of other fine singles including "The Booty Green" and "Things I Used To Do," all fine efforts—but none reached the charts. Bobby stayed with Fire until the early Sixties when the label folded. Of course, this was just a minor obstacle for the ever ambitious Marchan.

"Otis Redding and I were very close friends. See I lived in Macon, Georgia for a time, and we did some jobs together in colleges. Then Otis had a hit with 'These Arms Of Mine' and I brought him over to New Orleans and he heard Irma sing 'Ruler of My Heart'; he liked it and changed the words to 'Pain In My Heart.' That was a big hit.

"After that he talked to Jim Stewart (Stax Volt producer) for me and told him I had a nice voice. So Jim Stewart said he'd like to record me also. Booker T and the MG's backed me up. I did a couple of things but they really weren't up to standard."

If you're ever lucky enough to hear "What Can I Do" on Volt 106, you might disagree with Bobby. The side is a classic Memphis soul ballad with a great Marchan rap on the flip.

Next, it was on to Dial Records and a long association with producer Buddy Killen in Nashville. "I had known Joe Tex for a long time, and he was with Dial records at the time (1965) and spoke to Buddy Killen about me. So I got with Dial and Buddy. We had a hit with 'Shake Your Tambourine' that Buddy released to

Bobby Marchan, 1982

Cameo. That was a Top 50 hit (on the Soul Charts)."

Bobby continued to criss-cross the country with a number of different bands. At one time he worked with Marvin Marchan, his son in Florida.

Come the Seventies, Bobby began penning songs for other artists with some success. He wrote "Body English" for King Floyd and "Get Down Get With It" for Slade, their million seller. "I'm glad they did it, 'cause I started getting them big royalty checks! I got more money from that than on my own records."

Bobby renewed his association with Johnny Vincent, who attempted to reactivate Ace in 1975. Bobby cut one record and helped produce a minor hit for Willie Dixon, covering Al Green's "God Blessed Our Love." Marchan had been working in Florida with Dixon, who had been billing himself as Al Green Jr., and brought him to Jackson to record.

Then it was back to New Orleans for a release on Sansu, "Shake It Don't Break It" b/w "Do You Want To Dance." Bobby has little use for Sansu. "Sansu was very stupid. Marshall Sehorn had 'Separate Ways' there [written by Marchan but recorded by Z.Z. Hill, a big Southern hit on the soul charts]. I begged him to release 'Separate Ways' every day, but he put it on the shelf and hurried to get a disco record out. A year after he wouldn't release it, Z.Z. Hill called me and asked me if he could do it. I told him yes, indeed, and he got a hit out of it. Then Sansu called me up and asked me if they could put it out and I told them 'No.' In fact I told 'em, 'Hell no! Don't even call me about it.' "

Since then Bobby has worked regularly as the emcee at Prout's Club Alhambra. "When Mr. Prout opened his club he asked me to work there, and he also needed an entertainment manager. I helped Prout's with the booking too."

Bobby's shows are usually riotous affairs. He most often appears in cocktail dresses and evening wear of his own design that he sews himself. Marchan never has a problem loosening up an audience, being able to handle any crowd.

Bobby also emcees a regular Gong Show at the Club 2004 that has been a weekly affair for years now.

What occupies most of Bobby's time now is hyping his new group Higher Ground, a funk band that is comparable to Cameo. It is in speaking of his new group that Bobby Marchan comes to life. "My band Higher Ground, in my estimation, is one of the highest bands in the country. Four horns, they work very hard rehearsing. Every club we play we get return engagements. I've had my band just six months, and as you know we just cut our first record, 'Shake 'Em Up,' Part One and Part Two. Alan Rubin, the president of WMOT, signed us. We may be on our way at last."

Higher Ground works Prout's, J.J.'s in Algiers, and on weekends they sometimes work around South Louisiana. Bobby works hard finding them jobs and promoting shows, and he financed Higher Ground's recording sessions.

Although at times a frustrating interview, you still have to admire Bobby for always having his thumb on trends and the public's taste. He has virtually been a master of it for the past thirty years.

When quizzed on what keeps him going in the music business after all these years, he says, "I've never wanted to do anything but be an entertainer. I love to entertain the people."

FRANKIE FORD
Feel Like Jumpin'

Frankie Ford works five nights a week at Lucky Pierre's, a rather notorious Bourbon Street nitery. Watered-down mixed drinks are a steep $5 and the girls who sit at the piano bar eyeball all who enter. Every inch of the room seems to be covered in mirrors or imitation leather. Frankie renders versions of "MacArthur Park," "Feelings," and "Tie A Yellow Ribbon" from behind an oversized brandy snifter that is generally stuffed with tips. When someone asks him to play one of his hits he will generally furrow his brow like a scolding school teacher and whisper, "This is not the kind of place for rock and roll."

Frankie Ford will forever be known for his 1959 hit "Sea Cruise." He was born Frank Guzzo, August 4, 1939, the only son of Mr. and Mrs. Vincent Guzzo. Frankie grew up in Gretna, Louisiana, a suburb of New Orleans, located directly across the Mississippi River on the West Bank.

From his childhood Frankie was groomed to be an entertainer. "I used to sing in the backyard when I was about six," says Frankie, pausing during a break. "The lady next door heard me and told my mother, 'You know, he's better than some of these kids on the radio. You ought to see about sending him to some lessons.'"

Voice lessons aside, Frankie grew up like most other adolescents, "except maybe I was a little spoiled" — listening to the likes of Bing Crosby, Frank Sinatra and Kay Starr on the radio. At the age of twelve, Frankie won a talent contest that was sponsored by the Monteleone Hotel's Parisian Room on Royal Street. The award was a trip to New York to appear on the *Ted Mack Hour*. By the time Frankie entered high school he had joined his first band, the Syncopators. "We had four horns, every band in New Orleans had a bunch of horn players," points out Frankie. "We were just playing pretty much Top 40."

Growing up in New Orleans afforded Frankie the unique opportunity to learn what happens musically when the white and black cultures meet and mix. "Around the middle Fifties the radio stations started slipping in black records, and we really liked it. I remember sneaking into the Joy Lounge when I was under age to go see Sugar Boy and the Cane Cutters. Then we'd go stand outside the Labor Hall to hear Little Willie John or Ray Charles, because we couldn't get in. I saw Huey Smith and Fats Domino at the auditorium too.

"Then I got together with the sax player and we learned 'Hearts Of Stone' by the Charms. I guess that was about 1954. When the radio started to turn over instead of being strictly Top 40, the band started turning around too. By '56 we were a complete rock and roll band."

With the city teeming with musical activity during the 1950s, it didn't take too long for Frankie to catch the eyes and ears of an eager record company. "A friend of mine—Paul Marvin—cut a couple of records for Deluxe, and one for Verve. Joe Caronna was his manager, and he also had the Ace Record distributorship in New Orleans. Joe asked Paul if he knew of any other acts around that were good.

"He said, 'Yeah, there's a good friend of mine in a band that's real good.'

"So Joe came across on the ferry one night and listened to us rehearse. After the rehearsal he asked us if we were interested in cutting a record.

"I said, 'yes, definitely!'

"We didn't hear from Joe for about three or four weeks, until one morning he called from Cosimo's Studio and asked, 'Can you be down at the studio this afternoon?'

"Well I got the guys together and rushed down to the studio. He asked if we had any original songs and I played him 'Cheatin' Woman' and 'Last One to Cry.'

"So Joe said, 'Okay we're gonna cut that.'

"I was in perfect awe. I was working in the same studio with Huey Smith, Charles Williams, Robert Parker and Red Tyler. I just couldn't believe it."

Always sensitive to trends in the music business, Ace's owner Johnny Vincent convinced Frankie and Joe Caronna to change Frankie's professional name from the awkward Guzzo. Since it was 1958, the age of hot rods, why not use a catchy name like Frankie Ford? Originally Vincent wanted to use Frankie Lee Ford, mimicking Sun Record's Jerry Lee Lewis, but Frankie balked, and they settled simply on Frankie Ford.

"When the record came out, we had to travel," continued Frankie, "but a lot of the guys had jobs, or were in school. So we

Frankie the Teen Idol, 1959

broke up the band and Joe formed my first professional group. We had Paul Stahli on drums; Earl Stanley, bass; Leonard James, tenor; and Mac Rebennack, guitar (Mac is a distant cousin of Frankie's). I was singin' and playin' a little piano.''

The record, which appeared on Ace 549, was a modest New Orleans hit. Oddly it generated some airplay in Philadelphia, where it was assumed that Frankie was black, largely due to the fact that Ace was primarily an R&B label at the time. Frankie still laughs when recalling his first trip to Philadelphia. "I was booked into the Uptown Theatre to do the Georgie Woods Show. I got there to rehearse and it was a completely black theatre. Georgie saw me and said, 'Oh my God, you're white!'

"So I said, 'Well, nobody's perfect.'

"Georgie said, 'This is a black theatre, I just don't think it will happen.'

"He was gonna pay me and send me home. But I told him, 'I'm not gonna take your money if I'm not gonna work. At least let me rehearse.'

"Doc Bagby's Orchestra was working as the house band, and I rehearsed 'Hallelujah,' the Ray Charles thing. That had not hit except with the blacks up north. Georgie just shook his head and said, 'Okay, you're on the show.' Well the audience really liked me, and right after that I did my first spot on 'The Dick Clark Show.'"

It was Frankie's second record that was to change his entire life, though it was cut practically by accident. "I was flying back from that trip to Philadelphia with Joe and Johnny Vincent, who had been at a record convention in New York," he relates. "On the Tuesday after we got back, Joe called me and said, 'Get down here right away, we've got a track we want you to cut.'

"While I was in Philadelphia, Huey Smith had cut 'Sea Cruise,' as a follow up to 'Don't You Know Yokamo.' But Huey and Bobby Marchan (the Clowns' lead singer) were having some kind of argument, and couldn't cut it. Johnny had seen me performing some of Huey's things and thought I sounded close enough to Bobby to try 'Sea Cruise.'

"I walked into the studio, and had not even heard 'Sea Cruise.' I didn't even know any of the lyrics. Huey sat down with me and wrote out the words. The first thing we cut was 'Roberta,' and then we did 'Sea Cruise.' We had two mikes in the studio — me on one, the Clowns on the other one. When Johnny mastered the record, he sped the tapes up just a bit, so I sounded even more like Bobby."

The record was simply a classic. Huey's boogie-woogie piano set the launching pad for the riffing horns and Frankie's enthusiastic vocal. Initially "Sea Cruise" was released only in New Orleans to test its sales potential. It got about half way up the local charts and then fell off. But when the record was released nationally, it was an immediate smash and Frankie was suddenly in the national spotlight. In 1959 "Sea Cruise" rose to #14 during its 17-week stay in *Billboard's* Hot 100, and #11 in the R&B charts. Frankie began touring, headlining a series of rock and roll caravan shows with the likes of Chuck Berry, Frankie Avalon, Paul Anka, The Fleetwoods, The Skyliners, and the Coasters, among others. He had his own fan club, and made regular appearances on *American Bandstand*, lip syncing his hit. Frankie recalls, "We worked six months, with only two days off. We travelled in a bus, starting in New York and working all the way across the country."

When he did finally come in off the grind of one-nighters, Frankie went back into the studio under the production wing of Huey Smith, who was then arranging material for Ace. According to Frankie, Huey was not the least bit upset about him having the hit with "Sea Cruise," because "Huey didn't travel. He just stayed home and produced records. So Johnny told Huey to just create a another artist. He already had a record in the charts at the time anyway." ("Don't You Know Yokomo.")

So Huey wrote and produced the hilarious "Alimony," whose infectious New Orleans rhythm picked up right where "Sea Cruise" left off, and Frankie had another national hit, even if only briefly.

Frankie also cut the humorous "Morgus The Magnificent" on Ace's sister label Vin under the guise of Morgus and The Three Ghouls. Morgus was a popular New Orleans TV personality who hosted horror movies every Saturday night. The record is well remembered in New Orleans for its way-out lyrics and Mac Rebennack's smoldering guitar break.

After two full-tilt rock and roll hits, Frankie's style went in another direction, as evidenced by releases like "Chinatown" and "Time After Time." "I was growing then," explained Frankie. "Johnny just didn't want to go in any different direction. I had to really fight to do 'Time After Time.' As a producer, he just couldn't think in that direction. He could only think in terms of rock and roll and R&B."

Not so for Ace's other teen idol, Jimmy Clanton, who cut a long string of smoochie singles. "Jimmy and I were very close," says Frankie. "We were roommates on the road. He was a nice guy and talented. I was probably closer to him than any other Ace artist. I was close to Earl King too, he was gonna write some stuff for me, but I'd left Ace and it just didn't happen."

After six singles and an album, Frankie and Joe Caronna decided to split from Johnny Vincent, with money apparently being one of the factors. "We really thought there were more records sold than the statements indicated. Some of the royalty statements were hilarious, just hilarious." Frankie also cited his need for more artistic freedom than Vincent could afford.

Frankie's first step towards independence was the formation of Spinet Records with Caronna in 1959. The duo immediately had a monster local hit with another novelty tune, "Chinese Bandits."

"That was the year that LSU (Louisiana State University) had the best football team in the country. So Joe said, 'Look, I'm not kidding, LSU is gonna be number one.' So we came up with this topical thing, Chinese Bandits.' (Chinese Bandits was the alias for the LSU defense, partly because of their yellow uniforms.) I wrote the chorus, and Huey and I got together and made a deal to split what we'd make. We had to call ourselves the Cheerleaders, because our contracts with Johnny hadn't expired yet."

The record still gets plenty of local airplay throughout Louisiana and has become a collector's item with R&B record collectors and LSU football fans alike. Frankie still vividly recalls the confusion that surrounded the release of the record. "We sent some dubs out to the radio stations, and people started calling in like crazy asking where they could get the record. The first thousand records came without labels, but we just told 'em to send 'em on, because the stores were just screaming for them. We couldn't even get a stamp to stamp the labels, we had to write the titles on by hand. We had to put 1,000 records on a turntable to see which side was which. We had to hand deliver them to the stores because it was Saturday and the distributorship was closed."

Spinet had seven other releases by some local singers and a couple of groups Huey and Frankie threw together, but none caused as big a stir as "Chinese Bandits." "Joe really just set up Spinet to give me a little business experience. But we really didn't do too bad for a small independent."

It wasn't until after Spinet that Imperial came into the picture. "Joe Banashak, who distributed Imperial in New Orleans, told Joe, 'I'll talk to Lew Chudd about Frankie, and see if he's interested.'" Imperial turned out to be very interested, offering Frankie a $10,000 signing bonus."

With Dave Bartholomew handling all the Imperial sessions in New Orleans, Frankie now found himself under the musical guidance of the man with the golden touch. Frankie still speaks very highly of Bartholomew. "What can you say about a guy who has 50 million records to his credit? He knew how he wanted to have things. I certainly wasn't gonna question him. You simply can't argue with success."

Frankie Ford's first Imperial release became a hit, though it came by way of the back door. "Joe Jones had cut this thing, 'You Talk Too Much,' for two different companies (Ric and Roulette). They put injunctions on one another, and neither could get the record out. So Dave called me and asked me if I thought I could sound like Joe Jones. I said, 'Yeah sure,' I'd had to sound like Bobby Marchan once before.

"We cut the record on a Monday, using the same musicians that worked on the Joe Jones sessions — except maybe one. They shipped the tape out Tuesday, pressed it on Wednesday in Los Angeles, on Thursday they shipped the record, on Friday it was in the shops.

"When people came into the record shops and asked for, 'You

Talk Too Much,' they didn't know who it was by. So they bought mine because it was the only one available. Quite honestly, I made more money off 'You Talk Too Much' than 'Sea Cruise.'"

Frankie's Imperial releases totalled five. "Seventeen" was a fair-sized national record, while his other releases, the best of which were "Saturday Night Fish Fry" and "A Man Only Does," generated enough local sales to keep Imperial interested in more sessions. Frankie stayed busy between records, making a string of one-nighters throughout the country. "I didn't carry a band because most of the clubs had good house bands back then. We just sent the arrangements ahead and did a few run throughs when I got there."

Just when Frankie was enjoying his career the most, he got a call from Uncle Sam. Rather than make a fuss, Frankie made the best of the situation. "It wasn't that I didn't want to go," says Frankie sheepishly, "but it just came at a bad time.

"I started out as just a regular boot. I was stationed in Fort Leonardwood, Missouri for my basic training. At first nobody knew who I was because I enlisted under my given name. But Imperial let it leak to a radio station.

"They transferred me to information school after that, and then into the Soldier's Chorus. We did shows for the troops in Japan,

Vietnam, and Korea. I even had my stint extended a few months to be on the 1964 *Bob Hope Christmas Show* in Korea."

When Frankie returned to New Orleans in 1965 the music scene he had left had changed radically. "Imperial had sold out," says Frankie, shaking his head, "so I didn't have a record company to come back to. At that time the English sound was everywhere, and all the clubs were hiring guitar bands. Horn players were all out of work. Cosimo had moved his studio from Governor Nicholls to Camp Street, but few sessions were going on then. No one seemed to know where to go or in what direction the music business was headed. I stayed here until October '65, then moved to San Francisco until '67.

"When I came back I had this song written by Eddie Marshall, who had also written 'Venus' for Frankie Avalon. So I got together with Allen Toussaint, and he helped me with 'I Can't Face Tomorrow.'"

The single appeared on Doubloon, a label formed by Frankie and Ken Elliott, a disc jockey known locally as "Jack The Cat." The record did well in New Orleans, but they couldn't find an outside distributor.

During the late Sixties, Frankie became a fixture on Bourbon Street, where he continues to work to this day. "The first club I worked on the strip was the Ivanhoe," says Frankie. "I got a raise on the second day, and the owner brought me down the street to tell me if I stayed with him, he would let me open the new club he was going to build. That's how the 'Backstage Club' came about. With the exception of the year I spent at the Fountain Bay Hotel, I've been on the street ever since.

"I've built up a reputation," he continued. "All the clubs I've worked at are pretty intimate, with an elite clientele. People just don't fall in off the street."

Recordwise, Frankie hasn't experienced the same success he experienced between 1959 and 1961. "The biggest thing I had was 'Blue Monday,' on ABC, but they killed it," says Frankie, still frustrated. "They were changing presidents about every fifteen minutes then and they decided to push another Three Dog Night record, just as mine was getting ready to hit the charts. It was good, too."

Frankie even tested out the country music business, but his success has so far been negligible. "I was really doing country before it was fashionable," claims Frankie. "I leased a record to Paula that I cut up in Memphis, and I also went up to Nashville to do some stuff for Cinnamon. I guess I got a little nibble on that."

The biggest thing that happened to Frankie in the Seventies was his cameo appearance in *American Hot Wax*. Frankie explains the circumstances.

"The executive producer, Fred Gallo, called me and said he was interested in using 'Sea Cruise' in the movie. He wanted to know if I was overweight and if I had my hair," laughs Frankie. "So I sent him some recent photos, and he sent me a contract."

In the movie, Frankie portrays himself in a fictionalized and far-out takeoff of the recording session that produced the classic. Even though he was then 38, he looked two decades younger as he stormed through his hit.

Recently Frankie returned from a ten-day tour of England where he got rave reviews, performing an entire New Orleans set. And he's booked to return again in the future.

He also returned to the studio to cut an album at Sea-Saint, for the Southern Yat Club (yes that reads right). "There's some good things on there," contends Frankie. "It's a little blues, a little country, a little funk. It was a real old time New Orleans session." Presently Sea-Saint Studio is trying to land a deal with a major record company.

> **tagged for stardom...**
>
> **frankie FORD**
>
> **I CAN'T TELL MY HEART**
> (WHAT TO DO)
> b/w
> **ALIMONY**
> Ace #566
>
> Thanks, Music Merchants, for all your help on "SEA CRUISE"— I know you'll like my latest...
>
> personal management: JOE CARONNA
> bookings: GAC
> exclusively: ACE RECORDS
>
> *Billboard June 22, '59*

Frankie is somewhat baffled by his hometown's apathy towards his performing, only recently has he been invited to appear at the New Orleans Jazz Festival, which spotlights the city's musical talent. "I don't know what it is," he muses. "When I go to other cities the reviews are great." But, he quickly points out, "some people *only* work the Jazz Fest."

Despite his many ups and downs, Frankie's outlook remains positive. "I love to work," he states simply. "I tried to take three months off last year, but after a few weeks I started going bananas.

"I feel like I've been a success. I can pretty much pick and choose where I want to work. I've got one of the best jobs in town. What's there to complain about? I'm happy to be doing what I've been trained for all my life. I love it, and I'm making a good living at it. What else can a person ask for?"

JESSIE HILL
Puttin' Some Disturbance On Your Mind

Jessie Hill is looking . . . for what, even he doesn't know for sure. But it really doesn't matter, because he's not likely to ever find it.

Jessie lives in a modest half shotgun, only a few blocks away from where he was born on December 9, 1932. Outside, the traffic continually rumbles by on Caffin Avenue, and next door two men are busy painting the flowers on Fats Domino's white wrought iron fence pink and red.

Inside Jessie is perched on his couch wearing a beige polyester safari suit. His toothy grin and thick round glasses give him an odd Oriental look whenever he removes his ever-present cowboy hat, and reveals his balding head. A few of Jessie's friends fill up the front room and the conversation dwells on an upcoming engagement at Tipitina's the following week. Jessie is repeating for the third or fourth time that "this time I'm really gonna get it together," and that "this is just a tune up gig until I starts playin' the Hilton and Fairmont hotels." But when Jessie Hill is pressed for details it becomes apparent he's not at all certain who's going to play in his band for the Tipitina's gig.

Jessie hails from the same extended Ninth Ward musical family that produced Prince La La, Walter "Papoose" Nelson, Popee, Melvin, David and Betty Ann Lastie. Obviously Jessie came up in a musical environment. "Can't remember when I wasn't beatin' on somethin' tryin' to make some racket," he recalls.

"I used to go to McCarthy school back over here. When I was seven or eight, I'd leave the house early to go light the lamps at the church, and go practice on the drums afterwards, 'cause that's where they use' to keep the instruments."

Besides his musical family, Jessie also befriended Eddie Bo and Oliver Morgan as a youth. "When we was comin' up, we would be jammin' everyday." Jessie's drumming improved as he got older, and by the time he was 15, he used to sit in with Kid Arnestine's Dixieland Band on drums, which also featured Harrison Verret, Fats Domino's mentor. "It was kicks man," laughs Jessie. "Them old mens use' to like me. They carried me to Buras, Sunrise —

everywhere. Then I started playin' with Freddie Domino's band, Fats' cousin, before I got my own group together."

Jessie's first group, "The House Rockers" (the name he carries on today), contained both David and Melvin Lastie, as well as guitarist Little Eddie Lang. David Lastie recalls, "We worked mainly hillbilly joints down in St. Bernard." Mr. Google Eyes also remembers using the group to back him at the Club Desire occasionally. "They had a pretty good little band. I was surprised as hell when I heard him sing. 'Cause he [Jessie] use' to stutter so bad, nobody could hardly understand him."

The House Rockers stayed together for a year, including a trip with Bobby Marchan and a troupe of female impersonators to Dayton, Ohio, and a couple of other Northern cities in 1953. The band broke up upon their return, with Eddie and David hitting the road with Guitar Slim before getting back together with Jessie in 1954.

In the meantime, Jessie teamed up with Professor Longhair and Papoose to work "back-a-town." By Fess' own admission, Jessie was one of the few percussionists that could keep up with his unorthodox style of piano.

"See I been knowin' Fess all my life," continues Jessie. "We use' to open the curtain at The Blue Eagle, playin' in front of Muddy Waters, Little Willie John, Jimmy Reed and all those guys. See I was so far advanced with my playin'," maintains Jessie, "that I could only play with Fess. All this stuff you hearin' drummers play now, they's playin' what I was playin'." Oddly enough, Jessie never did get to record with Professor Longhair, giving way to the likes of John Boudreaux, Earl Palmer and John Woodrow on his recording sessions.

In the late Fifties, Jessie took over the drummer's stool for a short time with Huey Smith's Clowns. Remarkably, during Jessie's stint with the Clowns, the group also featured the likes of James Booker, James Rivers, Geri Hall, Raymond Lewis and Bobby Marchan, all of whom went on to cut successful records under their own names. Jessie recalls playing a number of famous theaters on package tours, and hanging around the Dew Drop when he got back to New Orleans.

The year 1958 saw Jessie leave the Clowns and get the House Rockers back together to work gigs in and around New Orleans. David Lastie rejoined the group that also contained Alvin "Shine" Robinson, guitar; Richard Payne, bass; and John Boudreaux, drums; now that Jessie had abandoned them in favor of singing and playing the tambourine.

Jessie at home, 1983

It was at this point that Jessie picked up the idea for his hit. David Lastie recalls that Jessie got the words to "Ooh Poo Pah Doo" from a blues piano player, "Big Four," who hung out at Shy Guy's Place. Apparently Jessie wrote the words to the song down on a paper sack, and stuffed it in his back pocket.

Jessie concurs, adding, "We started playin' 'Ooh Poo Pah Doo' as a gimmick. It got real popular everywhere we'd play, so I'd say, 'Y'all ready for my new record? We're gonna cut it pretty soon.' So they was all singin' it on my lil' circuit. They was ready for it when it did come out. So I kept at Larry McKinley [Minit Record co-owner] to record it."

Joe Banashak, Minit's other owner, recalls initially hearing Jessie's tape at an audition at WYLD that also netted Benny Spellman, Aaron Neville, Allen Toussaint and Ernie K-Doe for the fledgling label in January 1959.

"Jessie came in with this tape," began Banashak. "It was so pitiful looking. It was all spliced, and it kept breaking when we tried to play it. But me and Larry listened to it and I told Larry, 'Man he's got a good thing goin'.' "

Allen Toussaint was added to Jessie's regular group for the session, which turned into the first production hit for Toussaint and

Minit. "The record was a giant here real quick," continued Banashak, "but we had trouble at first getting it anywhere else."

According to Banashak, the local One Stop that supplied records to other cities stayed off "Ooh Poo Pah Doo" for as long as they could because of a disagreement between him and Joe Assunto. After Banashak arranged some phony long distance calls to the One Stops, the record began to break in Baltimore, and then San Francisco, before it eventually rose to #28 nationally in 1960.

How did Jessie handle this overnight national success? "I hit the road!" he exclaims incredulously. "The Apollo Theater, the Uptown, man I went all 'cross the country. I was makin' more money than I ever saw in my life."

"You couldn't tell Jessie nuthin!" contends David Lastie, still looking back frustrated. "He'd try to bullshit ya' instead of payin' you. I just got fed up with him, and the band broke up in Washington."

When Jessie got back to the studio, things started going downhill there too. Even though he briefly got back into the *Billboard* Hot 100 with "Whip It On Me," Jessie just couldn't get another hit.

"He just wouldn't learn any new material," claims Banashak. "He went back home and lit candles and had gris-gris stuff all over his house. He just couldn't get it together."

His other releases like "Highhead Blues," "Scoop Scoobie Doobie" (included on Minit's outstanding *Home Of The Blues* collection), "I Got Mine," and "Oogzey Moo" couldn't capture the magic of his first release, even if they were rollicking examples of energetic New Orleans' newer style of R&B.

Banashak vividly remembers one of Jessie's sessions at Cosimo's Studio, then on Governor Nicholls. "The whole family was in there — all his relatives — and they were in there fightin' like cats and dogs. They were callin' each other every name you could think of. Popee had Papoose down on the ground in a fist fight! Of course that session was a write off."

Banashak also recalls that Jessie didn't drive at the time. When Jessie wanted to get money from the Minit office on Baronne Street, he would visit a car dealership in the Ninth Ward and tell them he was Jessie Hill and interested in buying a car for his chauffeur to drive him in. Naturally, with the smell of a commission from selling a big limo in his nose, some unsuspecting salesman would get behind the wheel and drive Jessie anywhere he wanted. Jessie would direct them to Banashak's office, where he'd promptly jump out and say "see you later!"

MINIT RECORDS

Minit Music, Inc.

c/o Imperial Records
Hollywood, Calif.

Minit Music, Inc.
BMI - 2:35

INSTRUMENTAL
Record No.
616

HIGHHEAD BLUES
(J. Hill - D. Lastie)
JESSIE HILL
(SO:719)

Jessie bowed out with Minit in 1962, ironically with "I Can't Get Enough Of That Ooh Poo Pah Doo." "I left with Joe Jones to play a job in Houston," continues Jessie. "But I wasn't makin' money fast enough, so I got on a Greyhound bus and come out to L.A. I never was hungry or lonesome in my life 'til I got to California," says Jessie sheepishly.

As it turned out, Jessie's move to California proved to be the most successful move of his career. After a chance meeting with J.R. Fullbright, who arranged some jobs up for Jessie, and got him on his feet, Jessie ran into transplanted New Orleanians Harold Battiste and Mac Rebennack, who got him involved with writing material for other artists. So Jessie put performing on the back burner and directed his energy towards writing songs.

It didn't take long for Jessie to become one of the busiest and most successful writers on the West Coast during the Sixties. He penned songs for just about every major label, and groups like Ike and Tina Turner, Sonny and Cher, and Aretha Franklin recorded his material. Jessie even co-authored material with country star Willie Nelson.

"I must have been makin' money," boasts Jessie. "I was writin' 30-40 songs a year. I was busy all the time."

At last count Jessie has written well over 150 songs, not counting the songs he sold outright, like to his neighbor, Fats Domino. Some of his most successful tunes were co-written with Mac Rebennack. "I been knowin' Mac since way before he became Dr. John, from hangin' out at Cosimo's. I'm the one that made him start singin', he use' to sound like Alfalfa [a character on the "Lil' Rascals" series] 'til I got him straightened out."

A close listen to Dr. John reveals that many of Dr. John's vocal mannerisms mirror Jessie's to a T. Commenting on his relationship with Jessie, Dr. John reveals, "Me and Poo still got our publishing company. It's lyin' dormant, but one of these days when we get out of litigation... It's like a bond you know, we couldn't break it even if we wanted to."

Periodically Jessie also recorded during this period for one of Huey Meaux's labels as a soloist, and did an album's worth of duets with Shirley Goodman (Shirley and Jessie) during the late Sixties. His last recorded effort was the album *Naturally*, which only hinted at his earlier glories, but the album is worth finding, even if only because of the bizarre album jacket, which includes a pinwheel with a dozen or so poses of Jessie.

David Lastie, who briefly moved to the West Coast too, recalls, "Jessie was doin' beautiful out in L.A. Big car, two houses — he was hustlin'. But he started borrowin' money and runnin' up bar tabs. Jessie milked L.A."

The California heydays abruptly ended when Jessie quit the production firm he wrote for after a disagreement with Harold Battiste. But to add insult to injury, Jessie's Cadillac was stolen, containing all his material, while he was in the L.A. County Jail — for an accumulation of traffic warrants. Virtually back at square one, Jessie's "mind told me to come on home."

Since returning from Los Angeles in 1977, Jessie's pretty much been spinning his wheels. When he first returned, he worked around Jed's and was a fixture around Tipitina's when it first opened, playing with a series of pickup bands.

Even though he's appeared at each Jazz and Heritage Festival since he's returned, without a recent record, or most importantly, a dependable band, work slowed to an all but intolerable level. To make ends meet, Jessie resorted to driving his own cab — "The Poo Cab" — until it was wrecked.

In 1981, Jessie was to have taken part in Alligator Records' aborted New Orleans Rhythm and Blues Anthology. The project's failure didn't worry Jessie much though. "They weren't hardly

The Music REPORTER
R & B BiG 50

Pos. 2/22	This Week	Weeks On Chart	Position 2/22	This Week	Weeks On Chart
1	**1** BABY .... 5 Wa_s'.ngton & Benton Mercury 715		33	**26** TOO MUCH TEQUILA ...... 2 Champs—Challenge 59063	
14	**15** DON'T LET THE SUN 7 Ray Charles Atlantic 2047		☆	**40** WHO ARE YOU GONNA LOVE ...... 1 Ray C... s-ABC-Para. 10081	
17	**16** LET IT ROCK .... 6 Chuck Berry Chess 1747		47	**41** I KNOW IT'S TRUE 3 James Brown Federal 12369	
16	**17** OW ABOUT THAT 14 Dee Clark Abner 1032		38	**42** ROOSTER BLUES .. 13 Lightn'n' Slim E...lo 2169	
24	**18** HARBOR LIGHTS .. 3 Platters Mercury 71.03		34	**43** NOT ONE MINUTE MORE ...... 13 Della Reese—RCA Victor 7644	
18	**19** RUNNING BEAR .. C Johnny Presto.. Mercury 71474		49	**44** JUST A LITTLE MORE ...... 3 Robert Mosely—Coed 524	
13	**20** HARLEM NOCTURNE ...... 7 The Viscounts—Mad...on 12.		☆	**45** OOH POO PAH DOO 1 Jessie Hill Minit 607	
☆	**21** TOO POOPED TO POP ...... Chuck Berry—Chess 17-7		☆	**46** CINDY ...... 1 ..d[.]y Vann . e-X 101	
25	**22** SHAKE A HAND .. 6 LaVern Baker Atlantic 2048		35	**47** HONEY HUSH .... 9 Joe Turner Atlan..ic 1001	

✱

gonna pay me no money. It weren't hardly no good deal neither." But he adds, "I'm ready to record, but I'm gonna wait 'til the money's right. Then it's gonna be real nice."

At 9 p.m., the night of the Tipitina's gig, Jessie's busy on the club's phone frantically calling musicians so he'll have enough to make the 10:30 opening set. Amazingly he assembles five musicians on the bandstand by showtime, which was broadcast over WWOZ-FM. Some of the members of the "band" had never even met each other. But, precisely at 10:30, Jessie Hill and the House Rockers, who are playing for the door, kick off before 16 people who have paid the $3 cover charge.

While the House Rockers struggle through a couple of instrumentals, Jessie plays his tambourine and eyes the sparse crowd before deciding to head for the bar in the middle of the second tune. Between numbers the musicians desperately shout out song titles to each other, trying to find one they all know how to play.

The group struggles through a handful of Sixties soul standards — "Mustang Sally," "Something You Got," "Try Me." Even though the songs are stretched out to inappropriate lengths, Jessie puts all he can into each number, flailing his tambourine, twisting and turning like a worm on a hook. His delivery is closer to shouting than singing, but his exuberance covers up any of his vocal deficiencies. One or two couples get up to dance dishearteningly, but most just drink up, and look like they'd rather be someplace else.

The musicians look relieved when the first set grinds to a halt. Jessie returns to the bar muttering about being sabotaged by his musicians before asking "How'd we sound?" knowing what the answer is all the time.

The band plays again for another hour, trying to field requests from the dwindling audience, repeating many of the songs from the first set. Jessie does his best to keep the gig from falling completely apart by encouraging the band and the audience. But even Jessie catches himself stifling an occasional yawn. Mercifully the manager asks Jessie to wind up early because it's a slow night. Jessie concludes with his four-million seller, "Ooh Poo Pa Doo." At the end of the night, Jessie and the band had $90 to split among them.

KING FLOYD
Back In The Groove?

During the first ten years of his career, King Floyd sold more than five million records, and then simply vanished. No records, no public performances, no word, nothing. He simply disappeared, leaving many people asking, "Whatever happened to King Floyd?"

"I had the need to travel," states King simply. "I was looking for something different — I needed that inspirational thing. I wasn't satisfied with myself. I had all those hits, and then I couldn't get nothing. I was like a baseball player who gets nothing but homeruns, and then suddenly can't even get a bunt. My feeling for writing just suddenly dried up. I needed something different, and fortunately, travelling brought it back."

King Floyd III was born in New Orleans and raised in Kenner, Louisiana, in adjacent Jefferson Parish. Although he is reluctant to give out his age ("Let's just say I'm in my thirties") King developed an interest in music at a relatively early age. "I started singing when I got to be about eleven or twelve. I started hanging around the One Stop on Rampart Street. From there I got to know people like Earl King and Willie Tee. I decided I wanted to be a musician, and the best way to learn was by being with the people that were doing it for a living.

"Mr. Google Eyes got me my first job at the Sho-Bar on Bourbon Street, around 1961. I really got inspired watching people like Ernie K-Doe, Tommy Ridgley and Irma Thomas at the Holland Gym, down where Causeway is now [Jefferson Parish]. My uncle used to book the bands so I'd get in free. I also dug Otis Redding, Sam Cooke, Joe Tex and Jackie Wilson. I was caught between the local people and the national thing."

King's influences were markedly different from many of his contemporaries however. "I left New Orleans and went into the military when I was real young. I got out in 1963 and started working for Shaw Artists, who did a lot of booking around New York. I began to work around Manhattan, and getting some exposure. I started hanging out with J.J. Jackson and Don Covay, who gave me some hints on writing. But the one thing that really inspired me to write was Barbara Lynn's "I Know." I figured it was easy to write a song like that. I stayed in New York about a year, and then people started telling me that things were happening in California, so I moved to Los Angeles."

Once in Los Angeles, King bumped into a few people he had known back in New Orleans who were willing to help him: "I met Harold Battiste out in L.A.—I had known him through Barbara George in New Orleans, I used to go over to his house because he had a piano. There was this kind of atmosphere around Harold that inspired me to write. By hanging out with Harold I got to meet Jimi Hendrix and Sonny and Cher. I was learning something from everybody.

"I met Buddy Keleen, a deejay who introduced me to Jimmy Holiday. They helped me produce my first record on Original Sound, 'Walkin' and Thinkin' and 'Why Did She Leave Me?' It did very well on the West Coast. Record hops were real popular then, and I worked a lot of those off the record.

"I ran into Mac Rebennack too. Funny I never met Mac in New Orleans, but we started to write some stuff together. We wrote some of the songs for my first album."

King's premier album was arranged by Harold Battiste; *King Floyd — A Man In Love* was released on Pulsar, a subsidiary of Mercury Records in 1967 (later reissued on V.I.P. as *Heart of the Matter*). It only hinted at King's later style as the Pulsar album was closer to pop than soul. King also supplemented his recording and occasional live appearances by writing for other artists. "I wrote for a lot of Harold's artists. I wrote something for Shine [Alvin Robinson] with Mac, 'She's About To Drive Me Mad.' I even wrote some songs that Jayne Mansfield recorded. I spent five years in L.A., but I hadn't reached the height I wanted. It just didn't happen on a big enough scale for me. I wanted to be known nationally, so I moved back to New Orleans in September 1969."

Now with a wife and a young daughter to consider, King decided it would be best to abandon music for the time being, and he got a job with the post office. "I was in town about a month," recalls King, "and I ran into Wardell Quezergue. He said he couldn't do anything with me at the time, but he'd ask around. Then I talked to Elijah Walker [local promoter], and he was gonna record C.P. Love, and Tommy and Sammy Ridgley. C.P. suggested to Walker that he record me in his place. That impressed Walker, so he asked Wardell if I had any material, and Wardell said, 'Yeah, he got some good tunes.' So one Sunday we all drove up to Malaco Studio

King Floyd, late 1960's

in Jackson. Walker, Wardell, Jean Knight, Tommy Ridgley, Bonnie and Sheila and myself. I'll never forget, that was May 17, 1970."

As it turned out, King almost missed the session entirely. "My car broke down on the way, and I had to be back at work that afternoon. I almost turned back. When we got there, everyone was waiting for me, and there was only a few minutes of studio time left.

"We cut two tunes. The first one was 'What Our Love Needs.' That took three takes, because I was saying 'hating' instead of 'hitting.' Then we did 'Groove Me.' It only took one take, boom-boom-bomp, and we did it on down. I was out of there in thirty minutes. I guess it was destiny."

Everyone involved chose "What Our Love Needs," as the A-side. "Groove Me" had been written by King, nearly five years before in California, and was only recorded as a B side. But things weren't to turn out that way. "I was real satisfied with the way the session went. I really liked the way Wardell arranged the funk things.

"When we got back to New Orleans we got together at Walker's office over in the Ninth Ward, to decide what we were gonna do with the record. Malaco was to make a lease agreement with Atlantic, but Jerry Wexler wouldn't call us back. We tried to get Stax interested, but couldn't. Stax thought I sounded like Otis Redding on

'What Our Love Needs,' but they didn't like 'Groove Me' at all. I couldn't figure out their reasoning, 'cause I was hung up on 'What Our Love Needs.'

"We couldn't get anybody to lease it, so Malaco decided they were gonna put it out themselves [on their Chimneyville label]. I got the record on August 2, and brought it to Hank Sample — he was a singing deejay — on WBLK. He started playing 'What Our Love Needs' for about a month or so. Then George Vinnett, who was with WYLD, bumped into me when I was on my way to the Post Office. He told me, 'King, I got great news, I just got your record in the mail, and I'm gonna take it to my niece's party tonight and give it a listen.' So he called me back around six the next morning and said, 'You got a hit record baby! I'm gonna play it on the air right now.' So I turned on the radio and he played 'Groove Me.' I called him right back and said, 'No George, you're playing the wrong side!'

"He told me, 'No way man. I took it to my niece's house, and that's the only record they played the whole night.' So everybody in New Orleans started playing 'Groove Me' on the radio. All the local jocks were on it, we had a double-sided hit. But it was 'Groove Me' that really took off. George Vinnett called Atlantic Records and told them what was happening here. Atlantic finally called Malaco back, and they came down to sign the papers."

"Groove Me" proved to be a milestone for both King Floyd and Malaco. The record was the first hit to come out of the Jackson, Mississippi studio. To get the rights to "Groove Me," Atlantic signed a long-term contract that put Malaco on its feet. Atlantic agreed to distribute all the products on Malaco's Chimneyville label, and to use the Malaco facility for recording.

The benefits for King were obvious. "Groove Me" was a breath of fresh air in the world of soul music, and a much needed uplift in the New Orleans' musical climate. Incorporating a funky backbeat that preceded reggae, King's style nested somewhere between James Brown's best and Otis Redding.

"After Atlantic picked it up," continues King. "WTIX picked up on it, and the other white stations too. Then I heard it on WLAC in Nashville, and some friends of mine came back from Chicago and said they heard it up there. That's when I realized I had a big record. George was getting all the Atlantic reports and he said, 'King, you got a monster on your hands.'"

"Groove Me" wouldn't stop until it topped the national Soul charts. On the Hot 100 it nearly did as well, before it stopped at number six, during its 20-week stay. Oddly enough the record stood on its own merits, since King hadn't sung in public since returning from California.

"I didn't do my first gig until late September of 1970, after the record was already taking off. I worked the I.L.A. Hall and made $150," laughs King. "Percy Stovall started booking me into all the small towns around New Orleans. It got real exciting. I quit my job at the post office and started working ten nights in a row before I'd get one off."

" 'Groove Me' was certified gold Christmas Day of 1970. After that I met Alex Hodges of Paramount Agency, and he asked me how much I was making. I said '$500 a night.' He told me, 'I can get you $1,200.' Twelve-hundred a night! I though, 'Hey I better go with him.'

"I started going all over the country then. Miami, New York, Chicago, Los Angeles — I just couldn't believe it. I made $104,000 in personal appearances in 1971."

Malaco was able to pry King away from his rugged personal appearance itinerary, to get him back in the studio for a follow-up single and album. "We came back with 'Baby Let Me Kiss You.' It started doing real well, but it got pulled off one of the big stations in New York, WABC, because they thought it was too suggestive. Sales just backed up after it got pulled." Still, "Baby Let Me Kiss You" managed to climb to a respectable #9 on the R&B charts, and his third Chimneyville release, "Got To Have Your Love," reached #35.

"It seemed like the sound kind of changed after that. Wardell and I started hearin' different things. I guess our egos started to come out. Everybody started clashing in the studio, and things don't work out when that happens."

King hit a temporary dry spell sales-wise. Malaco issued a string of fine singles and the excellent *Think About It* album in 1973, but they didn't catch on like the initial releases. Still King stayed busy working around the country, working off his earlier hits.

In 1974, Atlantic decided to pull a cut from King's first album and releases it as a single, which resulted in King's next big national hit. "We had cut 'Woman Don't Go Astray' for the album," explains King. "We'd been cutting new things, but we couldn't seem to come up with anything. My uncle and George [Vinnett] were after me to get Atlantic to release 'Woman Don't Go Astray.' Finally Atlantic did release it, and it did 600,000."

After "Woman Don't Go Astray" Malaco let their agreement

lapse with Atlantic. Instead they signed a leasing/production agreement with T.K. Productions, Henry Stone's Miami-based record company, in 1974. They also began producing King themselves, with mixed success. They coupled King with Dorothy Moore for one release, and also a fine *Well Done* album. King's sales remained respectable, but he couldn't break out with another big record.

In 1974, King travelled to Europe and the Caribbean. Europe lauded him as "the Soulful Highness." "I loved Europe," says King. "It was a real experience. I had a band from London that was fantastic. We worked England, Sweden, Germany and France. I wanted to bring 'em back to America. Talk about the Average White Band — these guys had 'em all beat."

His tour of the Caribbean also opened his eyes and ears to the music of the islands. "When we got there, they had a band that knew my material note for note; we didn't even have to rehearse. Everyone was musical there. If you went to the market, they had cats beatin' on steel drums. If you went to a hotel, they had bands in the lobby, if you went in the bar, they had another band in there.

"I'd had some hits in Trinidad, so some musicians came out to meet me. I got introduced to Bob Marley and Peter Tosh. The drum sound that they were using really intrigued me. When we got back to the studio, I wanted to incorporate the reggae thing into my stuff."

However both Malaco and King were increasingly frustrated by their continued lack of national success. Partly because of that, the two parted company in 1975. "It wasn't a matter of me not getting my royalties," reflects King on the split. "I got em. Sometimes late, but I got 'em. I had trouble communicating with the engineers. Tommy [Tommy Couch, Malaco producer] just wanted me to be an artist and a songwriter. But I wanted to engineer stuff too, because I thought it was gonna help. Tommy felt it would take away from me being a performer. I tried to tell 'em it wouldn't, but we couldn't come to any kind of agreement, so I just left."

Despite his success with Malaco, King also aired other frustrations between him and the company. "I felt like Malaco was only exposing me to the black public. I felt like I could have been doing rock concerts like Otis Redding had been doing, but they only concentrated on selling my records to a small audience. I thought I had a broader appeal, and 'Groove Me' proved that."

Malaco's version of their parting differs somewhat from King's. According to one source at Malaco, "King Floyd went out in left field: One day he came in with a feather and said he was an Indian."

King moved over to Mercury, but only one single, the fine "Can You Dig It?" appeared on the Dial subsidiary. Malaco unearthed some old sessions, and he even had a small hit with "Body English," in 1977. But that's been it as far as records are concerned for King Floyd up to the present.

"When the disco thing came in, I was still writing this funk stuff. That just about terminated my writing."

Without a recording contract that would insure promotion and publicity, work began to slow for King, and the more prestigious dates were becoming fewer, and far between. "I blew a lot of gigs too," admits King. "I wasn't taking care of business by rehearsing and I looked bad on some jobs. That kind of stuff gets around. I was supposed to go back to Europe but I messed that up. I was gonna get $50,000 for a month, but I lost my damn briefcase on the way back to America, and it had all my contacts in it. It seemed like everything started falling apart after that."

After a five-year ride at the top, it was a hard blow for King's ego to go back to scuffling for small local gigs. But to his own detriment King squandered virtually all of his money. According to his uncle, Cleon Floyd, King literally wasted "hundreds of thousands of dollars. King bought a brand new house out in New Orleans East and filled it full of brand new furniture that he bought on Royal Street. He and his wife [Jean Knight's daughter] lived there for two months and just left. They just left the house and the bank repossessed everything in it. He would buy brand new cars and just leave them on the side of the road if they had a flat tire.

"And clothes, King bought more clothes than you could wear in a year. He would send 'em to the cleaners and never pick 'em up. There's probably a hundred dry cleaners in the country with some of his clothes in them."

The last straw came in 1978, when the credit companies came after him and repossessed his Cadillac. King realized it was time to "try and get my head back together." So he headed back to Los Angeles to rebuild his faltering career.

The public hadn't completely forgotten about King Floyd. In early 1979, Malaco released a disco version of "Groove Me" by Fern Kinney, which did well on the black charts. But the best was saved until later in the year, when the Blues Brothers included a reggae version of "Groove Me" on their first album, which eventually went platinum. "I guess they drew on my reggae influence," muses King. "I enjoyed their version of it. Someone told me that Mick Jagger gave them the idea to do it."

King's time in L.A. was spent doing the odd gig and trying to get his songwriting skill back together. After he straightened out some of his personal problems, he returned to Kenner in the summer of 1981, to try and get his career regenerated.

It wasn't easy getting back on his feet. Local gigs in New Orleans were scarce and paid poorly. Through an old friend, Roger Redding, Otis Redding's brother, King got a few better paying gigs out of town in Miami and Houston. During the summer of 1982, King toured South Africa for a full month with an African band.

While back home, he got back into the groove of writing and by the end of 1982 he had enough new material of his own for a new album. But he grew frustrated about the lack of recording opportunities, returned to Los Angeles, and is still trying to land a record deal to get the real boost his sagging career needs.

"I'm the one who fumbled," he says. "That's why I'm back where I am. It seems like everything was going good for me. The door was open but I let it get slammed in my face. But I'm confident that I can do it again. I feel if anyone from New Orleans can do it, it's me. I'm young, I've got the knowledge now, the experience and the international appeal to do it. I have no doubt that it can be done again."

ERNIE K-DOE
The In-Kredible K-Doe

Few would argue that Ernie K-Doe is still the most colorful character still regularly performing rhythm and blues in New Orleans. Even though it has been nearly two decades since K-Doe has had anything that even mildly resembles a hit record, it would be hard to tell from listening to his own personal hype or from watching the hysteria of his on-stage performances. Even though he's now in his late 40s, it's not unknown for him to jump into an audience or to destroy a brand new suit with his frantic dance routines and perilous splits. "I don't like to brag," he says in obvious jest, "but I still believe I can out-perform any man in show business. Ernie K-Doe can stop any show at the drop of a hat."

The first the world ever heard of Ernie K-Doe was in 1961, when his record "Mother-In-Law" was the number one record in the country. But of course this certainly wasn't the beginning, nor the end of the "in-kredible" Ernie K-Doe story.

Born Ernest Kador, February 22, 1936, at New Orleans' Charity Hospital, he was the ninth of eleven children fathered by Ernest Kador Sr., a Baptist preacher. K-Doe was raised by his mother's sister, at 2419 South Derbigny Street in Uptown New Orleans. As a child, K-Doe befriended other up-and-coming singers such as Danny White, and Art and Aaron Neville, who lived in the nearby Calliope Projects. As a youth, Ernie was taken to the New Home Baptist Church by his aunt, and to his father's church in the tiny West Baton Rouge Parish town of Erwinville, where he got his first taste of gospel singing. K-Doe showed promise while still an adolescent, and he was invited to join the Golden Chain Jubilee Singers and the Zion Travellers—both gospel quartets that enjoyed local popularity.

One of K-Doe's most vivid childhood memories is going to gospel programs in the late Forties with his aunt. "There used to be a church where the St. Thomas Projects are now, called the Two Winged Temple. All of the gospel groups played the Two Winged Temple when they came to New Orleans. The Rocks of Harmony, The Highway QCs, Sister Rosetta Tharpe, Mahalia Jackson, The Soul Stirrers, the Five Blind Boys—I saw them all.

"My favorite were the Five Blind Boys (of Mississippi) because of their lead singer, Brother Archie Brown Lee. I always listened to how he sang, how he phrased words on his records so clearly. Some records you got to put your ear down to so you can hear what they're singing. But not Archie Brown Lee, that man *never* missed. Some people like to say that Mahalia Jackson was good, but to me she's not the best. Archie Brown Lee was the best.

"I wished people today could have seen him. He wasn't but 5'4" and about 145 lbs. But when he sang his voice must have weighed about 8 million pounds! I don't care what kind of song that man was singing, you had to move, you just couldn't keep still." It is still the image of Archie Brown Lee that K-Doe emulates to this day.

At the age of 15, K-Doe won a talent contest sponsored by radio station WMRY for his dancing and his singing. This inspired him to continue his singing while attending Booker T. Washington High School, where he was an all-around athlete, lettering in four sports. He still sang in church on Sundays, but when singing with kids in the neighborhood and with fellow students, K-Doe began getting a taste for blues.

Soon after he turned 17, he moved to Chicago where he joined his mother, who had moved there soon after WW-II to look for work. Even though he was under-age, K-Doe's mother often took him around to clubs that sponsored amateur shows and where other vocal groups often performed, like the Crown Propeller and the Club Bagdad. "My mama had to sign a paper for me to get into the clubs to sing," he explains. "I had to sit in the back room drinking soda pop. The only time I could come out was when they called me out to sing on the stage."

While in the Windy City, the teenager was introduced to groups like the Four Blazers, the Moonglows and the Flamingos, the latter group of which K-Doe claims to have performed and recorded. It was the Four Blazers, though, who introduced the teenager to Dave Clark, who worked as a producer and promotion man for United Records. Clark was impressed enough to do a whole blues session on K-Doe, on November 30, 1953, but to date the four-song session has remained unissued.

K-Doe returned to New Orleans in 1954, forming his own vocal group, The Blue Diamonds. The group became a regular attraction at the Tiajuana Club on S. Saratoga Street, where K-Doe also acted as unofficial master of ceremonies. "The Tiajuana really inspired youngsters like me," recalls K-Doe. "Johnny Ace used to sing

Ernie K-Doe, 1962

there, Chuck Willis, Bobby Marchan, Richard Penniman, Billy Brooks, Ollie Nightengale—a lot of singers and dancers. It was fun singing and watching people perform there too. It was like a school, I wanted to be a real good singer, so I watched the best singers when they came to the Tiajuana.''

When Lee Magid of Savoy Records came down from Newark, New Jersey to audition talent in June of 1954, K-Doe and the Blue Diamonds were one of the first in line at Cosimo's Studio. Magid liked the group well enough to cut a split session on the Blue Diamonds, with K-Doe singing the frantic lead vocal. Two sides were released, "Honey Baby" and "No Money," using Huey Smith, Earl Palmer, Lee Allen and Charles Williams as session men. The record failed to sell because of Savoy's lack of active promotion. As a result, neither the Blue Diamond nor any of the other New Orleans artists were invited back to record for Savoy.

Despite his initial disappointment, the mid-Fifties was an exiting period for a young New Orleans R&B singer, especially for one as electrifying as K-Doe (he was still spelling his last name Kador then). Borrowing much of his stage presence from his idol Archie Brown Lee, K-Doe's reputation spread, and he soon began to perform along with the Blue Diamonds at the Dew Drop, the

Sho Bar on Bourbon Street, and Jessie's Club in Marrero, Louisiana, along with the Tiajuana.

In 1955, Specialty Records got wind of K-Doe, who was now working solo, and arranged to record both him and a singer/pianist from Macon, Georgia, "Little" Richard Penniman. "Do Baby Do" and "Eternity" did little for K-Doe, but Little Richard's "Tutti Frutti," recorded just hours before K-Doe's two sides, went on to define rock and roll music.

K-Doe continued to build his local following with his wild on-stage antics and colorful costumes that often included a dazzling jeweled turban, a la Chuck Willis. In 1958, K-Doe got back into the studio, this time recording for the Ember label from New York. With Robert Parker's band providing the accompaniment, K-Doe waxed the trendy "Tuff Enough" which did well locally but not good enough to continue Ember's interest, although they would re-release it four years later once K-Doe had hit the bright lights.

By the turn of the decade, K-Doe was perhaps the hottest attraction in all of New Orleans. All he needed was a hot record to blast him off, and that was on the immediate horizon once he signed on with the fledging Minit label in 1960.

At the time K-Doe was being managed by WYLD disc jockey, Larry McKinley, who was Joe Banashak's partner at Minit Records. Allen Toussaint had been contracted by Minit, and arranged K-Doe's first release, "Make You Love Me" b/w "Where There's A Will, There's A Way." On the latter, K-Doe mimics his idol, Archie Brown Lee, to a tee, quite reminiscent of Ray Charles' then-popular gospel-blues style. Both sides did well enough in New Orleans to continue Minit's interest.

His second Minit release "Hello My Lover" b/w "T'ain't It the Truth," aided by Imperial Record's distribution network, did well enough to rack up 80,000, even though it didn't crack the national R&B charts. Both sides were superb Allen Toussaint productions, with the female chorus acting as a "choir," answering each of K-Doe's quivering pleas.

"In those days, Minit didn't have much money," says K-Doe. "So all the artists helped each other out on records. Allen Toussaint used to rehearse us in the front room of his parents' house in Gert Town. Benny Spellman, Irma Thomas, Willie Harper, Calvin Lee—they all sang on my records, and I helped out on all of theirs. When we got ready to record, we'd all go down to Cosimo's Studio in the French Quarter at night and cut. Either me or Allen wrote those early songs. Allen produced them."

The source of the phonetic spelling of K-Doe's surname, which began appearing on his Minit singles, has often come under speculation. But as K-Doe points out, it was Joe Banashak's idea to spell it K - D-O-E, instead of K-A-D-O-R. "Everybody called me 'Kay-doe,' but Joe said, 'Ernie, we got to get the people that buy records to say Kay-doe. Kador is just too hard to say. We need something catchy.' So he decided to spell it K, with a dash, D, O, E. After we started putting it that way on my records, I legally had my name changed to K-Doe, and it's copyrighted (sic) too."

K-Doe's third Minit single, released in March of 1961, proved to be a record that K-Doe will forever be associated with, "Mother-In-Law." Written by Toussaint, the record rose to #1 on the R&B and pop charts just a month after it was issued. "Mother-In-Law" was a natural hit, the title alone evoked interest. Instantly catchy, the record features K-Doe's persuasive vocal weaving its way between Benny Spellman's deep bass chorus, while still leaving just enough room for Toussaint's dancing piano rhythms.

According to K-Doe, "Mother-In-Law" was recorded as a lark. "Allen had wrote it and thrown it away," claims K-Doe. "He had just balled it up and threw it in the trash. I saw it in the garbage can and pulled it out. I looked at the words and said, 'Hey man this is good, I want to do this.' "

But, according to Toussaint, often a more reliable source, K-Doe's claim is slightly "exaggerated." Toussaint recalls, "I really had trouble writing songs for Ernie. He was into that spiritual church thing. He liked to holler and preach like the Five Blind Boys thing. I couldn't write a song like that.

"I was inspired by Danny White to write 'Mother-In-Law.' Danny didn't make a lot of records, but he was very popular in the city. We weren't recording Danny White at Minit, so when it came time to do a session on Ernie I thought, 'Well maybe we can get away with recording these songs I wrote for Danny White.' So K-Doe ended up recording 'Mother-In-Law.' "

The rest is pretty much history. Even though Dick Clark refused to play the record, citing it as offensive, it quickly won a gold record, and it became the first New Orleans record to peak at #1 in Billboard's Hot 100. Naturally K-Doe took off on a whirlwind national tour, headlining with the likes of Sam Cooke, Jerry Butler, James Brown, Maxime Brown and Little Willie John. K-Doe is still fond of telling the story about travelling the country and to Havana, during the height of the Cuban missle crisis, where he performed in an outdoor stadium before, by K-Doe's estimate,

100,000.

"They wanted Ernie K-Doe all over the country," he says, still relishing the days of overnight stardom. "The Apollo, the Peacock, the Regal—everybody wanted to hear me sing 'Mother-In-Law.' "

"Te-Ta-Te-Ta-Ta," penned by K-Doe himself, was a great followup, and it made it to #53 in the Hot 100 during the summer of 1961, just as "Mother-In-Law" was cooling off. Banashak was quick to release an Ernie K-Doe album (Minit 0002, now available as Bandy 70004) which collected his earliest singles and a number of songs previously unreleased. K-Doe himself proves to be no slouch of a tunesmith, penning the riotious dance number "Rub-Dub-Dub" (along with Robert Parker) and the stunning gospel-based "Waiting At The Station." In the latter, like a great quartet singer, K-Doe builds the song's emotion to a fervent crescendo. At the song's peak, K-Doe sings "I think I heard someone call my name." Just as his voice trails off, a member of the choir-like female backup singers shouts "K-Doe"—one of the high points of K-Doe's recorded work.

Minit and K-Doe continued their hold on the charts as both sides of K-Doe's next single "I Cried My Last Tear" b/w "A Certain Girl" hovered around the #70 spot in Billboard's Hot 100 during the month of November.

When 1962 arrived, Minit released K-Doe's "Popeye Joe" to satisfy the demand for the Popeye Dance craze, which outstripped the Twist in terms of local popularity. Even though there is evidence to the contrary, K-Doe claims to have debuted the dance at a New Orleans record hop. Nonetheless, K-Doe's colorful version of the story is worth relating.

"I was feeding my son, Little Ernie K-Doe, in the kitchen one morning," explains K-Doe. "I was playing an old Lowell Fulson record, 'The Old Time Shuffle,' and I was shuffling across the floor. My son said, 'Daddy what are you doing? You look like that old Popeye.' So I said, 'Maybe so.' So that's how I started the Popeye dance."

K-Doe's dance and exhausing stage routines made him a top attraction from coast to coast. One of his all time favorite stories concerns a 1962 show at Municipal Auditorium in New Orleans before a packed house. James Brown was then the hottest R&B attraction in the country, but New Orleans was K-Doe's home and he wasn't about to be outdone, even by "the hardest-working man in show business."

Benny Spellman, the "Mother-In-Law" Voice

"It was the biggest battle of my life," points out K-Doe. "Larry McKinley was the announcer, and he called me out first. You see it was a dressing thing. New Orleans against Macon, Georgia, and I sure wasn't gonna let New Orleans down. I had a royal blue smoking jacket on, but under that, nobody knew. Then James Brown came out in a brown suit, white shirt, brown polka dot tie. But while Larry was talking, everybody went to screaming! You see, when I pulled off that smoking jacket, guess what? Everything else I had on was ice blue! And on 'Certain Girl' I changed suits nine times! I had a clothes rack and a valet backstage. Everytime I'd get to a certain part in the song, I'd just run straight around to the side, change my suit and come back out the other side!

"Now those tricks I do with the mike stand, I learned how to do them by practicing with a broom and a #9 thread. See, to get real good at working that mike stand, it's gotta be part of you. It was rhythm. I can turn around and do my splits and I know that the microphone will come right back up to me."

After "Popeye Joe," K-Doe never again was able to break into the Hot 100. Even though he continued having local hits for the next 2 years with the likes of "Hey, Hey, Hey," "Beating Like A Tom Tom," "Get Out Of My House" (the inevitable answer to

"Mother-In-Law") "Easier Said Than Done" and "Pennies Worth of Happiness," the growing rift between Imperial's Lew Chudd and Joe Banashak stalled promotion on all of K-Doe's Minit releases.

When Chudd sold Imperial to Liberty Records in 1963, K-Doe was effectively without a recording contract. Banashak, who later was concentrating his efforts on making Instant a growing record concern, salvaged four unreleased tracks produced by Toussaint (who was now in the army) and released two excellent singles. Both "Sufferin' So" and "Talkin' Out of My Head" did well in the local market, but due to Instant's fragmented distribution, couldn't break elsewhere.

Through Larry McKinley, who still acted as K-Doe's manager, he wound up on the powerful Duke label. "Don D. Robey was the owner of Duke Records," says K-Doe. "He had a big club over there in Houston, Texas, where I often appeared at the Bronze Peacock. He had a good label. They had Bobby Bland, O.V. Wright, Al 'TNT' Braggs, Little Jr. Parker and Buddy Ace."

Duke was able to catapult K-Doe back into the national R&B charts in 1967 with the gospel-tinged "Later For Tomorrow," which charted at #37, and the popish "Until the Real Thing Comes Along," which made it to #48.

For the most part however, K-Doe's Duke records lacked the spark of his Toussaint-produced New Orleans efforts. The Duke releases were marred by over production and overly complicated arrangements. "I spent 3 years at Duke," says K-Doe. "Most of my sessions were produced by Robey and arranged by Willie Mitchell. We had a lot of good records I thought; some things sold, some didn't." But, obviously, when they didn't, Robey let K-Doe's contract expire.

By 1970, K-Doe was back in Cosimo's Jazz City Studio, where he was reunited with Allen Toussaint for an album which was released on the Janus label. But the anticipated spark was mysteriously missing. Mike Leadbitter reviewed the disc in *Blues Unlimited* and said, "The distinctive sound of the city (New Orleans) isn't here; simplicity gives way to big arrangements. The whole thing is a lifeless bore." He was sadly correct.

Once K-Doe's record sales began to plummet, so did the demand for live performances. K-Doe was forced to stay closer to home, working the small soul clubs and nightspots in New Orleans. The Seventies remained an increasingly frustrating period for K-Doe, who wasn't, and still isn't, used to taking a back seat to anyone. He

Janus LP Jacket, 1970

had signed a contract with Marshall Sehorn, who chose to record K-Doe only sporadically.

K-Doe in turn blames Allen Toussaint and Marshall Sehorn for his fall from the public eye. "How can you be a popular performer when a record company won't put records out on you? Three records in nine years, that killed me. I found out they were using me as a tax write-off on my last record. Ernie K-Doe ain't no loser! I demanded my release when I found that out."

In 1982, K-Doe began hosting an R&B show on WWOZ, a popular community-sponsored New Orleans' FM station (he had previously worked at a Thibodaux station as an announcer for a short time in the Sixties). His on-air antics made it perhaps the most popular "underground" program of its type in the city. By backing up records, composing outlandish monologs and generally causing a ruckus deejays haven't caused in some time, K-Doe has only underlined his off-the-wall reputation.

Onstage K-Doe still cuts a dynamic stage profile, even as he nears fifty. Both on stage and off, K-Doe is his own best PR person. He still sings and dances with an array of pickup bands in small black clubs around New Orleans, and on "oldies but goodies" shows in St. Bernard and Jefferson Parish. Sadly, the bands are often hopeless, and often the audience consists of less than a dozen people. But K-Doe holds nothing back, singing, screaming, and shouting, surely with the picture of his idol Archie Brown Lee still etched in his mind. When he does get the audience he deserves, most notably at the New Orleans Jazz Fest, he only doubles his usual intensity, amazing everyone but himself.

After being on a 15-year skid, sometimes without another job lined up and his voice beginning to fray around the edges, one obviously asks what possesses a man to chase a memory that is all but unattainable. "Oh Ernie K-Doe slipped up," he admits. "But I have to believe that I'm going back to the top. The only thing I know is singing and dancing. Ernie K-Doe is going back to the top. That's all there is to it."

LEE DORSEY
Still Working In A Coal Mine

Lee Dorsey is a busy man to say the least. At one time or another he has been: 1. A former undefeated lightweight boxing contender; 2. One of the best body and fender repairmen in New Orleans. 3. One of New Orleans' most energetic and successful rhythm and blues entertainers. 4. The father of eleven children.

Yes, it's true, Lee Dorsey is a man of many talents. He developed into a contending lightweight boxing protegé, who retired undefeated. As a body and fender man, his work is unsurpassed, and he is a much-sought-after tradesman. And don't think raising that many kids is a cinch either.

But of course the world knows Lee Dorsey from his energetic performances that once earned him the tag "Mr. TNT," and his string of infectious hit records. Among New Orleans artists, only his childhood pal Fats Domino surpassed him in terms of national hit records.

Lee's major assets are hard work and talent. No one puts more of himself into his work. His love for making people feel good drives him to work long and hard. He's been known to do a full day in his body shop, work an early show at a concert, and finish up with a late night set at a club. Rather than tiring him, performing seems to revitalize the diminutive singer.

Lee Dorsey is a hard man to track down, but when he does sit down to talk about himself, he's just as open, vibrant and likeable as his music.

Born Irving Lee Dorsey, December 4, 1926, it has been mistakenly written that he was born in Portland, Oregon. "I never did bother to clear that up," shrugs the compact singer, relaxing at Sea-Saint Studio. "I was raised up right here in the Ninth Ward."

Music seemed to be very much a part of his growing up, and Lee doesn't recall when his mother *wasn't* singing. As an adolescent, one of his best friends turned out to be pretty musical too. "I was brought up with Fats. I was a couple of years older than Fats, but he was one of my closest friends. We used to tease him 'cause he couldn't play after school. His mom made him come home and practice on that raggedy piano. We just always called him Fats 'cause he was just a little ole fat kid. Everybody had a nickname then, 'Tee Neg,' 'Bum Bum,' fact they called me 'Bubba.' "

When Lee was 10, his parents and his two brothers moved to Portland, Oregon, where his father had gone to find work. Lee took the move in stride, growing up like any other youth. During this period he developed a passing interest in "hillbilly" music, and recalls tuning into the Grand Ole Opry, and even learned to yodel like Jimmie Rodgers.

Before Lee could decide what to do after high school, World War II started, and Uncle Sam wanted Lee in the Navy. Lee soon found himself in the heat of the battle for the South Pacific, serving as a gunner on a destroyer. Lee's tour ended when a Zero sprayed the deck and hit him in the leg as he tried to dive through a port hole.

After the war, Lee knocked around Portland until he got interested in prize fighting. "I knew some guys who went to the gym to box," says Dorsey throwing a phantom punch, "so I just started goin' with 'em. Once I saw I could whip some of 'em, I started gettin' fights too."

Dorsey adopted the colorful moniker, "Kid Chocolate," and became a respected fighter around the Pacific Northwest during the late Forties. "I liked boxing. I never once got whupped. I was fightin' feather-weight and lightweight, 128 - 131 pounds. I was a dirty fighter," chuckles Dorsey, behind his ever-present dark glasses. "I been knocked out on my feet, and guys hit me again and brought me back." Lee recalls that his biggest fight was on an Ezzard Charles card once.

In 1955, "Kid Chocolate" threw his last punch and became Lee Dorsey once again. "I just got cocky and quit," laments Dorsey. "I packed my things up in the car and drove straight to New Orleans. My manager tried to get me to come back, but I just told him to sue me, and that was that."

Once back in his hometown, Lee had to find a job, so he decided to study body and fender repair under the G.I. Bill. "I always liked to tinker with things and work on cars, so I thought I'd give it a try."

At the time Lee had no ambition of being a singer, but on his off hours he frequented the Dew Drop, and hung out on Rampart Street because "that's where the action was."

Lee began working for a local deejay, Ernie the Whip, who owned a body shop as a sideline. By 1957, Lee was married, with young ones already on the way. His only ambition was to save enough money to open up his own repair shop. But fate was to have other plans—at least for the time being.

"I use' to sing to make my work go easier. I wasn't thinkin' of makin' no records. But one day this guy came in to get his car fixed—Reynauld Richard (an independent record producer). I was up under a car hammerin' an' singin' away, and he said, 'Hey, you wanna make a record?' "

"I said, 'Sure.' I didn't think he was serious. But he was. That evening he left $50 and told me to come down to Cosimo's studio on Governor Nicholls.

"I went down that evenin' after I cleaned up from work. I didn't have any songs, but Richard asked me if I could write a poem. 'Sure,' I said, 'I can come up with that.' So I wrote 'Rock, Pretty Baby,' and 'Lonely Evening,' and as it turned out they made a little bit of noise."

The record appeared on Rex 1005, Cosimo Matassa's label, distributed by Ace. Up-to-date for 1957, the single did well enough for Richard to invite Lee back to Cosimo's for another session, just a month later.

"That's when I cut 'Lottie-Mo,' " laughs Dorsey. "That's the one that got me on American Bandstand." Issued originally on Joe Banashak and Irving Smith's Valiant label (later to become Instant), the record did so well on the local charts that ABC-Paramount picked it up for national distribution. The bubbly single didn't manage to crack the Hot 100, but ABC gave it enough of a push to get Dorsey's name around the country.

Besides being Dorsey's first hit, "Lottie-Mo" also initiated his association with Allen Toussaint—who produced the single—that lasts to this day. It also meant the lightweight body-and-fender whiz was going to have to appear on stage. Poor Lee had yet to sing in front of a live audience!

"I was always pretty shy about performing," admits Dorsey. "If I was sittin' in a club havin' a drink and they introduced me, I'd head for the door. Before they got my name out, I'd be out in the street. It took me a while before I got over that."

According to Allen Toussaint, it didn't take Dorsey too long to get accustomed to the role of being a performer, and the duo began sitting in at the Dew Drop regularly. After his American Bandstand appearance, Dorsey came in off the road. He began working with Lloyd Lambert's orchestra as part of a package show handled by Hosea Hill of Thibodeaux, opening for Guitar Slim.

As it turned out, the only real money Lee saw from his first two records was through personal appearances, as he had innocently signed his publishing royalties over to Richard.

"He just paid me $50 a wop," exclaims Dorsey, "I didn't know any better! After I told Allen about it he told me, 'Lee, don't you make no more records for that man for $50.' " So Lee let his contract with Richard expire. Besides, he still felt more comfortable with a hammer in his hand than a microphone. So after his brief brush with stardom, Lee went back to banging out fenders during the week picking up the odd weekend gig . . . at least for awhile.

Then in 1961, Marshall Sehorn, who was then working for Fire/Fury Records, happened to hear "Lottie-Mo" while in New Orleans on a promotion trip. At first, Sehorn thought Lee Dorsey was an alias for Ray Charles, but he found out Dorsey was employed by an auto wrecker. Sehorn took note of the fact and told his boss Bobby Robinson about him when he returned to New York.

Not long after, Robinson stopped off in New Orleans on his way back from a record convention in Miami and sought out Dorsey. The two came to terms, and Robinson was anxious to record Dorsey right away. But Lee didn't have any original material. Then, seemingly like magic, Dorsey and Robinson got the idea for Lee's biggest hit while they sat on Dorsey's porch. Lee picks up the story:

"I was livin' right next to a grocery store, and the kids use' to play the dozens in front. They were singin, 'Sittin' on the slop-jar, waitin' for my bowels to move,' and it was catchy the way they were singin' it. So that night I just jotted it down. 'Sittin' in La-La, waitin' for my Ya-Ya . . . ' " Robinson liked it too and arranged for Dorsey and Allen Toussaint to go over the tune the next day. But since Toussaint was under contract to Minit, he couldn't do the session, so he taught the piano arrangement to Marcel Richardson.

The infectious shave-and-a-haircut beat of "Ya-Ya" soon tore the charts open. It reached number one on the R&B charts and #7 on the Hot 100 in late 1961. It also earned Lee his first gold record.

So Lee had to pack his bags again and put his fender hammers in storage. "I really got in on the theatre circuit after 'Ya-Ya,' " remarks Dorsey.

Dorsey also formed his first group and worked with the likes of Big Joe Turner, Chuck Berry, Pigmeat Markham, T-Bone Walker, and even sixty-one consecutive one-nighters with James Brown and the Famous Flames.

Dorsey still has mixed feeling about being on the road. "Oh you make a lot of money, but you spend a lot too. You got to worry about your transportation, clean clothes, instruments, and the band. It was a lot tougher takin' a band on the road in those days, and, being black, you just couldn't stay anywhere. I got ripped off plenty of times by club owners who'd take off with the money from a full house. Man, I had to watch the door an' sing at the same time. It was rough."

Dorsey's next Fury release, "Do-Re-Me," written by Earl King, followed "Ya-Ya" into the charts, incorporating the same nursery rhyme approach that would soon become the Dorsey-Toussaint trademark. Fury followed with three more singles and the excellent "Ya-Ya" album, but they didn't catch the public's attention like his first two releases.

By 1963, Fire/Fury had folded and Toussaint had been drafted into the Army. None of this fazed Lee, however. He was just as happy under a car as under the spotlight. "I was just a regular guy," shrugs Dorsey. "I didn't know much about show business. I'd come in off the road and do a little body and fender work in shops around town to make some extra money. See, I went through a few bucks," he winks.

"I never had any trouble getting body and fender work. I had the tools and I knew the work. I love it. I never knew if I was a better body-and-fender man or a vocalist."

Lee didn't totally abandon music. Marshall Sehorn arranged sessions for Lee on Smash and Constellation, which Harold Batiste produced. Good records, but they stayed on the distributors shelves.

Sehorn decided to take things into his own hands, bringing Lee into Cosimo's studio in 1965 with Allen Toussaint producing. Sehorn planned to take the four-song session around and see if he could find a company to lease Dorsey's material. One of the tunes on the tape was "Ride Your Pony."

Sehorn eventually leased the session to Amy Bell Records, and Lee rode "Pony" back into the charts for the first time in four years. So once again he put away his tools, and became a full-time recording artist/performer.

"Ride Your Pony" kicked off an impressive string of hit singles on Amy. It also marked the beginning of the Sehorn-Toussaint partnership, with Dorsey being their vehicle to the charts. The year 1966 proved to be the trio's best year. The bluesy "Get Out Of My Life Woman" was followed by "Workin' In A Coal Mine"—Lee's second gold record—and "Holy Cow." Even then, with the British music invasion at its peak, the delightful Dorsey was able to sound vigorously fresh and alive.

Besides hitting the theatre/club circuit, Lee also made his first trip overseas in 1966, where he was an unqualified smash. Dorsey spent three months in England, which included dates with the Beatles and the Rolling Stones.

With Dorsey's records in the charts producing a steady revenue, Sehorn and Toussaint had enough money coming in to work on other projects. They set up a number of house labels to record local artists who would otherwise go unrecorded.

Lee's gravy days lasted into 1967, with "My Old Car," (originally a Coke commercial) and "Go Go Girl," making the charts. He continued to tour the country regularly between recording sessions, but he stopped long enough for Ebony magazine to photograph him in a smoking jacket, smiling between his black and white poodles!

Even though Lee managed to earn all the successful trappings of a celebrity—a big house and a couple of matching Cadillacs—his perpetual smile disappears from his face when he explains how the extended touring put a strain on his family life, resulting in a painful divorce.

Musically, the Dorsey-Toussaint sound matured on record, as the Meters were added as the rhythm section on Lee's recordings. Their funky sound was the perfect foil for Dorsey's 1969 hit, "Everything I Do Gonna Be Funky," so obviously illustrated.

By 1970, Marshall Sehorn had negotiated a deal with Polydor for the latest batch of Dorsey recordings. The result was the excellent, though moderately selling *Yes We Can* album, and three fine singles. The album contained such underground classics as "Freedom For The Stallion," "Sneakin' Sally Thru the Alley," "Tears, Tears, and More Tears" and "Riverboat," spotlighting Toussaint's producing and songwriting abilities as much as Lee's sparkling vocals. The "Yes We Can" single was the most successful song of the session. Even though it only slipped into the R&B charts at #46, it inspired a more successful version by the Pointer Sisters just a few years later.

It seemed that Dorsey was the perfect medium for Toussaint's art. "I guess Allen saves his best material for me," says Lee. "He knows what he's doin'. He can write a song to suit just about any style."

Recordingwise Lee slowed up during the early Seventies, as

Lee Dorsey and Marshall Sehorn

Toussaint and Sehorn's Sansu corporation built the Sea-Saint studio, and tried to lure outside record labels. He made a couple of sessions, but he was more than content going back to banging out fenders and making a few gigs in his gold plated Cadillac. In 1977, Lee crawled out from under his business long enough to record the bank-up-to-date *Night People* album. "I thought it was great," commented Lee. "It was today's thing."

Leased to ABC, the single and the album did well locally, but didn't get much further. "It just needed a little boost," says Lee with a trace of frustration. "The kids were singin' it in the streets; the words were really catchy. But I haven't seen a penny from it neither. Every time I ask Marshall about it he says, 'Well Lee, I guess that's one that got away.' Shee-it."

Not long after, Lee began working with his present group, "my funky li'l white band," SKOR, that had also been doing sessions at Sea-Saint.

But all of Lee's activities came to an abrupt halt in late 1979. Lee was driving his son's motorcycle one evening when he was broadsided by a car that was being chased by the police. "I broke my legs," shutters Dorsey. "He just got out of the car and ran away, and they never caught the guy. The doctor said I might never walk again, but I didn't believe that. I guess I'm a lucky son of a gun, I've used up nine lives—hope I've got about 9 more left, too!"

Incredibly Lee worked the 1980 Jazz Fest from a wheelchair, to the delight of thousands. By the fall, he was back on his feet, just barely, and was about to embark on one of the most bizarre tours of his career. Lee was invited to open for the Clash on their first North American tour. "I was surprised, but it worked out real well," remarks Dorsey. "I liked 'em, they're real straightforward people. We got along real well."

Today Lee still does what he enjoys best, splitting his time between assisting his son, Irving, with the body and fender shop, located on North Prieur, and singing in clubs around town weekends. He's also hoping to finish up a country-western album with Toussaint.

"It's something I've always wanted to do. I listen to country all day. I like the songs 'cause they all have a down-to-earth story."

Lee's also more selective these days about where and when he performs. "I've been working less and less in New Orleans lately. More out in the Parishes. I like to work for a crowd, I don't like workin' for tables an' chairs. If I can make you feel like you've enjoyed yourself, then I feel like I've done something."

EPILOGUE

Certainly no book concerning New Orleans rhythm and blues would be complete without a few words concerning Fats Domino. It would seem a tragic flaw not devoting a chapter to the Fatman and indeed one was prepared. However, at the time of the publication of this book, writer John Broven was researching an entire book on Mr. Domino. So that there would be no runover of material, I decided to donate my research to John so that he can tell Fats' story in more detail than I possibly could in the confines of a single chapter.

Imperial Records, Inc.
6425 Hollywood Boulevard
Hollywood 28, California
HOllywood 9-8193 Cable: Imperial Hollywood

August 13, 1958

Mr. Fats Domino
c/o Fats Domino Orchestras, Inc.
6425 Hollywood Boulevard
Hollywood 28, California

My dear Fats:

This release marks the tenth anniversary of your association with the Imperial label. I thought you would be interested in knowing that in the past ten years you have sold over 40,000,000 records, 3,000,000 albums and about 4,000,000 EP's.

This is quite a record. Please rest assured that today you are a household name throughout the world.

I know that you will duplicate these sales figures in the next ten years.

I remain, with kindest personal regards to you, your wife and your children,

Very truly yours,

IMPERIAL RECORDS, I .

Lewis R. Chudd

lrc:eb
P.S. Your new record YOUNG SCHOOL GIRL b/w IT MUST BE LOVE is a smash.

WINNIE'S LOUNGE:
Where The Music Plays On

Winnie's Bar and Restaurant, located on the corner of A.P. Tureaud (formerly London Avenue) and North Tonti, looks like any other Seventh Ward neighborhood bar. The Barq's chalkboard on the sidewalk announces you can get a home-cooked meal inside, and the defunct Jax sign over the front door still carries the names of the former owner, "Ruthie." Inside is a long bar, with lots of tables and chairs, underneath the newly installed ceiling fans. A jukebox stands against one wall, and a small bandstand rests at the far end of the room near the kitchen. On Sundays at about 8 p.m. Winnie's starts to fill up, and by 9 o'clock no seats are left. Sunday evenings mean good times at Winnie's, because for three hours there will be nothing but live rhythm and blues, the same kind that New Orleans has been producing for the last thirty years.

Rhythm and blues still lives here, with the young as well as the old. Fats Domino, Frogman Henry, and Lee Dorsey are still the big names around Winnie's. Drinks are inexpensive, the plate lunches tasty, and the atmosphere is a lot looser and noisier than other live music venues in the city. The clientele consists of folks from the neighborhood, and a number of New Orleans' best singers and musicians who come to sit in, to have a drink, and to see what their peers are up to.

The house band is led by the brilliant, but little-known guitarist Irving Bannister, who has been playing in New Orleans R&B groups for over two decades. He is perhaps best known for his work on Danny White's 1963 hit, "Loan Me Your Handkerchief." The musicians squeeze together on the bandstand and kick-off with "Honky Tonk," and a couple of jazzy instrumentals. The sound is loose, as the musicians try to find each other — raggedy at times, but right. After each number there is a flurry of applause and shouts for requests. "Down Home Blues," demands one rotund woman in a polyester jump-suit sitting at a nearby table crowded with drinks. Often a musician is dropped between numbers to bring drinks back for the rest of the band.

Although Winnie's has no dance floor, the aisles do nicely, and are used for that purpose much to the dismay of the fire marshal. By the time the band's featured vocalist, Joe Francois, takes the bandstand, the volume from the band is nearly matched by that of the audience.

Francois' short, energetic set features lots of contemporary fast-paced material. However, he handles the slow blues-ballads admirably, milking the appropriate lyrics for all they're worth, and often dropping to one knee to sing to the ladies at an adjacent table. Francois concludes his set amid howls for "one more," before turning the microphone over "to one of the celebrities in the house tonight."

Lee Dorsey, Guitar Slim Jr., Jessie Hill, King Floyd, Rudy Ray Moore, Dog Man, Robert "Barefootin" Parker, Ernie K-9, Tommy Ridgley, Sammy Ridgley, or Little Sonny Jones — they all like to sit in and do a couple of numbers. Free from the compulsion to play top 40 or disco, they can really let loose to an appreciative audience. Here you can experience the atmosphere, the feeling, or whatever you want to call it, that is just as much a part of rhythm and blues as the actual music.

Little Sonny Jones is a long-time Winnie's Sunday night attraction. Sonny was a featured vocalist with Dave Bartholomew's Imperial Recording Orchestra during the early Fifties. He waxed a number of sides with Imperial and later on the tiny Scram label, and often worked as a warmup vocalist for Fats Domino. Today he works a day job and sings for fun on weekends. But he still clearly enjoys his celebrity status at Winnie's. Sonny sticks to popular blues material, his versions of "Driving Wheel," and "Something On Your Mind" deservedly brings forth waves of applause, especially when he ventures into the audience to sing them.

Sonny's brief cameo also brings warm approval from David Lastie, Tommy Ridgley, and Ernie K-Doe. K-Doe has become somewhat of a regular around Winnie's, serving as the unofficial featured attraction every Sunday evening. K-Doe demands the lion's share of the attention and time, most evenings, and usually gets it, by continually hyping himself, shaking hands and acknowledging all the other performers. It might have been over two decades since "Mother-In-Law" was the number one record in the country, but you'd never guess it by the way K-Doe handles himself on and off the stage. Once he commandeers the microphone, K-Doe puts out like he was auditioning for the Ed Sullivan Show. Invariably he runs through his many hits — "Certain Girl," "I Cried

My Last Tear," "Hello My Love," "T'ain't It The Truth," and the inevitable "Mother-In-Law." The many years of shouting, and singing in smoky nightclubs, have taken away the smoothness in K-Doe's tenor, but still he remains one of the most electrifying singers in the field of rhythm and blues. He pushes the microphone stand down until it almost hits the floor, before he kicks it back with his heel, while he pirouettes and catches the mike behind his head. Most regulars at Winnie's have seen it more times than they care to remember, but it invariably brings forth howls of approval from behind the growing walls of Falstaff cans. K-Doe won't relinquish the microphone until he and the audience are limp with exhaustion.

Although sweat is usually pouring off Irving Bannister and the All Stars, it's not yet time to take a break. There's usually another singer waiting next to the bandstand who presses to "do just a couple of short numbers."

"I like to stop in when I'm passing through to see what's going on," says singer Tommy Ridgley, watching brother Sammy sing. "It's a fun thing, 'cause I know there's not big money involved. Usually I just like to watch, but I do a couple of numbers every now and then.

"Winnie's is the kind of place you go to get your act together. Really there aren't too many places in the city like Winnie's any more. I wish they had more, because the musicians and singers can learn from each other, sort of like school. In the old days the Dew Drop was like that, everybody'd rush over after their gig and line up to get a chance to play at the Dew Drop. And you know they'd do it for nothing, just to say they played at the Dew Drop."

"These cats put out," says saxophonist David Lastie, who had just come in after playing all day in the French Market. "I like to make it down here when I get the chance. Even if I don't play, I like to see what all these other cats is up to."

Winnie's proprietor is Winnie Lear, who got into the live music business quite by accident, "I was just tryin' to make it in the bar and restaurant business," he relates. "The idea to have music on Sundays wasn't mine, it was Sidney Quezergue's (brother of noted New Orleans arranger/bandleader Wardell Quezergue). We just started it a few years ago, and it surprised me just how many musicians make it. Not just the older cats like Johnny Adams and Little Sonny either. Lots of these hungry cats too," laughs Winnie, referring to the queue of performers waiting for their chance.

Some Sundays are more memorable than others, according to Winnie. "One night K-Doe had his birthday party in here, and it seemed like every musician in New Orleans was here. I mean to tell you they was comin' out the windows and the doors. Lee Dorsey brought his whole band in here, and nobody would leave until they got a chance to play. I think we ran out of beer, and I didn't get home 'til the sun was comin' up in the mornin'."

After a short break the musicians crowd back onto the bandstand. There'll usually be a few changes in the horn section, or perhaps a new bass or keyboard player is added to the lineup.

The time allotment for the featured singers is kept short, because there's always someone else waiting for their chance. Since the next day is a working day, the band usually tries to conclude around 1 a.m. More often then not the closing number is a rousing version of "Second Line." This brings most everyone to their feet in a hurry. The lights come up, and the musicians pack up as the last few patrons file out, not long after the last note is heard. But you can bet that they'll be right back in the same place come next Sunday evening.

Appendix A

New Orleans R&B Singles Chart Entries 1949-1971

This is a listing of hit singles by artists from New Orleans. It shows positions on *Billboard's* rhythm and blues charts. Data assembled from Joel Whitburn's *Top R&B Records 1949-1971,* available from Record Research, P.O. Box 82, Menomonee Falls, Wisconsin 53051.

Date	Pos.	Wks.	ARTIST — RECORD	Label
			Adams, Johnny	
6/30/62	27	5	Losing Battle	Ric 986
12/7/68	34	6	Release Me	SSS Int'l 750
4/21/69	8	12	Reconsider Me	SSS Int'l 770
10/25/69	45	3	I Can't Be All Bad	SSS Int'l 780
8/29/70	41	5	I Won't Cry	SSS Int'l 809
			Archibald	
6/2/50	10	2	Stack-A'Lee	Imperial 5068
			Bo, Eddie	
7/19/69	13	11	Hook And Sling (Part I)	Scram 117
			Booker, James	
11/27/60	3	10	Gonzo	Peacock 1697
			Brown, Roy	
11/25/49	3	8	Boogie At Midnight	Deluxe 3300
6/16/50	1	18	Hard Luck Blues	Deluxe 3304
9/15/50	2	11	Love Don't Love Nobody	Deluxe 3306
10/13/50	8	1	Long About Sundown	Deluxe 3308)
10/20/50	6	2	Cadillac Baby	Deluxe 3308
8/17/51	8	1	Big Town	Deluxe 3318
3/13/57	14	2	Party Doll	Imperial 5427
			Byrd, Roy	
8/4/50	5	2	Bald Head	Mercury 8175
			Clanton, Jimmy	
7/19/58	1	17	Just A Dream	Ace 546
11/16/58	28	1	A Part Of Me	Ace 551
1/17/60	19	9	Go, Jimmy, Go	Ace 575
			Darnell, Larry	
11/4/49	3	16	I'll Get Along Somehow	Regal 3236
11/4/49	1	22	For Your My Love	Regal 3240
7/28/50	4	6	I Love My Baby	Regal 3274
11/17/50	5	5	Oh Baby	Regal 3298
			Dixie Cups	
5/2/64	1	13	Chapel Of Love	Red Bird 10-001*

Date	Pos	Wks	Title	Label
7/18/64	12	9	People Say	Red Bird 10-006*
10/24/64	39	6	You Should Have Seen The Way He Looked At Me	Red Bird 10-012*
12/19/64	51	9	Little Bell	Red Bird 10-017*
4/10/65	20	4	Iko Iko	Red Bird 10-024

Domino, Fats

Date	Pos	Wks	Title	Label
3/24/50	6	3	The Fat Man	Imperial 5058
12/1/50	5	6	Every Night About This Time	Imperial 5099
12/21/51	9	1	Rockin' Chair	Imperial 5145
5/2/52	1	20	Goin' Home	Imperial 5180
12/6/52	9	1	How Long	Imperial 5209
4/18/53	2	14	Goin' To The River	Imperial 5231
7/18/53	5	12	Please Don't Leave Me	Imperial 5240
10/10/53	10	1	Rose Mary	Imperial 5251
12/19/53	6	11	Something's Wrong	Imperial 5262
3/31/54	10	1	You Done Me Wrong	Imperial 5272
3/9/55	12	5	Don't You Know	Imperial 5340
5/4/55	1	24	Ain't It A Shame	Imperial 5348
9/7/55	3	11	All By Myself	Imperial 5357
11/16/55	3	12	Poor Me	Imperial 5369
2/1/56	6	13	Bo Weevil/Don't Blame It On Me	Imperial 5375
4/11/56	1	21	I'm In Love Again/My Blue Heaven	Imperial 5386
7/25/56	6	11	When My Dreamboat Comes Home/So-Long	Imperial 5396
10/3/56	1	22	Blueberry Hill	Imperial 5407
12/26/56	1	15	Blue Monday	Imperial 5417
3/6/57	1	13	I'm Walkin'	Imperial 5428
5/22/57	4	11	Valley of Tears	Imperial 5442
10/26/57	14	2	Wait And See	Imperial 5467
5/10/58	15	5	Sick And Tired/No, No	Imperial 5515
7/12/58	15	2	Little Mary	Imperial 5526
11/30/58	2	15	Whole Lotta Loving	Imperial 5553)
1/11/59	26	3	Coquette	Imperial 5553)
3/15/59	13	7	Telling Lies	Imperial 5569
5/17/59	7	9	I'm Ready	Imperial 5585
8/16/59	1	13	I Want To Walk You Home	Imperial 5606)
8/16/59	22	4	I'm Gonna Be A Wheel Some Day	Imperial 5606)
11/15/59	2	14	Be My Guest	Imperial 5629)
12/6/59	19	5	I've Been Around	Imperial 5629)
7/17/60	2	11	Walking To New Orleans	Imperial 5675)
8/7/60	28	3	Don't Come Knockin'	Imperial 5675)
10/16/60	8	5	Three Nights A Week	Imperial 5687
11/20/60	7	12	My Girl Josephine	Imperial 5704)
1/15/61	28	1	Natural Born Lover	Imperial 5704)
2/19/61	19	7	Ain't That Just Like A Woman	Imperial 5723)
2/26/61	7	7	What A Price	Imperial 5723)
7/2/61	18	5	It Keeps Rainin'	Imperial 5753
8/6/61	2	12	Let The Four Winds Blow	Imperial 5764
6/16/62	22	2	My Real Name	Imperial 5833
11/9/63	24	2	Red Sails In The Sunset	ABC 10484
1/4/64	63	5	Who Cares	ABC 10512*
2/29/64	86	2	Lazy Lady	ABC 10531*
9/19/64	99	2	Sally Was A Good Old Girl	ABC 10584*
10/31/64	99	2	Heartbreak Hill	ABC 10596*

Dorsey, Lee

9/3/61	1	19	Ya Ya...............................	Fury 1053
2/10/62	22	5	Do-Re-Mi	Fury 1056
6/19/65	7	13	Ride Your Pony..................	Amy 927
1/15/66	5	10	Get Out Of My Life, Woman	Amy 945
8/6/66	5	11	Working In The Coal Mine..........	Amy 958
11/19/66	10	8	HolyCow.........................	Amy 965
10/28/67	31	5	Go-Go Girl	Amy 998
6/28/69	33	5	Everything I Do Gonh Be Funky	Amy 11055
11/7/70	46	4	Yes We Can	Polydor 14038

Dupree, Jack & Mr. Bear

8/10/55	7	11	Walking The Blues.................	King 4812

Floyd, King

10/10/70	1	22	Groove Me	Chimneyville 435
3/27/71	5	9	Baby Let Me Kiss You..............	Chimneyville 437
8/7/71	35	5	Got To Have Your Lovin'..........	Chimneyville 439

Ford, Frankie

4/12/59	11	7	Sea Cruise......................	Ace 554

Gayten, Paul & Annie Laurie

4/21/50	8	3	I'll Never Be Free..................	Regal 3258

George, Barbara

11/26/61	1	19	I Know...........................	AFO 302

Harris, Betty

9/28/63	10	9	Cry To Me.......................	Jubilee 5456
7/15/67	16	11	Nearer To You	Sansu 466
6/7/69	44	5	Cry To Me.......................	Jubilee 5653

Henry, Clarence

11/28/56	3	12	Ain't Got No Home................	Argo 5259
3/12/61	9	11	I Don't Know Why, But I Do	Argo 5378
6/4/61	11	7	You Always Hurt The One You Love..	Argo 5388
8/13/61	19	5	Lonely Street	Argo 5395

Hill, Jessie

5/1/60	3	11	Ooh Poo Pah Doo - Part II..........	Minit 607

Joe & Ann

12/18/60	14	4	Gee Baby........................	Ace 577

Jones, Joe

10/9/60	9	12	You Talk Too Much	Roulette 4304

Joseph, Margie

6/20/70	46	2	Your Sweet Loving	Volt 4037
4/10/71	38	2	Stop In The Name Of Love..........	Volt 4056

K-Doe, Ernie

4/9/61	1	16	Mother-In-Law	Minit 623
7/9/61	21	4	Te-Ta-Te-Ta-Ta...................	Minit 627
4/8/67	37	4	Later For Tomorrow	Duke 411
11/4/67	48	3	Until The Real Thing Comes Along...	Duke 423

Kenner, Chris

6/11/61	2	17	I Like It Like That	Instant 3229

King, Earl

3/17/62	17	5	Always A First Time	Imperial 5811

Knight, Jean

5/22/71	1	16	Mr. Big Stuff	Stax 0088
10/16/71	19	7	You Think You're Hot Stuff	Stax 0105

Laurie, Annie

2/20/57	3	11	It Hurts To Be In Love	De Luxe 6107
7/17/60	17	11	If You're Lonely	De Luxe 6189

Lewis, Smiley

8/29/52	10	2	The Bells Are Ringing	Imperial 5194
8/31/55	2	17	I Hear You Knocking	Imperial 5356

Little Richard

11/16/55	2	20	Tutti-Frutti	Specialty 561
3/28/56	1	16	Long Tall Sally/Slippin' And Slidin	Specialty 572
6/20/56	1	17	Rip It Up/Ready Teddy	Specialty 579
10/31/56	15	1	She's Got It/Heeby-Jeebies	Specialty 584
1/23/57	11	5	The Girl Can't Help It	Specialty 591
3/6/57	2	13	Lucille/Send Me Some Lovin'	Specialty 598
6/12/57	2	12	Jenny, Jenny/Miss Ann	Specialty 606
9/21/57	5	8	Keep A Knockin'	Specialty 611
2/15/58	6	8	Good Golly, Miss Molly	Specialty 624
6/21/58	15	4	Ooh! My Soul/True, Fine Mama	Specialty 633
10/26/58	12	7	Baby Face	Specialty 645
11/20/65	12	8	I Don't Know What You've Got But It's Got Me	Vee Jay 698
8/27/66	41	4	Poor Dog (Who Can't Wag His Own Tail)	Okeh 7251
6/13/70	28	4	Freedom Blues	Reprise 0907

Marchan, Bobby

6/19/60	1	15	There's Something On Your Mind	Fire 1022
10/8/66	14	11	Shake Your Tambourine	Cameo 429

Meters

2/1/69	7	10	Sophisticated Cissy	Josie 1001
4/19/69	4	12	Cissy Strut	Josie 1005
7/19/69	20	7	Ease Back	Josie 1008
11/1/69	39	3	Dry Spell	Josie 1013
12/6/69	11	9	Look-Ka Py Py	Josie 1105
4/4/70	11	8	Chicken Strut	Josie 1018
6/20/70	26	8	Hand Clapping Song	Josie 1021
9/12/70	21	7	A Message From The Meters	Josie 1024
2/6/71	42	3	Stretch Your Rubber Band	Josie 1026
6/12/71	47	4	Doode Oop	Josie 1029

Mitchell, Bobby

3/14/56	14	2	Try Rock And Roll	Imperial 5378

Neville, Aaron

10/2/60	21	2	Over You	Minit 612
12/3/66	1	17	Tell It Like It Is	Parlo 101

Parker, Robert

4/30/66	2	17	Barefootin'	Nola 721
2/11/67	48	3	Tip Toe	Nola 729

Price, Lloyd

5/23/52	1	26	Lawdy Miss Clawdy	Specialty 428
10/3/52	5	8	Oooh-Oooh-Oooh	Specialty 440
10/3/52	8	4	Restless Heart	Specialty 440

1/31/53	7	5	Ain't It A Shame	Specialty 452
2/27/57	4	12	Just Because	ABC 9792
12/21/58	1	19	Stagger Lee	ABC 9972
3/22/59	4	8	Where Were You (On Our Wedding Day)	ABC 9997
5/17/59	1	16	Personality	ABC 10018
8/23/549	1	13	I'm Gonna Get Married	ABC 10032
10/4/59	15	4	Three Little Pigs	ABC 10032)
11/22/59	2	13	Come Into My Heart	ABC 10062)
11/22/59	6	11	Wont'Cha Come Home	ABC 10062)
2/14/60	3	12	Lady Luck	ABC 10075)
5/1/60	26	2	Never Let Me Go	ABC 10075)
5/1/60	16	3	No If's - No And's	ABC 10102
7/17/60	5	12	Question	ABC 10102
10/19/63	11	6	Misty	Double-L 722
10/18/69	21	8	Bad Conditions	Turntable 506

Prince La La

10/1/61	28	4	She Put The Hurt On Me	AFO 101

Robinson, Alvin

6/6/64	52	8	Something You Got	Tiger 104

Shirley And Lee

12/13/52	2	11	I'm Gone	Aladdin 3153
8/17/55	5	25	Feel So Good	Aladdin 3289
7/25/56	2	17	Let The Good Times Roll	Aladdin 3325
11/14/56	5	8	I Feel Good	Aladdin 3338

Slim, Guitar

1/9/54	1	21	The Things That I Used To Do	Specialty 482

Smith, Huey

7/6/57	9	7	Rocking Pneumonia & The Boogie Woogie Flu	Ace 530
3/22/58	4	9	Don't You Just Know It	Ace 545

Spellman, Benny

6/16/62	28	1	Lipstick Traces	Minit 644

Spiders

2/13/54	3	17	I Didn't Want To Do It	Imperial 5265)
4/7/54	8	3	You're The One	Imperial 5265)
11/23/55	7	11	Witchcraft	Imperial 5366

Thomas, Irma

5/8/60	22	3	Don't Mess With My Man	Ron 328
* 3/28/64	17	12	Wish Someone Would Care	Imperial 66013
* 7/4/64	52	6	Anyone Who Knows What Love Is	Imperial 66041
* 11/7/64	98	2	Times Have Changed	Imperial 66069
*12/19/64	63	8	He's My Guy	Imperial 66080
2/24/68	42	2	Good To Me	Chess 2036

Turner, Joe

3/3/50	12	1	Still In The Dark	Freedom 1531
6/22/51	2	25	Chains Of Lve (Van "Piano Man" Walls)	Atlantic 939
4/4/52	4	5	Sweet Sixteen (Van "Piano Man" Walls)	Atlantic 960
9/19/53	2	25	Honey Hush	Atlantic 1001
1/30/54	9	1	TV Mama	Atlantic 1016

4/28/54	2	27	Shake, Rattle And Roll	Atlantic 1026
3/16/55	3	14	Flip Flop And Fly	Atlantic 1053
8/31/55	11	6	Hide And Seek	Atlantic 1069
1/18/56	13	2	The Chicken And The Hawk/ Morning, Noon And Night	Atlantic 1080
4/25/56	3	10	Corrine Corrina	Atlantic 1088
8/22/56	12	2	Rock A While/Lipstick, Pwder And Paint	Atlantic 1100

Williams, Larry

6/19/57	2	16	Short Fat Fannie	Specialty 608
11/9/57	9	9	Bony Moronie	Specialty 615

*Billboard did not publish an R&B chart for the entire year of 1964. These records did, however, chart in *Billboard* 1964 Hot 100.

Appendix B
Important Rhythm and Blues Clubs

The following is a list of important rhythm and blues clubs and musical venues. The information contained in parentheses refers to the period when these clubs featured live music.

Astoria, 235 S. Rampart St. (late '40s - mid '50s)
Beautiful Nile Auditorium, 1512 N. Claiborne Ave. (late '40s)
Bernard's Cocktail Lounge, 3611 Florida Ave. (late '40s)
Big 4 Nightclub, 1401 S. Galvez St. (late '40s)
Black Diamond Rest. & Bar, N. Galvez (late '40s)
Blue Eagle, Felicity & S. Rampart ('50s)
Booker T. Washington Auditorium, 1201 S. Roman St. (mid '40s to present)
Brass Rail, 1306 Canal St. (early '50s to mid '60s)
Brown Derby, Louisiana Ave. and Freret St. (late '40s - late '50s)
Cadillac Club, St. Claude and Poland Ave. (early '50s - early '60s)
Caldonia Club, St. Philip St. and St. Claude Ave. (late '40s - early '50s)
Cinq Sou, behind the Dew Drop (late '40s - early '50s)
City Park Stadium, City Park (mid '50s - early '70s)
Coliseum Arena, 401 N. Roman (late '40s - late '50s)
Congo Square, N. Rampart St. (continuously)
Club Baby Doll, St. Bernard Ave. & N. Dorgenois (late '40s)
Club Desire, 2406 Desire St. (late '40s - early '50s)
Club 4-U, 1414 Frenchmen St. (late '40s)
Club Rocket, 3000 Jackson Ave. (late '40s - early '50s)
Cotton Club, 2924 Jefferson Hwy., Jefferson La. (early '50s)
Dew Drop Inn, 2840 La Salle St. (1938 - early '70s)
Dixie Bell Rest. & Bar, 1104 S. Rampart St. (late '40s)
Dog House, 300 N. Rampart St. (late '40s)
Downbeat Club, 712 S. Rampart St. (mid '40s - early '50s)
Dorothy's Medallion Lounge, 3232 Orleans Ave. (late '70s - present)
Dream Room, 424 Canal St. ('50s)
Dream Palace, 534 Frenchmen ('60s - present)
El Morocco, 200 Bourbon St. (late '40s - early '50s)
Foster's Rainbow Room, 2926 La Salle St. ('40s - early '50s)
F&M Patio, 400 Lyons St. (mid '50s - late '60s)
Gallo Theatre, 2122 S. Claiborne St. (late '40s - late '50s)
Gaudet School Playground, Gentilly Rd. (late '40s)
Gladstone Ballroom, 3435 Dryades St. (mid '40s - mid '50s)
Gold Leaf Club, 1202 Saratoga St. (late '40s)
Greystone Ballroom, Eagle & Cohn St. (late '40s)
Gypsy Tea Room, 1432 St. Ann St. ('40s)
Hide Away Inn, 2900 Desire St. (late '40s - mid '50s)

House of Blue Lights, 445 S. Rampart St. (early '50s)
Hot Spot Bar, 419 S. Rampart St. (early '50s)
I.L.A. Hall, 2700 S. Claiborne Ave. (late '60s - present)
Ivanhoe, 601 Bourbon St. (sixties)
J&M Music Shop, 1040 N. Rampart St. (late '40s)
Jed's University Inn, 8301 Oak St. (early '70s - early '80s)
Jimmy's, 8200 Willow St. (late '70s - present)
Kohlman's Kotton Club, 1129 S. Rampart St. (late '40s)
Labor Union Hall, Tchoupitoulas & Soniat ('60s)
La Ray's, 1819 Polymnia St. ('60s)
Le Rondevous Club, 7 Mile Post, Gentilly Hwy. (late '40s)
Lincoln Beach, Little Farms, La. (early '50s - early '60s)
Lincoln Theatre, Freret & Washington (mid '40s - mid '50s)
Lloyd's Esquire Lounge, 2100 Huey P. Long Blvd., Gretna, La. (late '40s)
Louis Hagen's Pavillion, 2119 Pauger St. (late '40s)
Mardi Gras Lounge, 333 Bourbon St. ('60s)
Manhattan Club, 1310 Canal St. ('50s)
Maple Leaf, 8316 Oak St. (late '70s - present)
Mason's Americana
   (later became Mason's Las Vegas Strip), 2309 S. Claiborne Ave. ('70s)
Monkey Bar, 1320 Canal St. (mid '50s - early '60s)
Municipal Auditorium, Basin St. (early '50s - present)
Natal's Lounge, 7716 Chef Menteur Hwy. (late '50s - early '60s)
Night Cap, 1700 Louisiana Ave. (early '70s)
Old Absinthe Bar, 400 Bourbon St. ('40s - present)
Original Big Apple Bar, 1101 S. Rampart St. ('40s)
Palace Theatre ('40s - '50s)
Pontchartrain Beach, Lakeshore Drive (late '50s - late '60s)
Pepper Pot, 4th St., Gretna (late '40s - mid '50s)
Pimlico Club, 2727 S. Broad St. (late '50s)
Prout's Club Alhambra Nite Club, 728 S. Claiborne Ave. (early '70s - early '80s)
Rip's Playhouse, London Ave. & N. Dorgenois St. (late '40s)
Robin Hood, 2059 Jackson Ave. (mid '40s - early '50s)
Rosenwald Center, S. Broad & Earhart Blvd. (late '50s - mid '60s)
Rose Tattoo, 500 Napoleon Ave. (early '80s)
Safari Room, 5047 Chef Menteur Hwy. (early '60s)
Sand's, 801 Jefferson Hwy., Jefferson La. ('60s)
San Jacinto Club, 1422 Dumaine St. ('40s - '50s)
Stereo Lounge, 1001 Causeway Blvd., Jefferson La.)'60s)
700 Club, 700 S. Rampart St. (late '40s)
Shadowland Club, 1921 Washington Ave. (early '50s)
Sho Bar, 228 Bourbon St. (late '50s - early '60s)
Shy Guy's Place, St. Bernard Hwy. (late '50s)
Starlight Cafe and Hotel, Forshey & Lowerline St. ('40s)
Talk O' The Town, 131 S. Rampart St. (late '40s)
Tiajuana Club, 1201 S. Saratoga St. ('50s)
Tick Toc, 235 S. Rampart St. ('40s)
Tipitina's, 501 Napoleon Ave. (late '70s - early '80s)
Walnut Room, New Orleans Lakefront Airport ('60s)
Winnie's Lounge, 2304 London Ave. (late '70s - present)

Appendix C
Album Discography

Over the past few years, most of the best material from the classic New Orleans rhythm and blues era has been reissued. Since New Orleans has consistently been a singles market, many of the reissue labels have taken the burden from us collectors by compiling a number of "greatest hits" type packages on many performers. A number of fine anthologies have also been made available that are well worth investigating. The following is a listing of currently available albums (spring 1984), with regards to value and content. It only includes albums currently in print and excludes bootlegs.

Johnny Adams
Heart & Soul, SSS 5, Charly 30154 (England)
   A fine collection of Johnny's early R&B sides recorded for Ric and his successful late Sixties SSS country/soul material, including his biggest hit, "Reconsider Me."
The Many Sides of Johnny Adams, Hep' Me 158
   An excellent album that captures Johnny's contemporary style well.
Christmas In New Orleans, Hep' Me 159
   Johnny adeptly handles the best songs of the Christmas season. Worth acquiring.
From the Heart, Rounder 2044
   Recorded in 1983, Johnny proves once again that he is perhaps America's finest balladeer.

Lee Allen
Down On Bourbon Street, NOLA 16 (England)
   This is largely a reissue of the *Walkin' With Mr. Lee* album originally recorded in the late Fifties for Ember. Of course all are instrumentals.

James Booker
New Orleans Piano Wizard: Live! Rounder 2027
   A solo album recorded in concert at the 1977 Zurich Boogie Woogie and Ragtime Contest, and it finds Booker in fine form.
Classified, Rounder 2036
   This is the album discussed in the James Booker chapter. It speaks for itself.

Roy Brown
Laughing But Crying, Route 66-2 (Sweden)
   Excellent compilation of many of Brown's hottest sides, originally recorded on Deluxe and King between 1947 and 1959. Powerful.
Good Rocking Tonight, Route 66-6 (Sweden)
   More of the same, but with the important inclusion of the song that really started it all. Recordings date from 1947 to 1954.
Saturday Night, Mr. R&B 104 (Sweden)

Compiles most of his overlooked, but excellent, rock 'n' roll-influenced sides recorded under Dave Bartholomew on Imperial. A handful of earlier hits from King also are included. 1952 to 1959.
Hard Luck Blues, Starday/Gusto 5036
   A budget priced double album that presents some of Brown's biggest hits from the King label. No duplication from the Route 66 LPs.

James "Sugarboy" Crawford
Sugarboy Crawford, Chess-2-9215 or Chess/Vogue (France)
   An interesting two-album anthology that presents all of "Sugarboy's" mid-Fifties Chess sessions, with a crack New Orleans band.

Lee Dorsey
Gonh Be Funky, Charly 1001 (England)
   A greatest hits-type anthology that collects Dorsey's most successful singles from Fury and Amy.
All Ways Funky, Charly 1036 (England)
   Contains a wide variety of material recorded between 1961 and 1978.

Frankie Ford
Let's Take A Sea Cruise, Ace 67 (England)
   An essential collection of Ford's rockin' Ace sides and a few Imperial jewels thrown in to boot.

King Floyd
Body English, Chimneyville 202
   Fine mid-Seventies soul effort. This will have to do until the classic *Groove Me* LP is reissued.

Guitar Slim
The Things That I Used To Do, Specialty 2120
   An essential collection of material recorded in the mid-Fifties by this devastating and influential singer/guitarist.

Jessie Hill
Can't Get Enough of That Ooh Poo Pa Doo, Bandy 70016
   Indispensable collection of Jessie's rockin' Minit singles, produced in the early Sixties by Allen Toussaint.

Ernie K-Doe
Ernie K-Doe, Bandy 70004
   The quintessential set that contains "Mother-In-Law" and all the other Minit hits. Produced by Allen Toussaint.
Ernie K-Doe: Vol. 2, Bandy 70004
   More of the same, but with less emphasis on the hits.

Chris Kenner
Land Of A Thousand Dances, Peavine 6172 (Japan)
   This is a great reissue of the Kenner album that was leased to Atlantic in the mid-Sixties. Still sounds great.
The Name of the Place, Bandy 70015
   Contains some runoff from the original LP, but with the inclusion of many of Kenner's more obscure but enjoyable sides.

Earl King
Let The Good Times Roll, Ace 15 (England)

Great collection of Earl's Ace and Rex sides, including "Those Lonely, Lonely Nights."
Trick Bag, Pathe Marconi 83299 (France)
Contains all of Earl King's Imperial material recorded in the early Sixties. Essential.
Street Parade, Charly 2021 (England)
Recorded in 1972 at Cosimo's Jazz City Studio, it presents Earl in a variety of enjoyable settings.
Good Old Rock and Roll, Sonet 719 (Sweden)
Interesting mid-Seventies recordings of new material with a crack New Orleans rhythm section. Sounds rushed at times, but still worth investigating.

Smiley Lewis
Hear You Knockin', Vivid 301 (Imperial)
A reissue of the ultra-rare Imperial LP, which contains many of Smiley's biggest records.
Hook Line and Sinker, K.C. 102 (England)
Collects a number of great, but obscure, singles from Imperial. Hopefully the two album anthology, "The Smiley Lewis Story," will again be released.

Bobby Mitchell
I'm Gonna Be A Wheel Someday, Mr. R&B 101 (Sweden)
This album spans the entire recording career of Bobby Mitchell. Great accompaniment from the cream of New Orleans' studio musicians.

Professor Longhair
New Orleans Piano, Atlantic SD 7225
This includes all of Longhair's astounding Atlantic sides. Had he recorded no other material, Longhair's legend would have still stood on these sides.
"Mardi Gras In New Orleans," Highthawk 108
Despite some runover from the Atlantic album, this invaluable release presents the ultra-rare Folk Talent, Mercury, Federal, Wasco and Ebb sides.
Rock 'n' Roll Gumbo, Mardi Gras 1002
Interesting 1977 recordings, with Gatemouth Brown in tow, that originally appeared on the French Blue Star label. Quite enjoyable.
Crawfish Fiesta, Alligator 4718
Released the day after his untimely passing, this captures Longhair's 1970's sound by far the best. Dr. John helps out with some tasty guitar fills as well.

Shirley & Lee
The Best of Shirley & Lee, Ace 47 (England)
Great collection of "the Sweethearts of the Blue's" biggest singles, originally recorded on Aladdin.
Shame, Shame, Shame, Vibration 128
Shirley's solo disco LP still pops up in the bargain bin. Worth picking up just for the title selection.

Huey "Piano" Smith
Rockin' Pneumonia and The Boogie Woogie Flu, Ave 9 (England)
A collection of Huey's biggest hits on Ace. A must for any rock 'n' roll or rhythm and blues record collection.
The Imperial Sides 1960-61, Pathe Marconi 1546731 (France)
A collection of Huey's underrated Imperial sessions. Interesting.
Coo Coo Over You, Bandy 70018
Contains his late Sixties soul influenced work recorded for Instant.
Rockin' & Jivin', Charly 2020 (England)

A disappointing late Seventies recording that doesn't capture the spark of his earlier material.

Irma Thomas
Irma Thomas, Bandy 70003
   An engaging package of Irma's Minit recordings.
Time Is On My Side, Kent 010
   Excellent collection of Irma's biggest national records recorded on Imperial, with a few of her earlier Minit releases sprinkled in as well.
In Between Tears, Charly 1020 (England)
   Interesting soul production produced by Swamp Dog in 1971.
Hip Shakin' Mama, Charly 2019 (England)
   Brilliant live set recorded at the 1976 New Orleans Jazz Fest with Tommy Ridgley's band backing.
Soul Queen of New Orleans, Maison de Soul 1005
   An interesting late Seventies recording consisting primarily of remakes of old hits.
Safe With Me, RCS 1004
   A recent effort which proves Irma can still sing with the best of 'em.

Allen Toussaint
Allen Toussaint Sings, Bandy 70017
   A collection of some rare early vocal efforts and a few instruments by the influential producer/pianist.
The Stokes with Allen Toussaint, Bandy 70014
   A collection of bouncy instruments recorded on ALON during the mid-Sixties.
Southern Nights, WEA 8585 (Japan)
   A reissue of the classic Warner Brothers album, reflecting one of Toussaint's artistic peaks.

Tuts Washington
New Orleans Piano Professor, Rounder 2041
   Tuts' first solo outing, recorded in 1983. Tuts reels off some stunningly accurate and infectious blues and boogies. Simply essential.

Anthologies
The Ace Story, Vol. 1, 2, 3 & 4 Ace 11, 12, 55, 98
   These present a broad cross section of Johnny Vincent's Ace label. Artists included are Huey Smith, Frankie Ford, Eddie Bo, Mac Rebennack, Earl King, Alvin "Red" Tyler, Bobby Marchan, Jimmy Clanton, etc.
Ace Rock n' Roll, Rock & Country 1012 (Sweden)
   Less emphasis on the New Orleans sound, but excellent tracks by Frankie Ford, Big Boy Myles and "Huey "Piano" Smith."
Vin Rock n' Roll, Rock & Country 1021 (Sweden)
   Contains material from Vincent's subsidiary label. More of a rockabilly anthology, but still contains material by Huey "Piano" Smith, Albert Scott, Danny Ray and Jimmie Lee.
Sehorn's Soul Farm, Charly 1032 (England)
   A mixed bag of late Sixties-early Seventies soul sides, recorded by a stable of Sehorn-Toussaint artist including Warren Lee, Earl King, Benny Spellman, Aaron Neville, K-Koe, etc.
Home of the Blues, Bandy 70007
   This is a reissue of the classic Minit LP. Jessie Hill gets the lion's share of titles, but Aaron Neville and Les Diamond contribute fine sides too.
We Sing the Blues, Bandy 70010
   Another reissue of a classic LP. Includes such Minit-ALON-Instant artists as Willie Harper, Jessie Hill, Chris Kenner, Aaron Neville and Irma Thomas.

All These Things, Bandy 70007
  This is the old "Solid Gold" package that was first released on Instant in 1969. Contains some great local hits, from the likes of Roger and the Gypsies, Raymond Lewis, Huey Smith, The Stokes and Huey Smith.

Love You New Orleans, Bandy 70008, "Plenty More, Keep Score," Bandy 70011, "It's Raining," Bandy 70012
  All three of these compilations present material originally recorded for one of Joe Banashak's many labels. Artists include Irma Thomas, Jessie Hill, Little Buck, Benny Spellman, Chuck Carbo, Allen Toussaint, Eskew Reeder, the Boogie Kings, Huey Smith, K-Doe, etc.

Mardi Gras In New Orleans, Mardi Gras 1001
  An indispensable album that includes all the classic R&B songs of Carnival by Professor Longhair, Al Johnson, The Hawkettes, Earl King, the Wild Magnolias, etc.

Going Back To New Orleans, Sonet 5021 (Sweden)
  Excellent set of strong blues influenced New Orleans material recorded for Specialty. Artists include Guitar Slim, Earl King, Lil Millet, Roy Montrell, Art Neville and Lloyd Lambert.

Real Blues From New Orleans, Bandy 70009
  This features the real downhome blues, recorded in the late Fifties-early Sixties, by Boogie Jake, Edgar Blanchard and Polka Dot Slim.

Ace Sound of New Orleans, Vivid 1013 (Japan)
  Eddie Bo, Bobby Marchan, Jesse Allen, et al.

New Orleans Blues, P-Vine 9034 (Japan)
  Contains material originally recorded for Deluxe and Regal during the late Forties. Artists include Dave Bartholomew, Mr. Google Eyes, Chubby Newsome, etc.

This Is How It All Began, Vol. 2, Specialty 2118
  An "oldies" type collection which presents big hits by Guitar Slim, Art Neville, Little Richard, Jerry Byrne, Lloyd Price, Larry Williams, etc.

Southern Blues, Savoy 2255
  Contains many of the rare Savoy singles recorded by Billy Tate, George Stevenson, Earl King and Little Eddie.

Aladdin's Rock 'n' Roll Sock Hop, Pathe Marconi 64791
  A compilation of great sides from the Forties and Fifties, including sides by Lee Allen, Calvin Booze, Gene & Eunice, etc.

New Orleans Rhythm 'n' Blues 1949-1967, Krazy Kat 7403
  A mixed bag of material as the time span would indicate. Still there are fine tracks as expected by Chris Kenner, Dave Bartholomew, Roy Brown, Huey Smith, etc.

The Official Rhythm and Blues Anniversary Album, Deese Days 101
  1984 remakes of some of New Orleans biggest records. Artists include Jean Knight, K-Doe, Earl King, King Floyd, Robert Parker, etc.

Other Albums of Interest

Archibald
  The New Orleans Sessions, Krazy Kat 7409 (England)

Bobby Charles
  Bobby Charles, Chess 2009 (England)

Jimmy Clanton
  Just A Dream, Ace 93 (England)

Larry Darnell
  I'll Get Along Somehow, Rt. 66-19 (Sweden)

Diz and the Doorman
Bluecoat Man, Ace 54 (England)

Dr. John
Gumbo, WEA 8253 (Japan)
Dr. John Plays Mac Rebennack, Clean Cut 705
Brightest Smile, Clean Cut 707

Fats Domino
Fats Domino, United Artists 9958
Fats Domino, Archive of Folk & Jazz 280
Fats Domino, Archive of Folk & Jazz 330
The Fabulous Mr. D, Liberty 10136
Here Stands Fats Domino, Pathe Marconi 82621 (France)
This Is Fats, Pathe Marconi 83289 (France)
I Miss You So, Pathe Marconi 83295 (France)
Walkin' To New Orleans, Pathe Marconi 1546621 (France)
What A Party, Marconi 1546631 (France)
Million Sellers, Pathe Marconi 83297 (France)
Reelin' & Rockin', Charley 1054 (England)

Jack Dupree
Rub A Little Boogie, Krazy Kat 7401 (England)
The First 16 Sides From Joe Davis, 1944-1945, Red Pepper 701 (England)
Blues From the Gutter, Atlantic 40.526 (France)
Blues For Everybody, Starday/Gusto 5037

Snooks Eaglin
Possum Up A Simmon Tree, Arhoolie 2014
Snooks Eaglin, Sundown 70904 (England)

Paul Gayten & Annie Laurie
Creole Gal, Route 66-9 (Sweden)

Betty Harris
In the Saddle, Charly 1002 (England)

Clarence Frogman Henry
You Always Hurt The One You Love, Viking 1009 (Austria)
Bourbon Street, Maison de Soul 101

Little Richard
Here's Little Richard, Specialty 2100
Little Richard, Specialty 2103
The Fabulous Little Richard, Specialty 2104
The Biggest Hits, Specialty 2111
Little Richard's Grooviest 17 Original Hits!, Specialty 2113

The Meters
Second Line Strut, Charly 1009 (England)

Art & Aaron Neville
The Best of Art & Aaron Neville, Bandy 70013

Lloyd Price
The Original Recordings, Specialty 2105
Lloyd Price, MCA 1503

Tommy Ridgley
Through the Years, Sounds of New Orleans 1007

Benny Spellman
Benny Spellman, Bandy 70018

Spiders
I Didn't Want To Do It, United Artist 301 (Japan)

Wild Tchoupitoulas
The Wild Tchoupitoulas, Island/Antilles 7052

Larry Williams
Here's Larry Williams, Specialty 2109

Walter Washington
Leader of the Pack, Hep' Me 157

Most of these albums are available from: Down Home Music Inc., 10341 San Pablo Ave., El Cerrito, California 95430. Floyd's Record Shop, P.O. Drawer 10, Ville Platte, Louisiana 70586. Round Up Records, P.O. Box 147, Dept. W. East Cambridge, Massachusetts 02141.

PHOTO CREDITS

Cover Design: Kathleen Joffrion
Front Cover Photo: Richard Olivier
Back Cover Photo: Lee Crum
Introduction Photos:
    Mr. "G" - Joe "Mr. G" August
    Ray Brown - Teddy Riley
    and Bobby Mitchell - Lynn Abbott

PAGE	COURTESY OF
7, 9, & 11	Tuts Washington
25 Left	Dave Booth
25 Right	Mike Smith
30	Parker Dinkins
41	Dave Booth
43	Leo Gosserand
47	Shirley Goodman
49	Rounder Records
57	Marshall Sehorn
66	New Orleans Jazz & Heritage Festival
73, & 77	Teddy Riley
85	Mr "G"
97	Pathe Marconi Records
116	Percy Stovall
137	Joe Banashak
139	Bobby Mitchell
141	Joe Banashak
163	Marshall Sehorn
174	Richard Olivier
179	Earl King
183	"Mrs. Slim"
186	Laura Painia Jackson
188	Dave Booth
191, & 195	Earl King
203	Alec Duncan
209	Percy Stovall
211	Shirley Goodman
213	David Booth
223, & 227	Irma Thomas
247	Leona Robinson Kelley
261	James Crawford
269	Percy Stovall
273	Dave Booth
277	SSS Records
285, & 287	Bobby Mitchell
300	Percy Stovall
305	Kathleen Joffrion
309, & 315	Ken Keene
316	Dave Booth
327, & 335	Cleon Floyd
339	Percy Stovall
349	Marshall Sehorn
352	Dave Booth
All Others	From Author's Collection

INDEX

Adams, Johnny, 83, 201, 202, 219, 223, 227, 230, 267-280
Adams, Placide, 241
Algere, Ray, 64
Allen, Lee, 22, 48, 58, 86, 100, 110, 196, 198, 213, 223, 239-249, 252
Allen, Jesse, 100
Allen, William B., 26, 86, 128, 136
Anderson, Andrew, 12
Anderson, Elton, 141
Archibald (Leon Gross), 3, 11, 100, 110
Arnestine, Kid, 317
Armstrong, Louis, 96
Assunto, Joe, 22, 25, 272
August, Joseph (Mr. Google Eyes), 71, 83-94, 123, 150, 318, 325

Banashak, Joe, 42, 59, 60, 61, 62, 63, 135-160, 228, 293-298, 312, 319, 320
Bannister, Irving, 259, 260, 355
Bartholomew, Dave, 11, 20, 22, 42, 46, 57, 69, 79-82, 95-104, 123, 124, 130, 131, 174, 192, 199, 200, 209-214, 240, 243, 249-257, 260, 264, 282, 292, 293, 312
Bates, Lee, 42, 293-300
Battiste, Harold, 59, 144, 216, 234, 274, 326
Bellaire, Lloyd, 282
Bernard, Alfred, 260, 261
Big Will, 28
Billington, Scott, 52, 53
Blackwell, Bumps, 113, 222
Blackwell, Nolan, 260
Blanchard, Edgar, 75, 198
Bo, Eddie (Eddie Bocage), 38, 130, 131, 155, 156, 192, 223, 228, 272, 274, 287, 317
Bocage, Frank, 282
Boogie Jake (Mathew Jacobs), 143
Bolden, Isaac, 159
Boogus, 3
Booker, Bea, 299
Booker, James, 12, 15, 41, 45-54, 127, 131, 213, 302
Braun, Jules, 74, 76, 97, 248
Brown, Clarence "Gatemouth", 31, 177, 178, 196, 198

Brown, Roy, 69-82, 85, 86, 96, 109, 124, 220
Butler, Joseph, 21
Byrd, Alice, 29-34

Cade, Melvin, 10
Cane Cutters, The, 259-266
Carbo, Chic, 114
Carbo, Chuck, 114, 115, 184
Carona, Joe, 41, 133, 308, 311
Cayou, Red, 8, 9
Celestin, Oscar "Papa", 11, 109
Chapaka, Shaweez, 259-266
Charles, Ray, 193
Chase, Dooky, 84
Chess, Leonard, 261-263
Christian, Buddy, 3
Chudd, Lew, 79, 98, 99, 100, 102, 115, 138, 139, 145-150, 200, 201, 231, 249, 255, 282, 293, 312
Clanton, Ike, 131
Clanton, Jimmy, 114, 131-133, 199, 264, 311
Clayton, Kid, 9
Clowns, The, see Huey Smith
Collins, Al, 130
Coleman Brothers, 86-88
Cooke, Roland, 36, 37, 192, 196, 197, 213
Cotton, Lawerence, 184
Crawford, James "Sugarboy", 259-266
Country Jim, 100

Darnell, Larry, 43, 96, 158, 220
Davenport, Lawrence, 293
Davis, George, 29
Davis, Quint, 26-32, 299
Demain, Louis, 9
Diamond, Lee, 144
Diamond, Joe, 64, 166
Dixie Cups, 205
Domino, Antoine "Fats", 4, 12, 15, 22, 38, 50, 57, 95, 99-104, 106, 110, 111, 125, 138, 172, 174, 180, 189, 196, 200, 201, 205, 229, 240, 241, 242, 253, 281, 298, 299, 343, 353
Dorsey, Lee, 23, 59, 63-67, 115, 148, 149, 165, 200, 237, 243-350, 358

Doucett, Salvador, 89, 240
Drive 'Em Down, 16, 170
Dupree, "Champion" Jack, 3, 18, 125, 169

Eaglin, Ford "Snooks", 27, 28, 56, 103, 259, 262
Easterling, Skip, 43, 156, 158
Emeralds, The, 115
Erikson, Jesse, 20
Ernie The Whip, 46, 123, 344
Ertegun, Armet, 22
Estes, Dorothy, 256
Evans, David, 174

Fayard, Al, 151
Fields, Frank, 22, 174, 214, 240, 252, 259, 262
Floyd, Cleon, 331
Floyd, King, 83, 237, 305, 325-332
Ford, Billy, 87
Ford, Clarence, 214
Ford, Frankie (nee Guzzo), 41, 42, 103, 131, 132, 307-318
Francois, Joe, 356
Franks, Edward, 46, 49, 50, 240, 263
Franks, Leo, 249
French, George, 201
French, Papa, 9

Gayten, Paul, 47, 74, 85, 86, 87, 96, 109, 124, 239, 240, 249, 286
George, Barbara, 149, 205
Goodman, Shirley, 205-218, 235, 243, 322
Gordon, Izzacoo, 39
Green, Candy, 72, 73
Guitar Slim (Eddie Jones), 111, 125, 129, 130, 177-189, 192, 197, 201, 318

Hall, Clarence, 98
Hall, Gerri, 40, 206, 303
Handy, Captain John, 9
Hardesty, Herb, 100, 252
Harper, Willie, 61, 64, 151
Harris, Betty, 64, 205
Harris, Joe, 98, 252
Harris, Joel, 73, 74
Harrison, Kid, 95
Hayes, Roy 285
Henry, Clarence "Frogman", 241, 285
Hess, Norbert, 51
Hezekiah, 8

Hildebrant, Henry, 151, 272
Hill, Hosea, 187
Hill, Jessie, 40, 60, 135, 144, 229, 317-324
Hirt, Al, 59, 61, 154, 157
Holmes, Eldridge, 61, 64, 150, 151, 166
Honey Boy, 29
Humphrey, Willie, 95

Jack The Cat (Ken Elliot) 137, 139, 151, 314
Jackson, Emile, 225, 236
Jefferson, Thomas, 9, 12, 264
Joe & Ann, 205
John, Deacon, 83, 93
John, Papa, 249
Jones, Mathilda, 206
Jones, Senator, 93, 276-278
Jones, Sonny, 157, 356
Johnson, Noon, 10, 256
Johnson, Smokey, 24, 117, 201, 259
Johnson, Sporty, 75, 83
Joseph, Frog, 241
Josepth, Pleasant (Cousin Joe), 109

Kari, Sax, 156, 157
Kaslow, Allison, 26-34
K-Doe (Kador) Ernie, 23, 59, 60, 63, 64, 83, 135, 142-150, 166, 192, 229, 230, 256, 333-342, 357
Kelly, Leona Robinson, 245
Kennedy, Meyer, 252
Kenner, Chris, 60, 103, 135, 148-152, 201, 230, 291-300
Kerr, Clyde Jr., 157
Kid Stormy Weather, 3, 8, 16, 170
Kimball, Jeanette, 11
King, Earl, 24-26, 31, 37-39, 47-58, 83, 93, 103, 107, 110, 115, 127-131, 177-205, 230, 252-256, 272, 292-300, 347
King, Jewel, 98, 110, 205, 311
Kittrel, Christine, 205
Knight, Jean, 158, 327

Labostrie, Dorothy, 219, 225, 271
Lambert, Lloyd, 36, 181-188, 195, 345
Landry, George (Big Chief Jolly), 167
Lang, Eddie, 156, 180, 318
Lastie, David, 44, 180, 259, 261, 317-319, 357
Laurie, Annie, 74, 75, 85, 86, 109, 124, 226, 240, 249

Leadbitter, Mike, 26
Lear, Winnie, 357, 358
Lee, Archie Brown Lee, 334
Lee, Leonard, 210-219
 (Also see Shirly & Lee)
Lee, Warren, 64
Levy, Charles, 296
Lewis, Raymond, 40, 150, 197
Lewis, Smiley (Overton Lemons), 9-11, 15, 37, 39, 47, 96, 100, 103, 109, 125, 190, 198, 240, 245-258, 281
Lil' Millet, 128, 222
Little Richard (Richard Pennimen), 38, 48, 112, 113, 164, 222, 239, 336
Lubinsky, Herman, 74
Lynn, Tammi, 206, 216, 235

Magid, Lee, 196, 335
Mancuso, Frank, 137
Marchan, Bobby, 39-41, 44, 48, 63, 127-131, 301-306, 310, 312
Matassa, Cosimo, 75, 107-118, 123, 133, 152, 181, 182, 202, 208, 219, 228, 240, 269, 345
McKinley, Larry, 95, 142, 209-215, 241, 319
McLean, Ernest, 98, 240, 252
McMurry, Lillian, 38, 195
Mercy Baby, 130
Merineaux, Black, 8
Mesner, Eddie, 138, 209-215, 241
Meters, The, 15, 64, 166, 167
Mingo, Joe, 20
Mitchell, Bobby, 230, 281-288
Modeliste, Zigaboo, 29
Mollier, "Kid" Ernest, 248
Montgomery, Little Brother, 8, 16
Montgomery, Robert,
Moore, Curley, 40, 114, 158, 166, 199, 202
Morgan, Isaiah, 9
Morgan, Oliver, 155, 156, 317
Morgus The Magnificent, 311
Morton, Jelly Roll, 38, 169
Munez, Ed, 230
Myles, Edgar "Big Boy", 23, 259
Myles, Warren,

Nelson, Walter Sr., 246
Nelson, Walter Jr. "Papoose", 10, 20, 21
Nettles, Willie, 36, 189, 196

Neville, Aaron, 59-64, 135, 144, 147, 230, 333
Neville, Art, 46, 47, 150, 333
Neville, Cyril, 53
Neville, Naiomi, See Toussaint, Allen
Neville Brothers, 67
Newsome, Chubby, 205

Okey Dokey, (James Smith, 106, 140, 226)
Orange, Allen, 59, 144
Otis, Johnny, 88

Palmer, Earl, 22, 98, 99, 174, 214, 243, 252
Pania, Frank, 12, 36-40, 128, 181, 184-195, 261
Papa Stoppa (Clarence Holoman), 86, 137, 226, 283, 284
Parker, Robert, 20, 21, 40, 103, 116, 117, 192, 230, 272, 308
Parsons, John, 53, 54
Penn, Ernest, 12, 56
Perrillat, Nat, 213
Pichon, Fats, 8, 84, 96, 109
Picou, Carlton, 42
Pitts, Nolan, 194
Poka Dot Slim, 156
Price, Lloyd, 37, 50, 100, 101, 138, 139, 192, 196, 209
Prince La-La, 317
Professor Longhair (Roland Byrd), 3, 4, 10, 15-34, 53, 111, 125, 132, 168, 175
Purnel, Alton, 9, 75, 83

Queserque, Wardell, 23, 24, 103, 202, 274, 326

Rankin, LeRoy "Batman", 76
Ray, Eddie, 231
Rebenack, Mac "Dr. John", 15, 31, 67, 114, 115, 127, 132, 234, 239, 271, 272, 309, 321-326
Reeder, Eskew (S. Q. Reeder, Esquerita)
Rena, Kid, 9
Rhapsodizers, The, 203
Richard, Reynauld, 345
Ridgley, Tommy, 31, 56, 98, 99, 110, 111, 124, 223, 228, 241, 325-327, 357
Riley, Teddy, 75-80
Rivers, James, 40, 150
Roberts, Rip, 23

377

Robey, Don, 49, 50, 197
Robinson, Alvin, 296
Robinson, Sylvia, 216, 217
Ruffino, Joe, 23, 133, 144, 150, 201, 223, 228, 271
Rupe, Art, 23, 113, 128, 185, 194, 222

Sample, Hank, 328
Samuels, Clarence, 75, 76
Santiago, Burnell, 8
Scott, Albert, 192
Scramuzza, Al 223, 274
Seale, Herman, 9, 48, 249
Sehorn, Marshall, 44, 55, 63-65, 117, 148, 154, 161-168, 200, 235, 278, 305, 346, 359
Sha-wees, 23 (Also see Crawford, Sugarboy)
Sheba, 28
Sheik, Kid, 9
Showmen, The, 60, 135, 149
Shirley & Lee, 39, 40, 47, 57, 205-218, 239
Shuler, Wayne, 141
Singleton, James, 52
Singleton, Shelby, 274, 275
Smith, Huey "Piano", 15, 35-44, 48, 57, 103, 127-134, 140, 159, 181, 194-199, 213, 302-306, 310, 312, 318
Smith, Irving, 148-152, 157, 293, 345
Smith, Wilbert, 144
Spellman, Benny, 59-61, 135, 144, 149, 154, 230
Spiders, The, 184
Stahli, Paul, 309
Stanley, Earl, 155, 309
Stergil, Dick, 23, 128, 130, 140
Stevens, George "Blazer Boy", 37
Stevens, George "Tex", 267
Stewart, Dell, 202
Stokes, The, 61, 62, 154
Stone, Roland (Roland Leblanc) 131, 199
Stoval, Percy, 36, 178, 181, 230, 272, 292-296, 329
Sullivan Rock (Rocky Sullivan), 3, 16, 18, 170

Tate, Billy, 36, 192, 263
Tee, Willie, 117, 202
Tex, Joe, 47, 48, 51, 144
Thomas, Irma, 23, 59, 60, 63, 135, 144, 150, 205, 223-236, 256

Toppers, The, 282-285
Toussaint, Allen, 4, 12, 15, 31, 40, 55-68, 92, 144-154, 160, 166-170, 199, 202, 213, 229, 230, 232, 255, 256, 319, 337, 345-349
Turbington, Earl, 29
Turner, Joe, 112, 241
Tyler, Alvin "Red", 48, 52, 53, 58, 96, 98, 127, 131, 148, 198, 240, 252, 263, 308

Valdeler, Patsy, 96
Verret, Harrison, 172, 317
Vidocovitch, John, 52
Vincent, Johnny, 37-43, 48, 58, 114, 115, 127-134, 140, 181, 182, 192-200, 264, 303, 308-311
Vinnett, George, 328

Walker, Elijah, 326-329
Washington, Bernadine, 103, 200
Washington, Isidore "Tuts", 5-14, 16, 17, 46, 56, 170, 190, 246-258
Washington, Walter, 223, 267-269, 278
Webb, "Boogie" Bill, 171-176
West, Willie, 64
White, Al, 157, 228, 230
White, Danny, 202, 333, 337
Wild Magnolias, 26, 31
Williams, Charles "Hungry", 36, 40, 48, 196, 198, 252, 308
Williams, John "Scarface", 40, 64, 303
Winslow, Vernon (Dr. Daddy-O), 75, 96, 101, 119-126, 226, 260

Young, Al, 137, 240